PRIESTS AND PRELATES OF ARMAGH, 1518–1558

Priests and Prelates of Armagh in the Age of Reformations, 1518–1558

HENRY A. JEFFERIES

FOUR COURTS PRESS

This book was typeset by
Woodcote Typesetters
in 10 on 12 point Ehrhardt for
FOUR COURTS PRESS LTD
Fumbally Court, Fumbally Lane, Dublin 8, Ireland
e-mail: fcp@ indigo.ie
and in North America for
FOUR COURTS PRESS
c/o ISBS, 5804 N.E. Hassalo Street, Portland, OR 97213.

A catalogue record for this title
is available from the British Library.

ISBN 1-85182-336-0

Printed in Great Britain
by Hartnolls Ltd, Bodmin, Cornwall

To my wife, Úna

Contents

List of Illustrations

Preface

ACKNOWLEDGMENTS

I wish to acknowledge the guidance of Mary O'Dowd, my supervisor at Queen's University, Belfast. I wish to express my gratitude to Colm Lennon for his advice in preparing this book for publication. I am indebted too to my mentors at University College Cork, K.W. Nicholls and Donnchadh Ó Corráin, and to Steven Ellis and Bob Hunter who helped to bring this work to fruition. Most of all I want to express my appreciation to my wife for her encouragement and patience while I was engaged on this magnus opus. Finally, I wish to acknowledge the support of Dr Deirdre Mullan RSM, and a grant from the Religious Sisters of Mercy in Derry which helped to fund the research upon which this book was based.

ABBREVIATIONS

As far as possible the clergy are identified by their contemporary titles; hence graduates were titled 'Magister', abbreviated to Mgr; non-graduate priests were simply titled 'Dominus', abbreviated to Dnus.

Abbreviations used in the notes are given on p. 175 below.

MONETARY VALUES

Unless otherwise stated all monetary values given below are in Irish pounds. The Irish pound is reckoned to have been worth 13s. 4d. sterling.

NATIONALITY

I have employed the term 'English-born' to denote any person who was born and came from England. The people of English descent and loyalty in County Louth regarded themselves simply as 'English' in the early sixteenth century but I have employed the term 'Old English' to distinguish them from English-born individuals.

Introduction

Armagh is exceptional among Irish dioceses as a very substantial portion of its archives has survived from the later middle ages.[1] Circa 1630 Archbishop Ussher bound the seventeen surviving books of medieval records into the seven volumes which have since been known as the Armagh registers. The registers are now preserved in the Public Records Office of Northern Ireland.[2]

This book draws heavily upon the last two of the Armagh registers, those attributed to Primates Cromer and Dowdall.[3] Both of these registers are artificial constructs; each was created by conjoining two sixteenth-century books inside one cover. Their survival offers a unique opportunity to thoroughly explore a diocese of the Irish church of the sixteenth century from within, using its own records.

The range and volume of documentation available for Armagh makes it possible to examine how the diocesan church actually provided pastoral care to the Christian community over a significant part of Ireland, and to explore how effectively the church was governed. In addressing the critical issue of the provision of pastoral care this study seeks to throw new light on one of the greatest lacunae in our knowledge of the church in sixteenth century Ireland.

The first part of this book presents a thematic study of the institutional church in the archdiocese of Armagh in the first part of the sixteenth century. It is primarily concerned with the diocesan church and its personnel, while the regular clergy are studied only in so far as they affected the church's pastoral ministry. It presents some considerable evidence to show that, contrary to the conventional historiography of the church in late medieval Ireland,[4] the diocesan church in Armagh was in good order on the eve of the Tudor reformations. It reveals that the southern parishes of the archdiocese were closely and very effectively administered, while in the northern parishes the archbishop exercised much of his authority indirectly, though not without effect. The church authorities in Armagh are shown to have worked constantly to maintain, and even to raise, standards of divine worship and moral conduct among the clergy and the laity.

This book reveals that the pastoral needs of the people in the archdiocese of Armagh were met through a surprisingly dense network of parish churches and chapels of ease, staffed by a priesthood which was generally satisfactory. The parish clergy are shown to have been very poor as a body. Their need to impose fees for various services may have given rise to some friction between them and some of the laity, though nothing so strong or widespread as to be characterised as 'anti-clericalism'. The training of the parish clergy was not at all as rigorous as that which would be required by the Council of Trent. The cost of a university education would have been prohibitively expensive for the great majority of priests, and the incomes from the parochial livings were generally too poor to allow a graduate to recoup his expenses. Nonetheless, the parochial clergy of Armagh on the eve of the Tudor reformations seem generally to have served a long apprenticeship before acquiring a benefice, and they seem to have ministered in their parishes as well as circumstances made possible at the time. They were judged to be adequate, if in need of some modest improvement, by the standards expected by the church authorities and their parishioners.

The second part of the book traces the impact of the Tudors' religious programmes on the diocesan clergy of Armagh up to the close of 1558, when the death of Mary Tudor made another major shift in the crown's religious policies most likely. The English crown's increased involvement in the life of the Irish church is reflected in the considerable volume of documents relating to the church among the state papers from that time. Nonetheless, the Armagh registers are a vital source of information about the church during the early Tudor reformations and during the Marian restoration. Their records of the routine administration of the church offer an opportunity to define patterns of change and continuity within the life of the church, such is possible for no other Irish diocese in that critical period.

Perhaps the most striking aspect of this part of the book is the degree to which the Henrician schism was made effective in the southern parishes in Armagh archdiocese. At the same time, there was an equally remarkable degree of continuity in the ways in which the archdiocese was administered internally, and in the ways in which the priests continued to serve their parishes throughout the early Tudor reformations. The pope's jurisdiction was effectively curtailed in the southern rural deaneries, but the liturgy celebrated by the clergy, as well as other religious practices, remained Catholic with little, if any, break into the early years of Elizabeth's reign. Unlike the situation in England it does not seem that the early Tudor reformations corroded clerical or popular commitment to Catholicism.

The opportunity for Catholic restoration and reform in Mary's reign was seized upon eagerly by the church authorities in Armagh. It may well be the case that by the time of Mary's unexpected death in 1558 the Catholic church in Armagh was in sufficiently good order to survive the Elizabethan reformation. This is not to say that the failure of Elizabeth's religious settlement was in any way inevitable in the archdiocese of Armagh. It is simply being suggested that that failure might not have occurred if the Catholic church in Armagh had not proved to be as resilient as it showed itself to be. In any event, it can be shown that the progress of the early Tudor reformations in the archdiocese was retarded by clerical opposition, with the connivance from the secular authorities at local and national levels. It is apparent from this study that the diocesan clergy made a very real difference to the course of the Tudor reformations in Armagh.

The Parishes and Priests of Armagh
inter Anglicos

The parish was the basic territorial unit in the late medieval church, both in terms of administration and also for the provision of pastoral care. To understand how the church actually ministered to the people and helped to shape their lives it is necessary to see what was happening at the parish level.

Drogheda, with Dundalk and Ardee, the chief towns in County Louth, were the centres of the groups of parishes known as the rural deaneries of Drogheda, Dundalk and Ardee respectively. Collectively these rural deaneries formed the key administrative unit of the archdiocese known as Armagh *inter Anglicos*. Here the church functioned within the framework of the English common law, under the jurisdiction of the English crown. The urban and rural elites in this region, and a proportion of the common people, were English by descent and identity. It was an environment which, despite the fact that most of the inhabitants were Irish, would not have been very alien to someone newly arrived from England.

Beyond the marchlands north of Dundalk the traveller entered a recognisably different region. The landscape was more mountainous, with extensive boglands and some wooded areas. There were fewer churches compared with County Louth, and few stone houses. There was only one truly urban centre in this portion of the archdiocese, the metropolitan city of Armagh. Bishop Chiericati described it in 1517 as being 'very desolate, the best thing in it being an abbey of the canons regular'.[1] The lower density of stone buildings and of urban centres suggests that the economy of the northern parishes of the archdiocese of Armagh was less commercialised compared with that in County Louth.

The parishes of the see of Armagh north of County Louth were organised into two rural deaneries; those of Orior and Tullyhogue. Together these formed the administrative unit known as Armagh *inter Hibernicos*. This area was dominated politically by O Neill, the most powerful lord in Ulster. O Neill was independent of the English crown and exercised virtually sovereign authority in his own right. His subjects were entirely Irish, with the exception of a few English-by-descent merchants based in Armagh.

The late medieval archbishops of Armagh struggled to exercise their authority directly in this, the greatest portion of their archdiocese. In Armagh *inter Hibernicos* much of the church administration had to be delegated to the senior Irish clergy who actually resided in this separate part of the archdiocese. *Inter Hibernicos* the archbishop retained ultimate responsibility for the spiritual welfare of the clergy and laity but the region was less firmly under archiepiscopal supervision than was the portion of the archdiocese *inter Anglicos*.

The divisions created difficulties in the administration of archdiocese, especially for one who was the English crown's appointee. Yet, Archbishop Cromer's predecessors had succeeded in establishing *modi operandi* which he too could use to promote the church's pastoral mission throughout Armagh, *inter Anglicos* and *inter Hibernicos*.

In this study the parishes of the three southern rural deaneries of the archdiocese – those *inter Anglicos* – will be discussed separately from those *inter Hibernicos*. This differentiation is necessitated by the different character and volume of source materials which are available for each of the two districts. More than that, the division of the archdiocese into two reflected the considerable differences in the conditions in which the church functioned.

THE GEOGRAPHICAL AND HUMAN SETTING

The three southern rural deaneries of the archdiocese of Armagh, namely those of Ardee, Drogheda and Dundalk, were virtually co-extensive with the county of Louth. The great majority of the land in the deaneries is low-lying and very fertile, drained by a series of rivers running west-east into the Irish Sea. It is capable of supporting a wide range of agricultural practices, and in the sixteenth century would have had the potential to be very productive indeed. To the north of Dundalk are the foothills of the Slieve Gullion range, though the mountains themselves are situated in the rural deanery of Orior. The only mountains within the three southern rural deaneries are those on the Cooley Peninsula. The peninsula has a narrow coastal strip of fertile land, especially on its eastern extremity, but the interior is marginal land with limited agricultural potential.

The fertile lowlands of Uriel attracted a great intensity of English settlement following the Anglo-Norman conquest of the late twelfth and thirteenth centuries. The lowlands of County Louth were divided fairly evenly into small manors.[2] Jocelyn Otway-Ruthven observed that above the 600′ contour there is little sign of Anglo-Norman settlement anywhere in Ireland,[3] and the same holds true of the uplands of the north of County Louth. The Anglo-Normans were unable to settle beyond the 'Gap of the North'. The archdiocese of Armagh remained divided throughout the later middle ages, with most of the three southern rural deaneries being under English rule while the two northern deaneries remained in Irish control.

The first half of the fifteenth century saw the O'Neills of Tyrone capture much land in the north of County Louth, and successfully impose a 'black rent' of £10 on the town of Dundalk.[4] The O'Hanlons exercised some lordship over Omeath on the Cooley Peninsula. However, from the mid fifteenth century the balance of power between the English and the Irish in the archdiocese shifted in favour of the former. The Old English lords of County Louth began to fortify the county in depth with tower-houses and expanded their lordships at the expense of their Irish neighbours.[5]

Harold O'Sullivan highlighted the strong divide within County Louth which was

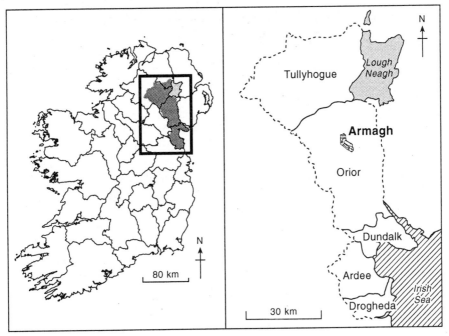

1   The rural deaneries of Armagh

reflected by the Pale ditch erected in 1488.[6] To the south and east, protected by the walled towns of Dundalk and Ardee, a string of tower-houses and the Pale ditch, was an area which was peaceful, highly anglicised and fairly prosperous. The marchlands to the north and west of the Pale ditch were more exposed to Irish attacks, had fewer Old English inhabitants and agriculture was less intensive and less prosperous. In this area the tide of English recovery seems to have ebbed somewhat; in the Cooley Peninsula by the late 1520s, and elsewhere in the marchlands in the 1530s, with consequent difficulties for the parish system in the troubled areas.[7]

At the lowest levels of society, but also the most populous, Irish people were predominant.[8] This pattern may have been true of all of County Louth except, possibly but not certainly, beyond the extreme south. The Irish parliament of 1465 observed that across the Pale generally Irish people 'exceed greatly the English people'.[9]

The economy in County Louth in the early sixteenth century was based upon agriculture. Farming there was favoured with fertile lowland, good drainage and, particularly in the south and east, by a high degree of political and social order. These conditions facilitated the maintenance of a well-developed agriculture. The land was intensively farmed by Irish standards. A three-course rotation of winter corn, spring corn and fallow was general on the fertile lowlands in the sixteenth century, as evidenced by the reckoning of tithes in 'couples' in the monastic extents.[10] This relatively high intensity of agricultural productivity formed the foundation of a market economy, which traded mainly in agricultural produce. The records of parochial tithes reveal that the economy to the south and east of the Pale ditch was significantly more prosperous than that to the north and west of it. The countryside around Drogheda and Termonfeckin struck Bishop Chiericati, the papal nuncio to the court of Henry VIII and erstwhile pilgrim to St Patrick's purgatory on Lough Derg, as 'a fairly rich territory'.[11]

County Louth had a modest urban hierarchy with four walled towns, headed by the port of Drogheda with a population estimated at 2,000 or more, followed by Dundalk which appeared 'rather ruinous' to Bishop Chiericati in 1517,[12] together with some smaller boroughs like Louth and Termonfeckin, and also a network of villages.[13] These provided the agriculturalists with a local market for foodstuffs. Surplus production could be sold through the towns to either the neighbouring Irish lordships or to England through the ports of Carlingford, Dundalk and especially Drogheda.[14] It is commonly held that the sea-borne trade of Drogheda rivalled that of Dublin itself. This seems unlikely because recent studies of the Irish trade done at Bristol and Chester, by far the most important English entrepots for Irish exports, revealed that trade with Drogheda was significantly less than that with Dublin, and the volume of trade with both centres declined in the second half of the fifteenth century.[15] Nonetheless, it was one of the chief ports in Ireland in the later middle ages. The volume of trade in County Louth allows one to presume that internal communications in the county were reasonably good even in the sixteenth century.

The trade engaged in by the merchants of the towns of County Louth, together with some small-scale manufacturing, sustained the populations of urban centres which were significant by Irish standards. Little is known of manufacturing industry in late medieval Ireland though it is assumed to have been small-scale and geared only to local needs. However, there are reflections of Drogheda's industrial base in the Armagh registers which identify five cobblers (all with Irish names) and three glovers (two with English names) resident in the city in 1518.[16] Margaret Spicer of Drogheda made ecclesiastical vestments, a specialist task requiring much skill and some experience.[17]

The spate of late medieval church and tower house building indicates that the economy of County Louth probably expanded from the middle of the fifteenth century. In the sixteenth century County Louth was dominated by an elite gentry class which was English by descent, culture and loyalty.[18] Their typical residences, the ubiquitous tower houses, survive in sufficient numbers today to bear witness to their near-monopoly of economic power and high status in the countryside. They controlled the land, and wielded great authority over the peasantry on their estates. Not only did they as landlords have the power to evict tenants (rarely exercised apparently as farmers were in short supply in the later middle ages), but they also billeted 'men of war' on the homes of their tenants, through a custom which was widely known as 'coign and livery'. A convocation of the clergy of Armagh *inter Anglicos* in 1492 condemned the practice as extortionate, apparently to no avail.[19] The economic power of the gentry was reinforced by its concomitant political power. The gentry volunteered their services in local government, helping to defend the English lordship against the Ulster Irish and working with the crown in law enforcement.

In the corporate towns of County Louth, as in Ireland as a whole, the powers of local government were exercised by merchant oligarchs.[20] In the frontier towns of Ardee, Dundalk and Carlingford, several of the merchants lived in tower houses which were akin to those of the gentry in the countryside reflecting, not just a consciousness of danger but also, most probably, similarities in outlook and aspiration.[21] Drogheda was quite a large and prosperous centre and may have been more 'cosmopolitan' than the smaller towns of Louth. Steven Ellis' work on the provision of secular justice in the Pale revealed that the people of the Pale, including those in the countryside and in the towns of County Louth, were effectively regulated by the English common law towards the close of the middle ages.[22]

The sedentary and well-ordered population in most of County Louth presented the church with the kind of milieu in which the parish system functioned best. The economy generated revenues for the church which were reasonably high by Irish standards, and there is evidence to suggest that economic conditions in County Louth had improved in the later middle ages, a development which would have benefited the church directly through its possession of lands and the right to levy tithes.

To conclude then, the church in the southern rural deaneries of Armagh in the early sixteenth century operated in a region dominated by Old English gentry and by oligarchs of English descent. They were able to define and control the political, social and economic structures in the county, giving it its 'English' character. They were able to ensure that men of English blood received preferential access to freehold properties, especially the larger ones, in the county. Irish people formed the majority of the population in the county but were disproportionately numerous among the small-holders, cottiers and landless labourers who were very rarely named in sixteenth century sources. The church in Armagh *inter Anglicos* had to extend its ministry to this Irish majority as well as to the English elites.

PARISHES

As occurred elsewhere in the colony parish boundaries were often made to coincide with the extents of the Anglo-Norman manors. Indeed, several medieval churches in County Louth are situated in very close proximity to Norman mottes.[23] It is difficult now to define the boundaries of the medieval parishes of County Louth, but the civil parish boundaries recorded by the Ordnance Survey in the last century preserve a record of the great majority of the late medieval parish boundaries.

One of the greatest challenges facing historians of the church in medieval Ireland is to identify which parish churches and chapels were served by a priest at any point in time. This is not, however, impossible for the archdiocese of Armagh *inter Anglicos* in the first half of the sixteenth century. Primate Dowdall's register preserves a virtually comprehensive visitation list of all of the rectors, vicars and curates in charge of churches *inter Anglicos c.* 1543–4.[24]

From Primate Dowdall's visitation list it is possible to identify twenty-four churches in the rural deanery of Drogheda, as well as the abbey church of Mellifont which served as a parish church to the local population. One may add the church of Killineer to this total, since the church was in existence throughout the first half of the sixteenth century and its curate was referred to in 1540.[25] This indicates that the average size of area served by a priest with a cure of souls in the rural deanery was only 2,147 acres. If one took account of the chapel attached to the convent of nuns at Callystown near Kilclogher, whose chaplain served the local people until the dissolution, the average size of area served by a church or chapel would fall to only 2,060 acres. There are also archaeological remains of a chapel at Barmeath in Dysert which seem to date from the later middle ages.[26] The rural deanery was clearly well endowed with parish churches and chapels.

Primate Dowdall's visitation list identified twenty-five churches in the rural deanery of Ardee. To these may be added three other churches, namely those at Castlering, Clonkeehan and Kilcrony which were served by priests according to Archdeacon Roth's records in 1535.[27] Primate Cromer's records for the same period indicate that there were also priests serving the churches at Mapastown and at Ash, north of Louth.[28] The average area served by the priests who staffed these thirty churches on the eve of the Henrician reformation was about 2,488 acres. There was a church at Crowmartin which became defunct some time before December 1518 when the parishioners made a vain attempt in Armagh's consistory court to force the *firmarius* and the vicar of Clonkeen to provide them with their own curate again. According to an extent made in 1541 the church at Crowmartin had been wasted by the Irish of Farney.[29]

Priests for only thirteen churches and chapels in the rural deanery of Dundalk were listed by Primate Dowdall. However, there is uncertainty as to how many churches on the Cooley Peninsula still functioned in the early sixteenth century. There are no references to Omeath in the registers of Primates Cromer or Dowdall. At Irish Grange there are remains of a fortified church which may have had a late medieval window.[30] It appears to have been in use until 1529 when the O Neills of the Fews and the O Hanlons of Orior destroyed the castles and churches at Grange and Templetown, and wasted the land.[31] The district was still uncultivated twelve years later. There was a priest to serve the parish of Roche in 1522, but in 1540 its tithes were worth nothing because of Irish raids.[32] The prebend of Kene was part of the corps of the archdeacons of Armagh in the first half of the sixteenth century and was presumably worth something before 1538 when it was recorded as being worthless in the Irish Valor.[33] Hence, it seems clear that the rural deanery of Dundalk was far better served with churches at the start of the sixteenth century than was subsequently the case after Irish raids in the 1520s and 1530s.

It may be concluded that the areas served by priests responsible for a cure of souls in Armagh *inter Anglicos* were small in extent and some were very small indeed, like Philipstown (Louth) and Parsonstown. The size of such areas mattered a great deal to the priests whose duty it was to serve them. The compact nature of the cures in the southern rural deaneries of Armagh facilitated the ministry of the parish clergy, allowing them to exercise a significant level of supervision and exert some influence on the parishioners. The priest's house would have been readily accessible, and the priest was well placed to visit the sick and dying throughout his cure. The priest must certainly have been a familiar figure in such small communities.

For any study of the parishes and priests of Armagh, a consideration of the church buildings as the focal point in each community, and the place in or around which the

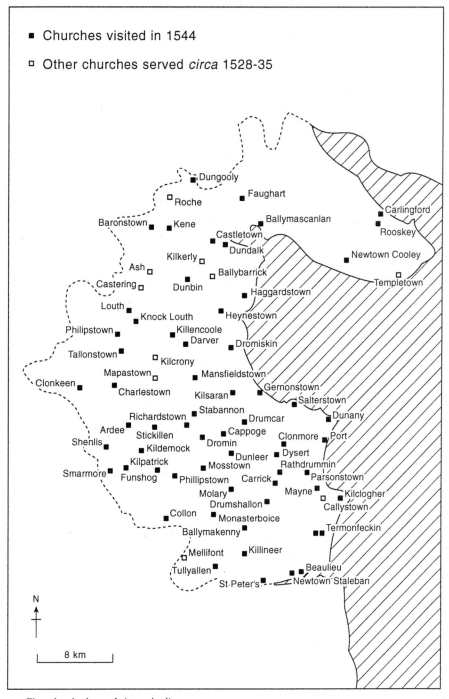

- ■ Churches visited in 1544
- □ Other churches served *circa* 1528-35

Dungooly
Faughart
Roche
Carlingford
Baronstown
Kene
Ballymascanlan
Rooskey
Castletown
Dundalk
Newtown Cooley
Kilkerly
Ash
Ballybarrick
Templetown
Castering
Dunbin
Haggardstown
Louth
Heynestown
Knock Louth
Philipstown
Killencoole
Darver
Dromiskin
Tallonstown
Kilcrony
Mapastown
Mansfieldstown
Clonkeen
Charlestown
Gernonstown
Kilsaran
Salterstown
Stabannon
Richardstown
Drumcar
Dunany
Ardee
Cappoge
Port
Stickillen
Clonmore
Shenlis
Dromin
Dunleer
Dysert
Kildemock
Kilpatrick
Mosstown
Rathdrummin
Smarmore
Parsonstown
Funshog
Phillipstown
Carrick
Molary
Mayne
Kilclogher
Drumshallon
Callystown
Collon
Monasterboice
Termonfeckin
Ballymakenny
Mellifont
Killineer
Beaulieu
Tullyallen
St. Peter's
Newtown Staleban

N

8 km

2 Churches in Armagh *inter Anglicos*

liturgy and so many of the rites of passage were celebrated, is very important. Also, the church buildings of County Louth may be used as an index of the 'state of the church' in the later middle ages.

Substantial remains of thirty-six late medieval rural churches, and at least two fragmentary remains, have been identified in the *Archaeological survey of County Louth*. Some remains also survive of the late medieval parish churches of Drogheda, Dundalk, Ardee and Carlingford. Geographically, the greatest number of rural church ruins (twenty eight in number) lie south and east of the Dundalk-Darver-Ardee Pale boundary. The remainder are found in the north of the county. Oliver Davies indicated that there was an 'unconfirmable report' that the church at Parsonstown was built in 1528.[34] Virtually all of the rural churches which possess diagnostic features are 'late medieval', that is, they were constructed in the fifteenth or early sixteenth centuries. The small number of earlier churches all show signs of having been renovated or much altered in the same period. The concentration of surviving buildings in the area between the Dee river and the Collon ridge is striking. Possibly the existing ruins reflect a higher intensity of church building in the relatively prosperous south and east of County Louth in the later middle ages, with the likelihood that some fabric of those newer buildings were better able to survive to the present than were older buildings.

The average width of the ruins of thirty-six late medieval rural churches is only about 5.7 metres.[35] Indeed, twenty-two of the churches were between 5 and 6 metres wide, twenty-eight between 4.5–6.5 metres, while only one is narrower than 4 metres or wider than 8 metres.[36] The length of the churches varied more. The average length of twenty-five unicellular churches is 14.2 metres, with twelve churches being longer and only two shorter than 10 metres.[37] Ten of the thirty-five substantial ruins had a separate chancel and nave.[38] In at least two of those, at Faughart and Stickillin, the chancel was comprised of a twelfth- or thirteenth-century church to which a long nave had been added in the later middle ages.[39] It is not possible to indicate why the other eight were designed as chancel and nave churches when most others in Armagh *inter Anglicos* were unicellular. It seems to have made no difference whether the rectory was impropriated or not, or whether the church was served by a beneficed clergyman or not. Nor was it only the wealthiest parishes which had a divided church. One can only suggest that the style of the church buildings reflected the wish of the parishioners, or at least that portion of them who financed the building. Undoubtedly some of the churches were built with money from the local gentry,[40] but others are likely to have been built through the joint efforts of all of the parishioners.[41]

The rural churches of County Louth were built to a common pattern. They were orientated along an east-west axis, with the altar below a window on the east side, a bell-cote on the west gable, and one or two doorways on the side walls near the west end of the church.

Little survives of the internal furnishings of the churches. The stone altars were removed from Armagh's medieval churches since the reformations, and none is known to have survived. On the eve of the Tudor reformations each altar had to be covered with a special altar cloth before Mass could be celebrated. This is apparent from the records of a case brought before Armagh's metropolitan court in 1520 in which the

defendant was severely punished for removing the altar cloth in order to prevent the
incoming vicar from celebrating Mass in the parish church of Molary.[42]

There is evidence for the existence of timber rood-screens in three rural churches
in Armagh *inter Anglicos* – at Castletown, Parsonstown and Templetown.[43] There was
also a rood-screen in the church of the priory at Louth which served as the parish
church for local people.[44] There may have been another in St Mary's church, Ardee.[45]
Others probably existed. These highly decorated screens between the chancel and nave
usually displayed a cross (or rood) at the top, flanked by images of the Blessed Virgin
and St John the Evangelist.[46]

Some of the windows behind the altars were adorned with stained glass, perhaps
showing religious images.[47] The church at Mayne has a recess to the left of the altar
which would have accommodated the statue of the church's patron saint.[48] Such statues were a standard feature in late medieval Irish churches. The provincial synod of
Cashel in 1453 insisted that every church in the southern province possess such an
image.[49] In the Armagh court book for the years 1518–22 there are a number of references to penitents being ordered to stand before the statue of the patron saint in their
church, holding a wax candle, during Sunday Mass.[50] The implication here is that the
statue always occupied a prominent position at the front of the church.

Also in the chancel of the church at Mayne is a sedilia or in-built altar seat for the
priest, and a piscina or basin for rinsing the sacred vessels.[51] Other piscinas survive at
Kildemock and Templetown.[52]

The floor of the chancel of some rural churches were tiled, as at Smarmore,[53] though
the custom in Ireland of having burials within the walls of ruined medieval churches
has obliterated most of the evidence for floor tiles. It is clear, in any case, that such tiles
were a rarity in the late medieval rural churches. Heather King referred to floor tiles in
such a church in Meath diocese as a 'luxury'.[54] Consequently, one may well imagine
the muddy state to which the rural churches could descend. Lord Deputy Sussex, in
1556, complained that the churches of Ireland 'not only in the north but also through
the most of Ireland, (were more) like stables for horses and herd houses for cattle, than
holy places to minister with due reverence the most blessed sacraments in'.[55] In 1571
Edmund Tremayne, clerk of the Irish privy council, also described the Irish churches
as being 'only like stables'.[56] That there was a pervasive problem in this regard is indicated by the Cashel legislation of 1453 which decreed that all churches were to be kept
neat and clean and that animals, corn and such things belonging to the laity should not
be kept in the buildings. It also decreed that cemeteries were to be walled in at the
parishioners' expense, and kept clean.[57]

In the church at Salterstown archaeologists found plaster still adhering to the inside walls.[58] It is probable that the late medieval churches were generally plastered and
the walls decorated with religious imagery (similar to that discovered in St Audeon's
church in Dublin),[59] but centuries of exposure to the elements have erased all traces of
what might have been. A number of late medieval fonts have survived from churches in
Armagh *inter Anglicos,* some of which were ornately carved, like the early sixteenth-
century font which was made for St Peter's church, Drogheda.[60] Some holy water stoups
are still in place in the ruined churches of County Louth.[61]

Eamon Duffy has highlighted the key role of images, in sculpture, glass or paint in communicating aspects of the faith to the illiterate Catholics of late medieval England.[62] We may assume that the images in their churches helped to represent the spiritual to the rural parishioners of Armagh *inter Anglicos,* though on a lesser scale than that which prevailed across the Irish Sea. The rural churches in Armagh *inter Anglicos* were not at all as impressive as those in the wealthier parishes of south eastern England.

The parish churches of the towns of Armagh *inter Anglicos* were much more elaborate than those in the countryside. St Peter's, Drogheda, was clearly a very impressive edifice.[63] It had a long nave with ten bays, north and south aisles, two large side chapels flanking the chancel, and a great tower at the crossing of the nave-chancel and the transepts.[64] Its steeple was reputed to be 'one of the highest steeples in the world' in the mid sixteenth century.[65] The church had at least ten chantry chapels endowed by successive archbishops of Armagh, and generations of Drogheda's patricians: viz. the chapels dedicated to St Anne, St Mary, St John, St Michael, St James, the Holy Rood, St Erasmus, St George, the Trinity and St Laurence.[66] Not only did the patricians continue to endow chantries to the very eve of the Tudor reformations; they also made very substantial investments in the fabric of the church. In 1515 John Wyrall, mayor of Drogheda, had a great window erected in St Mary's chapel within St Peter's church.[67] In 1525 the construction of the south aisle was completed, and its windows glazed through the generosity of Thomas Bath, William Pastow, James White and Thomas Thunder, all of whom were Drogheda merchants.[68] The great decorated market cross of St Peter's parish was erected through the gift of John Ballard in 1501.[69] Dr King has identified what she believes is a fragment of this cross.[70] It is decorated with an image of the pieta, a representation of the Lady of Pity which was increasingly popular in late medieval England.[71]

St Peter's was likened to a pro-cathedral by Aubrey Gwynn, and it certainly played a key role in the ecclesiastical life of the archdiocese.[72] Synods were held in the church, as were most of the sittings of the consistory court of Armagh. Even in the mid-fifteenth century St Peter's Church had a choir comprised of lay people.[73] It can be taken for granted that in the early sixteenth century, if not much earlier, the choir was accompanied by organ music. Primate Octavian purchased an organ in 1482 from Kilkenny for Armagh cathedral.[74] Obviously that entrepreneur from Ormond found customers enough in Ireland to keep him in business, and the wealthy patricians of Drogheda had the money and aspirations to emulate the liturgical achievements of other parish communities in Ireland, as well as England.

A memorandum among the Armagh registers from 1542 establishes the order of precedence in processions of the vicar of St Peter's, the twelve chantry chaplains, the holy water clerk and the sexton.[75] It must have made an impressive display when High Mass was being celebrated.

St Nicholas' church, Dundalk, was replaced (as was St Peter's, Drogheda) in the eighteenth century but there is evidence to demonstrate that it too received major benefactions in the later middle ages.[76] The late medieval church was very large, greater than 37.9 metres in length. It had a south aisle and transept too. Its bell-tower was incorporated into the present Protestant church. It appears to have been a late medieval construction. Also incorporated into its Protestant successor is a very elaborate sixteenth-century window with three round-headed lights, each 4′ x 1′6″, from which some original coloured glass fragments have been discovered.[77] Decorated floor tiles from the later medieval chancel have also been identified.[78] There were at least five chantries in St Nicholas' in the mid sixteenth century – St Mary's (1324), St Katherine's (1418), St Richard's (confirmed in 1485), Holy Trinity (*c.*1539) and another founded by Thomas Feld of Dundalk who died in 1536.[79] Additional priests were employed at old chantries, to increase the number of Masses which could be celebrated for the souls of the dead.[80]

The medieval church of St Mary's, Ardee, was replaced in 1812 by a Protestant church which incorporated much of the medieval fabric of its predecessor.[81] St Mary's too was a large church, 97′ long, with a nave 24′ wide, and a south aisle which was 18′ wide. John Bradley has suggested that the south aisle was constructed in the fifteenth century, and the chancel in the sixteenth. Ardee too had its chantry priests. The Valor in Hibernia reveals that the chantries of St George, St Katherine, St Mary, Holy Cross, and St John were each endowed with revenues of between £4 and £6 13*s. 4d.* per annum.[82] There was an impressive college built for the chantry priests at Ardee *c.*1487, much of which still stands.[83] The great decorated stone cross outside the west door of St Mary's church, with a representation of the crucifixion on one side and a Madonna and child on the other, may date to the early sixteenth century.[84] Dr King has suggested that it may possibly be associated with the Guild of the Holy Cross, a new confraternity which was licensed for Ardee in 1534, another indication of the strength of Catholic piety in the town on the very eve of the Tudor reformations.[85]

All in all, there is substantial evidence of late medieval beneficence towards the church in Ardee, Drogheda and Dundalk. Unfortunately, little evidence survives about the medieval parish church at Carlingford. However, Paul Gosling has recently argued that the tower in the former Church of Ireland church (now Carlingford's heritage centre) is of late medieval date.[86] He suggests that the chapel of St Michael referred to in the will of Christopher Dowdall in 1485 may be identified with a chapel beside the lough which was subsequently removed by marine erosion. In the medieval borough of Louth the priory church of St Mary, which served as the parish church, has been shown to have had a new nave built late in the fifteenth century.[87]

The prevailing view of decline in the late medieval Irish church is belied in Armagh *inter Anglicos,* at least, by the evidence of widescale church building, extension and ornamentation. The building of so many new churches in the countryside, and the significant extensions made to the urban churches, in such a short span of time must reflect a period of strong economic growth. The gentry of County Louth were replacing their former residences with tower houses at this same time. Similar tower houses were built in the towns by some of the urban oligarchs.[88] The same coincidence of church building and economic growth occurred in other parts of Ireland, in Wales, England, and across much of mainland Europe.[89] It indicates that the increased investment in the church was a result of increased prosperity and not simply of an increase in piety. Nonetheless, the scale of re-building and/or extension of churches in Armagh *inter Anglicos* is remarkable and demonstrates a high level of commitment of the people to their local churches up to the Tudor reformations. It seems more than likely that the priests and people in Armagh *inter Anglicos* looked to the future with a certain confidence as they worshipped in their new or beautified churches in the early sixteenth century.

There are two major conclusions to be drawn from this discussion of the parishes. First, in the first half of the sixteenth century the parishioners of Armagh *inter Anglicos* were served by a very dense network of churches staffed by at least one priest. This should have ensured that the people had ready access to a church for liturgical services, and to a priest for his ministrations. Second, the evidence of massive church building, extension and ornamentation suggests that the churches enjoyed considerable lay support before the Tudor reformation. Indeed, the levels of lay investment in their parish churches suggests considerable lay concern with the ministry of the Catholic church in general, and of the parish clergy in particular. More than that, one might infer that the enormous capital invested in the church buildings may be seen as indicating a considerable degree of positive lay appreciation of the ministry of their priests. Had the parish clergy been generally negligent it is inconceivable that their parishioners would have shown themselves so committed to their churches. This inference will be explored in detail in the section below which deals with the parish clergy. Nonetheless, the number of churches which functioned in Armagh *inter Anglicos* in the early sixteenth century indicates that the structures existed for the diocesan church to meet the pastoral needs of the laity, while the laity's investment in their churches may be taken as evidence of a considerable level of lay commitment to the diocesan church before the Tudor reformations.

FINANCE

Parochial revenues reflected the interplay of several factors; the size of a parish, its physical geography, the socio-economic environment, and also local customs of financial support for the church, as well as any endowments the church may have possessed.

It has been suggested above that economic productivity on the fertile lowlands of County Louth and in its towns was high in the early sixteenth century, with the uplands and the marchlands exposed to Irish raids being less productive. The valuations of twenty-five benefices recorded in the Irish Valor ecclesiasticus and in Primate Dowdall's register, together with information contained in the monastic extents for County Louth, can be used to give a good impression of the revenues received by parish churches in the archdiocese of Armagh *inter Anglicos c.*1538–40.

The Henrician valuations in the Irish Valor ecclesiasticus were compiled by commissioners in 1538–9.[90] The act of 1537 charged the chancellor or keeper of the seal to send commissioners to each diocese to determine the values of all tithes, offerings, emoluments (spiritual and temporal) of each benefice and chantry: in effect they were to survey every part of the clergy's income derived from ecclesiastical sources. Deductions were allowed for rents, the fees payable to stewards, bailiffs and auditors, for synodals, for alms which the benefice holders were obliged to pay, and for any pensions payable from the revenues of benefices.[91] Such information would have taken some time to compile. It is apparent, however, that the crown commissioners did not carry out inquisitions through local juries similar to those used to compile the monastic extents. Instead they drew their information from diocesan records of the kind which were kept for calculations of diocesan procurations and synodals, and particularly for the annual clerical subsidies imposed by the English crown.[92] Fifteenth-century records among the Armagh registers show that crown subsidies were met in part by fixed-rate levies upon benefices, indicating that the value of benefices was known with some precision. Because they were compiled by the diocesan administrators they are likely to be as accurate as any financial figures available for the sixteenth century. The fact that the figures of 1538 were revised in 1544, and probably on other occasions too, gives added grounds for confidence in their usefulness as indicators of clerical incomes.

The printed text of the 1538 valuations made for the Irish Valor has information for only two prebends, six rectories, nine vicarages and nine chantries in Armagh *inter Anglicos*.[93] Fortunately, a full text has been preserved in a copy of the Valor from *c*.1590, and another has been preserved in the record of the crown visitation of the archdiocese of Armagh in 1622.[94] Primate Dowdall's register preserves a valuation of the benefices in Armagh *inter Anglicos* which were liable for the twentieth tax in 1544.[95] These give data for two prebends, nine rectories and fourteen vicarages across County Louth.

A comparison of the 1538 Valor and Primate Dowdall's 1544 valuation lists reveal that the revenues of fifteen benefices were unchanged over the period, six benefices were worth less in the later period, while the values of two benefices had increased. Those benefices which had a lesser valuation for the twentieth tax in 1544 included two – Drumcar and Darver – whose incumbents had recently retired and were probably paid a pension by their successors.[96] When Dnus Patrick Galtrim, former prior of the house of the Crutched friars at Dundalk, resigned as vicar of Termonfeckin in 1542, the archbishop allowed him a pension of £2 14s. 8d. to be paid by his successor.[97] Evidently the retired vicar had died before 1544.[98] Under the terms of the act for the twentieth tax on clerical benefices, pensions were exempt from the tax. Most of the lower values may confidently be ascribed to the payment of pensions, though the lesser valuations of the northern parish of Killincoole may possibly be related to the depredations of the Ulster Irish in 1539 which devastated wide areas of the border lands in the north and west of County Louth.[99] Most significant, though, are the great majority of valuations which remained unchanged in the interval, despite the inevitable fluctuations in weather conditions and consequent variations in crop yields and their effects on prices. They suggest that parochial revenues were relatively fixed by custom, not only for assessments of episcopal or crown levies, but also for their collection from the lay community.

The Irish Valor and Primate Dowdall's register give simply a gross monetary value for the benefices they record. They give no indication as to the constituent sources which went to make up the income of the benefice. Fortunately the monastic extents are a little more informative in this regard, giving at least some idea of the values of the great tithes and altarages for several parishes in Armagh *inter Anglicos*. The monastic extents for County Louth were compiled in 1540 and 1541 through sworn juries from a number of locations across the county. The jurors sometimes included former members of the recently dissolved religious communities.[100] They obviously had access to monastic estate records to compile such detailed information in a reasonable space of time. The jurors who conducted the inquisition into the properties of the priory of Louth referred explicitly to 'the ancient evidences of the priory' as one of their sources.[101] The juries of County Louth, doubtless following the accounting practices of the religious houses whose extents they reported, provided information on impropriated benefices in different forms. The former extents of the Hospitallers of Kilmainham within the county of Louth detail the number of tithe couples in each townland of the parishes impropriate to it, and also indicate the value of the altarages of each parish.[102] The former extents of the Cistercian abbey at Mellifont, on the other hand, do not specify the number of tithe couples in the parishes, and give no indication as to the value of altarages.[103] These variations in accounting practices mean that the monastic extents are more useful for the study of some parishes' revenues than others in Armagh *inter Anglicos*. A further problem is that the price at which the tithes were leased by a religious community might not bear a very close relationship to their true value; for example, the rectory of Drumcar was leased for £9 6s. 8d. per annum, but was sub-leased for £20 by the farmer.[104]

Great tithes

The tithes of parishes in County Louth were divided into two categories. The term 'tithe' usually signified the 'great tithes' on corn and hay.[105] The corn tithes were collected annually by 'couples' of acres of grain in accordance with the custom of the county: one acre from every ten acres of wheat and one from every ten acres of oats.[106] The corn tithes were generally gathered in sheaves before being brought to a haggard for storage.[107] James Murray, in his study of tithe practices in the archdiocese of Dublin in the sixteenth century, showed that there were local customs there which determined whether the corn tithes were gathered in sheaves or collected as threshed grain.[108] It is conceivable that similar variations in local customs were also found in Armagh *inter Anglicos* though the evidence is wanting.

The religious houses invariably leased their great tithes.[109] Interestingly, the leases stipulated a fixed number of 'couples' for the tithes of parishes, and often even of townlands, and the tithe-farmers were charged a fixed rate per 'couple', regardless of market prices.[110] Hence the Hospitallers of Kilmainham took 10s. per 'couple', while the Cistercians of Mellifont and St Mary's leased their great tithes for 13s. 4d. per 'couple'. No information is available to show how the tithe-farmers in County Louth levied the tithes from the landlords and peasantry, but it is likely that they did so according to a fixed customary basis to minimise contention and facilitate collection.

Since most of the parishes in Armagh *inter Anglicos* were impropriated to religious houses it is highly probable that the customs pertaining to levying the great tithes in the remaining parishes were similar, if not the same. Some rectors took charge of tithe collecting themselves. Mgr William Mann, rector of Heynestown, successfully sued a layman in Armagh's consistory court in 1518 to secure the full amount of the tithes due to him.[111] Others may have leased the tithes for convenience, or in the expectation that a powerful layman might secure a greater volume of tithes, even after allowance had been made for his commission.[112]

The value of the great tithes varied across the parishes of Armagh *inter Anglicos* as one would expect. In the peaceful and prosperous south and east the corn tithes were considerable.[113] In the exposed borderlands of the north and west of County Louth there was sometimes no corn cultivated at all. This was especially true in the aftermath of 'rebellions'. In such exposed borderlands landlords and farmers adjusted to the atmosphere of insecurity by depending on pastoral farming to a greater degree than tillage farming. Cattle, which could be driven off to a place of safety, were less vulnerable to enemies than were cornfields and granaries which offerred an easy target for an incendiary's torch. This, however, posed great difficulty for the church in Armagh *inter Anglicos* as no tithes were paid on pasture land there. Indeed, lands which were entirely given over to pastoral farming were described as being 'waste' in the monastic extents.[114] Hence in parishes where pastoral farming was important, especially if it dominated the local economy, the church was denied a most significant source of revenue. That this was a widespread problem for the church in Ireland in the early sixteenth century is indicated by a statute of a provincial synod of the province of Dublin in 1518.[115] It meant that tithe revenues were greatly depressed over a very large part of Ireland.

Altarages

The second category of parochial revenues were termed 'altarages'. Altarages included the 'small tithes' or tithes on agricultural produce other than grain and hay; fish tithes; personal tithes which were levied on the profits of trade or waged incomes; and the various offerings known as 'oblations'.[116] The monastic extents record the total value of the great tithes and altarages for only six areas in County Louth in 1540, precluding the possibility of serious analysis.[117] Yet, from this small sample one might tentatively infer that the altarages comprised a significant proportion of parochial revenues across Armagh *inter Anglicos*, but are likely to have been especially important in poorer parishes in the marchlands, or wherever pastoral farming was predominant.

TABLE 1	Relative values of 'great tithes' and altarages		
Church	*Great tithes*	*Altarages*	*Percentage*
Kilsaran	£8	£2	20
Dysert	£4 10s.	£2	31
Port	£2 10s.	£1	29
Callystown	£2	10s	20
Tallonstown	£1 15s.	£2	53
Monasterboice	£1	£1 6s. 8d.	46

At Ardee, and presumably in some other places in County Louth, not only was the produce of gardens considered liable to the 'small tithe', but so too was turf.[118] At Carlingford there was a customary tithe on butter, though the fact that the townspeople of Carlingford considered that they had some grounds for ceasing to pay the butter tithe in 1521 suggests, perhaps, that it was not a universal custom in the rural deaneries of Armagh *inter Anglicos*.[119] At Dromiskin there was a customary tithe on beer.[120]

The tithe on fish was especially valuable at the port of Carlingford, being worth no less than £6 in 1540.[121] One may assume that they were also valuable in other coastal areas, like Kilclogher (alias Clogherhead).[122] It is not known how the fish-tithes were collected. Perhaps there was a fixed levy on the local fishermen, as Murray found for the fishermen at Lusk, County Dublin.[123] Freshwater fish were also liable to tithes, and possession of the fish-tithes of the River Boyne were disputed by the priories of Louth and Llanthony in the early fifteenth century.[124] On smaller rivers too tithes were demanded on salmon and other fish, but were not always given willingly.[125]

Personal tithes

The church endeavoured to collect personal tithes on the profits of shop keepers and merchants, and on waged incomes. Such tithes were notoriously difficult to assess and collect, however. A provincial synod of Armagh in the late fourteenth century legislated to secure the full payment of personal tithes from traders and merchants.[126] The provincial synod of Cashel in 1453 insisted that doctors, poets, goldsmiths, carpenters and such like, were liable to pay tithes 'notwithstanding the custom to the contrary'.[127] For the sixteenth century there is evidence from England, and suggestions for Dublin, to indicate that the church continued to have difficulty securing personal tithes.[128]

However they were collected, personal tithes were a critically important source of parochial revenue in many urban areas. Yet, Murray found that with the exception of the fashionable St Audeon's parish, Dublin's city parishes were very poorly financed by personal tithes.[129] The urban parishes of Armagh *inter Anglicos* were more fortunate in this respect in that they all embraced extensive rural hinterlands around the towns and were not solely dependent on personal tithes.[130] The urban parishes of County Louth were well-financed in the first half of the sixteenth century.[131]

Offerings

To supplement the revenues from tithes, the priests in Armagh *inter Anglicos* received offerings from their parishioners three times a year. These payments were not strictly voluntary, and the curates of Kilclogher and Termonfeckin sued some parishioners in Armagh's consistory court for failing to pay their dues as before.[132] Offerings were generally taken on major feast days, doubtless to ensure a good collection at times when church attendance was likely to have been better than usual. The value of the offerings is impossible to determine, but their significance to the parochial clergy is suggested by a statute of the provincial synod of Cashel in 1453 which decreed that mendicant friars were not to 'quest' on feast days on which the parochial clergy were accustomed to receive the offerings.[133]

Fees

Fees for the administration of certain sacraments, including baptism, weddings, funerals and for the churching of women after childbirth were required throughout the late medieval Catholic church. They were an important source of income for the clergy. There is little evidence about them from Armagh *inter Anglicos*. The presentments taken from juries in the south east of Ireland in 1537 show that they could be quite burdensome. The commons of County Kilkenny complained that the clergy there would not baptise a child until they received 6d or a dinner.[134] Murray found a little evidence that the fees for christenings in Dublin may have been more modest.[135] Perhaps the experience of Armagh *inter Anglicos* was more akin to that of Dublin than of the south east. Their contribution to parochial revenues is impossible to assess, but the amount of money involved would have depended on the number of ceremonies performed (which was obviously related to the size of the parish population), and the ability of the recipients to pay.

Mortuaries and the 'canonical portion'

The church in Ireland, as throughout Latin Christendom, claimed the best garments of the deceased as a mortuary.[136] The 'canonical portion' was a levy exacted on the moveable goods of the estate of the deceased. The 'portion' taken varied from place to place, in most of Ulster it was about 10%,[137] though in Derry diocese it was 20%.[138] In Dublin archdiocese the canonical portion was no less than 33%.[139] The inventory of the goods of Henry Gafney of Termonfeckin, dated 20 February 1489, indicates the size of the 'portion' in Armagh *inter Anglicos*.[140] Gafney's estate was worth £4 14s. 5d. after all demands had been met from it. From this 27s. 8d. was taken as the 'canonical portion', a levy of about 29%. In the English lordship the canonical portion went to the parishes, as shown by the fact that two suits concerning canonical portions brought before the consistory court of Armagh were promoted by the farmers of the parochial revenues.[141]

K.W. Nicholls has suggested that the canonical portion was the most oppressive of all the church exactions, and bore most heavily on the poor.[142] The archdiocese of Armagh had synodal legislation to regulate the imposition of the levy on poorer people. A case brought before Armagh's consistory court reveals that estates worth less than 21s. were exempt from the 'canonical portion'.[143] Synodal legislation also decreed that where widows and young orphans were left with estates of only one animal the priests were to levy no more than 12d. for an adult beast, or 6d. for a calf.[144]

Manses and glebes

Many parishes *inter Anglicos* possessed a manse and glebe. The royal visitation of 1622 includes many references to old or ruined manses in Armagh *inter Anglicos*, reflecting pre-reformation resources.[145] The extent of the glebe was largely fortuitous, depending on the generosity of the grantee(s) of the parish endowment. The glebelands of County Louth may be assumed to have been generally small; those of the neighbouring barony of Slane, County Meath, ranged from two to twenty acres in size, with a median size of five acres.[146] For Armagh *inter Anglicos* it is possible to use the Civil survey to determine the sizes of the glebes of Killincoole, Mansfieldstown and Darver; they were, respectively ten acres, ten acres and a half of an acre.[147] A parochial rector enjoyed full possession of the manse and glebe. However, when a parish was impropriated to a religious community the vicar might have to lease the manse and/or glebe from them, as did the vicar of Kildemock who paid 12d. for his vicarage in 1540.[148]

The maintenance of the parochial manse was the responsibility of the incumbent. An inquisition was held to assess liability for the delapidation of the church and manse of Dromin parish by the official principal of the archdiocese in 1539.[149] Evidently the church authorities expected to make good the defects by taking a levy from the estate of Dnus William Corbaly, the late vicar of the parish. In an earlier instance, in 1521, Dnus Conor Duff, the incoming vicar of Molary, sought to sue the benefactor of his predecessor's estate for the repair of the manse.[150] To judge by the absence of further references to the problem of delapidated manses it seems not to have been very common before the Tudor reformations.

Clerical incomes

Rectors received the full extent of the parochial revenues, and enjoyed freehold possession of a manse with, in all probability, a glebe around it. Depending on the size of the glebe a rector might be able to grow a considerable proportion of his own food. Eleven of the churches in Armagh *inter Anglicos* in the first half of the sixteenth century were held by individual rectors. When a parish was impropriated to a religious house or other institution the impropriators retained most of the parochial revenues in their own hands, and endowed the vicarage with the rest. In Armagh *inter Anglicos* the vicars were typically assigned the altarages and some small portion of the 'great tithes' for their living.

To calculate the incomes of the rectors and vicars I have used the complete text of the Valor for Armagh *inter Anglicos* preserved in an unpublished manuscript from c.1590.[151] The eleven rectories valued in 1538 were worth £6 10s 7d (Stg£4 7s. 0½d.) on average. If one excludes the worthless parishes of Kene and Baronstown the average rises to £7 19s. 7d. (Stg£5 6s. 4½d.). On the other hand, if one also excluded the exceptionally well-paid rector of Clonmore from the sample, one finds than that the remaining eight rectories were worth on average only £6 2s. 11d (Stg£4 1s. 11½d.). To calculate the average values of the vicarages I have included the vicar of St Peter's, Drogheda, who was not listed in the Valor but whose stipend is known to have been £10. The fifteen vicars received on average £7 4s. 9d. (Stg£4 16s. 6d.). If one excluded the exceptionally well-paid vicar of Stabannon, the average falls to only £6 11s. 7d. (Stg£4 7s. 8d.). If one combined the revenues of the nine rectors and fifteen vicars one finds an average income of only £7 10s. (Stg£5).

	Valor in Hibernia	TCD 567	Dowdall's
TABLE 2	Values of benefices *inter Anglicos*, 1538–44		
Archbishopric	£183 17s. 5½d.	£183 17s. 5½d.	£183 17s. 5½d.
Prebend of Kene	0d.		
Prebend of Dunbin	£1 6s. 8d.	£1 6s. 8d.	7s. 6d.
Rector of Clonmore	£22 13s. 4d.	£22 13s. 4d.	£22 13s. 4d.
Rector of Killincoole	£7 9s. 0d.	£7 9s. 0½d.	£4 8s. 9d.
Rector of Darver	£6 14s. 0d.	£6 14s. 0d.	£3 13s. 4d.
Rector of Heynestown	£6 6s. 8d.	£6 6s. 8d.	£6 13s. 4d.
Rector of Mansfieldstown	£6 6s. 8d.	£6 9s. 0½d.	£11 8s. 9d.
Rector of Beaulieu		£6 2s. 1d.	£3 2s. 1d.
Rector of Rathdrummin	£5 4s. 1½d.	£5 4s. 1½d.	£5 5s. 0d.
Rector of Carrick	£4 11s. 4d.	£4 11s. 4d.	£3 10s. 10d.
Rector of Baronstown		0d.	£3 6s. 8d.
Vicar of Stabannon	£16 8s. 7d.	£16 8s. 7d.	£16 8s. 8d.
Vicar of Dromiskin	£11 9s. 2d.	£11 9s. 2d.	£11 8s. 8d.
Vicar of Ardee	£10 10s. 4d.	£10 10s. 4d.	
Vicar of Dundalk		£10 0s. 5½d.	£10 0s. 5d.
Vicar of Dromin	£9 14s.10d.	£9 14s.10d.	£9 14s. 7d.
Vicar of Mansfieldstown		£7 12s. 6d.	£7 12s. 6d.
Vicar of Drumcar	£5 16s.11d.	£5 16s.11d.	£5 8s. 9d.
Vicar of Molary	£5 4s. 1d.	£5 4s. 1d.	£5 4s. 2d.
Vicar of Dunleer		£4 2s. 0d.	£4 2s. 1d.
Vicar of Carlingford	£3 13s. 8d.	£3 13s. 8d.	£3 13s. 9d.
Vicar of Dunany		£2 3s. 0½d.	£2 3s. 4d.
Vicar of Clonkeen	£1 7s. 2d.	£1 7s. 2d.	£1 7s. 1d.
Vicar of Kildemock	£1 1s. 1d.	£1 1s. 1d.	£1 1s. 3d.
Vicar of Termonfeckin		£9 7s. 0½d.	£9 7s. 6d.

Peter Heath, in his impressive study of the English parish clergy on the eve of the reformation, reckoned that Stg£15 would seem a 'desireable and reasonable' income for an incumbent with a chaplain, or where there was no chaplain Stg£10.[152] Only nine parish incumbents received more than Stg£5 while five of the twenty-four received less than Stg£2 10s. Whatever was the purchasing power of money in Ireland in the first half of the sixteenth century, it is clear that the vast majority of the beneficed clergy in Armagh *inter Anglicos* were poor, and five may be considered desperately poor indeed.

Yet the value of the benefices in Armagh *inter Anglicos* tells only a part of the story. There were twenty-four churches with benefices among the sixty-four churches *inter Anglicos*. However, the monastic extents reveal that there were several impropriated rectories in Armagh *inter Anglicos*, particularly among those held by the Hospitallers,

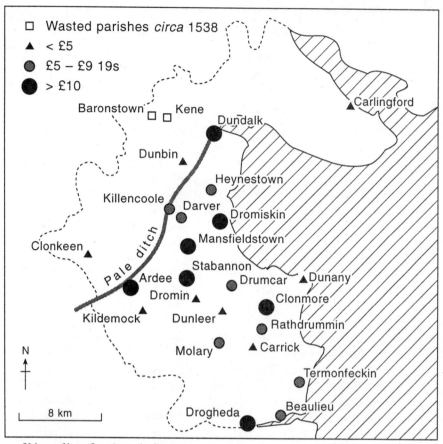

3   Values of benefices *inter Anglicos*

which had no vicarage in the sixteenth century. In such parishes the entire cure of souls was committed to stipendiary priests, the equivalent of an English 'perpetual' curate. These parish priests had the same pastoral responsibilities and economic standing as the curates who served the churches impropriated to the Cistercians at Mellifont and the Crutched Friars at Ardee, though the monastic extents referred to their impropriated churches as chapels. Nonetheless, the priests made responsible for those churches served the cure of souls in well-defined areas, and were entitled to the altarages therefrom. Such areas were occasionally referred to in the extents as parishes, as in the case of Knock Louth, Moorestown and Tallonstown. They subsequently became civil parishes. They may not always have been parishes 'de jure', but for the parishioners who lived around them those churches were the centres of their communal worship and, to judge by the money invested in the buildings, they were a focus of the laity's religious commitment. Any study of the church in Armagh *inter Anglicos* which fails to take full account of the churches served by non-beneficed priests – the great majority of all the churches – provides a very inadequate impression of the church in Armagh.

Only 33% of the churches known to have been served by a priest *c.*1535, or 37% of the churches served in 1544, were in the charge of beneficed clergymen. Furthermore, a number of the beneficed clergy, not just the prebendaries, were either absentee or pluralist benefice-holders, and their parishes were actually served by curates. The crown inquisitions on absenteeism in County Louth in the first half of the sixteenth century show that five beneficed clergymen were generally non-resident, whether for study, pilgrimage or whatever cause, and their parish cures had to be served by curates.[153] The pluralists included not only the often absent Mgr William Mann, rector of Mansfieldstown and vicar of Ardee, but Archdeacon White who was also the vicar of Termonfeckin in order to supplement his income. Yet it has to be observed that the archdeacon normally resided at Termonfeckin and carried out much of his responsibilities as vicar there in person, in addition to his archdiaconal duties, and he employed a curate, and supported a chaplain at Termonfeckin once a week as well.[154]

There is no list of the stipends paid to curates in Armagh *inter Anglicos* in the first half of the sixteenth century. The visitation report for Armagh in 1622 indicates the values of stipends paid to curates in charge of churches then.[155] The stipends recorded are meagre indeed. However, the one curacy for which a direct comparison of stipend may be made from the early period with the 1622 record shows a marked difference: the curate of Haggardstown received a stipend of £4 13s. 4d. in 1540,[156] but in 1622 the stipend was a mere 10s.[157] Such a discrepancy makes it impossible to make use of the 1622 figures for the first half of the sixteenth century.

Apart from the curate of Haggardstown the only other stipend for which we have data from the first half of the sixteenth century is that of the curate of Callystown who received £2 10s. 8d.[158] In general it may be stated that the curates' stipends were low. The priory of St John's, Ardee, allowed the altarages of the churches it held impropriate as the stipends of the curates who served the cures.[159] The same was true of the churches held by the Cistercians of Mellifont.[160] It has been shown that the values of the altarages specified in the monastic extents ranged from 10s. to £2. Evidence of the values of altarages in the neighbouring dioceses of Meath and Dublin confirm the impression that altarages were generally small in value.

The most striking indication I have found of the plight of some curates in charge of parishes relates to the parish of Heynestown. Mgr Caroll O'Cahan, rector of Heynestown and a member of the metropolitan court of Armagh, made an indenture with Dnus Roland Leyden on 9 December 1531 stipulating that the latter would serve the parish cure for one year, keep the chancel of Heynestown church and the manse in good repair, meet the ordinary obligations on the rector, and pay £10 to Mgr O'Cahan for the year in return for possession of the revenues of the parish.[161] On 10 December 1532 Mgr O'Cahan made a similar indenture with Dnus Hugh Mc Colkin for a three year period, but now he required an annual payment of £11 6s. 4d., together with hospitality for himself, his servants and horses should he visit the rectory.[162] The indentures are remarkable in that the rectory was valued at only £6 6s. 8d. in the Valor in Hibernia in 1538.[163] After the curate had paid Mgr O'Cahan his fee, and met the charges upon the parish, it is hard to imagine much being left for the curate's sustenance, let alone profit. No less remarkable is the fact that Mgr O'Cahan could have the indenture with Dnus

Mc Colkin guaranteed by a 20 mark bond (£13 7*s.* 8*d.*) from a relative of Mc Colkin's, possibly his father.[164] One can only conclude that the increase in terms demanded by Mgr O'Cahan over the course of one year, and the bond he extracted to guarantee fulfilment of those terms, show that clerical employment was in very short supply and employers were in a position to dictate very stringent conditions indeed.

Lower in status even than the curates in charge of churches were the assistant curates or chaplains employed by several of the better paid beneficed clergy in Armagh *inter Anglicos.*[165] There were also chantry priests, employed to celebrate the Mass at a specific altar for the souls of their patrons and their families, living and dead. The two types of priests were not consistently differentiated in the Armagh registers and it can be shown that the duties of the chantry priests could and did overlap with those of the assistant curate. Hence, the chantry priest who served the altar of the Blessed Virgin Mary in St Fechin's church, Termonfeckin, celebrated Mass four times a year for the nuns of the Cistercian convent at Termonfeckin, and was also obliged to assist the vicar and curate of Termonfeckin parish at confessions, baptisms, purification of women after childbirth, and other sacraments, and in return the nuns fed him every Wednesday and the vicar fed him every Saturday.[166] A number of chaplains seem to have rented no more than a room for their domicile.[167] Others were more fortunate and held a house.[168] The chantry priests of Ardee were endowed with a college to 'reside there in common in a hall and rooms fittingly laid out and constructed' in 1487. The ruins of the residential apartments of this impressive structure still stand today as a testimony to the benificence of its founder, Walter Verdon.[169] Clearly some of the assistant curates or chantry priests lived in reasonable comfort. Dnus Thomas Halpin, a chaplain in Dundalk, had his own servant boy.[170] Others, one suspects, can hardly have received more remuneration than their food and board in the parish manse. Some chaplains leased property to make ends meet.[171]

Below these impoverished priests there were holy water clerks in several parishes in south eastern County Louth.[172] It was the lowliest ecclesiastical post within the parishes.[173] These men, who may not have proceeded to priest's orders, feature in a number of suits brought before the consistory court of Armagh between 1518–22. It seems as though their low status and low incomes made many of these clerks frustrated, and liable to ill-discipline.[174]

The primates of Armagh were conscious of the need to compel the impropriators of parochial revenues to remunerate the clergy who served the cures of souls to a satisfactory level. A provincial decree insisted that vicars be paid a proper salary, and the Armagh registers include a record of a suit wherein the curate of Tullyallen sued the monks of Mellifont to increase his stipend in 1518.[175] The curate of Dromiskin parish, who probably served the parish cure in the absence of the vicar, Dnus Robert Rathcliff, a canon of St Patrick's cathedral, Dublin, sued the vicar and the monastic impropriators in 1523 to increase his stipend.[176] However, clerical poverty could not be legislated away. Some priests, particularly the curates and chaplains, were tempted to supplement their meagre stipends by various means. Some leased tithes from monastic houses.[177] Dnus Thomas Lery, assistant curate to the vicar of Termonfeckin, untruthfully claimed that a dying parishioner had appointed him as tutor to his children. The consistory court of Armagh found Dnus Lery guilty of illegal interference with a will and he was suspended from his priestly ministry. He was fortunate in that his vicar, Archdeacon James White, managed to persuade the court to lift the suspension.[178]

Unfortunately, the registers give no indication as to what was considered as an acceptable 'minimum wage' for vicars or curates. Whatever it was, it was far more typical of the 'average income' of the priests of Armagh *inter Anglicos* than the values of benefices recorded in the Valor in Hibernia because two thirds of the churches were actually served by unbeneficed curates.

Despite their low incomes considerable financial demands were made on the parish clergy of Armagh *inter Anglicos*. Each rector was responsible for maintaining the chancel of the parish church, the laity were responsible for the nave.[179] Each rector was responsible for maintaining the manse in good order, as too were the vicars who enjoyed possession of one.[180] A delapidated manse would not only make an uncomfortable residence, it could prove to be a financial liability. The manse of Rathdrummin was found to need repairs costing £2 in 1431, a heavy burden as the incumbent's annual income was assessed at only £5 4s. 1½d. in the Valor in Hibernia.[181] Furthermore, the priests who served impropriated parishes did not always enjoy automatic possession of a manse. The vicar of Kildemock, as was shown above, was obliged to pay an annual rent of 12d. for his manse to the impropriators of the rectory.[182]

All priests with cures in Armagh *inter Anglicos* had to attend an annual synod, usually in St Peter's Church, Drogheda. They had not only to pay for the expense involved in travel and in finding lodgings, but they were also obliged to pay a fee called a synodal even when, as in the case of the 1534 synod, it was adjourned without carrying out any business. In Armagh archdiocese the synodals were graduated according to clerical incomes: the wealthiest incumbents paid 2s., the poorest paid 6d and the others paid 1s.[183]

Procurations were more burdensome charges which were due to the archdeacon as well as to the archbishop of Armagh. These were payable by the rectors of the parishes, either the priests or the institution which held the rectory impropriate. The highest fee in Armagh archdiocese was £1 6s. 8d. from St Peter's, Drogheda, while the average fee for the remaining parishes *inter Anglicos* was much lower at 4s. 5d. The precise amounts charged as procurations were related to clerical incomes, but the charges varied (sometimes significantly) from one list to another.[184]

The beneficed clergy of the Pale were obliged to pay an annual subsidy to the Dublin administration which, in the mid fifteenth century in Armagh *inter Anglicos*, was paid by a levy of between 8.75% to 13.74% on incumbents' incomes.[185] The local gentry probably imposed cess on the clergy as well as lay freeholders, as occurred in other parts of the colony.[186] The convocation of the clergy of Armagh *inter Anglicos* attempted to legislate against the practice in 1492, though to what effect is unknown.[187] The provincial synod of Cashel in 1453 demanded that the clergy there should not be cessed more than once a year, and never on a Saturday or Sunday so that the clergy could attend to their religious duties in peace and quietness.[188]

A final, unassessable burden was the obligation on priests to be hospitable to the poor, the ill, the pilgrim and the stranger. However, good hospitality was expensive and it seems as though many of the clergy *inter Anglicos* were poor enough to appreciate some charity for themselves.

The discussion of parochial revenues and clerical incomes has served to make clear that many of the parishes in Armagh *inter Anglicos* were poorly financed, particularly in the exposed marchlands to the north and north west. However, the widespread impropriation of parochial revenues to religious communities magnified the economic problems of the parishes. The majority of the clergy in Armagh *inter Anglicos* were forced to depend greatly upon the altarages. Indeed, many of the unbeneficed priests had no other means of support. Consequently the poverty of most priests compelled them to be fairly rigorous in exacting fees, possibly causing a degree of friction between the priests and some of their parishioners. Nonetheless, the priests' financial dependence on their parishioners would have served to ensure that the priests could not afford to neglect the needs and wishes of the laity. Few of the priests in Armagh *inter Anglicos* were in the enviable position of the vicars of Drogheda, Ardee and Dundalk with their secure and substantial incomes. These facts would have an important bearing upon the clergy's disposition towards the Tudor reformations.

THE PRIESTHOOD

Education and training

The Third Lateran Council in 1179 decreed that every cathedral should endow a master 'to teach the clergy of the church and, without payment, poor scholars as well'. The Fourth Lateran Council in 1215 reiterated this injunction and added that every metropolitan see should also employ a theologian.[189] The archiepiscopal city of Armagh is reported to have possessed a large school in 1462.[190] Mgr Rory Mc Gillamurra (+1570), a Céile Dé at Armagh, was a bachelor in divinity and lectured in the subject.[191] Hence, it appears that Armagh maintained both a school and a theologian in the later middle ages as directed by the Lateran councils. Since so many of the clergymen who served the parish cures *inter Anglicos* were Irish the education offered in Armagh, and in the other schools *inter Hibernicos,* probably had a direct effect on the ministry offered to a great many parishioners in County Louth.

The priests drawn from County Louth itself may have attended more local educational establishments, or had the benefit of private tuition. There were, in fact, very few schools in the English lordship in Ireland on the eve of the reformations other than the schools maintained in monasteries. There was a couple of reputable grammar schools in the Ormond territories, and a common school in Dublin.[192] There was a school too in St Peter's parish, Drogheda, as one would expect for so important a city. In the mid fifteenth century Primate Mey excommunicated some men who polluted St Patrick's fountain near Drogheda's house of scholars, preventing the scholars from having refreshment therefrom.[193] William Servant, 'master of the scholars', appears as a witness to an appeal to Rome made in Drogheda in 1483.[194] There is no evidence to show that the chantries in County Louth had any pedagogic functions.[195]

Monastic schools seem to have been important providers of education. On 21 May 1539 Lord Deputy Grey and the council of Ireland appealed to Cromwell to preserve five monasteries and a convent in which 'young men and children, both gentlemen's children and others, both of man kind and woman kind, be brought up in virtue, learning and in the English tongue and behaviour, to the great charge of the said houses; that is to say, the woman kind of the whole Englishry of the land, for the most part, in the said nunnery, and the man kind in the other said houses'.[196] It seems clear from this letter that all six houses maintained schools, and it is most improbable that the council would highlight the pedagogic utility of monastic schools if their only students were aspirants for the religious life. The tenor of the appeal suggests otherwise. That the six identified by the council were not the only religious houses to maintain schools in the colony is indicated by the appeal itself which referred to the education given 'in these houses commonly, and in others such like'. Furthermore, there exists the text of an earlier appeal to Cromwell from the sovereign and council of Wexford for the preservation of the local monastery of Selskir which, the council stated, kept many poor folk as 'scholars and orphans'.[197]

The monastery of Mellifont, near Drogheda, may safely be assumed to have kept a school. It possessed one of the largest communities of monks in Ireland before the dissolution and, together with St Mary's Abbey, Dublin, which was named by the council of Ireland in its 1539 appeal, was reported to have been in exceptionally good order at the end of the fifteenth century.[198] The reason why St Mary's and the other monasteries were named in the 1539 appeal, and Mellifont was not, may simply have been due to the fact that none of the councillors came from County Louth. The cause of the two Ormond monasteries named in the appeal must reflect the interest of Councillor James Butler.

There was, of course, no university in Ireland despite the repeated efforts made to establish one in Dublin. In 1465 an attempt was made to found a university in Drogheda, but the project failed to reach fruition.[199] Only a privileged minority of the clergy from Ireland could afford to acquire a university education overseas. For the favoured few Oxford was the most popular choice, though some ventured further afield to Cambridge or Glasgow, or to universities on mainland Europe.[200] Of the five graduates who may be identified among the diocesan clergy of Armagh in the early sixteenth century, three were Oxford graduates, one graduated at Cambridge and the *alma mater* of another has yet to be identified. It seems to be generally true that the universities produced more canon lawyers than theologians. A training in canon law opened the way to promotion in diocesan administration.

Acquiring an education was an important step towards priesthood, but neither the grammar schools nor universities actually trained men to become priests. It was left to the aspirants for ordination to learn for themselves the liturgical aspects of their profession. Much could be learnt through observation at mass, and by imitating the priests conducting services. For a satisfactory knowledge of theology and canon law requisite in one who was to have the *regimen animarum* it would have been necessary to study books such as *Ignorantia Sacerdotum* which Primate Cromer instructed all of his clergy to acquire in 1526, or else a little priest's manual such as that which Dnus Sean O'Connor of Roscommon (+1405) is thought to have translated from Latin into Irish.

TABLE 3 Parish clergy *inter Anglicos*

Church	Position	Name	Dates	Sources
Baronstown	Rector	*Dnus Peter Mc Gonyll*	1531	Cromer's, II, f. 58v (139).
		Dnus John Bermingham	1531	Cromer's, II, f. 58v (139).
Beaulieu	Rector	Dnus Robert Lagan	1509	Octavian's register, no. 181
			1528	Cromer's, II, f. 37v (86).
		Dnus Thomas Bocome	1528	Cromer's, II, f. 37v (86).
Carrick	Rector	Dnus Thomas White	1480	Octavian's register, no. 150.
			1501	Octavian's register, no. 651.
Clonmore	Rector	Dnus Octavian Rounsele	1508	Octavian's register, no. 289.
Dromin	Rector	Dnus William Palmer	1500	Octavian's register, no. 394.
			1518	Cromer's, I, f. 4 (11).
Heynestown	Rector	Dnus Robert Tatayo	1515	Octavian's register, no. 212.
		Mgr William Mann	1518	Cromer's, I, f. 1v (2).
			1528	Cromer's, II, f. 39v (93).
		Mgr Carroll O Cahan	1528	Cromer's, II, f. 38 (88).
Kene	Prebend	Mgr James White	1530	Cromer's, II, ff 56–56v (131).
		Mgr Cormac Roth	1530	Cromer's, II, ff 56–56v (131).
Mansfields-	Rector	Mgr Thomas Darcy	1528	Cromer's, II, 39v (93)
town		Mgr William Mann	1528	Cromer's, II, 39v (93)
Ardee	Vicar	Mgr Thomas Darcy	1524	Cromer's, II, f. 13v (30).
		Dnus William Mann	1524	Cromer's, II, f. 13v (30).
Carlingford	Vicar	*Dnus Rory O Culean*		
			1518	Cromer's, I, ff 18v–19 (40).
		Dnus Simon Betagh	1521	Cromer's, I, f. 9v (19).
Clonkeen	Vicar	*Dnus Patrick Mc Laughlin*	1497	Octavian's register, no. 38.
		Dnus Robert Mc Laughlin	1518	Cromer's, II, f. 3v (6).
Dromiskin	Vicar	Mgr John Ricard	1520	Cromer's, II, f. 7v (12).
		Dnus Robert Rathcliff	1520	Cromer's, II, f. 7v (12).
Drumcar	Vicar	Dnus Nicholas Birrell	1521	Cromer's, I, ff 96–96v (121).
Dunany	Vicar	*Dnus Thomas Fenan*	1520	Cromer's, I, f. 54 (72).
				Cromer's, I, f. 107 (135).
Dundalk	Vicar	Dnus William Bryane	1503	Octavian's register, no. 186.
		Dnus Alexander del Palatio	1518	Cromer's, I, ff 6v–7v (20).
Dunleer	Vicar	*Dnus James Brune*	1518	Cromer's, I, f. 3 (9).
		Dnus John Brune	1519	Cromer's, I, f. 37 (56).
		Dnus John Ardagh		Cromer's, I, ff 106–106v (134).
			1524	Cromer's, II, f. 13v (30).
Kildemock	Vicar	*Dnus Thomas Duffy*	1518	Cromer's, II, f. 3 (4)

Church	Position	Name	Dates	Sources
Mansfieldstown	Vicar	Dnus Robert Serle	1530	Cromer's, II, f. 52 (125).
Molary	Vicar	*Dnus Eamon Duff*	1520	Cromer's, I, ff 60–60v (79).
			1521	Cromer's, I, f. 92 (116).
		Dnus Conor Duff	1521	Cromer's, I, f. 85 (108)
		Dnus Patrick Mc Eguyr	1522	Cromer's, I, f. 108 (137).
St Peter's	Vicar	Mgr Michael Golding	1499	Octavian's, no. 160.
			1519	Cromer's, I, f. 49 (67).
Termonfeckin	Vicar	Dnus Simon Geffry	1503	Octavian's, no. 190.
		Mgr James White	1519	Cromer's, I, ff 49–51 (67)
			1530	Cromer's, II, ff 56v–57 (132).
		Mgr Cormac Roth	1530	Cromer's, II, ff 56v–57 (132).
Ballymakenny	Curate	*Dnus Nelan O Donnelly*	1521	Cromer's, I, f. 92v (116).
Castletown	Curate	Dnus Patrick Taafe	1522	Cromer's, II, f. 1 (1).
	Curate	*Dnus Liam O Macriell*	1522	Cromer's, II, f. 1 (1).
Charlestown	Curate	*Dnus James Mc Dueny*	1518	Cromer's, II, f. 3 (4).
Drumcar	Ast curate	*Dnus William Rayly*	1520	Cromer's, I, f. 55 (73).
Drumin	Ast curate	*Dnus Thomas O Carroll*	1518	Cromer's, I, 13 (30).
		Dnus Patrick Mc Roddan	1518	Cromer's, I, 13 (30).
Drumshallon	Curate	*Dnus Nelan O Donnelly*	1520	Cromer's, I, f. 63 (81).
Kilclogher	Curate	*Dnus John Geragh*	1518	Cromer's, II, f. 3 (4).
Killincoole	Ast curate	*Dnus Turlough O Daly*		Cromer's, I, f. 101v (127).
Killineer	Curate	*Dnus Nicholas Lorcan*	1519	Cromer's, I, f. 28 (46).
		Dnus William Wyly	1521	Cromer's, I, f. 78v (100).
Kilsaran	Curate	Dnus Robert Ardagh	1530	Cromer's, II, f. 47 (121).
Mayne	Curate	*Dnus John Gruyr*	1520	Cromer's, I, f. 63 (81).
			1530	Cromer's, II, f. 47 (121).
Monasterboice	Curate	*Dnus Donal O Highran*	1521	Cromer's, I, f. 71v (93).
		Dnus John	1530	Cromer's, II, f. 47 (121).
Moorestown	Curate	*Dnus Thomas Duffy*	1518	Cromer's, II, f. 3 (4).
		Dnus Thomas Silke	1521	Cromer's, I, f. 87 (110).
Port	Curate	*Dnus Thomas Fenan*	1521	Cromer's, I, f. 102v (134).
Roche	Curate	*Dnus Donal O Lughran*	1522	Cromer's, II, f. 1 (1).
Salterstown	Curate	*Dnus Patrick Mc Egyr*	1521	Cromer's, I, f. 71v (93).
Smarmore	Curate	*Dnus Eamon Mc Eneny?*	1530	Cromer's, II, f. 47 (121).
Stabannon	Ast curate	*Dnus Nicholas Seskyn*	1522	Cromer's, I, f. 109v (110).
Staleban	Curate	Bro Robert Bowden		Cromer's, I, f. 44v
Termonfeckin	Ast curate	Dnus Thomas Lery	1520	Cromer's, I, f. 55v (74).
Tullyallen	Curate	Dnus Nicholas Birrell	1518	Cromer's, I, f. 1 (1).
			1520	Cromer's, I, f. 63 (81).
		Dnus Richard Heny	1531	Cromer's, II, f. 60v (146).

As in the rest of Christendom most priests in Ireland are likely to have been trained through a form of apprenticeship. In return for a period of service as a server and/or servant, a priest might prepare a young man for ordination. In 1514 Dnus William Ledwych, parish chaplain at St Audeon's, Dublin, remembered accompanying Dnus John Kearney, vicar of Dundalk, forty years previously when he gave extreme unction to a dying man.[201] Ledwych was eighteen years of age at the time, and may well have been undergoing training with the parish priest. In 1519 another young man of eighteen years of age, John Lymerick of Dundalk, described as 'literatus' (literally a learned person or scholar), was present at the death bed of Dnus Thomas Halpin, a chaplain of Dundalk, with Dnus Laurence Lymerick, another chaplain.[202] Presumably John was being trained by his relative. John Lymerick was a clerk in Dundalk in 1522.[203] Some years later he became a chaplain of Archbishop Cromer.[204] This system of training would have produced variable results depending on the qualities of the teacher and the student. Yet, in practice, the training probably equipped the average priest in Ireland as well as his counterparts in other countries for his vocation. A priest lacking a higher education was not necessarily unable to serve well the needs of his parishioners.

Promotion

It is clear from Primate Cromer's register that there were many more priests in Armagh *inter Anglicos* than there were benefices, or even parishes, to employ them. Many priests spent their entire clerical careers as auxiliary chaplains, at a chantry chapel, or in a lord's household, or as an assistant curate. Some went on to take charge of a church on their own. A minority went on to get preferment to a benefice. Clerical careers are extremely difficult to trace in late medieval Ireland but it is possible to follow a number of priests in Armagh *inter Anglicos* through their different ministries in the first half of the sixteenth century. The sample is biased towards the clergymen who succeeded in gaining a benefice and who were thus most likely to feature in diocesan records.

The differing careers of the two eighteen year old men, Ledwych and Lymerick, are instructive. Dnus Ledwych left his native County Louth to find employment in Dublin. Yet at the age of 58 years Dnus Ledwych was still a chaplain, and consequently lowly paid and poorly esteemed.[205] Dnus Lymerick was more fortunate. He became one of Primate Cromer's chaplains and in 1540, at the age of 39 he was promoted to his first benefice. Indeed, not only did Dnus Lymerick become the rector of Baronstown in north County Louth but he was made prebendary of Kene and thus a canon of Armagh.[206] In 1544 Dnus Lymerick was appointed to the more lucrative rectory of Darver.[207] By 1557–8 he had succeeded in becoming the vicar of his native Dundalk, a post he held until 1561 at least.[208] The contrasting fortunes of these two men reflect the varying fortunes of almost all of the diocesan priests of Armagh *inter Anglicos* of that time, though it should be observed that some clerics may never have enjoyed permanent employment as these two priests did.

The archbishop's patronage was extremely restricted in Armagh *inter Anglicos*. He could collate priests to two prebends; the prebend of Kene which was financially worthless in 1538 and 1544, and the prebend of Dunbin which was worth only £1 6s. 8d. in

1538 and 16s. in 1544.[209] The primate could also collate a priest to the prebend of Duleek which lay within the diocese of Meath.[210] These prebends were positions of honour. As was observed in 1540 when Dnus Lymerick became a canon of Armagh, 'a canon without a prebend is like a fish without water'.[211] The prebend of Kene was held by Archdeacon James White until 1530, and then by Archdeacon Roth from 1530 until 1540.

Primate Cromer had the right to collate priests to only two rectories *inter Anglicos,* Clonmore and Heynestown, and to the vicarage of Dromin on two occasions out of three.[212] However, the archbishop's freedom to collate priests to benefices was further restricted by the occupancy of these benefices by incumbents who had been appointed prior to his arrival. Dnus Octavian Rounsele had been collated to the rectory of Clonmore by Primate Octavian del Palatio in 1508 and he held the benefice until the eve of Archbishop Cromer's death in 1542.[213] Only then was Primate Cromer able to place his own man in the benefice. Mgr William Mann was already the rector of Heynestown in 1518, before Primate Cromer arrived in Ireland.[214] Not until he resigned the rectory in 1528 was Primate Cromer able to collate Mgr Caroll O'Cahan, a leading member in the consistory and metropolitan court of Armagh, to Heynestown.[215] Mgr O'Cahan first appears in Armagh's consistory court records in 1508, and clearly waited a long time for his benefice.[216] He was, however, made the prebendary of Clonallan in Dromore diocese also, a post of honour if of modest income. When he died in 1534 the rectory of Heynestown was united to the archdeaconry of Armagh for the lifetime of Mgr Cormac Roth, the official principal of Armagh.[217] Archdeacon Roth left the benefice in 1539 and it was held from then until 1542 by Dnus Ralph Colley. In 1542 Primate Cromer collated Dnus Hugh O'Shiel, one of his chaplains and a long-serving member of the archbishop's staff in the consistory and metropolitan court and, since 1539, vicar of Dromin, to the rectory of Heynestown.[218] Dromin was the third parochial benefice *inter Anglicos* in the primate's gift. Dnus William Palmer had been vicar of Dromin from 1500 until some point after 1518.[219] He resigned the vicarage to become the rector of St Anne's chapel in St Peter's church.[220] This title was honorary since St Anne's was simply a chantry chapel. Perhaps ill-health prevented Mgr Palmer (he was a graduate by 1518) from exercising a cure of souls. Mgr Palmer was succeeded by Dnus Thomas Ledwych who served as vicar of Dromin until his death in 1531. The archbishop then promoted Dnus William Corbally to the benefice.[221] After Dnus Corbally's death in 1539 the archbishop collated Dnus Hugh O'Sheil, his chaplain and member of his court, to the vicarage.[222] Dnus O'Sheil resigned the vicarage in 1544, having been promoted to the rectory of Heynestown.[223]

The foregoing graphically illustrate the strikingly limited scale of Primate Cromer's patronage within Armagh *inter Anglicos.* The archbishop was constrained to use the benefices at his disposal to remunerate a couple of the key men in his archdiocesan administration, particularly the lawyers who operated his church court. The needs of the parishioners in these parishes were met by curates who were usually poorly paid.[224]

The patronage of eight benefices, usually their manorial church, was in the gift of lay patrons.[225] These laymen would have wanted priests of good standing to serve their local church, but their choice of candidate was occasionally influenced by family interests. The parish of Clonkeen best exemplifies the way in which family connections could be used by priests to secure preferment to a benefice. The vicarage of Clonkeen was in the gift of Lord Taafe of Ballybragan. In 1532 Peter Taafe of Ballybragan presented Dnus Patrick Taafe to the benefice. Dnus Taafe had been a chaplain in Castletown ten years earlier and probably deserved his preferment, yet the coincidence in surnames is suggestive.[226] There were few members of gentry families who entered the priesthood, and the gentry enjoyed the patronage to few benefices, so family ties probably accounted for only a fraction of preferments in Armagh *inter Anglicos*, but they could be very useful for individual priests. Again, in the case of Clonkeen, it can hardly have been coincidental that the vicarage was held successively by Dnus Patrick Mc Laughlin and Dnus Robert Mc Laughlin (who resigned the benefice in 1518) about the time that one John Mc Laughlin was the tithe farmer of the parish.[227] Archbishop Octavian del Palatio collated Dnus John del Palatio (+1504) to the rectory of Heynestown in 1500.[228] He probably helped Dnus del Palatio to become vicar of Termonfeckin.[229] He collated Dnus Alexander del Palatio to the rectory of Clonmore in 1510, but the collation failed to take effect when its incumbent regularised his position by securing a certificate for his collation.[230] Dnus Alexander del Palatio had to make do with a pension of 5 marks until he became rector of Killincoole sometime prior to 1518. He was presented to the lucrative vicarage of Dundalk in 1522.[231] The last benefice was offered to Dnus Alexander del Palatio after the death of Archbishop del Palatio and must have owed something to his own abilities. Nonetheless, given the uniqueness of the surname 'del Palatio' in Ireland one may suspect that family connections with the archbishop had some role to play in the preferment of Dnus John and Dnus Alexander del Palatio to benefices in Armagh.

Local ties to a parish could also prove useful in securing a benefice. Dnus John Lymerick, one of Primate Cromer's chaplains, was from Dundalk. He was presented to the rectory of Baronstown in the north of County Louth in 1540, by its patron, Bellew of Roche. Dnus Lymerick was subsequently presented to the vicarage of his native Dundalk c.1557–8, another living in the Bellews' gift. Mgr William Mann, rector of Heynestown, was presented to the vicarage of Ardee in 1524.[232] He was probably from Ardee, as were Nicholas Mann, a layman of Ardee, and a Dnus George Mann, a priest of Ardee.[233] Finally, the family of Ardagh included among its number the vicar of Dunleer in 1519 and another of 1524,[234] the rector (*recte* curate?) of Roche in 1520, a chaplain of Dysert in 1535 who went on to be vicar of Mansfieldstown in 1544. The success of the priests of that surname must have owed something to their connection with the gentry family of Ardagh.

The majority of the parishes were impropriated to religious houses.[235] Generally, the livings of those parishes were almost invariably in the gift of the heads of the respective houses. Occasionally, though, as in the case of the vicarage of Ardee, the presentation to a benefice might be disputed between a powerful layman and the religious community. Nonetheless, the religious orders had the power to choose the priests who served almost 80% of the churches in Armagh *inter Anglicos*. This clearly gave them tremendous power over the appointment of the clergy in the southern rural deaneries of the archdiocese. It was not unusual, though, for the monastic impropriators to leave the choice of curate to the tithe farmer.[236] The archbishops were occasionally able to use their influence to have their candidates promoted by religious houses or by lay patrons. For instance, three successive archdeacons of Armagh in the first half of the sixteenth century were presented to the vicarage of Termonfeckin, a parish impropriated to the Augustinian priory at Louth. In 1542 Archbishop Cromer was given the opportunity to present a priest to the vicarage of Clonkeen by Sir Patrick Barnewall who enjoyed the patronage of the benefice during the minority of Nicholas Taafe, son and heir of Peter Taafe of Ballybragan.[237]

Patrons, the archbishop, gentry and religious communities alike, were generally keen to promote graduates. The archbishop, as one would expect, drew his administrative team primarily from among the graduates in the diocese. Mgr Cormac Roth, bachelor of both laws, was president of Armagh's metropolitan court from 1521 to 1540. He was vicar of Mansfieldstown until he resigned the benefice to become archdeacon of Armagh, prebendary of Kene and vicar of Termonfeckin in 1530.[238] Mgr James White, his predecessor as archdeacon, enjoyed possession of the same benefices until his death in 1530, and is also likely to have had a legal training.[239] Mgr William Mann became a MA at Oxford in 1513–14.[240] He held the rectory of Heynestown from some time before 1518 until he resigned it in 1528.[241] He was made vicar of Ardee in 1524, a living which he retained to his death in 1546.[242] He was rector of Darver in 1524 and kept the benefice until his resignation in 1544.[243] In 1528 he became rector of Mansfieldstown and remained so until his death.[244] Mgr Mann's plurality of benefices was most rare within Armagh archdiocese, and it reflected the value put upon his qualifications by the clerical and lay patrons of the several benefices he held at one point or another. The problem of losing graduate ministers to Dublin is well illustrated by the case of Mgr Thomas Darcy, a canon lawyer who graduated from Oxford.[245] Darcy was the official principal of Dublin archdiocese in 1516.[246] He secured a crown grant of the office of keeper of the rolls of chancery with a fee of £20 of silver in 1522.[247] In 1522 too he gained the prebend of Howth in Dublin archdiocese. However, Mgr Darcy was also vicar of Ardee until he resigned the benefice in 1524, and rector of Mansfieldstown until his resignation in 1528.[248] Inevitably, he was absent from the archdiocese of Armagh and his cures would have been served by unbeneficed curates.[249] Not until his promotion to the deanery of Dublin did he give up the last of his benefices in Armagh in 1528.[250]

Mgr Reginald Drummyn MA was presented as vicar of the very important parish of St Peter's, Drogheda, by Cardinal Wolsey in 1528 though he seems not to have secured the benefice.[251] Instead, Mgr Golding was succeeded by another graduate, Mgr William Hamlin BA, in 1533.[252] At £10 a year the vicarage of St Peter's was one of the best benefices in Armagh archdiocese, but Mgr Hamlin was licensed to hold the vicarage of Mansfieldstown *in commendam* from 1546 until his death or resignation *c.*1556.[253]

The graduate clergy were clearly a privileged minority, blessed with a university education and rewarded with the best, and often a plurality, of benefices. The parochial duties attached to their benefices were often delegated to non-graduate curates. The parishes of St Peter's, Drogheda, and Ardee, are likely to have been the only parishes in

Armagh archdiocese normally to have been served by a resident, graduate priest in the first half of the sixteenth century, and even at Ardee Mgr Mann MA, was often absent. An inquistion of 1524 found that Mgr Mann was not resident in either of his benefices.[254] This may have been because he was studying in England. Yet an inquisition of 1537 found that he had been absent from both of his benefices for the past three years.[255] The next recorded inquisition, from the year 1541, found him non-resident in Ardee, though he seems to have been resident in 1542.[256] It is clear that, if a priest had significant academic achievements to his credit, they did not automatically bring immediate benefits to the parishioners in his charge, though they may have been useful in the administration of the diocese as a whole. In any case, a good education did not necessarily produce a good pastor of souls, though the *Antiphonry of Armagh* records of Mgr Rory Mc Gillamhura BD, a Céile Dé, prebend of Dunbin (1551–?), rector of Clonmore (1557–?), and vicar of Ardee (?–1570), that he was 'a most reverend, extremely prudent, humble, affable, and charitable man who was loving towards all'.[257]

Working in the diocesan administration, even without graduate qualifications, was another path to advancement. Dnus Hugh O'Shiel was a chaplain at Dundalk in 1521, worked in the consistory court for some years before becoming Archbishop Cromer's chaplain, the curate of Ballymakenny and, eventually, he was made vicar of Dromin in 1539, and rector of Heynestown in 1542.[258] He resigned from Heynestown in 1544 and vanishes from our records thereafter. Dnus O'Shiel was not a graduate, but he probably had a legal training in an Irish *studium particular.*[259]

For priests who were not graduates nor blessed with the favour of a patron preferment could take a protracted period of time, or never happen at all. Dnus Robert Serle, for instance, was a chaplain at Termonfeckin in the late fifteenth century, and only became vicar of Mansfieldstown as late as 1530 and died within the subsequent six years.[260] Dnus Nicholas Byrrell was curate of Tullyallen for some years before becoming vicar of Drumcar in 1521.[261] He remained in this benefice until his retirement in 1542.[262]

Like Dnus Birrell, most priests who secured a benefice were likely to have stayed in their benefices for life. As well as Dnus Serle and Dnus Byrrell above, one may add Dnus Patrick Mc Gonyll who was rector of Baronstown from 1474 until 1531.[263] Mgr Michael Golding was vicar of St Peter's, Drogheda from before 1499 until his death in 1533.[264] Dnus Octavian Rounsfelde became rector of Clonmore in 1508 and held the benefice until 1542.[265] Dnus Thomas Duffy was vicar of Kildemock in 1518 and remained at Kildemock until his retirement in 1548.[266] Dnus Robert Mc Laughlin, having resigned as vicar of Clonkeen for the more tranquil parish of Rathdrumin in 1518, remained in his new parish for thirty eight years before his death in 1556.[267] Mgr William Mann, was vicar of Ardee from 1524 until his death in 1546.[268] Dnus Thomas Fenane, vicar of Dunany from at least 1520, died in his benefice in 1541.[269]

Yet most priests never succeeded in securing a benefice.[270] Circa 1522 William Corbally, James Hoper and two other men received dimissorial letters from Archdeacon White to allow them to seek ordination in another diocese since Armagh did not have a resident bishop at that time.[271] Dnus Hoper features in the registers as a chaplain in Ardee in 1524, but there is no further record of the priest.[272] Dnus Corbally is the only other man of the four who received dimissorial letters in 1522 who features in the Armagh registers. He became the vicar of Dromin in 1531 and died in 1539.[273] An inquisition after his death found that the parish church of Dromin was in need of repairs estimated to cost no less than £3 6s 8d.[274] After a career which included many years as a lowly chaplain Dnus Corbally died with a major debt being levied on his estate. Yet Dnus Corbally seems to have been by far the most fortunate of the four men who sought ordination in 1522.

Many curates who never secured a benefice may at least have been put in charge of a church with a cure of souls. The great majority of parish clergy in Armagh *inter Anglicos* were, in fact, unbeneficed. Such men, despite their poor stipends, were yet more fortunate than those priests who remained assistant curates or chaplains throughout their careers. Dnus Hugh Mc Conyll, for instance, was a chaplain in 1522[275] and seems never to have had a cure of souls. In 1532 Dnus Hugh Mc Colkin made an indenture with the rector of Heynestown which committed him to taking charge of the parish cure for a three year period under the most onerous conditions.[276] To secure even that difficult post Dnus Mc Colkin had to have John Mc Colkin, a merchant of Dundalk and perhaps his father, give a bond for 20 marks to guarantee that the priest would fulfil the terms of the indenture.[277]

It is quite possible that Dnus Mc Colkin was handicapped by being an Irish man in Armagh *inter Anglicos*. It is possible to identify, with a high degree of confidence, the beneficed clergy or the curates in charge of thirty one churches in Armagh *inter Anglicos* in 1518. This reveals that only seven of the nineteen benefices whose holders can be identified with certainty were held by Irish priests. Nonetheless, the number of beneficed Irish priests is remarkable because it ran counter to the Statutes of Kilkenny (1366) which decreed that no Irishman should hold a benefice within the English lordship. Presumably the Irish benefice holders in Armagh *inter Anglicos* had purchased a charter of denizenship to escape the legal disabilities of being Irish. Evidently there was also some anglicisation of Irish surnames. Hence, Dnus James Brune and Dnus John Brune, successive vicars of Dunleer in 1518–19, were probably members of the erenagh family of Mc Brune in the diocese of Dromore.[278] The Roth family, who provided officials principal for the dioceses of Armagh and Meath in the later middle ages, were originally surnamed Magherut or O'Rourke.[279] From 1521 Mgr Cormac Roth was president of the metropolitan court of Armagh. Mgr William Roth was official principal of Meath diocese about the same time.[280] Brother Stephen Roth was prior of St Leonard's, Dundalk, and seems to have been curator of wills in Armagh *inter Anglicos*.[281] The Leche family, which had earlier provided so many canon lawyers for Armagh were originally surnamed Kelly and had been forced to adopt an English surname to gain promotion in the church.

Not only did Irish priests hold only a minority of the benefices, they were generally to be found in the poorest benefices like Kildemock (worth £1 1s. 1d.), Clonkeen (£1 7s. 2d.), Dunany (£2 3s. 0½d.) and Carlingford (£3 13s. 8d.). In fact, for the churches which were served by stipendiary curates Irish priests predominated. Of the twelve curates in charge of churches who can be identified for 1518 nine were certainly Irish, while a tenth was probably an O'Reilly. Four benefices were held by absentees and the cure of souls would have been served by assistant curates, and the great majority of the assistant curates who can be identified in Armagh *inter Anglicos* were Irish priests. Hence it may be stated as fact that most of the priests in charge of churches whom we can identify were Irish. However, the sample of priests' names in 1518 is biased towards the south of County Louth since many of the priests could only be identified from the records of the consistory court of Armagh which was normally held in Drogheda or Termonfeckin. This bias is significant because it has been shown that this area was the most anglicised part of the archdiocese of Armagh in the sixteenth century. Therefore, one may make the inference that since Irish priests held more than a third of the benefices, and since two thirds of the churches in Armagh *inter Anglicos* were served by unbeneficed curates (who were generally Irish) it is possible to declare that the great majority of the priests in charge of all of the churches were, in fact, Irish.

Little can be said for certain about the backgrounds of the Irish clergy in County Louth in the first half of the sixteenth century. It has already been suggested that Dnus Patrick and Dnus Robert Mc Laughlin, successively vicars of Clonkeen up to 1518, may have been related to John Mc Laughlin, the farmer of the tithes of Clonkeen parish. Dnus James Brune and Dnus John Brune, successive vicars of Dunleer (*c.*1519), Dnus Liam O'Makrell, curate of Castletown in 1522, Dnus Thomas O'Rooney, chaplain at Termonfeckin in 1519 and Dnus Patrick O'Rooney, curate at Berlistown and then at Drumshallon in the 1530s all came from erenagh families in the diocese of Dromore.[282] Dnus Simon O'Culean, vicar of Carlingford in 1518, was a member of an erenagh sept in Armagh *inter Hibernicos* which held innumerable benefices *inter Hibernicos* in the later middle ages. Dnus Nelan O'Donnelly, curate of Drumshallon in 1521, and perhaps Dnus John Donyll, vicar of Stabannon from 1551–2, came from another sept with many churchmen, as did Dnus Donal O'Lughran, priest at Roche in 1522. The curate of Salterstown in 1521, Dnus Patrick Mc Egyr, shared the same surname as Mgr Eoghan Mc Egyr who was made treasurer of Armagh in 1527. Dnus Nicholas Lorkan of Killineer, chaplain in 1519, and Dnus Laurence O'Lorkan, curate of Monasterboice (–1547–1551–), came from a sept which originated around Lough Rorkan, in the north of the rural deanery of Orior, and provided many clergymen for the parishes of Armagh *inter Hibernicos* in the later middle ages. Few of these men ever succeeded in securing a benefice *inter Anglicos*.

It has been shown that the primate's right to present men to benefices in Armagh *inter Anglicos* was very limited. However, that is not to say that he had no authority at all when it came to appointing priests to parishes where he did not enjoy the patronage. Whenever a benefice became vacant the archbishop commissioned a panel of jurors to conduct an inquisition under the presidency of the archdeacon, or another senior cleric, to establish 1) how the benefice came to be vacant, 2) who had the right of presentation to the benefice, and 3) whether the man presented to the benefice was suitable. There was no fixed regulation as to the composition of the juries, other than that they be reasonably large, and that they included clergymen and laymen.

The inquisition into the vacancy of the vicarage of St Nicholas' parish, Dundalk, in 1522 was presided over by Archdeacon White and the jury included six priests, six clerics in minor orders and six laymen.[283] The inquisition into the vacancy of the vicarage of Ardee in 1524 was also presided over by the archdeacon and the jury was comprised of eight priests and five laymen.[284] Another inquisition of 1524 included seven priests and five laymen,[285] and one in 1533 had twelve clerics and two laymen.[286] There are many records of such inquisitions extant for the fifteenth and sixteenth centuries, and where they have not survived the format of the records of presentations and admissions to benefices, and the mandates for inductions generally record the information revealed in the inquisitions.

The inquisitions were important in establishing who enjoyed the right of presentation to benefices, but they were also useful in providing the archbishop with an assessment of the prospective incumbent. If the jury found the presentee satisfactory the primate would then institute him to the benefice, and have his archdeacon induct him into its temporalities. The system probably worked reasonably well in that the large juries are unlikely to have knowingly recommended an unsuitable priest, and the lay patrons, whatever calls were made upon familiy ties, are unlikely to have wanted a bad priest to serve their own parish. The primary weakness of the inquisitorial system is that it was only applied to benefices. For the majority of the churches, which were not served by a beneficed rector or vicar, the monastic impropriators, or lay patron if one existed, could appoint the curate in charge without much external interference. The curates were obliged to secure a licence of admission from the archbishop but it is clear from Archbishop Cromer's register that they often began to exercise their parish ministries before they had been granted admission by the ordinary. Indeed, the primate had frequently to cite curates at synods or at the consistory court to make them get their admissions.[287] The on-going difficulties experienced by the archbishop in this matter suggests that his influence over the appointment of curates in charge of churches was strictly limited.

The best that the primates could hope for, apparently, was to exclude unsuitable appointees if there were sufficient grounds to do so. One curate who is particularly prominent in the sixteenth century registers is Dnus Peter Bowden. Between 1518 and 1522 he was accused of fornication, allegedly assaulted and defamed by laymen, and was excommunicated for some reason by the consistory court. Already by 1519 he had served as a chaplain or assistant curate for sixteen years, and was still a chaplain in 1521 after which he disappears from our records. One cannot but suspect that his troublesome character hindered his prospects of promotion to a position of responsibility in the church. However, it must be added that Dnus Bowden was an exceptional character and no other priest attracted quite so much notoriety during the years for which some acta survive from Armagh's consistory court.

In conclusion, this section has shown that the archbishop had very limited patronage to benefices in Armagh *inter Anglicos*. Indeed, Archbishop Cromer had to use a couple of prebends in Dromore diocese, over which he was custos, to support some of the key administrators in his consistory and metropolitan court.[288] He could use the system of inquisitions to 'screen' candidates for benefices. He might even, on occasion, have been able to influence the monastic impropriator or lay patron of a living to present a candidate of his own choice. Generally, though, the archbishop could only exercise the power of veto to block the admission of a priest to a parish cure – if he had sufficient reason to believe that the priest was unsuitable – though there is no evidence of this power being exercised in practice. Hence the reality was that the archbishop had little power when it came to choosing the priests who served parishes in the southern rural deaneries. Rather, the primates had to try to ensure that, through exhortations during the annual synods, through supervision and inspection during visitations or, more drastically, by disciplining any delinquent in the consistory court, the parish priests met the required standards of pastoral care once they had been admitted to their office.

For the priests a university education offered a sure path to preferment in Armagh *inter Anglicos*. However, few priests could afford to study in a university and there were few benefices in the archdiocese which would have remunerated a graduate for the considerable expense entailed in acquiring a degree. A relationship with a lay patron was obviously helpful for the preferment of a fortunate few of the clergy. Being Irish, on the other hand, constituted a definite handicap when it came to preferment. Generally Irish priests were awarded the least remunerative benefices, or they became curates on miserable stipends, if they were ever fortunate to rise above the level of chaplain.

For priests who were not graduates preferment came after an extended period of training and service. After a number of years as an 'apprentice' to a priest, a man might serve for several more years as a chaplain or assistant curate, before a minority reached the position of parish priest. A parish priest, therefore, would have have some considerable experience of priestly ministry before he became responsible for his parish. It was likely to have been a rigorous preparation, and an effective one for their calling. It is clear that the life of a priest in Armagh *inter Anglicos* was not likely to have attracted men for whom worldly wealth and comfort was a priority. For all but a handful of the priests on the eve of the reformations the priesthood held the prospect of little more than frugal (for most, indeed, very frugal) comfort, and a sense that they were serving God.

Ministry

The effort to characterize the ministries of the parochial priests of Armagh *inter Anglicos* in the first half of the sixteenth century is made difficult by the absence of any visitation records. Fortunately, the act book of the metropolitan court of Armagh for 1518– 22 allows one to make an informed assessment of the pastoral care provided by the diocesan clergy about that time.

The most basic requirement made of a parish priest was that he be resident within his parish. In the absence of visitation records there are a number of useful crown inquisitions which identify the non-resident clergy in Armagh *inter Anglicos*. The inquisitions were carried out in pursuance of an act of the Irish parliament of 1458 which decreed that all benefice holders in Ireland were to be resident. The inquisitions appear to have been thorough in that priests who held more than one benefice were reported as being non-resident in the secondary benefice though they may have resided in the other.

In the inquisition of 1524 five priests were reported to have been non-resident.[289]

Dnus Alexander del Palatio was reported to have been non-resident in the parish of Killincoole, though he was not reported as being non-resident in his primary parish of Dundalk. Similarly, Mgr William Mann was probably resident at Ardee, but he was reported to be non-resident in his secondary benefices of Heynestown and Darver. Mgr Thomas Darcy, rector of Mansfieldstown, held high office in church and state in Dublin and was an absentee from Armagh archdiocese. Dnus Octavian Rounsele was reported to have been absent from Ireland, but he remained in his benefice until 1542 so it is safe to assume that he was licensed by the primate to go overseas, either on pilgrimage or for study in a university. Dnus Thomas Duffy, though reported to be non-resident in November 1524, can be shown (even with our imperfect sources) to have been resident in June 1524 and in January 1525.[290] Dnus Duffy remained in his benefice until his retirement in 1548.[291] If Dnus Duffy was not resident in his parish in November 1524 he probably had a valid reason for his absence since he was not deprived of his benefice by the archbishop.

In an inquisition in 1529 Mgr Caroll O'Cahan, rector of Heynestown, was the only priest reported to have been non-resident.[292] Mgr O'Cahan had only been presented to Heynestown in November 1528.[293] He was, moreover, a senior member of the consistory and metropolitan court of Armagh and he delegated the cure of souls pertaining to his benefice to a series of curates, with the archbishop's consent.[294] One may conclude that absenteeism was not a problem in the parishes of Armagh *inter Anglicos* on the eve of the Tudor reformations. There was a small number of parishes held in plurality by priests whom the archdiocese valued and sought to retain by offering them a level of income which was possible only by combining the revenues of a couple of modestly funded benefices. The pluralist, or priest who was absent for a legitimate cause, had to secure a licence from the archbishop, and licences were issued on condition that a suitable curate be employed to serve the cure of souls in his absence.[295] Absence without a licence was severely punished. Dnus Richard Garward, rector of Rathmeun in Meath diocese, was cited before the metropolitan court in 1518 and deprived of his benefice for non-residence.[296] The deprivation of an incumbent for non-residence in a suffragan diocese shows that the primates had both the will and the power to eject unlicensed absentees from benefices in Armagh too. At the synod of the clergy of Armagh *inter Anglicos* of 1533[297] Archbishop Cromer directed the rector of Carrick and the vicar of Clonkeen to reside in person, implying that they had delegated their cures to stipendiary curates. He cited Dnus John Birmingham, rector of Baronstown, to present reasons why he should not be deprived for non-residence. Unfortunately, Dnus Bermingham's answers to his citation have not survived. Nonetheless, Primate Cromer's insistence that every priest reside in his parish is clear.

The priest charged with a cure of souls had to celebrate Mass on Sundays and holydays, and on a number of other days during the week.[298] The priest had also to recite the Office publicly in his church on Sundays and holydays, and on some other days during the week.[299] The priest had to celebrate the key rites of passage, at baptisms, marriages, the churching of women after childbirth, and at funerals. Visitation of the sick and anointing the dying were other regular responsibilities of the priests. The priest was obliged to hear his parishioners' confessions, at least once a year, usually prior to reception of the eucharist at Easter. Finally, a priest was obliged to instruct the parishioners in the Catholic faith.

The religious instruction of the laity depended primarily on the efforts of the parish clergy, together with the parents and godparents of children. It is virtually a truism that the diocesan clergy in Ireland on the eve of the reformation failed to preach the word of God, though that belief is based only on a hyperbolic source.[300] There were few university graduates in the archdiocese of Armagh, and graduates were most likely to have had the skills necessary to compose a good sermon, though that is not to say that all non-graduates were incapable of preparing sermons. Certainly the preachers at the annual diocesan synods were not exclusively graduates.[301] It has been shown that the vicars of Drogheda and Ardee were often graduates in the first half of the sixteenth century, and should have been sufficiently educated to provide reasonably good sermons. Mgr Hamlin, vicar of Drogheda (1534–56), delivered the sermon at the diocesan synod of 1543.[302] In any event, while it may well have been the case that many of the parochial clergy were not capable of composing an extended sermon they were expected, nonetheless, to explain the essentials of the faith, and the meanings of the major Christian feasts, in homilies at Mass on Sundays and holydays.[303] To assist the parish clergy in their catechesis Archbishop Cromer directed his priests with cures of souls in 1526 to acquire a copy of *Ignorantia sacerdotum*.[304] This was a schema of Catholic instruction for the laity which was to be expounded to congregations in the vernacular four times a year. It was structured around fourteen articles of faith from the creed, the ten commandments, Christ's two central precepts to love God and neighbour, the seven principal virtues, the seven deadly sins and the seven sacraments. It was a comprehensive guide to Catholic belief and practice. *Ignorantia sacerdotum* was widely used in England in the later middle ages.[305] In 1518 Cardinal Wolsey insisted that the clergy of the province of York acquire a copy of the same book. Primate Cromer's demand that the priests of Armagh should all possess their copy of the book within a month of his synod indicates that the book was readily available for purchase within County Louth. One might even venture to suggest that it may already have been a required text for the clergy of Armagh before 1526.

The same kind of catechetical schema appears to have been normal in confessional practice in late medieval England, and conceivably in the Pale as well.[306] All Christians were obliged to receive communion at least once a year, usually at Easter. Anyone who failed to do so could be denied a Christian burial in the province of Cashel, and doubtless throughout Christendom. Communicants had to confess their sins before communion. Dr Duffy has shown that confession was an important opportunity for priests to instruct the laity in the essentials of the faith. Easter was a particularly busy time for confessions, and the pressures of numbers in a limited time-span obviously imposed constraints on the catechetical endeavours of priests, yet Duffy has argued that much was achieved nonetheless. The pressures of numbers seeking confession at Termonfeckin in 1519–20 are hinted at in an agreement made in the consistory court of Armagh to the effect that the chaplain was to assist the vicar and curate of Termonfeckin in hearing confessions, together with other duties, in return for the vicar maintaining him every Wednesday.[307] Confession could, of course, be more frequent and the Armagh registers contain a couple of records of lay people being granted licences to have a private confessor.[308]

Extended sermons were not generally expected of the parochial clergy before the reformations. The requirement throughout the later middle ages was for parish priests to provide their congregations with, at least, four sermons a year.[309] These could be given by another priest commissioned for the purpose if the parish priest lacked the ability to preach himself.

The comparative neglect of preaching by the parochial clergy was compensated for to no small extent by the vigorous pastoral activities of the mendicant friars. The mendicant orders were represented in all four of the walled towns of Armagh *inter Anglicos*. There were houses of the four mendicant orders in Drogheda, though there is evidence suggesting that the Dominicans experienced difficulties in maintaining their presence in the city towards the end of the fifteenth century.[310] The Franciscans, on the other hand, enjoyed a period of reform and renewal in the later middle ages with their community in Drogheda becoming 'observant' in 1521. There was a Franciscan friary in Dundalk, which also became 'observant' in 1521. There was a Carmelite friary in Ardee whose community would refuse to be dissolved in 1540. Finally, there was a Dominican friary at Carlingford which was in good order in 1540. One source hints at the relative levels of esteem enjoyed by the mendicant orders in County Louth and south Down: in 1485 Christopher Dowdall bequeathed 3s. 4d. each to the Franciscan communities at Downpatrick and Newry, 6s. 8d. to the Franciscans at Dundalk with 2s for the repair of their chapel, and another 6s. 8d. to the Franciscans at Drogheda. Dowdall bequeathed 1s. 8d. to each of the communities of the three other mendicant orders in the city.[311]

The author of the well-known reform tract of 1515 praised the friars as the only clerics among the Irish or English in Ireland to preach the word of God. The Irish annals regularly praised friars – though never the parish clergy – for their preaching. The friars went on extensive preaching tours and people were prepared to travel some distance, and pay bridge tolls en route, just to hear them.[312] Chapuys, the imperial ambassador to Henry VIII, informed his master in 1534 that among the Irish the observants were feared, obeyed and almost adored; even the lords held them in such reverence as to endure from them blows with a stick.

Compared with the parish clergy the friars were better trained and equipped for preaching. It seems to have been common for friars to deliver the obligatory quarterly sermons on behalf of parish clergy who could not preach themselves. The friars had to be licensed by the local ordinary for the purpose. It would seem that the preaching friars were rewarded by being allowed to collect alms from the congregation in the parish church.[313]

The zeal and piety of the mendicants was appreciated by the laity, sometimes to the disadvantage of the diocesan clergy. Inevitably, perhaps, some friction between the friars and the parish priests ensued. Some of the legislation of the provincial synod of Cashel in 1453 suggest that much of the friction was based upon competition for the laity's alms and bequests. The Cashel synod forbade the friars from questing on the days on which parishioners were accustomed to give their oblations to their parish priests, and it stipulated that the friars were to give to the parish priest one quarter of the goods bequeathed to them by any of his parishioners, or granted to them on the occasion of a parishioner's funeral.[314] Similar complaints were probably made in the archdiocese of Armagh but there is no evidence to suggest that they were more than a minor irritant. The parish clergy who invited friars to deliver the quarterly sermons must have appreciated the support of the friars in informing and inspiring the laity in their Christian faith, and this may have been the general attitude of the parochial clergy to their mendicant colleagues.

There is a widespread assumption that the parish system had broken down over much of Ireland by the later middle ages and that pastoral care had somehow become devolved upon the mendicant friars. That is certainly untrue of the archdiocese of Armagh. It has been shown that every church and chapel in County Louth (excepting the few in the marchlands destroyed in war) were staffed by a resident priesthood. Indeed, many parishes had assistant curates and chaplains to assist the parish priest in ministering to the parishioners. The mendicants were neither numerous enough, nor sufficiently dispersed in the countryside, to offer an alternative to the regular services provided by the parish priests, nor indeed was that their function. The role of the mendicants was that of auxiliaries to the parish clergy. The parish clergy were obliged to catechise their parishioners routinely, but the preaching of the friars may have added depth and greater insight compared with the regular homilies delivered by their parochial colleagues.

It is difficult to assess how well the parish clergy fulfilled their pastoral obligations, yet one may argue that they probably carried out their duties in a sufficient manner. Unsatisfactory priests were liable to be exposed in archdiaconal and archiepiscopal visitations, or be condemned directly by parishioners before the consistory court. Primate Bole removed a curate of Collon from his cure after the parishioners complained of his negligence.[315] It may be significant that this instance of neglect in Armagh, which is unique among the Armagh registers, concerned a Cistercian monk and not a diocesan priest. One may assume that the monk was placed in the cure as a cost-saving measure and that he felt neither the vocation nor the inclination for a parish ministry. This example shows that deprivation was a very real threat to negligent priests, but the fact that such deprivations were rare speaks for itself. Primate Cromer's register contains records of a number of court actions against priests for neglecting to maintain the chancels of their churches.[316] It can be shown that priests were punished for allegations proved against them by their parishioners in the consistory court.[317] Remarkably one of the trials took place within a week of the offence.[318] These acta reveal, not only that clerical misbehaviour could be speedily dealt with in Armagh *inter Anglicos*, but that there were effective institutional mechanisms in place for identifying, and correcting, clerical failings.

It is not being argued here that the secular clergy were paragons of priestly perfection. Throughout pre-reformation Europe rural priests in particular dressed and lived very much like their neighbours, though the church authorities endeavoured to stop them socialising in taverns and alehouses, gambling and playing football.[319] It has been argued, however, that the laity did not share the church authorities' concern in these matters, and that as long as a priest met their religious needs adequately they only desired that he be socially congenial and financially self-sufficient.[320]

Evidence of positive appreciation of the parish clergy *inter Anglicos* is scarce because the appropriate source materials have not survived. The most valuable source in this respect would have been the wills of lay people. Only a relatively small number of late medieval wills exist from County Louth to hint at the kind of positive evidence which may once have existed in abundance.

One may venture to suggest, by analogy with studies of the parish clergy in England on the eve of the Tudor reformations, that the lack of serious complaints made against the parish clergy may be seen as evidence that they served their parishioners to at least a minimum standard acceptable to the church authorities, and more importantly, to their congregations. The parish clergy of Armagh *inter Anglicos* were carefully supervised, and disciplined, by the archdiocesan authorities. The evidence of positive appreciation of the clergy has not survived to any significant extent, but the spate of church building and ornamentation in County Louth in the later middle ages, together with the wills that do survive are consistent with the impression that the laity *inter Anglicos* were as appreciative of the parish clergy as were their contemporaries in England.

CONCLUSIONS

The parish clergy in Armagh *inter Anglicos* served small, intimate communities which were well ordered and relatively sedentary. A favourable geography and a high degree of political order facilitated the maintenance of a well developed economy. In short the priests worked in an environment which was conducive to a good parochial ministry.

Evidence on clerical training is scant, yet the formation of the priesthood in the archdiocese seems to have been similar to that of priests throughout Latin Christendom. Candidates for the priesthood acquired a basic education for themselves, served a priest as an assistant for some years before ordination, and then served as a chaplain or assistant curate for several years more before they had a realistic chance of securing a benefice. Priestly training was, therefore, more practical than academic, and was probably the better for that in some respects. The non-graduate priest was well experienced in addressing the needs of the laity and could propound forms of religious practice and piety which were accessible to their largely illiterate congregations.

It would seem that the parish clergy *inter Anglicos* succeeded in performing their pastoral obligations to a degree which was acceptable to the archiepiscopal authorities and, more importantly perhaps, to their parishioners.

Although the parish clergy did not generally deliver extended sermons, they taught the faith to their congregations through homilies, explaining catechetical works such as *Ignorantia sacerdotum* and through reading synodal decrees. Many of the churches housed religious images which served to re-inforce the catechetical endeavours of the priests. Furthermore, the mendicant orders, which were established in the four walled boroughs of County Louth augmented the efforts of the parish clergy by preaching – frequently in the towns, and regularly in the country churches.

For the priests themselves their financial circumstances would have been a pressing concern. The parochial revenues of Armagh *inter Anglicos* were generally very modest. After the religious communities had syphoned off the bulk of the revenues of the parishes they held impropriate the vicars, and most especially the stipendiary curates who actually served the great majority of the churches, usually found themselves with incomes which were small indeed, and yet burdened with a range of expenses. The late medieval archbishops of Armagh had drawn up 'minimum wage' legislation in their synods, and acted through their courts to enforce it on niggardly impropriators, but the minimum stipend or income seems to have been very low. Clerical indigence made it necessary for the priests to demand fees for their services, despite the friction it might cause with the laity.

Possibly there were too many priests in Armagh *inter Anglicos* on the eve of the reformations to be comfortably maintained. Yet the laity insisted on having the numerous parish churches and chapels and chantry altars well staffed, and there were more than enough men being ordained to the priesthood to oblige them. The lay men and women demonstrated their attachment to late medieval catholicism, not only by endowing chantry priests and making bequests to the parish priests and the mendicants, but also by their remarkably high level of investment in their local churches in the later middle ages.

The discussion of the priests and parishes has been based mainly on the Armagh registers of the sixteenth century and hence it may create a false impression of stasis. It is not easy to correct this impression, both because no study has been made of the parish clergy of the archdiocese *inter Anglicos* for earlier periods and, more importantly, because of the lack of appropriate source materials to make comparisons with earlier periods possible. Nonetheless, there seems to be evidence enough to show that there was no general dissatisfaction with the church or its priests in Armagh *inter Anglicos* in the later middle ages. On the contrary, there is considerable archaeological evidence to show that the church in Armagh *inter Anglicos* was undergoing a period of revival and enjoyed great popular support before the Tudor reformations.

3

The Parishes and Priests of Armagh
inter Hibernicos

The volume of the material available to study the diocesan church in Armagh *inter Hibernicos* is not so great as that for the southern parishes of the archdiocese. The late medieval archbishops were obliged to delegate much of their supervisory duties in the north to administrative officers who were based *inter Hibernicos*, and whose archives have long since disappeared. Also, it appears that any records relating to the northern parishes which were kept by the archbishops' registrars were usually maintained in chests or volumes separate to those relating to the parishes *inter Anglicos*. Nonetheless, it is possible to construct a reasonably comprehensive image of the church in Armagh *inter Hibernicos* in the first half of the sixteenth century, and to present convincing answers to the kinds of questions about the priests and their parish ministries which have been addressed in the study of the priests and parishes *inter Anglicos*.

THE GEOGRAPHICAL AND HUMAN SETTING

The late medieval traveller from Drogheda to Armagh would have been conscious of entering a different environment as he or she ventured north into that part of the archdiocese of Armagh *inter Hibernicos*. The landscape encompassed more mountains, bogs and woodlands than in the rural deaneries *inter Anglicos*. Yet the geography of the northern deaneries was by no means uniform.

On the Lough Neagh basin, in east Tyrone and north of Armagh, the land was generally low lying and fertile. Indeed, a late sixteenth century English observer stated that Glenaul, the district between the Blackwater and Armagh city, was 'champion and fertile'.[1] Michael Glancy observed that the 1633 inquisition for the manor of Armagh listed the names of a great many sub-denominations within the townlands, indicating the existence of 'a large agricultural community'.[2] There were some marshy wastelands and woodlands close to the shores of Lough Neagh within the parishes of Ardboe and Clonoe, and around the confluences of the rivers Blackwater and Bann with the lough in Mc Cann's country and Oneilland, but they were relatively small.[3] On the evidence of the Maps of the escheated counties, 1609, the bogs and woodlands in this region appear to have been broken up to a very great degree. The soils are generally heavier than in County Louth, and the climate is less suitable for wheat to ripen. Yet these lowlands could have supported a relatively dense agricultural population.

On the western and southern rim of the Lough Neagh basin the physical geography was far less conducive to arable farming than were the lowlands. The Sperrins in mid Tyrone to this day support a very sparse farming population. Due south of Lough Neagh the Slieve Gullion-Carrigatuke range of mountains and hills still presents a difficult terrain for farming. Between that range and the marches of County Louth were The Fews, 'a very strong country of wood and bog', and Orior, an area 'for the most part without wood, but full of hills and bogs'.[4]

Philip Robinson constructed a map showing the pattern of townland density in Ulster *c.*1609 and used it to suggest that there was probably a higher population density on the Lough Neagh basin than on the uplands before the plantation.[5] The map confirms what one would have expected, that the agricultural potential of the mountains in mid Tyrone and around the Slieve Gullion-Carigatuke range was perceived as being low, then, as now.

The northern rural deaneries of Orior and Tullyhogue encompassed a great part of the O'Neill lordship of Tyrone. The O'Neills have been characterised as 'warlords', enjoying an autocratic authority based on their military power.[6] Katharine Simms has shown that the powers of the great Gaelic overlords, and of the O'Neills of Tyrone in particular, were very considerable. O'Neill was able to impose military service and to exact taxation and tributes on the population of his overlordship, from the Foyle in the west to the Bann in the east, from Castleroe on the north coast to the northern marchlands of county Louth.[7] Indeed, the town of Dundalk was compelled to pay a 'black rent' to the O'Neill in the early sixteenth century. Evidence from the late sixteenth century reveals that O'Neill had his officials count the number of cattle in his overlordship twice a year – a striking demonstration of his fiscal powers, and the sophistication of his administration.[8] Dr Simms has shown that there was an 'ever-increasing emphasis' on the overlord's responsibility for enforcing public order towards the end of the middle ages. Though the rule of O'Neill may have been 'despotic',[9] it is highly probable that the political and judicial stability imposed by the O'Neill lordship would have facilitated a higher level of economic activity than in the more troubled borderlands of the Fews or the marchlands of the Pale.

Conn O'Neill was O'Neill from 1519 to 1559. His demesne lands were situated around his chief residence at Dungannon castle.[10] Extending northwards from the demesne lands along the western side of Lough Neagh were the estates of O'Neill's *lucht tighe*; the O'Donnellys, O'Devlins, O'Hagans and O'Quinns, were to be found interspersed with church lands.[11] These lands were exempt from the onerous burden of billeting troops for O'Neill. Extending south westwards from O'Neill's demesne lands were the estates of the Mac Donnell gallowglasses who were based at Ballygawley.[12] To the south of these lands, in Largy and Kinard, Niall Óg, son of Conn O'Neill, held possession in the early 1560s, showing that O'Neill had almost certainly held these lands in the first half of the sixteenth century. In Muintirbirn and Tiranny Conn O'Neill's grandson, Henry Mac Shane O'Neill enjoyed possession in the early 1560s. Conn O'Neill certainly enjoyed possesion of Tiranny in 1544 and may have held Muintirbirn also.[13] The castle at Benburb was one of O'Neill's greatest castles.

Conn O'Neill held possesssion of much of the primate's lands in Glenaul and in

Tiranny.[14] In both places the primates continued to assert ownership over the lands but in 1544 Primate Dowdall's rental book gives no return for the lands held by Conn O'Neill, and the jurors who helped to compile the 1609 inquisition for County Armagh stated that they were unable to learn how much rent was payable for the lands of Tiranny.[15] One must conclude that O'Neill was the *de facto* possessor of those lands, not the primates. In Oneilland too, the archbishop claimed ownership and demanded certain rents of the O'Neills occupying the territory.[16] The 'Declaration of Shane's ordinary force' shows that in the early 1560s Shane O'Neill enjoyed virtually complete possession of Oneilland. The lordships of the Fews and Killetra were under the control of branches of the O'Neill dynasty.

O'Neill then enjoyed tremendous authority over the greater part of the lands encompassed by the archdiocese of Armagh *inter Hibernicos*. Of the lordships within the archdiocese held by *uirrithe* perhaps the O'Hanlon lordship of Orior was the most important.[17] The O'Hanlons were descendants of the Uí Nialláin but were displaced by the Mac Canns. By the fourteenth century they had become based at Castle O'Hanlon (now Tandragee) but they were hard pressed by O'Neill expansionism and their lordship shrank to a narrow strip of land beside the Glenree River bordering Mc Guinness's country.[18] In 1508 the great earl of Kildare forced O'Hanlon to cede Omeath on the Cooley peninsula to him.[19] By the second half of the sixteenth century, however, a branch of the O'Hanlons were in occupation of Omeath and the mountainous heart of the Cooley peninsula, a difficult area both in terms of its physical geography and the proximity of the towns of Carlingford and Dundalk. It must reflect the continuing O'Neill pressure upon the O'Hanlons to move southwards.

Within the archdiocese of Armagh the O'Neills of the Fews were the most unruly of Conn O'Neill's subordinates. Tomás Ó Fíach's study of the O'Neills of the Fews showed how they conducted wars against all of their neighbours, Irish and English, from the late fifteenth into the early sixteenth century.[20] The consequent turbulent environment was not very congenial for priests to have to minister in. The church enjoyed some degree of immunity, but it was not always respected.[21] As in the marchlands of County Louth, a war or even a major raid could bring about a temporary collapse of the church's ministry in a parish. The well-being of the church in Armagh *inter Hibernicos*, therefore, depended to no small degree upon the success of O'Neill of Tyrone in imposing order on his overlordship, and his *uirrithe* or subordinate lords. In 1533 Archbishop Cromer had to delegate his authority in a case of homicide from Armagh to the dean and the prior of the Céile Dé, and other Armagh clergymen, because a war between Hugh O'Neill of the Fews and O'Neill of Tyrone prevented the alleged killer being able to travel to Termonfeckin in safety to be examined by the primate in person.[22]

Mc Cann's country, beside Lough Neagh, was a minor lordship which was 'almost all wood and deep bog'.[23] It was firmly under O'Neill overlordship.

The Armagh registers have several records of primates appealing to O'Neill of Tyrone to act as the church's 'secular arm' and enforce decrees for which spiritual sanctions alone were insufficient to secure compliance to.[24] However, against the O'Neills themselves the church authorities were obliged to rely only on spiritual sanctions and pray for eventual success or compromise. On 16 February 1534 Primate Cromer called upon Conn O'Neill to act as the 'secular arm' in an appeal from the consistory court of Armagh to the Roman curia.[25] Later that same day the primate had to threaten O'Neill and a number of his men with excommunication and interdiction if they failed to make restitution for violently entering the archiepiscopal manor house in Armagh, for injuring the custodian, breaking the doors, and stealing goods pertaining to the manor.[26] The archbishops of Armagh had learned to live with such contradictions. They could only hope that O'Neill would defend the church and its liberties within his lordship. No one else was in a position to act effectively as the church's secular arm in the northern parishes. Furthermore, the O'Neills were not indifferent to ecclesiastical sanctions and reconciliations were invariably made.[27] In 1530 Nelan O'Neill complained to the metropolitan court of Armagh that certain churchmen, all erenaghs apparently, had disturbed him by fasting and ringing bells against him.[28] Doubtless, one of the bells rung against him was the famous Bell of St Patrick which was in the custody of the O'Mellan erenagh. In this instance it is very clear that Nelan O'Neill was upset by the churchmen's protests.

Evidence from the second half of the sixteenth century indicates that crop cultivation was carried out extensively in parts of the Tyrone overlordship.[29] Oats were part of the staple diet. The fact that flax was one of the four titheable commodities in the archdiocese of Armagh before the plantation, together with the high levels of exports of linen yarn and cloth from the north Pale ports, show that linen production was very important too in the local economy.[30] Pastoral farming was, of course, central to the economy of Ulster, as to Ireland generally.

For want of evidence, it is not possible to define the levels of economic production within the lordship. The contrasting densities of tower houses in the O'Neill lordship as compared with County Louth does not reflect economic conditions as one might have expected.[31] In Armagh *inter Hibernicos* the greatest cluster of tower houses was in the border lordship of the Fews, and not around the Lough Neagh basin as one would expect if economic conditions were directly associated with the density of tower houses. O'Neill of Tyrone had tower houses at Dungannon, Benburb, Omagh, Newtown, and Strabane, but at few other centres.[32] This low density of fortifications must have reflected a conscious decision on the parts of successive O'Neill overlords not to give hostages to fortune by founding too many castles/tower houses which could be used against them. In the winter of 1470/1 O'Neill had to conduct a six-month siege to recapture the castle of Omagh from some dissident subordinates.[33]

An examination of the values of benefices offers firmer evidence to show that economic productivity in Armagh *inter Hibernicos* probably was less than that in the parishes *inter Anglicos*. Yet, the different methods used to assess the laity's liability to tithes, and the varying degrees to which the tithes were effectively exacted, mean that the data does not exist which would allow for direct and reliable comparisons between economic conditions in the two sections of the archdiocese of Armagh in the first half of the sixteenth century.

The archiepiscopal city was the only truly urban centre in Armagh *inter Hibernicos* with its substantial community of clerics, its merchant community and other classes of laymen. There were English as well as Irish citizens in Armagh in the fifteenth century, and probably into the first half of the sixteenth century.[34] The town of Armagh was set on fire by English soldiers under Deputy Sussex in 1557 yet, according to the Lord Justice and council of Ireland, 'not a quarter of it was burned'.[35] This report seems to indicate that the town of Armagh was no mean size. The ruins of the stone houses of this urban population are visible in Bartlett's map of Armagh in 1601, and in the barony map of Armagh in 1609.[36] Indeed, in the barony map there are two tower houses drawn inside Armagh city, presumably the residences of local merchants, mirroring the pattern of wealthy merchant housing in the towns of County Louth. The archiepiscopal palace was at Drumarg, outside the city, to the south west.[37]

There was a weekly market at Armagh in the later middle ages.[38] It seems probable that the rents which had been collected in kind by the seneschals of O'Neill and the archbishop of Armagh were sold for cash, or traded for goods from the Pale or for more exotic items which had been imported through the sea ports of County Louth. The need to acquire money may have been widespread in Ulster before the plantation, as suggested by the considerable export trade in Irish linen. Since linen was domestically manufactured one might suggest that the small-holders in Ulster marketed some of the linen to earn some cash, either to help pay their rents or taxes, or to purchase such necessities as salt or iron goods.

It is now impossible to determine how extensive were the roads in Armagh *inter Hibernicos* prior to the plantation. The maps of the Lough Neagh Basin which were drawn in Bartlett's maps and the Maps of the escheated counties, 1609 reveal a relatively dense network of roads from Dundalk to Armagh and Dungannon. It is impossible to say whether these roads reflected a concentration of economic activity there, or whether the roads were mapped solely because of their military significance in the recent war. If the latter was the case it is likely that the density of roads across Ulster was greater than can now be ascertained. The quality of the roads is likely to have been poor. The English maps of the early seventeenth century show few bridges in Armagh *inter Hibernicos*. Nonetheless, it should be observed that the maps were drawn in a time of war, and bridges were likely to have been thrown down to hamper incursions by English armies. In 1458 Primate John Bole offered 40 days' indulgences to anyone who would support a carpenter who planned to build a bridge and a chapel at Kilcreevy, some kilometres south west of Armagh.[39] This record is interesting in that it throws a little light upon the economy of Armagh city in that the carpenter was clearly a man of some means. One cannot demonstrate that the bridge was constructed, but the chapel actually was built and in 1609 was classified as a parish church.[40] If communications within Armagh *inter Hibernicos* were indeed poor it should be noted that the quality of roads across Europe at the time was poor. Merchandise was normally transported by means of pack animals everywhere in Europe, with wheeled transport being extremely exceptional in the sixteenth century.[41]

Nicholas Canny, some years ago now, de-emphasised the contrasts between socio-economic conditions in the Pale and those in Gaelic Ireland.[42] He referred to the fact that the peasant population of the Pale in the sixteenth century was largely Irish, with the proportion of Irish people there increasing over time. Some of these peasants are known to have migrated from the Pale to better prospects in Tyrone. The exactions known to historians under the generic title of 'coign and livery' were imposed on the county of Louth as well as Ulster.[43] The lifestyles of the peasantry across Ireland, Canny suggested, were far from dissimilar. The discussion above would tend to support the views of Professor Canny.

The discussion of the socio-economic conditions within Armagh *inter Hibernicos* must needs be somewhat tentative and provisional in character. Yet these observations can be safely made. There were considerable spatial variations in the demographic and economic patterns in the region, which were largely determined by the physical geography of the area, but also by proximity to the Pale. Outside observers who first entered the overlordship of Tyrone from the Pale via the Fews or Orior encountered a landscape which was more mountainous, boggy and wooded than was the Pale itself. Yet around the Lough Neagh basin there was much fertile land which was widely cultivated and which probably maintained population densities which were not dissimilar to those of the northern Pale. O'Neill was able to impose a high degree of order on the region encompassed by the archdiocese of Armagh *inter Hibernicos*, a fact which facilitated economic productivity and a climate of peace. However, in the event of a dispute between O'Neill and the church, the churchmen usually had to cede most ground.

PARISHES

Primate Dowdall's taxation record for the beneficed clergymen of the rural deanery of Tullyhogue circa 1544 lists vicars and/or rectors for twenty-two parishes.[44] It is the only comprehensive list of parishes in Tullyhogue in the sixteenth century. The taxation list includes a rector of Donaghrisk and a rector and vicar of Drumcraw, two parishes which had been united to Desertcreat and Derryloran respectively in the fifteenth century, but which had clearly become independent again before the mid sixteenth century.[45] The list includes Killoon which was a parish church in the fifteenth and sixteenth centuries with a rector to serve the cure, at least until 1544.[46] Inexplicably, the rector of Lissan was not included on the taxation list, though Primate Dowdall's visitation record for 1546 shows that the rector of Lissan was resident in the parish and fathered two children within the previous two years.[47] Hence, one may conclude that there were twenty-three parishes in the rural deanery of Tullyhogue in the first half of the sixteenth century.

The 1609 Ulster inquisitions offer the most systematic account of the pre-plantation parishes available in any source.[48] According to the inquisitions there were then twenty parishes in the rural deanery of Tullyhogue which were served by beneficed clergymen.[49] The former parish church of Donaghrisk is recorded as a chapel in 1609, while there is no reference to either the church of Drumcraw or Killoon. However, in addition to Donaghrisk, four chapels were identified by the jurors.[50] In the map of Ulster among the maps of the escheated counties, drawn in 1609, there is a ruined church mapped at Killoon, just south of the Ballyclog, though there is no reference to it in the inquisitions. The church of Drumcraw, opposite to Derryloran, was neither

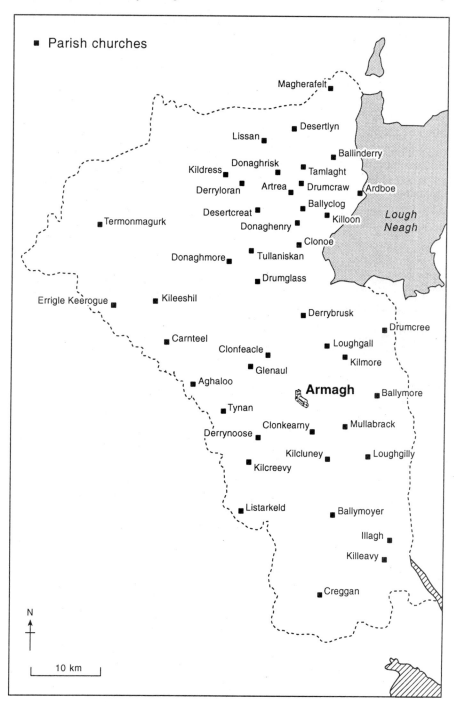

■ Parish churches

Magherafelt ■

■ Desertlyn

Lissan ■

■ Ballinderry

Donaghrisk
Kildress ■   ■   ■ Tamlaght
Derryloran ■   Artrea ■ ■ Drumcraw   ■ Ardboe

Desertcreat ■   ■ Ballyclog
Donaghenry   ■ Killoon   *Lough Neagh*

■ Termonmagurk
Clonoe ■

Donaghmore ■   ■ Tullaniskan

■ Drumglass

Errigle Keerogue ■   ■ Kileeshil

■ Derrybrusk
■ Drumcree

■ Carnteel
Clonfeacle ■   ■ Loughgall
■ Kilmore
■ Glenaul

■ Aghaloo   ⌂ **Armagh**   ■ Ballymore

■ Tynan
Clonkearny ■   ■ Mullabrack
Derrynoose ■
Kilcluney ■   ■ Loughgilly
Kilcreevy ■

■ Listarkeld   ■ Ballymoyer

Illagh ■

Killeavy ■

■ Creggan

N
↑
|— 10 km —|

4 Parish churches *inter Hibernicos*, 1544

mapped nor recorded in 1609, but the ruins of the church of Drumcraw were observable to the commissioners who drew up the civil survey of County Tyrone in the mid seventeenth century.[51] The ruins of chapels which were mapped in 1609, but not noted by the inquisition juries of that year, include one called Killetragh near Tamlaght, another at Eskragh near Killeeshil, while there are two churches at Killeeshil itself in place of the one recorded by the Ulster inquisitions. There were chapels mapped at Plaister and Killyneery near Carnteel, at Grange near Ballygawley and at Sess Kilgreen north of Errigal Keerogue.

Hence, in addition to the twenty-three parishes in the rural deanery of Tullyhogue which can be identified from sources from the first half of the sixteenth century there are twelve chapels which can be identified from the 1609 inquisitions and the maps of the escheated counties. None of these sites have been excavated by archaeologists and none possesses walls or other features which might allow one to demonstrate their use in the sixteenth century. The reasons why I would argue that these chapels were in use in the later middle ages are as follows. Firstly, the fact that these chapels are identified as such in the inquisitions and maps, and not merely as graveyards, must indicate that church buildings stood on them at the start of the seventeenth century.[52] Secondly, given the upsurge in violence as the conflict between the English crown and the O'Neills intensified from the mid sixteenth century it is most unlikely that the church buildings were newly founded during the period of the Tudor reformations.[53] Finally, a study of the churches and chapels in Derry diocese (a diocese contiguous with Armagh and also under O'Neill overlordship) reveals that were many chapels there which were most probably served by priests in the pre-plantation period.[54]

The average area served by a parish church in the rural deanery of Tullyhogue in 1544 was no less than 13,333 acres. If one took account of the ten chapels which are likely to have been served by a priest in the first half of the sixteenth century (which number excludes the second church at Killeeshil because it would not have improved access to services significantly and the ruined church at Killetragh since the latter was incorporated into Tamlaght-Killetragh in 1609[55]) the average area served by a church or chapel falls to 10,575 acres.

Given the lack of cartographic detail for mountainous mid Tyrone in the maps of the escheated counties it is conceivable that there were other chapels to serve that extensive district. Twenty per cent of the rural deanery was subsequently encompassed by the enormous, mountainous civil parish of Termonmagurk. If one excluded that district from the calculations one finds that the parish sizes fall to an average of 11,281 acres, while the areas served by parish churches and chapels was rather less at 9,192 acres. These are still quite extensive areas by comparison with the average size of area served by the churches and chapels in Armagh *inter Anglicos*. However, it should be observed that the lowland areas to the east and south of the rural deanery were served by a relatively dense network of churches and chapels and, to judge from the distribution of the ballyboes, this was also the area with the highest agricultural potential and probably of population density. A similar pattern of church and chapel distribution has been observed for the diocese of Derry before the plantation.[56]

Twenty-three parishes may confidently be identified in the rural deanery of Orior for the first half of the sixteenth century, with at least three chapelries identified in early seventeenth century sources. The average size of the parishes would have been about 14,085 acres. Even if one included the three chapelries the average size of area served remained high at 12,459 acres. On the other hand, it is by no means certain that all of the chapels which were served by priests in the first half of the sixteenth century are known.

The parish of Creggan was the most extensive parish in Orior rural deanery; the later Church of Ireland parish of Creggan, with 36,845 acres, gives some indication of its extent. Yet there were no chapels within this enormous area which can be identified from the 1609 maps or inquisitions. Nonetheless, it seems likely that there was at least one chapel of ease within the parish of Creggan before the area was devastated in the course of the Tudor wars against Ulster.[57] Henry Bird informed Sir Robert Cecil on 10 May 1600 that the English garrison at Carlingford launched innumerable raids on south Ulster 'killing men, women and children, burning their homes and taking from them many of their cattle and horses and driving ... terror' into the population.[58] He cited the devastation wrought upon the people around Lough Lorcan in the rural deanery of Orior as an example of the campaigning of the Carlingford garrison. A subsequent report by Mountjoy to Cecil stated that the English garrison at Newry had laid waste all of the land within twenty miles of Newry – an area which would have encompassed all of O'Hanlon's lordship and the Fews.[59] Bishop George Montgomery's survey of the parishes of Derry diocese indicates that in districts which had been thoroughly wasted by the crown forces during the Nine Years War chapels of ease were likely to go unrecorded in the eve-of-plantation surveys, apparently because they ceased to be served by a priest and were therefore defunct.[60]

It is impossible to define the boundaries of the parishes of Armagh *inter Hibernicos*. The civil parish boundaries are often very different from the parish boundaries recorded in the Civil Survey and Down Survey of the mid seventeenth century. Furthermore, these latter sources do not always record pre-plantation boundaries. The complex pattern of pre-plantation parochial boundaries, with discrete portions, which can be identified, in part at least, from the fifteenth century cannot be shown to have been maintained up to the mid seventeenth century.

Whatever their boundaries, it is clear that the parishes in Armagh *inter Hibernicos* were considerably larger on average than the parishes in County Louth. In the most extensive parishes, usually encompassing the most intractable terrain, regular Mass attendance would have posed real problems for the *cois mhuintir* living far from their parish church or chapel. The priests would necessarily have been infrequent visitors to the more distant corners of the parishes. Priestly instruction and spiritual guidance would have been physically hindered in such difficult environments.

Nonetheless, in one important sense the calculations of the 'average size' of the parishes in the rural deaneries of Tullyhogue and Orior are deceptive. The fertile lowlands were served by a dense network of churches and chapels, while only the mountainous districts, particularly in mid Tyrone and the south of the rural deanery of Orior, had very few pastoral care centres. It seems safe to suggest that the distribution of the churches and chapels might reflect the distribution of the lay parishioners, and their abilities to maintain parish ministries across the rural deaneries *inter Hibernicos*. Yet, it has to be pointed out also that the churches and chapels of Armagh *inter Hibernicos* were normally associated with erenagh lands. This in turn would oblige one to conclude that the distribution of the churches and chapels of Armagh *inter Hibernicos* probably reflected the pattern of population distribution, in so far as the distribution of erenagh lands (themselves a reflection of Early Christian endowments) facilitated the maintenance of a church to worship in.

Archaeological studies in County Louth revealed a remarkable phase of church building, extension and/or ornamentation associated with the period of economic growth from the mid fifteenth century. There is the likelihood that some of this economic growth would have filtered into Armagh *inter Hibernicos*. The extension of O'Neill lordship to the marchlands of County Louth would have imposed a greater level of political stability on the region, an important pre-condition for an increase in economic activity in Armagh *inter Hibernicos*.

The archaeology of the medieval church in the northern rural deaneries of Armagh has not received comparable attention as that of County Louth. The *Preliminary survey of the ancient monuments of Northern Ireland* is cursory indeed in its treatment of ecclesiastical remains. Furthermore, the state of archaeological knowledge was such that the contributors had great difficulty in distinguishing between church buildings of late medieval construction from those which post-dated the plantation.[61] A great problem with the Ulster churches is that it is not always clear if the planters built an entirely new church, or reconstructed an existing church. An even greater, and more general problem, is that too little remains of the great majority of pre-plantation church buildings to form the basis of any examination.

The greatest church *inter Hibernicos* was, of course, the cathedral church of Armagh. There were two lesser churches in its vicinity which were roofed and contained holy images inside them, suggesting that they were in use for religious services, until they were set on fire by English soldiers in 1557.[62] William Reeves stated that four carved panels in white alabaster, of Italian cinquecento design, from an altar or shrine in the convent church of Templenafertagh in Armagh survived the Tudor wars and Stuart plantation.[63] These interesting panels may owe their installation in a church at Armagh to the fifteenth century Italian primate of all Ireland, Octavian del Palatio (1477–1513). Also within the town were a Franciscan friary,[64] an Augustinian priory[65] and the house of the Céile Dé sited to the south east of the cathedral.[66]

Few church buildings survive in the rural deanery of Orior from the late middle ages. Among the best known are the churches at Killevy, where the ruins of a ninth century church and a thirteenth century church stand very close together.[67] One church was presumably reserved to the use of the nuns of the convent at Killevy, and the other served as the parish church.

The ruined parish church of Loughgall dates from the fifteenth century.[68] It was a substantial building (its dimensions are 90' x 30'), and rather larger than the average church in County Louth. Nothing survives of the medieval parish church at Creggan. However, tradition ascribes the building of the pre-plantation church at Creggan to Art O'Neill of the Fews in the early sixteenth century.[69] Given the proximity of the

O'Neill tower house at Glassdrummond, built in the late fifteenth century, this must be considered a real possibility. Tradition suggests that the chapel of Killyloughran in the parish of Creggan was abandoned at the same time. There are no surviving remains of any other late medieval churches in the rural deanery of Orior except, perhaps, the undated church at Eglish, formerly Glenaul.[70] Only part of the west gable and a fraction of the south wall still stand but the internal dimensions (15.4m x 5.5m) indicate that the church was about the average size of the late medieval rural parish churches in Armagh *inter Anglicos*.

Rather more church ruins survive in the rural deanery of Tullyhogue. Clonoe church has been ascribed to the fifteenth century and it too has a bell cote.[71] The east window, however, has been assigned a sixteenth or seventeenth century date. A fine pointed window with three lights and some tracery from the late medieval church at Donaghmore was built into the Church of Ireland church at Castlecaulfield. The window has been ascribed a fifteenth to sixteenth century date.[72]

The ruins at Ardboe have been dated to a period after the early sixteenth century, most probably the plantation period, though some fragments of thirteenth or fourteenth century stone work were found in the vicinity of the church.[73] Carnteel church was the subject of a detailed survey by Oliver Davies, and he posited a date of *c*.1550–1620 for the building.[74] Derryloran church has been definitely shown to be an early seventeenth century structure on medieval foundations, with some thirteenth century mouldings incorporated into the building.[75] The foundations of the medieval church indicate a width of 27' (almost 8m), making it quite a large church by the standards of those in County Louth. A hollow, 18m x 6m, is all that marks the site of the medieval church at Artrea.[76] This suggests that it was slightly larger than average compared with the rural churches *inter Anglicos*. The church ruins at Magheraglass date from the thirteenth or fourteenth centuries.[77]

The study of the archaeology of the churches in Armagh *inter Hibernicos* is made very difficult by the paucity of physical remains. Even excavations will not alter that fact significantly. All one may state is that there is little archaeological evidence, to date, of a surge in church building and ornamentation to parallel that in late medieval County Louth. However, it is possible that some increase did take place. From the mid fifteenth century there are records of parish churches at Donaghrisk, Drumcraw and Killoon in the rural deanery of Tullyhogue, and parish churches at Kilcreevy Otra and Etra, Illagh and at BallymcColgan in the rural deanery of Orior where there had not previously been beneficed clergymen.[78] In 1458 Art Mc Kearney, a carpenter of the city of Armagh, intended to build a chapel at Kilcreevy.[79] Kilcreevy had become a parish before the plantation, though it became defunct thereafter.[80] Until the mid fifteenth century BallymcColgan was part of the parish of Derrynoose. In 1430 the erenagh of Derrynoose complained to the primate that the impropriators of the parish, the Céile Dé of Armagh, were allowing too little remuneration for the vicarage of the parish to attract any priest to take up the cure.[81] The Céile Dé proposed that the tithes and altarages which had been diverted to support the curate who served the people of BallymcColgan and BallymcClemy in Derrynoose parish be given over instead to the vicar of the parish. However, since this would have required the vicar to serve those areas as well as the parish church and its area this compromise was not accepted and the impropriators were ordered by the metropolitan court to increase the area over which the vicar could exact tithes and altarages. This court case is most interesting in that it suggests that beneficed clergy and/or curates who served a subordinate part of a parish in Armagh *inter Hibernicos* were assigned the tithes and altarages of a certain area for their remuneration. By the first half of the sixteenth century the curate who served BallymcColgan had been replaced by a beneficed rector, as demonstrated by two procuration lists in Primate Dowdall's register.[82] This indicates that BallymcColgan had become a recognised parish in its own right. The parish did not survive into the seventeenth century.

Two conclusions may be drawn from this discussion. First, in the first half of the sixteenth century the parishioners of the fertile lowlands of Armagh *inter Hibernicos* were served by a comprehensive network of parish churches which were staffed by resident clergymen. Upland areas were poorly served by comparison. It is most probable that the parish churches were augmented by a number of chapels of ease which, to judge from evidence from the adjoining diocese of Derry, would have been staffed by curates. Second, while the evidence is lacking to indicate whether or not a surge in church building occurred in Armagh *inter Hibernicos* to parallel that known to have taken place in Armagh *inter Anglicos* on the eve of the Tudor reformations, it can be shown that the parish churches at Clonoe, Donaghmore and Loughgall, and possibly at Creggan, were built anew in the fifteenth or early sixteenth centuries and that would be consistent with the suggestion that there was a phase of renewal in the church before the Tudor reformations.[83] More significantly, though, is the fact that no less than six churches can be identified as having achieved parochial status from the mid fifteenth to the mid sixteenth centuries. This must surely reflect a period of growth in the pastoral ministry offered by the church in the archdiocese of Armagh *inter Hibernicos*.

FINANCE

Parochial revenues

Information on the composition of parochial revenues in Armagh *inter Hibernicos* does not become available until the 1609 Ulster inquisitions. Yet these inquisitions are important in recording many pre-plantation practices in ecclesiastical finances. The jurors at Dungannon reported that in Armagh *inter Hibernicos* tithes were levied in kind on corn, wool, fish and flax, and that 4*d.* was taken for every milch cow, a pig from every swine herd, and that no other tithes were paid in the archdiocese *inter Hibernicos*, either in kind or otherwise.[84] The inclusion of flax among the four titheable products is interesting in that it reflects the great importance of the crop in Ulster before the plantation. The 'flat rate' of a pig from each herd, regardless of its size, would clearly have burdened the small farmer much more than the wealthy. It is conceivable that the money tithe on milch cows replaced a levy in kind such as that imposed on swine herds, though the fact that the monetary rate was likely to have increased the tithe bills of the wealthy, those most able to resist unwanted change, suggests that it may not have been a novel imposition. It has been shown that the O'Neills of Tyrone had the ability to have the cattle in their lordships enumerated regularly for tax purposes, and that the taxes on cattle were paid in cash (or cash equivalents).[85] This shows that they possessed a mechanism through which the cattle tithes could have been collected, in return for a fee, for the church. Without the assistance of O'Neill or his subordinates it is difficult to conceive how the parish clergy could otherwise have gathered the cattle tithes. The exemption of dry cattle and sheep meat from liability to tithes in an economy where pastoral farming was very important would inevitably mean that the tithes did not reflect the full extent of agricultural output.

Primate Dowdall's register contains a record of the twentieth tax which he considered to be due from the beneficed clergy of fourteen parishes in the rural deanery of Tullyhogue *c*.1544.[86] The taxation figures are difficult to interpret because they were recorded for only two thirds of the parishes in the rural deanery and it is impossible to state why they were recorded and not the remainder. Also, in a region where monetarisation of the economy was not far advanced one cannot know how the figures were calculated, or indeed what the figures mean in terms of 'cost of living' in an economic environment which was significantly different to that *inter Anglicos*. Even so, the figures were gathered on the instruction of the archbishop and he, at least, expected that they would accord with reality to some considerable degree. Furthermore, work done on clerical incomes in the diocese of Dromore has found results broadly similar to those in Armagh *inter Hibernicos*.[87] Work on clerical incomes in Derry diocese, based upon the erenaghs' liability for the bishop's tertia, has provided similar results.[88]

In Armagh *inter Hibernicos* two thirds of the tithes were paid to the rector and one third to the vicar.[89] According to the 1609 inquisition the rectory of Donaghmore was then impropriated by the Céile Dé of Armagh.[90] The rectory of Clonoe was held by the rector of Donaghenry *in commendam,* with the obligation of supporting a chorister in Armagh cathedral.[91] In Primate Octavian's time (1481–1513) the rectory of Donaghmore was a prebend of Armagh cathedral, but the rectory of Clonoe was already united to the prebend of Donaghenry.[92] It is impossible to tell at what point the prebend of Donaghmore became impropriated to the Céile Dé.

Apart from the rectory of Clonoe, and possibly that of Donaghmore, all of the parochial revenues in the rural deanery of Tullyhogue were available to the parochial clergy. In some of the smaller or poorer parishes, viz. Ballinderry, Desertcreat, Donaghrisk, Drumglass, Tamlaght and Tullyniskan, there was no vicar at all and the rector received all of the parochial tithes.[93] According to Bishop Montgomery the parish rectory was often a sinecure, granted to men who undertook to take holy orders, to help to defray the costs of their education. However, Montgomery's own survey of the parishes of Derry diocese *c*.1607, before he had had time to make any adjustments to the diocese, demonstrates that only one rector in that diocese was a student.[94] In fact, rectors were normally expected to reside in their parishes, to celebrate Mass and to pray the Divine Office. Any rector who failed to perform these duties could be deprived of his benefice.[95]

The vicar was bound to perpetual residence and service of the parish cure.[96] As well as a share of the parish tithes the vicar (or rector if the parish was too poor to maintain a vicar) was entitled to the offerings of his parishioners, and the fees for the administration of the sacraments of the rites of passage.[97] Bishop Montgomery, writing in 1607 described such fees as 'small', but the fee for extreme unction across Ulster towards the close of the middle ages was a sheep, the 'caor olla'.[98] Unlike their counterparts in Armagh *inter Anglicos* it is possible that the parish clergy *inter Hibernicos* did not receive mortuaries.[99] The vicar (or the rector where there was no vicar) in the rural deanery of Tullyhogue invariably enjoyed possession of a house and garden close to his church.[100] In Derry diocese the vicarage was often made of stone and, given the proximity of these adjacent dioceses, it is likely that many of the vicarages in Armagh *inter Hibernicos* were stone buildings also.[101] Fourteen parishes can be shown to have had some glebeland for the priest who served the parish cure. The glebes, known as 'Fearann sagairt', were exempt from episcopal taxation. They were, however, generally small: eleven of the fourteen glebes pertaining to parishes in the rural deanery of Tullyhogue which were accounted for in the Ulster inquisitions ranged from one to six acres, with a median size of three acres.[102] Three were larger than the rest. The rector of Drumglass and the vicar of Termonmagurk had a sessiagh of glebe (= one third of a ballyboe or roughly eighty acres), while the vicar of Derryloran had half a ballyboe. For the incumbents fortunate enough to possess a glebe, the land would have been invaluable for growing at least a portion of their own food.[103]

Clerical incomes

The records of the twentieth tax on benefices in Tullyhogue in Primate Dowdall's register allows one to calculate the value of the benefices of fourteen rectors and eight vicars. It shows that the rector of Ardboe was reckoned to be the best paid cleric in the rural deanery with an annual income of £6 13s. 4d., but the average income of the fourteen rectors was only £2 2s. 9d. (Stg£1 8s. 6d.). Eight of those parishes also had a vicar. Their average wage was a mere £1 7s. 1½d. (Stg 18s. 1d.). It may be argued that the values of the parochial livings recorded in Primate Dowdall's register are incredibly low, and that the clergy may have been able to understate their incomes to an ordinary who was an infrequent visitor to their parishes. That is indeed conceiveable, but the consistency of the values across the rural deanery suggests otherwise, as does the fact that the Tullyhogue values are very comparable to the low values recorded of benefices in Cashel and Leighlin according to the Valor in Hibernia.

No comparable data exists for calculating clerical incomes in the rural deanery of Orior. A procurations list in Primate Dowdall's register suggests that parochial revenues were highest in the north of the rural deanery, and in the O'Hanlon lordship of Orior. This may be explained by reference to the soil quality, and more importantly by reference to the relatively stable political conditions in those areas, which would have facilitated a more intensive agriculture than that in the lordship of the Fews.

The parishes of the rural deanery of Orior were less well staffed than were the parishes in Tullyhogue. According to the Ulster inquisitions the dean of Armagh was, by right of his office, also the vicar of Armagh and Glenaul (the archbishop being the rector of each), and he received the rectorial tithes of the parishes of Kilmore, Drumcree, Loughgall, Loughgilly, Kilcreevy in Toaghy and Clonconchy.[104] The then vicars choral, the successors of the medieval Céile Dé, held impropriate the rectories of the parishes of Creggan, Derrynoose, Tynan, Ballymore, Mullaghbrack and the vicarage of Loughgall. While one might hesitate to accept such a relatively late source for the first half of the sixteenth century there are procurations lists which seem to confirm the details of the inquisitions. The lists are undated, but they are included among a series of documents dating from *c.*1544, though one of the documents is stated to have been taken from a register of Primate Octavian, now no longer extant.[105] In the lists of procurations the rectories impropriated to the dean of Armagh and the Céile Dé head the list, followed by the vicarages of the impropriated parishes, before the normal pattern of the rector and vicar of each parish being 'paired' begins.[106] The inquisitions also state that the chancellor of Armagh was the vicar of the parishes of Kilmore and Drumcree while the treasurer was rector and vicar of both of the parishes of Clonkearney Upper and Clonkearney Lower.[107] Furthermore, the rectorial tithes of the parish of Derrybrusk were impropriated to the archbishop's mensa.[108] This effectively meant that two thirds of the tithes of the great majority of the parishes in the rural deanery of Orior were diverted to the cathedral clergy at Armagh. Nonetheless, the cure of souls in the parishes was generally the vicars' responsibilities. Only the parishes of Armagh, Glenaul, Clonkearney Upper & Lower and Loughgall are recorded as having had their vicarage tithes impropriated as well as their rectorial tithes. The cathedral parish of Armagh and the adjoining parish of Glenaul are exceptional cases in that they were the parishes of the archiepiscopal manor of Armagh, and the deans of Ulster's cathedrals generally enjoyed the vicar's share of the tithes of the cathedral parish.[109] In the case of Loughgall it can be shown from a parish visitation of 1546 that there was a vicar in the parish.[110] That leaves Clonkearney unaccounted for. There is no reference to any vicar of Clonkearney in our records. It is probable, therefore, that the cure of souls there was delegated to unbeneficed priests.

TABLE 4 Values of benefices *inter Hibernicos*, 1544

Parish	Position	Value from Dowdall's register	Parish	Position	Value from Dowdalls's Register
Artrea	Rector	£3 6s. 8d.	Drumcraw	Rector	£1 0s.
	Vicar	£3 6s. 8d.		Vicar	£1 1s. 8d.
Ardboe	Rector	£6 13s. 4d.	Derryloran	Rector	£2 0s.
	Vicar	£1 6s. 8d.		Vicar	£1 6s. 8d.
Ballinderry	Rector	£1 1s. 8d.	Kildress	Rector	£3 6s. 8d.
Desertlyn	Rector	£2 4s. 2d.	Desertcreat	Rector	£2 4s. 2d.
	Vicar	£1 2s. 6d.	Donaghrisk	Rector	13s. 4d.
Magherafelt	Rector	£1 13s. 4d.	Carnteel	Rector	£1 6s. 8d.
	Vicar	16s. 8d.		Vicar	13s. 4d.
Lissan	Rector	£2 4s. 2d.	Tamlaght	Rector	£1 0s.
	Vicar	£1 2s. 11d.	Drumglass	Rector	£1 6s. 8d.

One may state, therefore, that the priests in charge of the cure of souls in the parishes of the rural deanery of Orior were usually vicars, though in Glenaul there must have been an unbeneficed priest to serve the church at Eglish. In the parishes of Clonkearney there were possibly one or two unbeneficed curates, and there would certainly have been curates serving the chapels of ease throughout the rural deanery. Many of the vicars had possession of a house and garden and some glebeland. The jurors of Armagh in 1609 were less informative about the parish church endowments than were their counterparts at Dungannon. They specified the extent of some glebes, but not others. From their inquisition it is still clear that the glebes of Orior rural deanery were arbitrarily distributed. The parishes of Aghaloo and Tynan, and possibly Ballymore, had none. The parish of Kilmore had only one acre of glebe, the parish of Clonfeacle had five acres (though the chapel of ease at Rowan had a sessiagh of glebe). The vicar of Loughgilly had the townland of Cornegrall as his glebe, the vicar of Derrynoose had two tates, and the vicar of Creggan had one and a half ballyboes as glebe. The contrasting sizes of the glebes show that the incomes of the parish clergy in Armagh *inter Hibernicos* depended very much upon chance.

It is impossible to make any assessment of clerical incomes for the rural deanery of Orior in the sixteenth century. It is likely, though, that the incomes of the parochial clergy in the rural deanery of Orior were broadly similar to those in Tullyhogue. It appears that throughout Armagh *inter Hibernicos* the incomes of the beneficed clergy were very low, significantly lower than those enjoyed by their colleagues in Armagh *inter Anglicos*, though very comparable with the incomes of many of the clergy in the south of Ireland.

Primate Swayne's register shows him intervening in 1430 to force the Céile Dé, the impropriators of the parochial revenues of Derrynoose, to remunerate the vicar who served the parish cure to an adequate level. Doubtless endeavours such as that had some beneficial effect. However, the archbishops of Armagh could not effectively counteract the pervasive problem of clerical poverty *inter Hibernicos*. Economic under-development, the dislocation which ensued with war or more local conflicts, and the difficulties in securing the full value of the tithes in such extensive parishes, conspired to depress clerical incomes throughout the later middle ages.

From their incomes the beneficed clergy of Armagh *inter Hibernicos* had to meet some great expenses, including the cost of maintaining their portion of the parish church. Normally the erenagh of the parish was responsible for maintaining two thirds of the church, with the rector and vicar responsible for the remaining third.[111] In the parish of Clonoe, however, the beneficed priests had to carry the full burden themselves.[112]

Procurations were a more regular obligation. The procurations lists for Armagh *inter Hibernicos* in Primate Dowdall's register vary greatly one from another.[113] The first, which was copied from a register of Primate Octavian (since lost), had charges for fifteen clergymen in the rural deanery of Tullyhogue.[114] The sums exacted for procurations ranged from 4s. 2½d. for the prebendary of Donaghenry with Clonoe to 8d. for the vicar of Killoon, with a median value of 14d. In the others, with charges for thirty three beneficed clergymen, ranged from 22d. for the prebendary of Ballyclog to only 4d. for the rector of Donaghrisk. In this second list the prebendary of Donaghenry with Clonoe was liable for only 6¾*d*. while there seems to have no longer been a vicar of Killoon. The rector of Killoon, though, was liable to a procuration fee of 12*d*. according to both lists. The median value of the second, seemingly later, procurations list was 8*d*. per beneficed clergyman.

Synodals were an annual levy demanded of the clergy of Armagh *inter Hibernicos*, like their southern counterparts. At the end of a record of the twentieth tax due from the benefices in the rural deanery of Tullyhogue, there is a statement that every rector was liable to pay 18*d*. in synodals, every vicar had to pay 8*d*.[115] The fees themselves were not too onerous, but the costs of travel and for food and accommodation when the annual synods were held in Armagh, must have created difficulties for some of the poorer priests.

The poverty of the parish clergy in Armagh *inter Hibernicos* has been starkly revealed here. It made the acquisition of an expensive university education impractical for the great majority of the clergy, and must have made it virtually impossible for the average priest to purchase any books, other than those required for the celebration of the liturgies, without having access to money from extra-ecclesial sources. Such circumstances would have made the priesthood an intellectually conservative body. On the other hand, the poverty of the priests ensured that they had to be attentive to the needs of their parishioners since altarages and offerings would have formed a crucial portion of their incomes.

THE PRIESTHOOD

Backgrounds and training

Very few of the clergy *inter Hibernicos* can be identified for the sixteenth century. Most of the papal records pertaining to Armagh are replies to delations, and there are only eleven such records in the printed calendars over the period 1482–1513.[116] These show an attempt being made by a delator to secure the benefice(s) of a priest(s) subject to an accusation made at Rome. Significantly, four of the Armagh delations were made by Clogher priests to secure a benefice in the parish of Termonmagurk, the most remote parish in the archdiocese from the primate's residence at Termonfeckin, and hence a vulnerable target for predatory legal action at Rome.[117] It is very rarely possible to determine the result of a delation. Delation records, then, are only useful when they identify the cleric who was being delated in Rome. The accusations themselves were motivated by mercenary ambition and may be disregarded, unless they can be confirmed from other sources.

The starting point of this analysis of the parish clergy of Armagh *inter Hibernicos* is a visitation list of the beneficed clergy in the rural deanery of Tullyhogue in 1460.[118] While one hesitates to draw upon material from the mid fifteenth century for a study which is focussed upon the first half of the sixteenth century the list is useful for these reasons: It is the only comprehensive list available of the beneficed clergy in one of the rural deaneries of Armagh *inter Hibernicos* for any point in time in the later middle ages. Secondly, it is the only source which allows one to examine how all of the benefices were staffed at a particular point in time. It helps to give meaning to the scattered records of clergymen which survive from the subsequent century. Furthermore, the relevance of the 1460 list for a study of the sixteenth century is suggested by its compatibility with the procuration lists for the (unnamed) beneficed clergymen *inter Hibernicos* in Primate Dowdall's register. Also the information on the staffing of the benefices in the rural deanery of Tullyhogue in 1460 is remarkably similar to Bishop Montgomery's survey of the parishes in the adjoining diocese of Derry made on the eve of the Ulster plantation.

The list of clergy reveals a striking pattern. A small number of surnames predominate. Two surnames alone, O'Lougheran (5) and O'Connellan (4) account for a third of the list between them. The same names predominate among the clergy of Armagh *inter Hibernicos* throughout the later middle ages. Several of these surnames can be identified as those of local erenagh families. Not all of the erenagh families in Armagh archdiocese can now be identified and so it is not possible to determine the proportion of Armagh priests who came from erenagh families, but in the neighbouring diocese of Derry it has been shown that most of the beneficed priests were from local erenagh families.[119]

The O'Lougherans were erenaghs of Donaghmore in the later middle ages, and members of the family usually held the positions of rector and vicar of the parish.[120] Primate Dowdall appointed Dnus Patrick O'Lougheran to the parish of Donaghmore in 1543.[121] The rector of Donaghmore was often the rural dean of Tullyhogue, as was Dnus Bernard O'Lougheran in 1518.[122] Other O'Lougherans were numbered among the rectors or vicars of half of the parishes in the rural deanery in the fifteenth century. As An tAthar Ó Doibhlinn observed of them in his study of Donaghmore parish: 'merely to list the names of these O'Lougheran clerics during the period is to get some idea of their influence and importance'.[123]

The O'Connellans are nowhere described as erenaghs but their number among the secular clergy of Armagh makes it likely that they were erenaghs.[124] Dnus Donal O'Connellan died as vicar of Derryloran in 1534, and was succeeded as vicar by Dnus Christian O'Connellan.[125] Meanwhile one Dnus Thomas O'Connellan was rector of Kildress.[126] In 1456 one Sawe O'Connellan founded a hospice in the parish of Donaghmore, another indication of this family's close association with the church in the later middle ages.[127]

The O Culeans were the erenagh family of Clonfeacle whose territory, Tuath Uí Chuiléin, comprised about ten townlands.[128] Several members of the sept served as rector or vicar of Clonfeacle.[129] Dnus Eoghan O'Culean was prebendary of Clonfeacle from at least 1518 and vicar of Kilmore until 1544.[130] Dnus Rory O'Culean was vicar of Carlingford in 1518.[131] Dnus David O'Culean was vicar of the archbishop's mensal parish of Derrybrusk until he retired in 1540, to be succeeded by Dnus Sean O'Culean.[132] O'Culeans were rectors or vicars of several other parishes in the rural deanery of Tullyhogue in the later middle ages.[133]

The Mc Cawells were another prominent clerical families *inter Hibernicos*. Dnus Éamon Mc Cawell was dean of Armagh from 1505 to 1549. In 1529 Dnus Denis Mc

Cawell was collated to the prebend of Ballyclog.[134] In 1542 Canon Patrick Mc Cawell, prebendary of Donaghenry and Clonoe died, and was succeeded in office by Dnus Muiris Mc Cawell.[135] The succession of Mc Cawells in Clonoe parish suggests the possibility that they were members of the erenagh family in that parish. The erenaghs of the parish of Errigal Keerogue were certainly Mc Cawells in the fifteenth century.[136]

The O'Donnellys were not among the beneficed clergy of Tullyhogue in 1460 but became prominent in the church in Armagh *inter Hibernicos* in the sixteenth century. Dnus Malachy O'Donnelly was rector of Ardboe in 1535.[137] Dnus Turlough O'Donnelly and Terence Danyell, a clerk, were granted a lease on the primate's land in the parish of Tullyniskin.[138] Terence's name is an anglicised version of the priest's name, raising the suspicion that they may have been father and son. Terence was subsequently ordained a priest and in May 1550 he succeeded Dnus Mc Cawell as dean of Armagh.[139] Dean Danyell was offered the office of archbishop of Armagh and he wrote to Cecil accepting the proferred promotion in October 1567, but ultimately he lost out to an Englishman.[140]

Other priests in Armagh *inter Hibernicos* in the first half of the sixteenth century include Dnus Eoghan O'Corre, rector of Ballyclog (ante 1518–post 1535).[141] The O'Corres were the erenaghs of the church lands in Ballyclog.[142] Dnus Art O'Renean, vicar of Ardtrea was also the erenagh of the church lands in that parish in 1534.[143] Dnus Patrick O'Heaney was the erenagh of the church lands in Ballymore parish in 1534.[144]

The pattern of clerical recruitment from the erenagh families is one which can be observed across Ulster in the later middle ages. Katharine Simms has shown that these erenaghs had a strong sense of duty and attachment to the church throughout the later middle ages.[145] My work on Derry diocese has shown how some of the descendants of erenagh families retained that sense of attachment to the church into the nineteenth century. This sense of tradition would have had a positive effect in fostering a sense of vocation to ministry in the church.

It is difficult to offer any assessment of the educational attainments of the clergy of Armagh *inter Hibernicos*. One may observe that university graduates seem to have been even more rare than among the clergy of Armagh *inter Anglicos*. Yet the education of the 'typical' parish priest in Armagh *inter Hibernicos* was probably no worse, and may often had been better than that enjoyed by his non-graduate counterpart in the southern rural deaneries.

Reference has already been made to the lecturers at Armagh, at least some of whom were graduates in theology. It seems certain that these teachers helped to educate some of the future priests of the diocese – for service *inter Anglicos* as well as *inter Hibernicos*, given the racial composition of the parish clergy throughout the archdiocese of Armagh. The houses of the Third Order Franciscans at Dungannon and Ballynasaggart near Errigal Keerogue, both founded *c*.1489, educated boys and did other pastoral work.[146] Also, there were *studia particularia* in which masters offered students a training in one or more subjects. The masters were drawn from families who followed as hereditary occupations the various learned professions, and usually were 'closely connected' with the church, often being drawn from erenagh families.[147] Katharine Simms described these institutions as 'a pale substitute for the non-existent university'. Edmund

Campion visited a *studium* during his time in Ireland in 1570–1.[148] He saw there ten students in one room, most of whom looked twenty years and more, and they were 'grovelling upon couches of straw, their books at their noses, themselves lying prostrate, and so to chant out their lessons by piecemeal'. The students learnt their lessons by rote, committing to memory the aphorisms of Hippocrates, or the Civil Institutes, and their Latin grammars too doubtless. The emphasis on memorisation suggests that originality was not fostered. Certainly, throughout the later middle ages there is little evidence of original scholarship in the writings of any but a handful of Irish clerics. The bulk of the prose produced at this time consisted of copies or translations of foreign works. Nonetheless, the same could be said, with small qualification, about institutes of higher learning across Europe. The *studia* were often run by graduates and aspired to a more advanced level of education than that available in the grammar schools elsewhere in Ireland. Matthew Ó Gríofa stated in 1458 that he had lectured publicly for four years in the faculty of canon law at Oxford university, before lecturing for four more years in various schools in Ireland.[149] Thomas Ruth or Magruhert, a cleric of Meath diocese, acquired a doctorate in law and, he declared in 1468, he had also studied and taught canon and civil laws for seven years in various schools in Ireland.[150] Such examples signify that the *studia particularia* in Ireland were not wholly isolated from wider intellectual currents abroad in Europe.

If one may judge from the legislation of the provincial synod of Cashel in 1453 some of the *studia particularia* offered an education intended only for candidates for the priesthood.[151] It is not clear whether such schools actually trained young men for the priesthood, or whether they simply offered lectures in theology or canon law. It would be quite remarkable if special schools had existed in Ireland to train priests as there were few such institutions anywhere in Europe at that time.

Bishop Montgomery's report on the priests of Derry and Raphoe prior to the plantation may be a little too late to be directly relevant for an attempt to judge the educational attainments of the clergy in Armagh half a century or so earlier but, assuming that no 'educational revolution' had occurred in Ulster in the second half of the sixteenth century, and that economic conditions in north west Ulster were not significantly better than in east Tyrone in the first half of the sixteenth century (both of which are improbable in view of the increased warfare attending the Tudor conquest), Montgomery's report may serve as a warning against unproven assumptions that the clergy in Ulster were generally ignorant in the sixteenth century.

Ministry

The clergy who served the parishes of Armagh *inter Hibernicos* had the same obligations as had their counterparts *inter Anglicos*. The dependence of the priests on fees for administering some of the sacraments, on the offerings made by their parishioners, and the laity's co-operation in paying tithes, ensured that the parish priests had to be attentive to the needs of their congregations. A negligent priest could be criticised before the rural dean of Tullyhogue or the dean of Armagh, and find himself cited before the courts of the ruri-decanal officials of Tullyhogue or Orior with Armagh city.

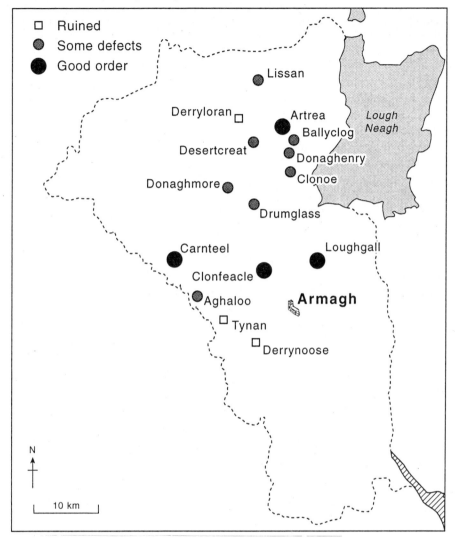

☐ Ruined
◕ Some defects
● Good order

Lissan

Derryloran ☐   Artrea   *Lough*
              Ballyclog *Neagh*
Desertcreat   Donaghenry
Donaghmore   Clonoe
              Drumglass

Carnteel   Loughgall
Clonfeacle
Aghaloo   **Armagh**
  ☐ Tynan
   ☐ Derrynoose

N

10 km

5   State of the churches in 1546

Any assessment of the actual ministry of the clergy of Armagh *inter Hibernicos* in the sixteenth century must start with the record of the visitation of the rural deaneries of Orior and of Tullyhogue which was conducted in 1546 by the bishop of Ardagh, and Dnus Nicholas Mc Grath, a canon of Clogher, acting as commissaries of Archbishop George Dowdall.[152] This report throws great light upon the church and priests in Armagh *inter Hibernicos*. It is unique, not only for the archdiocese of Armagh, but for any diocese of Ireland prior to the seventeenth century.

The rural deanery of Orior is represented by the parishes of Aghaloo, Clonfeacle, Derrynoose, Kilmore and Tynan. Eleven churches were visited in the rural deanery of

Tullyhogue. The first striking fact to emerge from the visitation was the poor condition of most of the churches. Only five of the sixteen churches were reported to have been in satisfactory condition. Four churches had some (unspecified) defect in their roofs while at Donaghmore the nave was in good condition but part of the chancel roof was missing. The churches at Ballyclog, Clonoe and Derryloran, and probably Ardboe also, had defects in both their roofs and walls. The church at Derrynoose was in a ruinous state with regards to its roofs and walls and the neighbouring church at Tynan was no better. Significantly, the rectorial tithes of the churches of Derrynoose and Tynan were impropriated to the Céile Dé, the rectory of Clonoe was impropriated to the prebendary of Donaghhenry. The provincial synod of Cashel of 1453 observed that it was a common experience that churches which were impropriated were often neglected by the impropriators.

The decay in the parish churches in Armagh *inter Hibernicos* was by no means exceptional. In the English lordship, beyond the inner Pale, there was a widespread problem with ruinous churches.[153] In Armagh *inter Anglicos* it has been shown that impropriators, rectors or lay people who allowed their portion of a parish church to fall into decay could expect to be cited before the consistory court and forced to amend their failings. It may be that the church courts *inter Hibernicos* were less effective in disciplining negligent clerics and erenaghs. However, the clergy could not always be held responsible for their churches becoming delapidated or ruinous.

The state of the churches probably reflects the low levels of parochial revenues in Armagh *inter Hibernicos*. The laity were not responsible for the maintenance of church buildings. The local erenaghs were generally responsible for maintaining two thirds of the parish churches, and the beneficed clergy the remaining third. Only at Clonoe do the priests seem to have been liable for the entire building.[154] The 1546 visitors found that the erenagh of Donaghmore maintained his part of the church in good order, but the beneficed clergy had neglected the chancel roof.

Churches were occasionally unroofed by severe storms. In 1478, for instance, 'a great wind wrecked many of the monasteries and churches and houses throughout Ireland'.[155] A similar storm unroofed 'many houses and churches' in 1487.[156] Another storm in 1528 wrecked many buildings.[157] In 1547 there was 'such a strange violent tempest, or rather hurricane, in the most part of Ireland that by force of it trees were rooted up, and churches and other edifices were quite blown down'. The storm blew down the steeple of St Peter's church, Drogheda, 'the highest in the world'.[158] There were also accidents, such as the fire which engulfed part of Armagh cathedral in 1511.[159] Most devastating of all, there were local wars and disorders which destroyed churches and impoverished the priests along with their people. It has already been shown that several churches in the marchlands of County Louth were ruined in war, and that tillage was abandoned in the aftermath of war, leaving whole districts 'waste' as far as church revenues were concerned. The erenaghs and clergy of Armagh *inter Hibernicos* would have encountered enormous difficulties in restoring their churches after such a set back.

The visitors to the churches in Orior and Tullyhogue in 1546 found that in almost all of the parish churches visited the sacred vessels and other equipment either in good or satisfactory order. Those of five churches were classified as 'good', in six others they were 'satisfactory'. The equipment at Derrynoose was good but for a chasuble. At Derryloran a chalice was found to be sub-standard. What was wrong with it was not stated, but the provincial synod of Dublin in 1518 legislated against the use of tin chalices, suggesting one possible problem.[160] The most serious deficiencies were found at Ballyclog whose rector, a cathedral canon, presented the church authorities with a severe headache: the primate had already visited him but had clearly failed to either reform or deprive him. No comparable information survives for the parish churches of Ardboe and Clonoe.

The 1546 visitors made enquiries as to the provision of Masses, and the recitation of the Office in the parish churches. The priests were questioned on oath at the altar after Mass, and some parishioners were asked to confirm what the priests had stated. The visitation report reveals that whatever the state of the churches – ruined, partly defective or in good order – the Mass was celebrated in the parish churches, and the Office was prayed. Only at one church, Ballyclog, was there a serious problem. The vicar served in Armagh cathedral, but the rector did not celebrate the Mass and there is no reference in the visitors' report to a curate. This grave situation was already known by the primate and was presumably being 'dealt with'.

The visitors were generally satisfied with what they learnt about the parish clergy *inter Hibernicos*. Eleven of them were reported to have been 'good'. The rector of Clonfeacle was called 'disobedient', though what was meant by that is unclear. The rector of Desertcreat was found to be 'good', but his curate was 'disobedient' towards him.

The greatest failing charged against the parish clergy was their susceptibility to concubinage. The rectors of Ballyclog, Clonfeacle and Desertcreat were believed not to have concubines, but the rector of Lissan had a son by his concubine in 1545, and a daughter by her in 1546. The vicar of Tynan claimed not to be concubinary, despite what some of his 'enemies' alleged to the contrary. The vicar of Clonoe seems to have have some allegations made against himself also. Of the eleven curates two certainly had concubines, some allegations were heard against two others, while two more had had concubines in the past and their former companions were still living in the vicinity of the parish churches. Five curates were stated to have been celibate, including the curate at Artrea who was said to be very old, and consequently beyond the age of susceptibility to female charms.

Older historians tended to be fascinated and/or shocked by clerical concubinage in late medieval Ireland. The scale of the practice is impossible to define, though the 1546 visitation record suggests that one should not assume that it was so common as to have been 'the norm' *inter Hibernicos*. Michael Haren found that the number of papal penitentiary dispensations for the archdiocese of Armagh between 1449 and 1533 was 64, significantly less than one a year and, since less than two thirds of all the dispensations from Ireland were secured from the sons of clerics, it seems safe to suggest that in the later middle ages as few as one son of a priest on average over each two year period secured a papal dispensation for illegitimacy in Armagh.[161] Furthermore, the rate of dispensation for illegitimacy was less in Armagh than in the adjacent dioceses of Derry,

Dromore or Clogher – a reflection, perhaps, of the efforts of the archbishops of Armagh to curtail priestly marriage.

Whatever its incidence it is necessary to see the practice in context. It was a canonically unlawful practice, but it was widely accepted in Ireland, and across much of medieval Europe as natural and permissible.[162] The custom of priestly marriage appears to have been more thoroughly established in the church in Wales than in Armagh archdiocese *inter Hibernicos*.[163] On much of the European mainland clerical marriage may have been at least as common, if not more so, than the visitation record suggests for the priests in the northern parishes of Armagh. Jean Delumeau quotes figures of 25% of priests in the Netherlands, and 33% of priests in the Rhenish dioceses as being informally 'married' on the eve of the reformation.[164] It appears that a great many priests and people had decided that whether or not a priest was married (a civil marriage, of course, not *facie ecclesiae*) was irrelevant where his priestly ministry was concerned.[165] Priestly marriage cannot be taken as evidence that a priest was a poor pastor. In a sense the Protestant reformers simply regularised a longstanding custom by encouraging their ministers to marry.

Historians have assumed that the fact that successive parochial incumbents in Ulster often shared the same surnames was an indication of 'hereditary succession' to benefices. This was not necessarily so. It may, instead, reflect the fact that benefice holders were normally drawn from local erenagh families.[166] It is a fact that very few sons could wait for their fathers to die in order for them to secure a benefice. The well-known example cited by John Watt was an exception, not the rule.[167]

The visitation report of 1546 is all too brief and, more importantly, for any judgement on its contents, it is incomplete, since a number of churches in Tullyhogue were not reported on. Some of the omissions may be accounted for by the relative inaccessibility of the churches in the extreme west and north of the archdiocese, though others like Tullyniskan were not so remote. All one can say is that the visitation was conducted in haste, as is obvious from the writing of the report. Nonetheless, it is invaluable in casting light upon the state of the church in Armagh *inter Hibernicos* and gives information on a large enough sample of churches to justify the following conclusions. The priests of the parishes in the northern rural deaneries served their parishioners regardless of the state of the churches. The laymen who gave evidence to the 1546 visitors did not make complaints about the provision of services in their parishes. Since several of the laity made allegations of concubinage against their clergy this may be taken as evidence that the priests attained at least a minimum standard (and there is no reason to believe that it was not much better than that) in their ministry which was acceptable to their parishioners. In this respect the presentments taken from south eastern Ireland in 1537, in which no criticism was made of the clergy for failing to provide pastoral care (though there were criticisms of some of the fees they charged) may offer a significant parallel to the situation in Armagh *inter Hibernicos*.

If further confirmation is needed for the thesis that the priests of Armagh *inter Hibernicos* generally served the needs of their parishioners in a satisfactory manner it may be found in the late medieval papal registers. Between 1482 and 1513 there are records of only eleven delations in the published calendars pertaining to the archdio-

cese of Armagh. Significantly, none of the delators made accusations of priestly misconduct or pastoral negligence, though such charges would greatly have helped their
case against the beneficed clergyman. Instead they resorted to allegations of a vague,
technical character, questioning the defendant's *titulus*. This is a pattern that can be
observed for all of Ireland on the eve of the Tudor reformations. Furthermore, there is
no record among the Armagh registers of a secular priest in Armagh *inter Hibernicos*
being deprived of his benefice for absenteeism or negligence.

CONCLUSIONS

The church in the archdiocese of Armagh *inter Hibernicos* functioned in an environment which was different to that *inter Anglicos* in a number of ways. In terms of its
physical geography it encompassed more mountains, bogs and woodlands than the
southern rural deaneries. Politically the region was independent of English control,
and yet enjoyed a high level of stability and order under the overlordship of Conn
O'Neill. Only in the south of the rural deanery of Orior where the O'Neill lordship
bordered on the Pale was there much disorder. Economically the region *inter Hibernicos*
was less developed, though the living standards of the bulk of the population in the two
portions of the archdiocese may not have been very different.

The differences between the church north and south of the Fews were formalised
by the gathering at separate synods of the priests *inter Anglicos* and *inter Hibernicos*. Yet
it has been shown that most of the parish clergy *inter Anglicos* were Irish, as were their
parishioners, and some of the priests were drawn from the rural deaneries of Armagh
inter Hibernicos or from the neighbouring diocese of Dromore which was under the
custody of the primate for most of the later middle ages.

This survey has shown that there was a marked contrast within the rural deaneries
of Armagh *inter Hibernicos* between the agriculturally productive fertile lowlands of
the Lough Neagh basin and the more marginal uplands of the rim. The parochial system reflected this contrast with the churches and chapels being concentrated on the
good farmlands. This, presumably, was where the bulk of the population *inter Hibernicos*
was to be found. Hence, although the average sizes of the parishes in the north and
south of the archdiocese were very different the people in the northern parishes may
generally have had to travel equivalent distances to their places of worship as their
counterparts in the south.

The parochial system in Armagh *inter Hibernicos* seems to have functioned well
into the mid sixteenth century, in the sense that the 1546 visitation showed that the
Mass continued to be celebrated and the priests prayed the Divine Office in their
churches while the lay representatives of the parishes had no complaint to make about
their priests' provision of pastoral care. That was despite the fact that the church buildings may not have always been in the same good condition as the churches of County
Louth. Absenteeism and neglect of the cure of souls was inherently unlikely in conditions in which altarages formed an indispensable portion of the clergy's modest incomes. The church authorities were able to deal effectively with unsatisfactory priests.

The mendicant orders, with only three houses in the northern rural deaneries, probably played a useful role in providing sermons for non-preaching priests but, as in Armagh *inter Anglicos*, their role was a supportive one to the parish clergy. The friars did not provide the regular masses in the parish churches and chapels, and the friars were not in a position to administer the sacraments whenever the laity needed them across the far flung parishes of Armagh *inter Hibernicos*. The parish priests were, as indeed one would expect, the mainstay of the church's ministry.

The living standards of the population in the northern parishes may have been little higher than subsistence and this probably precluded many clerical students from gaining a university education, but the lecturers at Armagh and the better masters of the *studia particularia*, and perhaps the teachers in the Third Order houses, may have offered a better substitute for a higher education than that available to the priests who were educated solely in County Louth.

Concubinage was clearly a widespread problem for the church authorities in Armagh *inter Hibernicos,* but the practice has probably received more attention from historians than it deserves. Seen in its sixteenth century context it was not unique to Ireland but was a common practice across much of contemporary Europe. In the southern rural deaneries concubinage was relatively rare on the eve of the Tudor reformations and clearly was effectively curbed by the church authorities.[168] Even there it was not regarded as an unforgiveable offense. At the convocation of the clergy of Armagh *inter Anglicos* in 1496 Dnus Simon Jeffrey, the newly installed rector of Beaulieu, was ordered to give twelve salmon to the primate as a penance for committing the sin of fornication.[169]

The most significant characteristic, perhaps, of the church in Armagh in the first half of the sixteenth century was its resilience. Already, the church there had been functioning for over a thousand years. It had continued to function despite political instability and economic difficulties over much of the middle ages and clearly possessed enormous inherent strengths before the onset of the Tudor reformations.

4

Archdiocesan Administrators

A NEW ARCHBISHOP

Dr George Cromer was provided to the see of Armagh on 2 October 1521.[1] He was granted the pallium as archbishop-elect on 25 October 1521. Henry VIII had supplicated the pope on his behalf. Nothing is known of Archbishop Cromer's family background, but he was probably drawn from 'a solidly established Kentish family'.[2] A letter of 1534 from John Cromer, onetime commissioner of the peace in Kent, indicates that the latter was familiar with Dr Cromer, though no evidence exists to directly demonstrate a family connection.[3]

George Cromer was a scholar of the university of Oxford in 1497.[4] He graduated as a Master of Arts. Henry VIII's *Book of payments* for 1518 records one Dr Cromer being given 20s by the king for going to Canterbury to give the king's offering to the shrine of St Thomas a Beckett.[5] This Dr Cromer, a cleric in the king's service, can be none other than the future archbishop of Armagh.

Dnus George Cromer secured a papal dispensation for pluralism in 1496/7.[6] He subsequently held a couple of benefices in plurality in the dioceses of Canterbury, London and Chichester. In 1512 Henry VIII presented Mgr Cromer to the college of Cobham in the diocese of Rochester.[7] Mgr Cromer remained the master of the college until circa 1532. The series of benefices which Mgr Cromer secured suggests that he had acquired a very powerful patron. Indeed, Henry VIII's presentation of him to Cobham may serve to indicate that he had entered the king's service. In his bull of provision to Armagh Dr Cromer was identified as one of Henry VIII's chaplains.

It is not possible to determine what precise qualities Dr Cromer possessed which commended him to Henry VIII for promotion to the primacy of Ireland. He was certainly well-educated, as indeed were virtually all of the English-born men whom the Tudors had the papacy provide to Irish dioceses.[8] Dr Cromer did not have much administrative experience to demonstrate his suitability for high office. Nonetheless, as a royal chaplain he had obviously impressed Henry VIII somehow. Service to the English crown or to Cardinal Wolsey, the leading crown minister for much of this period, provided many opportunities for promotion.

By the time of Henry VIII's reign the English crown enjoyed a virtual monopoly of all successful nominations to Irish sees.[9] The crown expected the archbishop of Armagh, by virtue of his high ecclesiastical office and his possession of sizeable estates inside the Pale and beyond, to play an active role in the maintenance of social and political, as well as spiritual, order in the north of the English lordship in Ireland.[10] It is significant that Dr Cromer, like Mgr Staples a few years later, was sent to Ireland to replace an absentee prelate. Almost from the moment of his arrival Archbishop Cromer became a member of the council of Ireland. He was lord chancellor of Ireland from July 1532 until August 1534.[11]

One may conclude that Dr Cromer may have been promoted to the archdiocese of Armagh by Henry VIII because he was a priest of some ability, and ambition, who had shown his devotion to the king in person, and who could be relied upon to be a conscientious, resident pastor in Ireland, and politically useful too. His provision to the see of Armagh was typical of a series of episcopal appointments made to the dioceses of the Pale before the Henrician reformation.[12]

The new archbishop was consecrated in December 1521 or January 1522, perhaps on his return to England from Rome.[13] However, Henry VIII did not grant Archbishop Cromer the restitution of Armagh's temporalities until 26 June 1523, though the grant was made retrospective to the date of his consecration.[14] It may be suggested that the king was ensuring that the money would be available to Primate Cromer to pay the often crippling demand for the 'first fruits', the incumbent's first year's income which had to be paid to the papal curia.[15]

The earliest reference to him in the Armagh registers is in a church court case record of 13 November 1523.[16] Given the incomplete nature of the registers, though, that cannot be taken as an indication that he had not come to Ireland before then. The new archbishop found himself responsible for a diocese which was deeply divided, whose divisions created difficulties in the administration of archdiocese, especially for one who was the English crown's appointee. Yet, Archbishop Cromer's predecessors had succeeded in establishing *modi operandi* which he too could use to promote the church's pastoral mission throughout Armagh, *inter Anglicos* and *inter Hibernicos*.

THE CAPITULAR BODY

The dean and chapter of Armagh played several important roles in the archdiocesan administration. Whenever the see fell vacant they became the guardians of the spiritualities and the spiritual jurisdiction in the archdiocese.[17] In practice, this meant that they held the powers to conduct diocesan synods and visitations.[18] The authority to conduct church courts in the archdiocese also devolved upon the dean and chapter. When Primate John Kite resigned during the course of a church court case in 1521 Mgr Cormac Roth, the president of Armagh's consistory court, had to be issued with a new commission by the dean and chapter so that he could continue with proceedings in the case.[19] Even the curators of wills had to be issued with fresh commissions by the dean and chapter.[20] Given the deep divide in the archdiocese it was, doubtless, inevitable that the Irish dean was obliged to appoint a sub-custodian for routine administration, including the power to institute priests into parish cures, in the church in the three rural deaneries *inter Anglicos*.[21]

The dean and chapter exercised their ancient right to elect the next archbishop of Armagh on a number of occasions in the fifteenth century.[22] However, although the chapter elected suitably qualified churchmen of English blood (but Irish birth), they failed to persuade the English crown to endorse any of their candidates. The Tudors were particularly anxious to impose English-born men on Irish dioceses, especially to the strategically significant dioceses of the Pale.[23]

Once the new archbishop took office he had to work with the dean and chapter in managing the archdiocesan church estates. All leases of archiepiscopal church lands or tithes had to be endorsed with the seal of the dean and chapter.[24] The seal of Armagh's chapter was kept under three locks, the keys to which were held by the dean, chancellor and precentor.[25] If one of these three dignitaries died the others were to hold the keys, but were not to use the seal until someone was promoted to the vacant office.[26]

The archbishop had to secure the endorsement of the dean and chapter in order to promote a priest to a dignitary or a canonry. New members had to be formally elected by the dean and chapter.[27] The archbishop could, however, insist on being present at elections.[28] He also had the power to confirm, or veto, the chapter's candidate.[29] In all probability the dean and chapter are likely to have rubber-stamped the primate's candidates to the archdeaconry and the couple of prebends situated *inter Anglicos*. On the other hand, the chapter expected the primate to take serious account of their recommendations when he was collating men to benefices and appointing canons in Armagh *inter Hibernicos*. When Archbishop Mey ignored their traditional rights in this regard the dean and chapter sued in Rome against his innovation.[30]

The archbishops of Armagh needed the consent of the dean and chapter in order to unite benefices, a practice resorted to occasionally to augment the remuneration of impoverished church administrators.[31] Also, proposed legislation in the synods for the priests and people of the rural deaneries of Orior and Tullyhogue had to be endorsed by the dean and chapter.[32]

Armagh possessed a cathedral chapter comprised of four dignitaries, a dean, chancellor, precentor and treasurer, together with a number of lesser canons who enjoyed an income from prebends, consisting of particular rectorial tithes. In Armagh, as in all Irish cathedrals, the archdeacon was an *ex officio* member of the chapter.[33] Because the dean and chapter exercised such wide powers in the administration of the archdiocese it was desirable, from the primates' standpoint, to be able to influence the composition of the chapter. Archbishop Mey attempted to re-constitute the cathedral chapter in the mid-fifteenth century. He clearly believed that there were too many prebends in Armagh *inter Hibernicos,* and too few *inter Anglicos*. He sought to annul some of the prebends in the rural deaneries of Orior and Tullyhogue without securing the consent of the dean and chapter, prompting them to appeal to the Roman curia against his unconstitutional actions.[34] On the other hand, he attempted to make canons of the vicars of Drogheda and Ardee, again without the consent of the dean and chapter.[35] The attempt failed and the two vicars became 'honorary' canons, entitled to wear the badge of office of a canon, without having a seat in the cathedral choir, or a vote in the chapter. Instead, the vicar of Ardee (and perhaps the vicar of Drogheda too) had to rest content with a promise of the next prebend which fell vacant.[36]

The dean and chapter of Armagh were predominantly Irish men in the first half of the sixteenth century. This contradicts the statement in the 1609 inquisitions which

claimed that there had been sixteen canons at Armagh cathedral, drawn in equal numbers from the rural deaneries of Armagh *inter Anglicos* and *inter Hibernicos*.[37] Apart
from the archdeaconry of Armagh, whose holder was an *ex officio* member of the cathedral chapter,[38] there were only two cathedral prebends in Armagh *inter Anglicos* in the
beginning of the sixteenth century. Another prebend, that of Ballyboys, is last referred
to in 1494–5 and appears to have become defunct thereafter.[39] The archdeacons held
the prebend of Kene in commendam before the Tudor reformations.[40] It was worthless
according to the Valor in Hibernia in 1538, and Dowdall's register in 1544.[41] The second prebend, that of Dunbin, was also impoverished, being valued at £1 6s. 8d. in
1538, and only 7s. 6d. in 1544.[42] There was also a third prebend *inter Anglicos*, but it was
the rectory of Duleek in the diocese of Meath.[43] In all then there were only two canons
and the archdeacon drawn from the church *inter Anglicos* in the first half of the sixteenth century.

As well as the four cathedral dignitaries, who were invariably Irishmen, there were
four prebends in Armagh *inter Hibernicos* according to a record taken from one of Primate Octavian's registers (now lost), and a procuration list in Primate Dowdall's register.[44] These were the prebends of Ballyclog, Clonoe, Donaghmore and Termonmagurk.
The rectory of Artrea was a prebend in 1534, possibly for the lifetime of its then holder,
Senkyn Mc Dewin, the primate's commissary in the northern rural deaneries.[45] The
rectory of Clonfeacle is described as a prebend in a patent roll of 1544 and, although it
was referred to as a simple rectory in the Armagh registers, one of the beneficed priests
of Clonfeacle served in Armagh's cathedral in 1546.[46] At any rate it is clear that the
dignitaries and canons *inter Hibernicos* could out-vote the canons *inter Anglicos*. It was
patently against the interests of the Irish members of the cathedral chapter to lose their
majority position to men of English descent or loyalty. Had that happened the Irish
men could have found themselves completely excluded from the chapter, as happened
in the chapter of St Patrick's cathedral, Dublin.[47]

The dean was the *ex officio* chairman of the cathedral chapter. He had the cure of
souls of all of the cathedral clergy, and he was responsible for all of their activities.[48]
The dean's pre-eminence in cathedral chapters was reflected in his income, which was
normally much greater than that of the other members.[49] The office of dean of Armagh
was stated to be worth no more than Stg£40 in 1492.[50] However, Dean Peter O'Molloy
(1487–1505) and Dean Éamon Mc Cawell (1505–1549) both held the priorship of the
Céile Dé in commendam, and that office was worth an additional Stg£4 in 1492. By
1505, though, the combined values of the deanery and priorship were stated to have
fallen to Stg£34.[51] The Henrician records for Armagh in the Valor in Hibernia excluded the benefices *inter Hibernicos* and so there is no value given for the deanery of
Armagh at that point in time. In the royal visitation of the church in 1622 the valuation
of the deanery of Armagh recorded in the King's book was £35, but the dignitary was
actually estimated to be worth no less than £120 in 1622.[52] It is probable that the figure
of £35 was derived from a sixteenth century valuation, as were those of all of the parochial livings in the rural deaneries of Armagh *inter Anglicos*. At any rate, an income of
Stg£34 or £35 would have placed the dean of Armagh well ahead of the rectors and
vicars of Armagh *inter Anglicos* whose benefices were valued, on average, at £6 2s. 11d.

and £7 4s. 9d. respectively in the Valor in Hibernia for 1538,[53] or the rectors and vicars of Armagh *inter Hibernicos* whose incomes were assessed to be, on average, £2 2s. 9d. and £1 7s. 1½d. respectively for the twentieth taxation of 1544.[54]

The dean's income was derived from some modest landholdings and rectorial tithes. The Ulster inquisitions of 1609 reveal that the dean of Armagh then held two small parcels of land equivalent to half a townland.[55] However, the dean of Armagh possessed a book which looked 'ancient' even then, claiming a further two and a half townlands as part of the corps of the deanery, though the lands had been lost to the church for some considerable time.[56]

It is probable that the bulk of the dean's income was derived from tithes. The dean was, *ex officio*, the vicar of the parish of Armagh with Glenaul (Eglish).[57] This encompassed some of the most fertile and best farmed land in Ulster. The 1609 inquisition also identified the rectories of Drumcree, Kilmore, Loughgall and Loughgilly, together with the rectory of the 'Luminaries' in Clonconchy, near Lisnadill, and the rectory and vicarage of Kilcreevy, as being impropriated to the dean.[58]

In their positions as prior of the Céile Dé, Dean O Molloy and Dean Mc Cawell also held impropriate the rectories of Ballymore, Creggan, Derrynoose, Mullaghbrack, and Tynan, and the vicarage of Loughgall.[59] In effect, the dean of Armagh drew one third of the tithes of Armagh parish, and two thirds of the tithes of most of the remaining parishes in the rural deanery of Orior.

The chancellor of Armagh seems to have been the second most important member of the chapter. Cathedral chancellors usually acted as the secretaries of the chapters, and supervised the cathedral schools.[60] In English cathedrals they also tended to be the archivists, but that may not have been the case at Armagh.[61] The landed corps of the chancellorship of Armagh was very modest, comprising certain houses and parcels of land in and around the cathedral city.[62] In 1367 the chancellor of Armagh's real estate was worth only £1, and Archbishop Sweteman united the rectory of Ballymore to the chancellorship to augment that modest income.[63] The 1609 inquisitions show that the chancellor of Armagh still held a small amount of real estate then, but also the revenues of the vicarages of Drumcree and Kilmore in Orior rural deanery.

The precentor was in charge of cathedral services, the liturgy, the music and the choir.[64] The corps of the precentorship were not identified in the 1609 inquisitions, possibly as the office was subsuming that of the 'prior of the vicars choral', the title given to the prior of the Céile Dé following the Tudor suppression of religious houses.[65] Fr Gwynn mistakenly believed that the precentorship was a 'new dignity' dating from the Tudor reformations,[66] but the Armagh registers show that the office was long established before the reformations.[67]

The treasurer was responsible for keeping the cathedral's treasures; its liturgical ornaments, relics and priestly vestments.[68] He made the ornaments and the bread and wine available for the masses and other services in the cathedral. The 1609 inquisition reveals that the treasurer of Armagh then held the revenues of the rectories and vicarages of the parishes of Clonkearney Upper and Lower as the corps of the treasurer.[69]

A peculiar feature of Armagh's cathedral chapter was the inclusion of the prior of the Céile Dé.[70] The Céile Dé were a religious community of ancient origin, yet they played an integral part in cathedral services throughout the later middle ages.[71] From the time of the reformation they were re-constituted as the vicars choral of Armagh cathedral.[72] The position of the prior and community of the Céile Dé before the reformations seems to have been directly analagous to that of the vicars choral of St Patrick's cathedral, Dublin. There were sixteen vicars choral in Dublin, but only their leader, the dean's vicar choral, had a fixed stall in the choir, and a voice on the cathedral chapter.[73] Cashel cathedral had a college of eight vicars choral in the sixteenth century, together with an organist.[74] Most Irish cathedrals on the eve of the reformations had modest colleges of just four vicars choral.[75]

It is not possible to offer an estimate of the size of the Céile Dé community at Armagh in the first half of the sixteenth century but William Reeves suggested that the community normally consisted of a prior and five brethren.[76] Despite its not inconsiderable land holdings, one suspects that the Céile Dé community at Armagh is likely to have been small on the eve of the reformations given that the priorship was worth only Stg£4 in 1492.[77]

Throughout Ireland, as in England, the canons other than the dignitaries had largely become sinecure non-residents before the sixteenth century.[78] Consequently, a proportion of the non-residents' incomes was assigned to their cathedrals' ' common fund' to augment the salaries of the resident canons, and to finance the college of vicars choral who took the non-residents' places in the choir. In Dublin in 1532 the non-resident canons had to give 20% of their incomes to the 'common fund', and thereafter were liable to further levies of 6s. 8d. for any of twelve specified holy days on which they were absent from cathedral services.[79] Armagh too had its non-resident canons.[80] However, it is not possible to give any indication as to the number of resident, as against non-resident, canons, nor is it possible to identify the size of the levy imposed on the non-residents for the common fund.

One may state that the archdeacons of Armagh did not reside in Armagh, and the prebendary of Dunbin is also likely to have been an infrequent visitor to Armagh. If the prebendaries *inter Hibernicos* were not always resident in Armagh themselves it appears that they could be represented in the cathedral by the vicar of the parish of which they were rector.[81] Hence the visitors of 1546 found that the prebendaries of Ballyclog and Clonfeacle resided in their parishes, while their vicars were serving the cathedral in Armagh.

A man of great importance for the cathedral at Armagh was the Master of Works. He was often a member of the Céile Dé, and had the responsibility for maintaining the fabric of the cathedral building.[82] Certain lands in Glenaul were set aside to cover the costs of maintenance.[83] Archbishop Cromer seems to have travelled regularly to Armagh and supervised the maintenance work done by the master of works and the dean.[84] The real estate set aside to fund the maintenance may have sufficed to cover the cost of routine works. However, major calamities, whether brought about by malice or misfortune, periodically overwhelmed the cathedral's resources. The Armagh registers have several records of primates seeking alms and offering indulgences to help restore the cathedral after a calamity.[85] In 1509 Primate Octavian granted the dues of the Office of

St Patrick to the dean and chapter to help restore the cathedral after it had fallen into a sorry state.[86]

When one attempts to examine how well the dean and chapter of Armagh carried out their primary responsibilities; those of maintaining the cathedral fabric and conducting an appropriate round of liturgical services, one is confronted by a lack of source materials. The archive of the cathedral chapter for the pre-reformation period has been entirely lost. It is clear that all was not well at Armagh in 1505 when Dnus Eamon Mc Cawell, vicar of Killevy, was provided to the deanery of Armagh and the priorship of the Céile Dé.[87] The revenues of these combined offices had fallen by some 15% between 1492 and 1505.[88] The cathedral was in a desolate state and its services were much diminished.[89] The fire of 1511 destroyed a great portion of the cathedral would have been an appalling setback. Nonetheless, Dean Mc Cawell and the chapter under his chairmanship set about rectifying this sorry situation. In 1509 they successfully petitioned the primate for additional resources to repair and adorn the cathedral building.[90] Primate Cromer took a special interest in the maintenance of the cathedral right up to the very eve of his death.[91] The primates, Dean Mc Cawell and the chapter of Armagh evidently ensured that the cathedral fabric was restored and subsequently well maintained for in 1553, just a couple of years after the death of the long-serving dean, Sir Thomas Cusack, lord chancellor of Ireland, remarked that St Patrick's cathedral, Armagh, was 'one of the fairest and best churches in Ireland'.[92]

There are several isolated pieces of evidence that are consistent with the suggestion that the cathedral services were well conducted. Not only was the cathedral building itself restored to good order in the first half of the sixteenth century, a fact conducive to the proper conduct of services, but in 1482 Primate Octavian bought a set of organs to enhance the quality of the liturgical services in Armagh's cathedral.[93] The 1546 visitors to the parishes of Armagh *inter Hibernicos* revealed that not only was the cathedral served by the dignitaries and the Céile Dé as one would have expected, but also by the vicars of some prebendal parishes.[94] They also reveal that Dean Mc Cawell, as ex officio rector of Loughgall, ensured that his portion of that parish church was very well maintained – an indication of his conscientiousness. The fact that Dean Mc Cawell remained in office for forty four years, through the episcopates of four primates, without being deprived, may tentatively be taken as evidence that he did not fall below at least the minimum standard expected of a churchman in his high position. Account should be taken too of the fact that the high offices held by the dignitaries, and even the prebendaries to a lesser degree, brought pressure to bear on the senior cathedral staff which would have helped to ensure that they abided by the standards expected of them by the primate and their colleagues. The dean and other dignitaries were men of power, their authority resting not only upon the offices they held, but also in the esteem which they enjoyed in men's eyes. Esteem has to be earned ... Furthermore, and quite probably of greater significance than the fear of the primate's court or the regard of their colleagues, the priests who served the cathedral church are very likely to have been motivated by a consciousness of their duty to God. Hence, in view of the attention given to the fabric of the cathedral church, the organ, the staffing of the cathedral by priests of prebendal parishes as well as the dignitaries and the Céile Dé, I suggest that, in all probability, the dean and chapter of Armagh conducted their affairs on the eve of the Tudor reformations in a manner which was at least satisfactory, and certainly in a better fashion than seems to have been the case at the turn of the sixteenth century.

THE ARCHDEACON

To support him in the routine administration of the archdiocese Archbishop Cromer could turn to his archdeacon. In Armagh *inter Anglicos* he was the senior clergyman subordinate to the primate, and an administrator whose local knowledge, long experience and expertise would be indispensible to an archbishop who was newly arrived from England. The archdeacon was the chief of the *ordinarii locorum* – clerics exercising a degree of ordinary jurisdiction at local level.[95] He was the *oculus episcopi*, literally the eyes of the bishop, with responsibility for the supervision, under the archbishop, of the clergy and laity. This supervision was carried out primarily through regular visitations of each of the parishes within his archdeaconry. The archdeacons of Armagh received procurations annually from the rectors and vicars of the churches *inter Anglicos* in the first half of the sixteenth century.[96] He had no other income by right of his office.[97] This supports the belief that archdiaconal visitations in the southern rural deaneries of Armagh were regular occurrences. Unfortunately, there are no surviving records of an archdiaconal visitation in late medieval Ireland, but the extant act book of the consistory court of Armagh does reflect something of the work of Archdeacon James White on the eve of Primate Cromer's arrival in Ireland.

The archdeacons of Armagh were expected to visit the parishes *inter Anglicos* in person. This is clear from records in Primate Mey's register for 1450 where Archdeacon Warren had to secure the written consent of the archbishop, the dean and chapter, and that of the priests *inter Anglicos* to employ commissaries to conduct visitations in his absence.[98] However, because the archdeacons were normally English by blood and loyalty they were personally active only in the three rural deaneries *inter Anglicos*. As late as the mid fifteenth century there are records of the archdeacons of Armagh employing commissaries to collect their procurations in the rural deaneries *inter Hibernicos*.[99] There is no evidence to indicate that this practice persisted into the sixteenth century but, given the nature of the sources, such a lacuna proves nothing.

During the course of their visitations the archdeacons were evidently empowered to process first instance suits and *ex officio* prosecutions. Archdeacon Warren was required to pronounce upon the validity of a marriage contract during his visitation of 1452.[100] Following a subsequent archdiaconal visitation Archdeacon Warren processed an *ex officio* suit against a Drogheda man who was denounced for bigamy.[101]

Archdeacon White appears to have conducted an archdiaconal visitation in 1518, or very late in 1517. He evidently found the parish church of Dunany to be in an unsatisfactory condition and he sequestrated the parish revenues until such time as the building's defect(s) had been put right. When the vicar and a layman of Dunany violated the sequestration the archdeacon had the violators cited before the consistory court of Armagh for an *ex officio mero* prosecution.[102]

Among the archdeacon's other responsibilities was the duty to conduct inquisitions into vacant benefices, and into the character of the candidate proposed for the benefice. Records for such inquisitions exist only for benefices in Armagh *inter Anglicos*. It may be that inquisitions were also conducted in the benefices in Armagh *inter Hibernicos* by the dean of Armagh and/or the rural dean of Tullyhogue, but with the loss of their records all evidence of such inquisitions has been lost.

Following inquisitions (where these were held) it was the responsibility of the archdeacon to induct the new incumbents into their benefices on receipt of episcopal mandates. Once again, the registers reveal that the archdeacons personally inducted clergymen into benefices *inter Anglicos*.[103] When mandated to induct priests into benefices *inter Hibernicos* the archdeacons seem always to have acted through commissaries. Archdeacon Roth generally delegated the task of inducting to benefices *inter Hibernicos* to one or more of the incumbents of neighbouring parishes.[104]

Archdeacon James White (1497–1530) was a law graduate who brought a sound legal training and twenty four years of experience in his post to Primate Cromer's administration. The English-born archbishop must have depended heavily upon him during the first years of his primacy. The importance of the archdeacon within the archdiocese was reflected in the fact that he had, *ex officio,* a vote in the cathedral chapter, and a stall in the cathedral choir.[105] The income of the archdeacon of Armagh is not recorded in any sixteenth century document, nor even in the Valor in Hibernia. Anthony Lynch found that the archdeacons of Armagh in the mid fifteenth century had an income of about £13 7s. 4d. by right of their office.[106] The archdeacons may have received a very similar sum in the first half of the sixteenth century. A list of the archdeacon's procurations in 1535 indicate that he levied £4 16s. 8½d. from the rural deanery of Drogheda, and a further £6 8s. 7½d. from the rural deanery of Ardee - making £11 5s. 4d. from two of the three rural deaneries.[107] The procurations for the rural deanery of Dundalk would have brought the archdeacon's income up to at least the fifteenth century figure. According to the royal visitation report for 1622 the archdeaconry was valued at a mere £2.[108] This incredibly low valuation can only have been derived from a now-lost source from the end of the sixteenth century. It suggests that the archdeacons lost the right to exact procurations during the course of the Tudor reformations.

Because the archdeaconry was worth such a modest sum in itself, it was necessary to supplement the archdeacon's income with other benefices. Archdeacon White held the prebend of Kene (worthless in the Valor) and the vicarage of Termonfeckin (worth £9 7s. in the Valor) up till his death.[109] If the Valor and visitation figures may be regarded as reasonable guides for the years up to 1530, they suggest that Archdeacon White may have drawn an income slightly in excess of £25 from his office and his benefices. This sum was far greater than that of the average rector and vicar in Armagh *inter Anglicos*.

It is not possible to establish how effectively Archdeacon White carried out his responsibilities as archdeacon. Mgr White was castigated as the 'blind archdeacon' by Christina Alin, a Drogheda woman, in 1518, presumably for failing to be as observant an *oculus episcopi* as she desired during the course of his recent visitation.[110] However, the archdeacon sued the woman for slander in the consistory court, and she confessed to the charge. Christina seems to have been a person who was all too loud in voicing her opinions. In 1522 she was prosecuted for slandering a woman by calling her a 'priest's whore', a charge to which she also confessed.

Archdeacon White often acted as a commissary of the president of the consistory and metropolitan court of Armagh.[111] He also witnessed many church court cases over which he did not preside.[112] That he enjoyed a reputation for integrity is suggested by a tithe dispute between the vicar and parishioners of Carlingford in 1521 in which the priest and laymen agreed to have the archdeacon act as arbitrator.[113] Interestingly too, the archdeacon paid most of Christina Alin's expenses in his suit against her, indicating that he was not a vindictive individual though he felt obliged to uphold the dignity of his office.

Archdeacon White's successor, Mgr Cormac Roth, was another law graduate.[114] By the time of his appointment in 1530 he had already served Archbishop Cromer as president of the consistory and metropolitan court of Armagh for nine years. Evidently he succeeded in impressing the primate for in 1534 Archbishop Cromer united the rectory of Heynestown (worth £6 6s. 8d. in the Valor) to the archdeaconry for Mgr Roth's lifetime in recognition of his 'great merits', and as a 'special favour'.[115]

The last two archdeacons before the Tudor reformations were well-educated men, with many years of experience in diocesan administration. It is probable that through their regular visitations both of the archdeacons in turn were more familiar figures in the parishes than was the archbishop. The good order of the parishes *inter Anglicos*, in terms of church buildings and personnel, must have owed something to the endeavours of the archdeacons, working for and with the archbishops of Armagh, in the decades prior to the Tudors' reformations.

RURAL DEANS

There were five rural deaneries in Armagh in the sixteenth century: the rural deaneries of Ardee, Drogheda and Dundalk which were *inter Anglicos*, and the larger rural deaneries of Orior and Tullyhogue which were *inter Hibernicos*. Normally the rural dean, or dean of Christianity, was a local incumbent resident in his rural deanery. He held office at the ordinary's pleasure, and served him as a supervisory officer.[116]

There were rural deans in Armagh *inter Anglicos* until the mid fifteenth century. No ruri-decanal archive has survived. However, among the Armagh registers are records of archiepiscopal mandates to the rural deans *inter Anglicos* directing them to perform such duties as citing parish priests and lay representatives of the parishes for an ordinary visitation, to collect the primate's procurations and synodals, and to collect the royal subsidy from their respective rural deaneries.[117] The office of rural dean was allowed to lapse in Armagh *inter Anglicos*, perhaps as financial exigencies compelled the archbishops of Armagh to collect their procurations and synodals directly at the annual diocesan synods, without recourse to intermediaries who would have expected fees of commission for their labours.[118] It is likely that the rural deans served little function in the three small rural deaneries of Armagh *inter Anglicos* since the archdeacon of Armagh was effectively compelled to confine his attentions to the same area. The office had obviously lapsed by the early sixteenth century. Indeed, there are few references to rural deans in any part of the English lordship in Ireland in the sixteenth century.[119]

There was a rural dean of Tullyhogue throughout the late medieval period, together with a ruridecanal official. In the peculiar circumstances in Tullyhogue, in which the archdeacon exercised no direct jurisdiction, and the primate was rarely if ever a visitor in the parishes west of the River Blackwater, it is probable that the rural dean of Tullyhogue exercised considerable authority in terms of church administration. Again, since the consistory court of the archbishop of Armagh rarely processed cases originating from that part of the archdiocese *inter Hibernicos*, the ruridecanal official may be presumed to have exercised jurisdiction over most first instance suits from the rural deanery, and also over a significant proportion of the lesser office cases.

A Scottish ecclesiastical text from the first half of the sixteenth century outlines the responsibilities of the rural deans in that country, and may serve to indicate the range of powers which could have been exercised by a rural dean in contemporary Ulster.[120] Scottish rural deans were obliged to conduct visitations within their rural deaneries. They were to collect synodals, procurations and any other dues owed to their bishop. They could also serve their bishop as a mandatory for holding inquiries into vacancies of benefices, and for the induction of parochial incumbents.

The Armagh registers show that the rural deans of Tullyhogue were issued mandates by the archbishops to cite clergy and lay people for visitations, and to cite people before the consistory court.[121] They received and published warnings of, or declarations of excommunications and/or interdicts on persons within their jurisdiction.[122] They were held accountable to the archbishops for certain revenues, probably the procurations and synodals due from priests within their rural deanery.[123]

The rural deans of Tullyhogue also exercised some judicial authority over the clergy and lay people in their jurisdiction, presumably to address sins uncovered in the course of ruridecanal visitations, rather like the archdeacon did in relation to his archdiaconal visitations.[124] The office of rural dean of Tullyhogue was said to be worth circa two marks in the mid fifteenth century, a modest sum which suggests that the office's revenues were derived from ruridecanal procurations, or from commissions for collecting archiepiscopal levies.[125] The office of rural dean of Tullyhogue survived into the sixteenth century.[126]

Since the archbishops and archdeacons of Armagh on the eve of the Tudor reformations exercised their respective authorities in the rural deanery of Tullyhogue indirectly through commissaries one may state that the office of rural dean there certainly had the potential to be useful and important. Whether it actually was so cannot be determined from the source materials. The fact that so many earlier rural deans were either disobedient and/or incontinent gives reason to doubt their efficacy as supervisory officers within the church.[127] Nonetheless, the state of the church in Armagh *inter Hibernicos*, as revealed in the visitation report of 1546, suggests that one ought not to form too negative an impression of the qualities of the church men there.

There was no rural dean of Orior. It is highly probable that the powers of a rural dean were exercised in Orior by the dean of Armagh's cathedral. This would certainly account for the visitational powers exercised by the dean of Armagh in the rural deanery of Orior in the 1540s.[128] This was an unusual arrangement, but it was paralleled in Waterford diocese where the dean of Waterford exercised a similar jurisdiction, and in Derry diocese where the dean of Derry's cathedral acted as rural dean of Inishowen.[129] In Orior most of the parishes were impropriated to the dean and chapter, and to the Céile Dé of whom the dean of Armagh was also prior since 1487.[130] The dean had, therefore, a direct interest in almost all of the parishes in the rural deanery of Orior before the reformations.

There was a ruridecanal official for the rural deanery of Tullyhogue, and another based in Armagh who was responsible for church court business within the rural deanery of Orior with Armagh city. Both officials were primarily legal officers, and their judicial functions are fully discussed below.

The official of Armagh also exercised important fiscal powers on behalf of the archbishop, as was highlighted by Aubrey Gwynn.[131] In 1531 Senekyn Mc Dewyn, official of Armagh (a.1522–1543) was granted a confirmation of his position as *custos* of the archiepiscopal palace at Armagh, and receiver of all the temporal revenues owing to Archbishop Cromer from his properties *inter Hibernicos*.[132] Senekyn was, doubtless, paid a commission for his rent-collecting work on behalf of the primate. In 1534 Archbishop Cromer united the rectories of Magherafelt and Ardtrea for Mc Dewyn's benefit for his lifetime.[133] This is a good reflection of the value which the archbishop ascribed to the work of the official of Armagh.

The ruridecanal officials of Tullyhogue may once have responsible for collecting the archbishops' rents west of the River Blackwater. A late fourteenth century official of Tullyhogue was cited to Armagh to pay the monies he had collected for the archbishop.[134] More interestingly, he was invited to discuss the state of the church with the archbishop and the dean and chapter in Armagh. Senekyn Mc Dewyn's commission of 1531 suggests that by the eve of the reformation whatever fiscal duties had once been carried out by the ruridecanal official of Tullyhogue had by then been concentrated in the hands of the official of Armagh.

It is not possible to assess the quality of the contribution of the rural dean of Tullyhogue and the dean of Armagh to the administration of the archdiocese of Armagh *inter Hibernicos*, though the fact that the priests continued to serve their parishes in a manner which seems satisfactory if one may judge from the 1546 visitation report, suggests that the deans *inter Hibernicos* did not fail in their duties.

CONCLUSIONS

In Archbishop Cromer the archdiocese of Armagh had a man with a good academic background, with close contacts in the court of Henry VIII. In facing his new responsibility Primate Cromer could draw upon the local knowledge, the long experience and the expertise of the senior clergymen within the archdiocese. He would find that his archdeacon an indispensable figure in his administration in the rural deaneries *inter*

Anglicos. The good order of the church in the parishes of Armagh *inter Anglicos* may be seen as an indicator that the archiepiscopal administrators of Armagh in the years prior to the Henrician reformation did their work well.

The dean, most of the cathedral chapter, and the rural dean of Tullyhogue, were Irish clerics whose backgrounds were very different to the primate. He probably met these men once a year and his relationship with them was inevitably less intimate than with the archdeacon who lived near the primate's castle at Termonfeckin. Yet, given the long-standing divide within the archdiocese Primate Cromer had to work with, and depend upon, these senior Irish clergymen to ensure that his authority was exercised effectively in the northern rural deaneries of his archdiocese. There is a dearth of evidence on which to make a definitive assessment of the state of the church in Armagh *inter Hibernicos* but, it has been shown in Chapter 3, that there is good reason to believe that priests *inter Hibernicos* made a reasonable effort in providing for the pastoral needs of their parishioners. The degree to which the pastoral ministry to the laity was efficacious would have reflected the effectiveness of the church administrators *inter Hibernicos*.

5

Archdiocesan Administration

Archbishop Cromer had three key instruments available to him to ensure that the secular clergy of his diocese met the pastoral needs of the laity in an adequate manner. The first of these was the diocesan synod. This presented the primate with an annual opportunity to set out his agenda to the parish clergy. He could outline his expectations of the priests, set goals for them, and exhort them to strive harder in their religious lives and in the performance of their priestly ministries. The second instrument was the visitation of the parish clergy. This allowed the archbishop to monitor the state of the church and clergy, to see that standards were being maintained, and that his synodal agenda was being implemented on the ground. Finally, the archbishop could employ his church courts to discipline any priests or laypeople who failed to meet the standards required of them. The courts gave 'teeth' to the synodal legislation and helped ensure that even the least motivated or obstreperous priest would implement the archbishop's wishes in his parish. In the discussion which follows these three instruments are examined separately, though in fact they were inextricably linked in the pursuit of the same goal of a better pastoral ministry.

SYNODS

Primate Cromer's register contains a record of almost all of the diocesan synods of the clergy of Armagh *inter Anglicos* from 1518 to 1535. These records are without parallel for the church in late medieval Ireland. They afford an invaluable opportunity to explore a central component of Primate Cromer's administration of the church in the archdiocese of Armagh before the Tudor reformations.

Diocesan synods inter Anglicos

The diocesan clergy of Armagh *inter Anglicos* came together for their annual synod every year in the last week of June or the first week of July.[1] The format of the synods was generally the same. The clergy met in St Peter's church, Drogheda, where Mass was celebrated in the morning. Some synodal records refer to a sermon being preached by a leading cleric of the archdiocese, usually exhorting the priests to strive for higher standards.[2] After the Mass the clergy processed out of the church in their surplices and caps[3] to the High Cross in the centre of Drogheda,[4] and sang the hymn *Veni Creator Spiritus*. The synod was then adjourned until midday.

The ringing of bells summoned the priests back for the resumption of the synod.

The president of the synod, who was invariably the primate if he were not detained by business in distant parts, usually sat close to the high altar in St Peter's. In the absence of the archbishop, the synods were presided over by the vicar-general.[5]

The proceedings of the synods were not always comprehensively recorded in the register. Yet this much is clear: the opportunity was not lost to exhort the priests at the synod to strive for higher standards. On the morning of the first synod over which Primate Cromer presided in person, on 5 July 1524, the archbishop exhorted the assembled priests to strive for the highest standards in their lives, their priestly ministry and in the administration of the sacraments.[6] In the afternoon session the primate engaged in further exhortation by referring the priests to many articles, and he did so again on the following morning with reference to more articles.

In the synod of 1525 Primate Cromer made repeated exhortations for a 'reformation of the clergy', a phrase to be understood in its contemporary meaning of 'reform', with no protestant associations as yet.[7] Similar exhortations are recorded for the synod of 1520 which was presided over by the vicar-general of the then-primate John Kite (1513–21), and in the synod of 1531 which was presided over by Primate Cromer's vicar-general.[8] Such exhortations to reform were by no means novel. Christopher Harper-Bill, in examining Dean Colet's famous convocation sermon of 1512, has shown that such calls for reform were a traditional feature of the medieval church, reflecting a desire for perfection rather than simply revealing a depressing vista of priestly failings.[9]

In the 1526 synod Primate Cromer ordered all of his parish clergy to acquire a copy of the *Constitutions of the province of Canterbury* by the time of the Feast of the Assumption (15 August) – or face a fine of 40s.[10] The constitutions, better known as *Ignorantia sacerdotum* after the opening words, were originally promulgated at a provincial synod held at Lambeth by Archbishop Pecham of Canterbury in 1281. Roy Haines has observed that the incipit 'with its rhetorical flavour may owe more to the fervour of the reformer than to the carefully qualified assessment of the administrator'.[11] Nonetheless, Primate Cromer's decree requiring all of his parish priests to have a copy of the *Constitutions* may have been intended to remedy a weakness which he perceived in at least some of his clergy.

Reference has already been made to 'articles' being expounded in synods to guide the clergy in their self-improvement. These generally seem to have been synodal and provincial statutes. Provincial synods were held regularly for the ecclesiastical province of Armagh, though few provincial statutes have survived.[12] Provincial statutes were regularly consolidated into comprehensive collections of canons outlining what was expected of parish clergy and the laity. The most comprehensive collections to have survived are those for the ecclesiastical province of Cashel which were issued in 1453 and, in revised form, in 1511.[13] The clergy of the ecclesiastical province of Cashel were directed to acquire a copy of the synodal decrees and to read them to their congregations in the vernacular four times a year.[14] This may well have been normal practice with all provincial statutes. The only near-comprehensive collections of provincial statutes to have survived for the northern province are those of Archbishop John Colton from 1383 to 1399, and those of Primate Nicholas Fleming which were issued in 1411.[15]

There were, of course, also some additional statutes enacted at provincial synods from time to time as circumstances required.[16]

At the synod of 1522 the provincial statutes were read to the assembled priests.[17] In synod after synod priests were repeatedly exhorted to observe the statutes ever more strictly.[18] In the synod of 1527 Primate Cromer stressed his concern to see that priests strictly adhere to the liturgical rubrics of the Mass.[19] This stricture is intriguing in that it seems to reflect a broader pattern across Christendom: not the negligence or care-lessness of the priest, but the response to a common belief that the efficacy of religious rites depended on their not being performed in exactly the same way each time: 'diver-sity was the key to the Mass's social value, for each variation in performance reflected local sensibilities far more than ... the priest's ignorance'.[20] Nonetheless, Catholic re-formers preferred to see the custom end. In the synod of 1530 the priests were re-minded of the legislation against priests committing fornication, and against leasing tithes without making a full inventory of the ecclesiastical charges to be levied on the benefices.[21]

Synods were used to address issues of ongoing concern. The synod of 1518[22] dealt with such recurring issues as the requirement for all priests exercising a cure of souls in the archdiocese to be properly instituted by the ordinary or his commissaries;[23] and the requirement that parish priests follow the proper procedures in drawing up wills for parishioners.[24] Whatever articles were emphasised in the individual synods the thrust of the agenda was always the same; to maintain and raise standards among the priest-hood, and see that administrative procedures were followed correctly.

The synods were used to process much diocesan business. A church court suit brought by Dnus Éamon Mc Cawell, dean of Armagh, against Dnus Eoghan O'Culean, rector of Clonfeacle, for slandering him as 'mean and base' in the doorway of Armagh cathedral, was dealt with in St Peter's church, Drogheda, on the day of the synod on 6 July 1518.[25] The prior of Louth monastery brought two tithe disputes to be dealt with by the primate to the synods of 1525 and 1535.[26] At the 1525 synod a letter from Pope Clement VII was read to clarify his intentions about dispensations for marriages within the forbidden degrees of affinity.[27] At the synod of 1530 Dnus. John, curate of Monaster-boice, was ordered not to serve the cure until he was properly instituted, while the rector of Rathnew in Meath diocese was ordered to bring his *titulus* (title) to the church auth-orities in Armagh, and the prebendary of Clonallon in Dromore diocese was ordered to employ a curate.[28] Clearly the synods could be used to deal with all sorts of problems.

An important, if mundane, aspect of the pre-reformation synods of the clergy of Armagh was the opportunity which they provided for the priests to settle their ac-counts with the archbishop and/or the archdeacon. This, presumably, explains why the monastic impropriators of benefices, or their proctors, were obliged to attend the synods. Again and again the synodal records report that those who failed to pay their synodals, or their procurations to the primate or the archdeacon, were threatened with the sequestration of their churches' revenues, or suspension or deprivation of their benefice.[29] However, the presidents of the synods of 1523 and 1529 had to threaten that any priest who violated such a sequestration imposed on his parish church would be subject to major excommunication.[30]

Some clergymen failed to attend the synods when cited to do so, and they were automatically fined and/or excommunicated.[31] Given the inevitability of punishment one can only suggest that the absentees may have hoped for more time to pay the charges which were to be collected from them at the synod. Not only did they have to pay their procurations to the archbishop and the archdeacon, but also their synodals. Synodals were fees for attending a synod, even when, as in the case of the synod of 1534 which was adjourned because of plague, no business was conducted.[32] The synodals at Armagh were graduated according to clerical incomes; the better off incumbents paid 2s., the poorest 6d., and the remainder 1s.[33]

The worst recorded spate of absenteeism occurred in 1528 when the impropriators of seven churches and nineteen parish clergy were declared to be contumacious.[34] It can hardly be an accident that the primate had expected to collect a 'voluntary' subsidy from the clergy at the synod, as had been requested in the convocation held in the previous April.[35] The rebellion was overcome by a compromise about the size of the subsidy. It is not possible to offer any calculation as to the 'normal' extent of failure to attend the annual synods *inter Anglicos*, yet the problem may not have been too severe. There were seventy two parishes or chapelries in the three southern rural deaneries, but in 1533 the impropriators of two churches and only two priests were found to be contumacious.[36] The primates were clearly able to ensure that the priests *inter Anglicos* attended the synods as directed, however much inclined some of them were to be elsewhere.

Diocesan synods inter Hibernicos

No record of a synod of the priests of Armagh *inter Hibernicos*, from the rural deaneries of Orior and Tullyhogue, survives for the sixteenth century.[37] All that exists is a note in the records of the synod *inter Anglicos* of 1 July 1522 declaring that the synod *inter Hibernicos* would be convened on 28 July 1522.[38] The records of a synod of the clergy of Armagh *inter Hibernicos* in 1462 may be representative of the other synods of which nothing can be known for certain.[39]

The synod *inter Hibernicos* of 1462 was held inside St Patrick's cathedral, Armagh. The archbishop, John Bole (1457–71), was present. Primates Mey and Bole were regular visitors to Armagh city and may have made a point of attending the northern synods. Primate Cromer (1521–42) may have been a regular visitor to Armagh city also. His conscientious character suggests that this is likely, and there is a reference from near the end of his life where he appointed commissaries to inspect the maintenance of the cathedral fabric since he was too ill to do so in person.[40] At any rate, whenever the primates did not preside at the synods *inter Hibernicos* it is virtually certain that the dean of Armagh would have done so.

At the synod *inter Hibernicos* of 1462 a series of (unspecified) diocesan statutes were read to the assembled priests and, with their approval, were ordered to be published and put into execution throughout the rural deaneries of Orior and Tullyhogue.[41] The significance of this synodal record is that it shows that synods *inter Hibernicos* were conducted in a similar manner to those for Armagh *inter Anglicos* and the northern synods had the same potential to advance reform among the secular clergy and in the parishes *inter Hibernicos*.

Convocations

Every time a parliament was to be convened in late medieval Ireland summons were issued to the archbishop of Armagh to attend, together with proctors to represent the dean and chapter and the parochial clergy of the archdiocese.[42] Invariably the archbishop replied that he would attend in person if the great council or parliament was held in the northern ecclesiastical province, but would otherwise be represented by two proctors.[43] The archbishop would explain that the dean and chapter were mere Irish and ought not to be allowed to attend parliament. The clergy *inter Anglicos* elected a proctor in a diocesan convocation to represent them in the third house of the Irish parliament.[44] The clergy in convocation bound themselves to pay their proctor's expenses for attending the parliament.[45]

The bishops and the clerical proctors who attended the parliament invariably agreed to grant a subsidy to the English crown. By the early decades of the sixteenth century the subsidy was £19 13s. 4d.[46] The subsidy of 1533 was a little less at £17 0s. 6d., possibly because of the depredations of the Ulster Irish in some border parishes.[47]

It was left to the clergy of Armagh *inter Anglicos* to decide how, and by whom, the subsidy was collected. In their convocations the priests set a levy on the benefices and on the church lands in the three southern rural deaneries. At their convocations the clergy elected a collector of the levies for each of the three rural deaneries *inter Anglicos*. The primate, or his vicar general, exercised the right to appoint the collector for the rural deanery of Drogheda.[48] There could be a contest for the position of collector in the other two rural deaneries *inter Anglicos*. In the convocation of 1520 Bro John Carroll, abbot of Knock Louth, and Dnus Thomas Duffy, vicar of Kildemock, each received four votes from the (beneficed?) clergy of the rural deanery of Ardee.[49] In the event the vicar-general chose the abbot of Knock Louth.[50] The vicar of Kildemock was, however, successful in being elected as collector in 1522 and in 1524.[51] Not only did diocesan and regular clerics covet the position of collector of the subsidies, so too did the laymen who farmed parochial tithes.[52] Evidently the position of collector was financially remunerative. The collectors in 1443 received 4d. per mark on benefices to cover their expenses.[53] This must be regarded as a modest yet useful sum for the not too onerous task of collecting a royal tax.

In most convocations there was no business other than the appointment of collectors for the royal levy, but occasionally there was. In the convocation of 1528 Primate Cromer asked for the appointment of a committee of experienced clergymen to seek a remedy for the tendency to rebellion shown by some of the English subjects, particularly in Louth and Meath.[54] In the convocation of 1535 a letter from Henry VIII was read concerning a new subsidy, together with another calling on the clergy to elect a proctor to represent them in the forthcoming parliament.[55] At the same meeting it was announced that the pope was no longer to be prayed for publicly – a statement which served to underline the likely drift of crown legislation in the forthcoming parliament.

On two occasions, Primate Cromer petitioned the convocation for a subsidy for himself, firstly in 1524 when he was newly arrived in Ireland, and next in 1528 before he set off for England on royal business.[56] The convocation of April 1528 is interesting in revealing something of the 'decision-making process'. The primate made a request to the convocation for a subsidy in the order of £1 from the monastic impropriators, 6s. 8d. each from rectors, 3s. 4d. from vicars, and 1s from unbeneficed parish priests. Some voices suggested instead that the convocation agree to pay the archbishop half of their usual procurations as a subsidy. However, the primate seems to have ignored this, less generous offer. It is apparent from the rebellion staged in the 1528 synod that he took the sullen silence of many of the priests present as a token of consent. At the synod, however, a compromise had to be arrived at.[57]

In exceptional circumstances it is clear that the convocation could take on something of the character of a synod. In Cromer's register the terms 'synod' and 'convocation' are quite distinct. In the convocation of November 1518 the clergy addressed a range of problems which were, evidently, too pressing to leave until the synod of the following July of 1519.[58] There was a discussion about the problem of 'vagabond' friars exercising a cure of souls and seeking alms without a licence from the ordinary.[59] The presiding vicar-general took the opportunity to suspend services in the church of Charlestown, County Louth, because of its delapidated condition. He also suspended two priests for 'auctioning' the services of their churches. The convocation of 1496, under the presidency of Primate Octavian, affords another example of such a convocation.[60] At that assembly the primate ordered the rector of Beaulieu to dismiss his concubine, and to pay a fine of 12 salmon for his sin. The archbishop also decreed that whenever thunder and lightning occurred the priests should, under pain of fines of 3s., 2s. or 1s. according to rank, ring the church bells while darkness continued.

Hence, while the annual convocations were normally concerned only with the task of electing the collectors of the royal subsidies, they were sometimes used for ecclesiastical business, even to the extent of becoming an extraordinary synod if the need arose.

Conclusions

One may conclude that the annual synods in Armagh were recognised as important instruments of reform, and that they were well employed as such. Primate Cromer availed of them as regular opportunities to exhort his parish priests to ever higher standards in their personal conduct, in the celebration of the liturgy and in the provision of pastoral care to the laity. The reading of *Ignorantia sacerdotum*, and the synodal statutes, may be seen as a form of 'in-service training', if one may be forgiven for employing modern jargon. The synods were also used to address current issues affecting the church's ministry at diocesan level. Doubtless too the regular gatherings at synods and convocations helped to foster an *esprit de corps* among the parochial clergy who otherwise worked and ministered in their separate parishes throughout the year. On the other hand, the holding of separate synods for the clergy of Armagh *inter Anglicos* and for those *inter Hibernicos* reflected the persistent divide created by the English presence in part of the archdiocese. In the diocese of Ely a dinner had become an established part of the synod by the mid sixteenth century, and the same seems to have been true at Armagh in Primate Cromer's time.[61] A memorandum of July 1542 records the cost of the archbishop's dinner as being 5*s*. 4*d*.[62] Clearly the annual synod could be a convivial occasion, not unlike some clerical gatherings of modern times.

It is clear from the synodal records for the years immediately prior to Primate Cromer's arrival in Ireland that his exhortations for reform were by no means novel. Rather the archbishop was able to employ the well established synodal traditions in the archdiocese to promote the ideal of perfection. One may conclude by observing that exhortations of themselves were not likely to have a lasting impact. If reform was to be achieved in the parishes the archbishop would have to investigate the implementation of the synodal decrees, and discipline anyone who failed in their obligations.

VISITATIONS

Every bishop was required to conduct regular visitations of his entire diocese. None of the visitation books of the archdiocese of Armagh has survived, and there are few references to parish visitations in the registers attributed to Primates Octavian and Cromer. The gapped records available in earlier registers suggest that the visitations were conducted annually in the fifteenth century.[63] One may suggest that this continued to be the case into the sixteenth century, if for no other reason than the fact that the primates needed the procuration fees associated with visitations.[64] Certainly, the synodal records in Primate Cromer's register show that the priests of Armagh *inter Anglicos* were reminded to pay their archiepiscopal procurations virtually every year.[65]

The visitation could be of two kinds. It could be a peremptory meeting between the assembled clergy and laity of a rural deanery and the ordinary, or his commissaries, at a designated location. Alternatively, the archbishop could decide upon a more thorough visitation in which he, or his commissaries, personally visited the parish clergy and laity in their churches.

It is impossible to tell how often Primate Cromer or his predecessors conducted the first kind of visitation, as against the latter. The one visitation record from the sixteenth century which has chanced to survive among the Armagh registers is of a more thorough kind.[66] If one may hazard a guess, one might suggest that the first visitation of each new primate was likely to be of the thorough kind. This suggestion may be supported by the presence in Primate Dowdall's register of a complete list of the functioning churches in Armagh *inter Anglicos* to be visited in 1544, the year after the archbishop's consecration.[67] Furthermore, it is clear that Primate Dowdall had visited Armagh, and possibly Clonfeacle, in person before 1546.[68]

The format of the peremptory visitations of the archdiocese is clear from the Armagh registers. Generally the clergy and 'faithworthy laymen' of each of the five rural deaneries were summoned to assemble at a key church within each deanery on consecutive days:

the clergy and laity of the rural deanery of Drogheda at St Peter's church, Drogheda;

the clergy and laity of the rural deanery of Ardee at St Mary's church, Ardee;

the clergy and laity of the rural deanery of Dundalk at St Nicholas' church, Dundalk;

the dean and chapter, the Céile Dé, the clergy and laity of the rural deanery of Orior at St Patrick's cathedral, Armagh;

the clergy and laity of the rural deanery of Tullyhogue at St Jarlath's church, Clonfeacle.[69]

The archbishops often, but not always, conducted visitations of the archdiocese *inter Anglicos* in person.[70] In Primate Mey's register there are letters from the vicar of Ardee and the vicar of Dundalk declaring that the hospitality which they had given to the primate while on visitation was not intended to establish a precedent which might form the basis of a legal obligation in the future.[71]

Some primates, most notably Archbishops John Mey and John Bole, travelled to the cathedral city of Armagh regularly to visit the dean and chapter, the Céile Dé and the monastery of SS Peter and Paul. One late reference suggests that Primate Cromer was also a regular visitor to Armagh city.[72] While at Armagh the archbishops could reside at their archiepiscopal palace, though some tended to stay in a chamber of the house of the Céile Dé instead.[73] The archbishops sometimes chose to visit that portion of Armagh *inter Hibernicos* through commissaries.[74] The commissaries usually included a senior member from the cathedral chapter, or the ruridecanal official of Orior with Armagh city.[75] Indeed, the only visitation record to survive for the archdiocese of Armagh in the sixteenth century is of one conducted by two commissaries, one of whom was a canon, in the parishes *inter Hibernicos*.[76]

It is not possible to determine at what time of year diocesan visitations were carried out in Armagh in the sixteenth century. It is conceiveable that diocesan visitations in Armagh may have been used to ensure that new synodal legislation was being implemented in the parishes. Such a visitation may have been particularly useful in 1526 to see whether all of the priests had acquired their copy of *Ignorantia sacerdotum* within the period of time stipulated at the diocesan synod(s).[77] On the other hand, the synodal records in Primate Cromer's register show that some of the kinds of problems normally uncovered in visitations were addressed in the annual synods; fornication, liturgical practices, non-residence, the leasing of tithes, and the proper institution of unbeneficed priests into their cures.[78] Priests were obliged to show their 'titles' to their parish cures to visitors,[79] and the synodal record of 1530 includes a directive to the rector of Rathnew in Meath diocese to bring his 'title' to the vicar-general as a matter of urgency, indicating that that synod almost certainly followed an ordinary visitation. Furthermore, the unpaid procurations due from visitations were paid at the diocesan synods *inter Anglicos*.[80]

The visitors would have used a set of articles of inquiry to give focus to their investigations. They would also have attended to any presentments made to them against any priests or lay folk during the course of their visitations. The visitors would have been particularly concerned to investigate the parish clergy's performance of their pastoral responsibilities, to see that synodal legislation was being observed by the priests and people, and that, at least minimum, standards of morality and religious observance were being maintained. By interviewing the lay people on the day subsequent to the examinations of the priests the church authorities clearly hoped to arrive at a true picture of the state of the church in the individual parishes.

Unfortunately, the books of the visitation of the clergy and people of the late medieval archbishops of Armagh have long since perished. All that survives is a loose paper document which records the visitation in 1546 of the two northern rural deaneries *inter Hibernicos* by two commissaries of Primate George Dowdall (1543–58). Nonetheless, this record is most useful in throwing light on the manner in which visitations were conducted in Armagh, as well as illuminating the state of the church and clergy in the northern deaneries before they were affected by protestantism.

The 1546 visitors appear to have drawn their information from personal inspection of the church buildings and liturgical equipment. The clergy were questioned on oath, after they had celebrated the Mass. The visitation articles investigated the priests' performance of their duties of celebrating Mass, recitation of the divine office, and celibacy. Further enquiries were made among lay parishioners.

Following an ordinary visitation injunctions were normally issued ordering the remedying of any failings uncovered. The *comperta*, or charges against delinquent priests or lay people, could be dealt with by the visitors during the course of the visitation[81] or, in extreme cases, a delinquent could be arraigned before the consistory court to be prosecuted *ex officio*.[82] Unfortunately, the absence of any act book for the 1540s precludes the possibility of examining the judicial outcomes of the findings of the 1546 visitation *inter Hibernicos*.

Visitation records, like the other curial documents historians normally rely on to study the late medieval church, tend to be bureaucratic and formalised, and they can obscure the bishop's very real importance as a pastor to his clergy. The 1546 record indicates that Archbishop Dowdall had recently visited Armagh city in person, as the primates often did, and interviewed some of the parish clergy from the rural deanery of Orior. He had discussed with a number of his clergy the issues which concerned them and he knew the rector of Clonfeacle, for one, well. As the bishop of Ardagh and Canon Magrath, the archbishop's commissaries, did in 1546, Primate Dowdall would have spent time exhorting and persuading the clergy to strive for higher standards.

It was, for instance, impractical for the primates to suspend every priest in the rural deaneries *inter Hibernicos* who was guilty of fornication. Primate Mey's agreement with the O'Neill to seize the goods of clerical concubines, and divide the spoils between himself and the church, seems not to have been continued by subsequent primates.[83] Progress could yet be achieved in persuading individual priests, like the parish priest of Tethnan O Nellan, to put their female companions aside and to live chastely.[84] Such off the record conversations are likely to have been far more common than one might imagine. Obviously, they were not always fruitful. When Maurice Doran OP, bishop of Leighlin (1524–25), exhorted his archdeacon, Maurice Cavanagh, to lead a purer life he was killed for his efforts. Clearly, prudence was a very necessary virtue in addressing sins in such an age.

The visitation was a long established and potentially effective instrument of epis-copal oversight, particularly of the parish clergy, and of the religious communities within a bishop's jurisdiction. However, to be effective visitations had to be reasonably fre-quent, thorough and be followed up by corrective action to deal with the failings which were uncovered.

It is difficult to assess the effectiveness of the archiepiscopal visitations in Armagh on the eve of the reformations. No doubt every visitation was preceded, rather like a school inspection today, by a flurry of activity by those about to be visited. Nonethe-less, by taking evidence through personal observations, from the clergy on oath, and by drawing information from lay parishioners, the visitors could form a reasonably true estimate of the state of the church and clergy in the parishes.

It is surely significant that the lay people interviewed by Primate Dowdall's com-missaries in 1546 told the visitors of several priests who broke the rule of celibacy, but in only one case was a priest reported for failure to perform his pastoral duties. There can hardly be much doubt but that the laity in late medieval Ulster would have been far more concerned about a priest being negligent in carrying out his priestly functions, than they would have been about his marital status, though it is interesting to note that the lay representatives of the parishes visited in 1546 did make presentments against concubinary clergy. It seems probable, therefore, that the visitations succeeded in re-vealing something of the true state of the church and clergy in the parishes.

It has been argued above in Chapter 3 that, if the 1546 visitation report is reliable, it indicates that the priests in the church in Armagh *inter Hibernicos* ministered to their people in a satisfactory manner (at least), whatever about the incontinence of some of their number. As for the rural deaneries *inter Anglicos* it appears from the study of the consistory court records below that the clergy there were well disciplined in the pre-reformation period. The degree of success of the church authorities in addressing the problems which may have been identified during the course of visitations depended upon the effectiveness of the church courts.

THE CHURCH COURTS OF ARMAGH

The church court was a vital instrument in the administration of the church in that it gave the ordinary the power to enforce the legislative programmes endorsed in the synods, and it allowed the bishop to discipline persons for religious or moral failings which were uncovered during the course of episcopal or archdiaconal visitations, or which were brought to the court's attention by third parties. If Primate Cromer's ad-ministration of the archdiocese of Armagh was to be efficacious he needed to have church courts which were active and effective.

Book 1 of Primate Cromer's register is an act book of the consistory and metropoli-tan court of Armagh.[85] It is comprised of records of the acta or acts of the court during the period 1518–22 and offers a tantalizing glimpse of how Armagh's church courts functioned on the eve of the Tudor reformations. William Lukin, the court registrar, envisaged a two-fold division of his book.[86] Court proceedings were to be recorded in the first part of the book, with depositions confined to the 'third quarter of this volume' or 'the end of the book'.[87]

The trial records were generally arranged in chronological order according to the date of the first hearing of each suit. Normally each case record was written from the top of a new folio, though occasionally an entry was added later below a brief record.

The Armagh court book was not a day by day record. It is comprised of copies or summaries of original court records. The book is obviously incomplete. At this point it is not possible to calculate the extent of the loss of records from the period of time covered by the court book, but it may well have been very great indeed. For 1521 there are records of twenty six suits, of which nine were first heard in the month of July. That more than 34% of the cases of that year received their first hearing in a single month seems improbable. Less probable still is that 30%, i.e. six of twenty, of the cases dealt with in 1520 received their first hearing on a single day; 30 October 1520. It seems more likely that there were many more suits of which no record now survives.

It will thus be clear that any conclusions about the volume of business processed by Armagh's metropolitan court, any calculations of the average length of time taken to process suits, and even simple statements about the number of suits which reached conclusions, must be based on very unsatisfactory evidence. One cannot even be sure how representative are the records preserved in the Armagh court book of the normal litigious business of the court. Nonetheless, the court book offers a unique opportunity to examine, if only in an impressionistic fashion, how Armagh's church courts functioned on the eve of the reformations.

The nature of the church courts

The church courts claimed competence in all matters concerning faith and morals, a very wide remit indeed.[88] The courts dealt with all manners of failings among the clergy, including non-residence, negligence and any moral faults. They were also concerned with the fabric of church buildings, the state of graveyards and the condition of church ornaments. They acted against anyone withholding lawful revenues from the church. They investigated claims to possession of church revenues or presentations to parish benefices. Sacrilege, immorality, assaults on spouses and clerics, and failure to attend Mass might be punished by the church courts. All matrimonial matters fell within their jurisdiction, as did the correction of all sexual sins except rape which was reserved by the civil courts. Questions of illegitimacy, accusations of slander and defamation, and the upholding of oaths were also dealt with by the ecclesiastical courts. Finally, all testamentary matters, including the granting of probate, lay within the prerogative of the church courts. It may be seen that the jurisdiction of the church courts was very extensive. It related to many aspects of people's lives, including the most intimate. It was founded on the premise that the church courts functioned in a Christian society which was committed to Christian values.

The litigious business brought before the courts may be divided into two broad categories. First there were the office cases in which the court proceeded against persons who had, or who were suspected to have, infringed the canon law of the church, or local synodal decrees.[89] If such a person had come to the attention of the church authorities and was charged directly by them the judge acted *ex officio mero*. If the defendant had been charged by someone else the judge acted *ex officio promoto*, in which case the individual who promoted the court proceedings had to bear the costs if the charge proved unfounded.[90] The second category of business comprised instance cases, which were brought to the courts at the instance of one party against another.

The distinction between office and instance suits was less clear in practice than it seems in theory. Some matters, such as suits alleging slander of clerics or suits by clerics to secure what they regarded as customary dues, could be promoted *ex officio promoto*, or as an instance suit.[91] In Armagh's consistory the president of the court dealt with both office and instance cases. Normally instance business was delegated to an official principal, while office cases were delegated to a different judge known as a commissary.[92]

To initiate an instance suit the plaintiff had first to present the court with a statement of charges against the defendant(s), called a libel, which was read aloud in the court.[93] A court officer called an apparitor was then commissioned to issue citations to the plaintiff(s), the defendant(s) and any known witnesses, ordering them to appear before the court on a specified day.[94] There was one apparitor for each of the three rural deaneries *inter Anglicos*. The accused was given a written copy of the libel, together with the citation.[95] Every defendant had to be given sufficient time in order to prepare his or her defence.[96] Each party in an instance case was free to choose a proctor to represent them in court.[97]

Documentary evidence was highly valued by the church courts for making judgements.[98] In a case of alleged bigamy the metropolitan court of Armagh ordered the defendant to secure a death certificate for his wife's previous husband to prove his innocence.[99] However, the predominant form of evidence in instance cases comprised oral statements taken from witnesses on oath. Depositions were taken in open court, with the deponents liable to further questioning if it seemed that they were withholding evidence.[100] The depositions were recorded for the court by a notary, and copies could also be made available to the defendant(s).[101]

If the witnesses were unable to attend the court for any legitimate reason the judge could establish a commission to take depositions outside the court. Alternatively, the court itself could be transferred to a more convenient location to process a case.[102] The court issued *aggravatoriae* whenever it was necessary to compel reluctant witnesses to give testimony.[103]

The archbishops of Armagh often presided over their courts in person. In 1521 Mgr Cormac Roth was appointed as commissary and president of the metropolitan court by the dean and chapter of Armagh.[104] Roth was subsequently confirmed in his offices by Primate Cromer.[105] Whoever was judge had to weigh the proffered evidence, and issue his decree or sentence. The sentence was recorded in a notorial instrument of judgment, a copy of which was given to the plaintiff.[106]

Far less evidence survives on the procedure of office cases in Armagh's court than for instance cases. Some of the office cases in Armagh's court must have originated in presentments made against malefactors in the course of diocesan or archdiaconal visitations. Apparitors could also bring suspected malefactors to the court's attention. Other office proceedings were promoted by private individuals.[107]

Office cases were invariably dealt with by summary proceedings. The defendant was charged upon oath to make a true answer to the articles exhibited against him. If he denied the charge he was ordered to purge himself in public by means of his own oath, and those of a number of compurgators who would swear on his behalf.[108] There is no record of a defendant purging himself before the consistory court in the Armagh act book, though one may find references to compurgation in earlier Armagh registers, for example, when Dnus Cúconnacht O Higha, rector of Aghaloo, purged himself in 1455 of the charge of maintaining a concubine.[109] A defendant who failed to purge himself before a church court was usually ordered to perform penance. If a defendant purged himself, and there was yet evidence brought against him, he could then employ an advocate or proctor to represent his cause.

The structure of the church courts in Armagh

Many of the late medieval archbishops of Armagh were English by birth or ancestry and a number of them had been reluctant to venture often into the northern parishes *inter Hibernicos*, resulting in the jurisdiction of the consistory court being largely confined to the rural deaneries *inter Anglicos*.[110] The court was peripatetic within the archdiocese of Armagh *inter Anglicos*, with sessions held regularly in churches at Drogheda, Termonfeckin, and, less frequently, at Dundalk.[111] Sessions seem to have been held twice a month.[112]

Much of the church court business in the rural deaneries *inter Hibernicos* was delegated to the courts of the ruridecanal officials of Tullyhogue and of Orior with Armagh city.[113] Senkyn Mac Dewyn, the official of Orior with Armagh city, was empowered by Primate Dowdall in 1543 to deal with 'all matrimonial cases, and ... everything known to belong to the office of the officialty'.[114] The officials obviously exercised jurisdiction over first instance suits. Anthony Lynch has shown that in the early fifteenth century the ruridecanal officials also enjoyed jurisdiction over office cases, and even dealt with some criminal matters such as rape and theft – which were reserved to the civil courts in colonial Ireland.[115] It is likely that the ruridecanal officials *inter Hibernicos* continued to exercise some jurisdiction over office cases in the early sixteenth century though there is no evidence to demonstrate that they did so.

Appeals could, of course, have been made from the ruridecanal courts to the metropolitan court of Armagh. Yet the surviving records in the court book virtually all pertain to cases which originated in the rural deaneries *inter Anglicos*, or from the suffragan dioceses of the north. From the archbishop's court a litigant could appeal to the Roman curia. The judge issued 'apostles' if he recognised the validity of the appeal, or 'refutory apostles' if he refused the right to appeal.[116] The metropolitan judge would issue tuitory letters to legitimate appellants who appealed to Rome from any of the church courts of the northern ecclesiastical province, including the courts of Armagh.[117]

There is no evidence to demonstrate clearly whether or not the archdeacons of Armagh had a separate court of their own in the sixteenth century, like their counterparts in England and Scotland. They obviously possessed some disciplinary powers to punish malefactors identified in the course of archdiaconal visitations.[118] However, Archdeacon White had to sue the vicar of Dunany in the consistory court for violating the sequestration which he had imposed on the parish revenues.[119] He also had to sue a woman in the metropolitan court for defamation, which suggests that he had no court of his own.[120] Instead, one finds that the archdeacon presided over the metropolitan court as a commissary of the vicar general or of the president of the court.[121] The matter cannot be proved beyond question without more evidence, though there seems to be sufficient reason to doubt the existence of an archdiaconal court on the eve of the reformation. Presumably the small size of the archdiocese *inter Anglicos* made the existence of the secondary court superfluous.

Armagh's consistory court cases, 1518–1522

The cases brought before Armagh's consistory court between 1518 and 1522 mainly concerned instance business, together with a minority of office cases. The following analysis is based upon the records of some 113 cases preserved in Book 1 of Primate Cromer's register which can be made to yield significant results. Given this relatively small number of case records, the short span of years, and the uncertainty as to why the proceedings of these particular cases were copied into the register, they cannot form the basis for a convincing statistical analysis of the court's business. Instead the different types of suits outlined below can only indicate in an impressionistic fashion the relative frequency with which such cases were processed by Armagh's consistory court on the eve of the Tudor reformation.[122]

Of the 87 first instance cases recorded in Primate Cromer's register no less than twenty-one concerned matrimonial disputes.[123] Sixteen of those suits called upon the consistory court to pass judgement on marriage contracts. Many women sought the court's recognition of extra-ecclesial marriages they had entered into *per verba de praesenti, carnali copula subsecuta*, generally because the continued commitment of their male partners was in doubt. In a number of suits only one witness was presented to the court. One woman stated that all the witnesses to her wedding had died, except for her mother.[124]

Six women brought suits to have their marriages annulled, four of them on the grounds that their husbands were impotent.[125] The charges were rigorously investigated for fear of collusion between the spouses. Two husbands were examined by commissions of seven and nine men respectively.[126] While the suits were being processed the litigants were ordered to live together as man and wife, presumably to see if the alleged problem could be overcome. One couple was imprisoned in the archbishop's jail for failing to live together as the court directed.[127] One man sued for an annulment on the basis of an alleged previous marriage contract, but the court decided that his current marriage was perfectly valid.[128]

Two women sought annulments on the grounds that they were coerced into marriage. One woman proved to the court that she had not given her assent to her marriage, but had been forced to the altar.[129] In the other case the plaintiff presented witnesses to declare that she had been dragged to her wedding by two men, while she wept and tore her clothes in protest.[130] The court investigated one marriage which was rendered invalid by an impediment of affinity.[131]

Two women brought violent husbands to Armagh's consistory court. One won a court order binding her husband to keep the peace on pain of forfeiting a 20-mark bond.[132] The other secured a divorce *a mensa et thoro*, in effect a legal separation without the right to re-marry.[133] The court demanded 3s. 4d. from the defendant as a surety for his good behaviour, and it ordered him to return his wife's dowry since no reconciliation was anticipated.

There were two suits concerning dowries. In one a woman succeeded in having the court order a man to return the dowry of her deceased daughter, as she had died before the wedding.[134] In the second instance a husband successfully sued his parents-in-law for a dowry for his wife, although they had opposed their daughter's wedding to him.[135]

A striking feature of the matrimonial suits recorded in the Armagh court book is that no less than eighteen of the twenty one plaintiffs were women. The court regularly recognised the validity of marriages at the behest of the female partner. It acted against a man whose wife claimed that he had deserted her.[136] It defended wives with violent husbands. The court granted an annulment to a woman who had been compelled to marry without her consent, and to another because her husband was unable to consummate the marriage. It ordered the restitution of dowries which had been unlawfully detained by would-be husbands. By contrast with the high rate of success enjoyed by female litigants, two of the three male plaintiffs lost their matrimonial suits.[137]

Women were frequently plaintiffs in defamation suits, usually to defend their characters against sexual slurs. Quite often, however, women featured as defendants for abusing other women as 'whores' or men as thieves. Women defended their interests in testamentary and debt disputes before the consistory court. One may conclude that the courts offered women a degree of security, and an important avenue for redress, in their relationships with men.

There are records of twenty-four first instance suits for defamation or slander preserved in Primate Cromer's register, together with two counter-suits.[138] There are records of two further defamation trials which were dealt with *ex officio*.

Twelve laymen sued for slander, six of them against people whom, they alleged, had publicly accused them of theft.[139] One of the more interesting of the other suits was brought by Thomas Bayth jnr, a merchant of Drogheda, against Alexander Rownsele, another merchant, for attributing to him the dangerous statement that Lord Deputy Kildare was a traitor.[140]

Four women claimed to have been defamed by being called 'a priest's whore', usually by other women.[141] One of these latter responded with a counter-suit alleging that she had first been called a 'common whore, a priest's whore, a monk's whore, and a whore to all other men besides' by the plaintiff in the first suit.[142] One woman claimed that she had been defamed by being called 'a witch'.[143] One widow brought a suit against a man who said that she had caused the death of her husband by denying him wine and whiskey.[144] He responded with a counter-suit alleging that she had called him 'a deceitful clot'.[145] Both lost their suits.

Priests were responsible for five defamation suits. The rector of Rathdrumin, sued his relative Thomas Mc Laughlin for alleging in public that the priest had intercourse with his wife.[146] Dnus Thomas Gruyr, curate of Mayne, successfully sued a layman for abusing him as 'a false whore of a priest' in a dispute about the canonical portion of his late father's estate.[147] Dnus Peter Bowden, another curate, failed in his suit against a layman who allegedly abused him as a 'fornicating priest'.[148] The most bizarre suits must surely be those of Dnus Patrick Mc Egyr, curate of Salterstown. This priest first sued Dnus Donal O'Highran for publicly preaching that he had stolen the head of St Boice from the church of Monasterboice.[149] The suit lapsed when he was arrested by the bishop of Meath and taken before the metropolitan court. Dnus Mc Egyr purged himself and subsequently sued Dnus Gabriel for accusing him of stealing the relic before the bishop of Meath, thus prompting Dnus Mc Egyr's arrest.[150] In the end the litigating parties reached a private settlement.

There were two office cases alleging defamation. Mgr James White, archdeacon of Armagh, successfully sued a woman from Drogheda who had called him 'the blind archdeacon', presumably in relation to his supervisory duties in the church.[151] In the other suit the dean of Armagh, denounced Dnus Eoghan O'Culean, rector of Clonfeacle, for abusing him as mean and base at the doorway of Armagh cathedral.[152] No further record survives of the suit.

Partial records from the proceedings of eighteen testamentary suits are preserved in Primate Cromer's register.[153] These suits represent merely a fraction of all of the testamentary business processed by the church courts in Armagh. Probate of wills was normally delegated to commissaries appointed by the archbishops. John McCafferty has suggested that Brother Stephen Roth, prior of St Leonard's, Dundalk, may have been responsible for granting probate for all the wills in Armagh *inter Anglicos*, at least while Mgr Plunkett was vicar general.[154] Generally testamentary suits were brought before the consistory court only if a dispute arose.

The consistory court of Armagh was regularly called upon to settle disputes about the appointment of executors for estates. Evidently the appointment as executor to some estates was much coveted. Most testamentary disputes concerned some aspect of the property of the deceased person's estate. To avoid conflict the church authorities took great pains to ensure that wills were properly drawn up. Hence, for instance, the synod of the clergy of Armagh *inter Anglicos* in 1518 decreed that the local priests were to register the wills made in their parishes. The wills were to name the proposed executors, legatees and witnesses. A full inventory of the extent of the estate, together with an account of the legitimate claims to be met from it, were required.[155] However, people sometimes died without having made a will, or they were alleged to have altered their will, or they claimed property for their estate which they may or may not have owned, or they failed to detail their debts comprehensively.

As one would expect executors did not always meet the claims made on estates to everyone's satisfaction. Several disputes were brought before Armagh's consistory court for that reason. In six of the nine such suits the conflicting claims were either referred to arbitration or settled out of court.[156] Two claims were validated by the court.[157]

Any transaction undertaken with the support of an oath rendered all of the parties concerned liable to the church's jurisdiction in the event of nonfulfilment. There were seven suits alleging perjury recorded in Book 1 of Primate Cromer's register.[158] In a case in which the defendant was found guilty he was given an exemplary public penance, reflecting the church's anxiety to uphold the sanction of oaths. The culprit had to walk around the cemetery at Termonfeckin, clothed in white linens, on six different Sundays, to fast on bread and water for three days, and to pay 12*d.* for the expenses of court, and give 3*d.* to the poor.[159]

There were five suits brought before Armagh's consistory to secure the full payment of revenues owed to parish churches. Two concerned tithe disputes.[160] Another concerned the payment of laity's offerings.[161] Two laymen, presumably acting as church procurators, each sued other layfolk for monies owed to their church.[162]

In another case the vicar of Molary sued an unbeneficed curate for the cost of repairing the manse at Molary.[163] The curate denied responsibility for the maintainance of the house, and the case was settled by agreement. The curate of Tullyallen sued his employers for the payment of his stipend, though to what effect is not recorded.[164]

The procurators of the Office of St Patrick, whose task it was to collect a levy for the support of the primate, sued a layman who had promised to present certain lands to the Office, but subsequently reneged on his promise.[165] Normally these procurators collected their levy through the local clergy in return for a small commission. Some priests claimed a quarter share of the levy by custom, though this was disputed in a test case before Armagh's consistory court.[166] The sentence in neither case is recorded in the court book.

Six trials relating to matrimonial or sexual matters may be considered to be office cases. These include trials for charges of adultery, of fornication, of bigamy, of marriage within the forbidden degrees, of interrupting the progress of a wedding, and the prosecution of a priest who married a couple in contravention of an interdict.[167]

There were six cases wherein clerics, including a monk, charged laymen with assaulting them.[168] Naturally the church authorities took a dim view such attacks. One of the men had already been convicted by the archdeacon of assaulting the priest of Stabannon, but failed to atone for his crime by burning a two pound wax candle before our Lady's statue in Stabannon church, as the archdeacon had ordered.[169] Two laymen who fought each other inside the church at Port were each ordered to place a one pound candle before the statue of St Columba in the church, and to walk around the graveyard dressed in white linen on two different holy days.[170] The chief culprit had also to give 3*d.* to the poor, 8*d.* to the curate for his expenses in promoting the case, and 12*d.* for the court's expenses.

The procurators of the parish church of Drumcar sued the holy water clerk of the parish for breaking a bell and, together with a number of other individuals, for detaining some property belonging to the church.[171] The procurator of the parish church of Termonfeckin, on behalf of the parishioners, sued the vicar of Termonfeckin and the prioress of Termonfeckin who held the rectory, for the maintainance of a chaplain for a chapel within the parish church.[172] The case was very protracted, but eventually the parishioners won their case. A layman sued his parish priest, Dnus Rory O'Culean, vicar of Carlingford, for a (unspecified) crime, and the vicar was temporarily deprived of his benefice.[173]

Office cases often followed from information gathered during a visitation. Primate Cromer's register has a record of some laymen being cited to pay their portions of the cost of repairing the nave of the church of the Holy Trinity, possibly that at Termonfeckin.[174] The parishes of Kildemock and Dunany had their revenues sequestrated because the parish churches had been allowed to fall into a delapidated condition.[175]

Clerical misconduct was severely dealt with. Two priests were suspended for simony.[176] Two priests who had eaten meat on a fast day were ordered to preach publicly that they had done so through a misunderstanding, and they were also directed to fast on bread and water on a subsequent date.[177]

There is a single so-called heresy trial recorded in the Armagh registers. It concerned a butcher of Drogheda who received the sacraments while labouring under a sentence of excommunication.[178] However, the butcher claimed that he knew nothing of the excommunication and threw himself upon the court's mercy. His demeanour in court, together with the fact that he desired the sacraments in the first place, make it clear that he was no heretic in the true sense of the word.

Discussion

In the mid fifteenth century it appears that Armagh's first instance business was dominated by suits alleging perjury or debt, followed in order of volume by suits for defamation, and then matrimonial suits. This pattern accords well with the composition of the instance business processed by the English church courts around the same time.[179] R.N. Swanson suggested that the English church courts lost their perjury business, not only because of writs of prohibition and the use of praemunire by the common law courts to take the business away from them, but also because the secular courts began to offer the possibility of monetary compensation, while the ecclesiastical judges were more concerned to secure the repentance of the alleged perjurer.[180] The rivalry of the common law courts had a definite impact on the business processed by Armagh's consistory court. Perjury and debt suits, which had constituted the 'bread and butter' business of the courts, constituted a small part of its business by 1518 to 22.

The rivalry between the ecclesiastical and secular judicial systems in Armagh *inter Anglicos* ought not to be exaggerated. The church courts played a significant role in helping to maintain social order by offering an avenue for the peaceful resolution of conflicts which might otherwise have resulted in violence. The temporal and ecclesiastical authorities appreciated the symbiotic relationship between the two systems.[181]

The church authorities, for their part, depended on the co-operation of the secular authorities in dealing with stubborn excommunicates.[182] Forty days after a sentence of excommunication the bishop could seek a writ of caption from the chancery requesting a reprobate's imprisonment until he submitted to the church court.[183] Not all excommunicates were signified by the judges of the Armagh consistory, a wise strategy to avoid exhausting the goodwill of the secular authorities. Even without signification the excommunicated person incurred disabilities which barred them from seeking judicial redress before the church or lay courts if ever they should need it. Since the sanctions of the ecclesiastical courts were strictly spiritual, the assistance of the secular powers was vital as a last resort against the most recalcitrant offenders.

About 90% of the instance suits brought before the consistory courts of Norwich and Winchester in the sixteenth century concerned matrimonial, defamatory or testamentary matters, or disputes about ecclesiastical revenues.[184] At Armagh such cases comprised approximately 85% of the consistory court's instance business which is recorded in the court book. This broad comparability is striking.

On the other hand, office prosecutions for sexual immorality were extremely common in English church courts prior to the reformation. In 1474, for instance, 110 of the 141 office prosecutions brought against laypeople in Canterbury's consistory court related to sexual irregularities.[185] Yet, records of only two such cases were copied into Primate Cromer's register, and one of the cases was abandoned by the individual who promoted it.[186] One might suggest that society in Ireland had a more tolerant attitude towards incontinence than was true of the English, and that local people were generally reluctant to bring illicit liaisons to the attention of the church authorities. The man convicted of adultery with his mother-in-law offended in a grievous fashion, and it may be the depravity of his misdeed which led to his being presented to Armagh's consistory court for punishment.[187]

It is difficult to make any definite assessment of the effectiveness of Armagh's consistory court. The incomplete nature of the records makes it impossible to calculate the percentage of cases initiated which concluded in a verdict or settlement, precluding the possibility of calculating the average length of time taken for a case to reach a conclusion.

If one focuses on instance suits it is a fact that verdicts or settlements are recorded for fifteen of the twenty one matrimonial suits in Primate Cromer's register. In the context of the incomplete nature of the register this suggests that matrimonial causes were dealt with expeditiously. Conclusions are recorded for eleven of the eighteen executory cases, with two more cases having reached the stage where the sentence was predictable, and the records of two further cases closing with the disputes in the hands of arbitrators. Four conclusions are recorded for the seven perjury suits. Instance suits for defamation and slander have conclusions for only twelve of the twenty six cases, six of which were settled out of court. Because of the gaps in the records these figures do not reflect the full number of cases which reached a conclusion. They do reflect the fact that some suits were simply less tractable, and hence took more time, than others. Because Armagh's consistory court acted also as the metropolitan court for the province of Armagh any appeal against a judgement of the consistory had to be made in the Roman curia. Only one such appeal from within Armagh, from a failed suit for defamation, is recorded for the years 1518 to 1522.[188]

Overall the evidence of the court book reflects a court which seems to have operated justly and relatively inexpensively.[189] That is not to say that some few individuals did not feel aggrieved when a court decision was made against them, or when they were faced with a large bill following a protracted suit. However, the judges seem to have done as much as they could to have cases settled amicably.

The records of the Armagh court book do not prove that religious and moral standards in Armagh *inter Anglicos* were irreproachable. The absence from the court book of any record of a trial for non-attendance at church, and the tiny number of recorded trials for sexual misbehaviour, are not necessarily indications that these failings were rare.[190] Instead, it may simply be that such offenders were rarely presented to the church courts by priests or church procurators. It must be recognised that the church courts did not operate in a vacuum. They were dependent on the willingness of local priests and people to present malefactors to the courts. This willingness was in turn conditioned by general attitudes at parish level towards behaviour which the church authorities regarded as sinful, but which the local communities may, or may not, have been more tolerant of. Historians of the church in England have repeatedly stressed the degree to which the business processed by the courts broadly reflected the interests of the wider society in which they operated.[191]

Within the social and juridical circumstances existing in County Louth it seems that Armagh's consistory court functioned rather effectively. It processed the cases brought before it in a very competent and conscientious manner. Every effort seems to have been made to arrive at the correct verdict. The judges endeavoured to ensure that the court's decisions were obeyed, and in this they seem to have enjoyed much success.

The church courts in Armagh *inter Hibernicos* encountered in the brehon law a less elaborate and bureaucratic judicial system than that operating in the Pale. The absence of surviving case records from the brehons or the church courts *inter Hibernicos* makes it difficult to say much about the interaction between the two judicial systems there.

Henry O'Neill appointed Canon Art Mc Cawell, official of Tullyhogue, as the brehon for the O'Neill lordship.[192] This combination of secular and ecclesiastical judicial authority in the hands of one churchman was not unique. A similar instance is known from the early sixteenth century when Feidhlimidh Mac Uinseannáin, official principal of Raphoe diocese, served as the brehon of O'Donnell of Tyrconnell.[193] If these were not isolated instances, and one suspects that they were not, one might propose that the 'dual mandates' were designed by the Irish lords to bolster the authority of their own judicial systems. Another possible explanation, which was offered by Katharine Simms, is that it was the training of these church officials in civil law which commended them to the lords' favour.[194]

The metropolitan court of Armagh felt compelled on a number of occasions to appeal to the secular rulers of the Ulster lordships to enforce its wishes against recalcitrants, lay and clerical.[195] It may be that spiritual sanctions counted for less among the Irish than they did in the Pale, and that the church's dependence on the secular arm was thus the greater. However, the O'Neills were sometimes the worst offenders. A striking illustration of the dilemma in which the primates could find themselves in is afforded by two decrees made by Primate Cromer on 16 February 1534.[196] In the first Cromer called upon Conn O'Neill, lord of Tyrone, to act as the 'secular arm' of the metropolitan court in a case under appeal to Rome. Later that day though, Cromer had to issue a solemn warning to the same O'Neill that he and his men would be excommunicated, and their lands placed under an interdict, unless they made restitution for having despoiled the archbishop's manor at Armagh, and wounding its custodian.

Obviously the church courts had to accept great limits to their operations in such an environment.

It is difficult to avoid the conclusion that Archbishop Cromer, and his immediate predecessors, wielded much less authority in the parishes *inter Hibernicos* than they did in the southern deaneries. Armagh's consistory court, the most powerful instrument to regulate the lives of the priests and people of the archdiocese, was largely inactive *inter Hibernicos*. The ruridecanal officials are not likely to have been able to exercise the same kind of authority as the primate's official principal.

An indication of the weakness of the ruridecanal courts is the widespread practice of clerical concubinage in Armagh *inter Hibernicos*. Anthony Lynch has observed that all of the rural deans of Tullyhogue between 1450 and 1490, on whom the primates depended to exercise oversight over the parish clergy, had themselves been charged by the archbishops, to no lasting effect, for keeping concubines.[197] One gets the impression from the 1546 visitation record that the church authorities in Armagh in the first half of the sixteenth century had to resort to persuasion to promote clerical celibacy in the northern deaneries. By contrast, a priest in Armagh *inter Anglicos* could find himself charged before the consistory court for unwittingly eating meat on a fast day.[198]

Since the weakness of the church courts in the rural deaneries of Armagh *inter Hibernicos* made it very difficult for the archbishop to enforce so basic a requirement as clerical celibacy, court action against lay people for any but the most serious sins seems unlikely. That weakness suggests that catholicism in much of late medieval Ireland may have already acquired something of the character of a 'voluntary' religion. If that was indeed the case then the success of the Catholic church in Ireland in surviving the virtually complete loss of its courts systems is a little easier to understand.

PRIMATE CROMER AND THE CHURCH COURTS OF ARMAGH

The records of the consistory court in Primate Cromer's time were entirely lost, apart from one unfinished record of a dispute about the right of presentation to the position of abbess of the Augustinian convent at Termonfeckin.[199] This document, although incomplete, reflects the same attention to detail, and persistence in addressing suits as one would expect after a study of the act book for 1518 to 22.

For Armagh *inter Hibernicos* the loss of church court records is also virtually complete. However, there are records extant of suits brought from Armagh *inter Hibernicos* directly to the primate's court. Archbishop Cromer imposed a heavy penance on one Sean Mc Eweyr of Armagh: viz. to appear at the processsion into Armagh cathedral, clothed in white linens as a penitent, and to place a 1 lb wax candle before the statue of St Patrick, every Sunday until such time as the primate had decided whether he could absolve him without recourse to the Holy See.[200] Meanwhile he was given a qualified absolution with prayers and penances. The nature of the sin was not recorded but, clearly, it was a grievous offence.

Another case involved the killing of John O'Callaghan, the messenger of the official of Orior with Armagh city.[201] The archbishop reserved the case to himself, but its acta have not survived. In June 1530 Nelan O'Neill complained to the primate's court that certain churchmen, apparently erenaghs of churchlands in Armagh *inter Hibernicos*, were 'fasting' and 'ringing bells' against him.[202] Archbishop Cromer commissioned the bishop of Raphoe and the official principal of Raphoe to examine the case. No further record of the matter has survived. In March 1531 James Mc Kywan, a tenant of the archbishop, obtained admonitory letters from the primate for the return of fifty one cattle stolen from him by Henry O'Neill and some of his men – to what effect is not known.[203] In February 1534 Primate Cromer denounced Conn O'Neill and some of his men, for plundering the archiepiscopal manor at Armagh.[204] In September of the same year the primate had to respond to the usurpation of church lands at Muintirheny by the O'Hanlons of Orior. The lands were held by O'Hanlons in 1609, suggesting that Archbishop Cromer's threats were ignored and that Dnus Patrick O'Heaney, his erenagh, did not recover his lands.[205]

These court records are inadequate for any kind of convincing analysis, but they do suggest that Archbishop Cromer took a direct interest in court actions from the northern rural deaneries, as well as those from *inter Anglicos*. The admonitory letters to the political leaders reflect the problems faced by the primate in the absence of consistent political support in Armagh *inter Hibernicos*. Within the archdiocese of Armagh Archbishop Cromer is likely to have maintained his consistory court at the same level of effectiveness as when he first arrived in Ireland, if he did not actually enhance its authority by his diligence. The archbishop took interest in church court matters from *inter Hibernicos*, though he would not have been able to discipline the clergy and laity there as thoroughly as was possible in the southern rural deaneries of the archdiocese. Nonetheless, the primate did exert real authority in Ulster as is shown by an instance in 1529. When Cathal O'Reilly, lord of East Breffny, raided the archiepiscopal manor at Julianstown in County Meath in August 1529 Archbishop Cromer excommunicated him and his followers, and placed them under an interdict.[206] Within a fortnight O'Reilly took an oath to make restitution to the archbishop's tenants and to do penance.[207]

CONCLUSIONS

One may conclude from this study of the administration of the archdiocese of Armagh that Primate Cromer recognised the value of the annual synods as instruments for promoting modest reform within the archdiocese. The synodal records show the primate constantly exhorting his priests to strive for higher standards in their priestly lives and ministries. The visitation system was long established in Armagh and could have been used by Archbishop Cromer to make regular surveys of the priests, people and church buildings throughout the archdiocese, checking that standards were being maintained, or even improved under the influence of his synodal calls for improvement.

There are very few church court records extant from the time of Primate Cromer's episcopate. Nonetheless, the act book for the years immediately prior to his arrival in Ireland show that the consistory court of Armagh worked reasonably well in the rural deaneries *inter Anglicos*. Since Archbishop Cromer showed himself anxious in his synods to raise standards in the archdiocese one may suggest that he would have employed the church courts to maximum effect in order to promote improvements. Certainly it is likely that Primate Cromer would have ensured that the church courts continued to function as well as they had done before he arrived in his see, and one suspects that he may have made them work better through close supervision.

The evidence does not exist for one to make categorical assessments of the effectiveness of the archiepiscopal administration under Primate George Cromer, yet the good order of the diocesan church in Armagh *inter Anglicos* especially, and perhaps to some degree *inter Hibernicos* too, may be interpreted as evidence showing that the church was well administered on the eve of the Tudor reformations.

6

Archdiocesan Finances

Archbishop Cromer succeeded to the possession of extensive church lands, some tithes appropriated to his *mensa*, and the right to levy a number of fees for carrying out certain functions pertaining to his offices as ordinary of his diocese and as metropolitan of the northern province of the Irish church. These were to maintain him with a household and lifestyle which were then deemed appropriate to maintain the dignity of his high office. The archbishop's revenues would help to pay the salaries of some of the officers who manned his temporal and spiritual administrations. They were to finance the level of hospitality expected of so exalted a pastor of God. Finally, they would have to meet the secular burdens imposed on the archbishop by the English crown in the south, and by O'Neill in the north. The archiepiscopal finances were of critical importance for Archbishop Cromer, and his successor. The status and authority which the primate enjoyed were related to the wealth he controlled. The efficient functioning of his administration depended upon adequate finance. Inevitably, then, even the least mercenary of pastors would find much of his time and energy would be taken up with the administration of his see's finances.[1]

ARCHIEPISCOPAL ESTATES 'INTER ANGLICOS'

The archiepiscopal estates in Armagh *inter Anglicos* and Meath were organised along manorial lines. A seneschal and bailiff administered each of the manors on the primate's behalf and rendered accounts of money rents, customs and profits of the manor courts such as would have been familiar to any bishop in England.[2]

The manor of Termonfeckin was the most important of the archbishop's estates in the sixteenth century. It had a small borough with a weekly market, and a pillory.[3] The archbishop's gaol was also located at Termonfeckin.[4] According to the Rental Book of Primate Dowdall, the manor was worth £31 3s. 8d. in 1544.[5] This meant that it was worth two and a half times more than the next most valuable manors and, on its own, accounted for no less than a sixth of the revenues of Primates Cromer and Dowdall.[6] The sixteenth century archbishops had a tower-house there which served as their chief residence.[7] The great majority of the documents in the sixteenth-century registers, whose place of composition is known, were composed at Termonfeckin. The annual convocations of the clergy of Armagh *inter Anglicos* in the first half of the sixteenth century were often convened in the parish church of Termonfeckin. Church court cases, and ordinations, were conducted in the church at Termonfeckin on occasions.[8] The archdeacon of Armagh, the archbishop's most senior administrative officer for church matters, was the vicar of Termonfeckin also in the first part of the sixteenth century, with a manse in close and convenient proximity to the primate's residence.[9]

St Peter's church, Drogheda, was a kind of 'pro-cathedral' for Armagh *inter Anglicos*. The annual synods of the clergy of Armagh *inter Anglicos*, and most provincial synods, were convened in St Peter's church. Visitations of the parish clergy of the rural deanery of Drogheda were often conducted therein. The consistory and metropolitan court of Armagh normally processed cases in St Peter's. Consequently, the late medieval primates found it useful to have a residence in its parish, inside the walls of Drogheda. In the time of Primate Octavian del Palatio (1482–1513) the archdiocese's registry was housed within the Drogheda residence, an indication of the house's long-standing importance in the administration of the archdiocese.[10]

The archiepiscopal manor of Dromiskin was well placed in the northern half of Armagh *inter Anglicos,* for holding visitations and conducting sessions of the archdiocese's consistory court. It had a pillory but, unlike Termonfeckin, no market.[11] The late medieval archbishops often resided there, at least until the last quarter of the fifteenth century.[12] Thereafter the manor appears in the archdiocese's records only as a source of revenue. It seems likely that financial exigencies compelled Primate Octavian to lease the archiepiscopal residence and mensal lands at Dromiskin around the same time as he was forced to lease the residence in Drogheda.[13] A rental of Dromiskin dated 1544 shows that one Thomas Daw held 30 acres of the archbishop for 'a pair of gloves', while one Patrick Mc Gartlan paid £1 1s. 9d. in rent for 30 acres, Patrick Cantoke paid £1 rent, and Richard Plunket paid 19s. 6d. rent for thirty acres each in Dromiskin.[14] This suggests that an archbishop of Armagh had leased the land at a nominal rent to Daw, or his predecessor, in return for a high (monetary) entry fee. Something similar may have occurred in the case of Sir Oliver Plunket who held thirty acres in Dromiskin for 10d. and a half pound of wax, and sixty acres in Whiterath in the same manor for half a pound of wax only.[15] Thomas Hanlyng of Drogheda held a messuage at Dromiskin for 'three corn wheats'.[16] Such expedients were probably unavoidable while the see of Armagh was over-burdened by demands for the 'first fruits'. Nonetheless, it left the archbishops of Armagh more impoverished thereafter.

According to one rental in Primate Dowdall's register the manor of Dromiskin was worth £10 3s. 10d. in 1544.[17] However, another rental in the register, also dated 1544, indicates that the manor was worth an additional £3 1s. 2½d., though why the additional figures were preserved separately from the rest is unclear. According to the Valor in Hibernia the manor of Dromiskin was worth £14 1s. 6d. in 1618, at a time when the Protestant archbishop's total income was £400.[18] In the royal visitation of 1622 its value is shown to have increased to £20, while the archbishop's revenues stood at £1,935 9s. 9d.[19] Even in the seventeenth century it seems that long-term leases at low rents kept the manor at a relatively modest value.

From the Newtown of Monasterboice the archbishop of Armagh received £10 7s. 8d., and from the Old Town of Monasterboice an additional £1 6s. 8d., according to Primate

Dowdall's rental of 1544.[20] There are no references to the archiepiscopal estates at Monasterboice in the Valor in Hibernia or the 1622 visitation record.

From the north of County Louth Primate Dowdall's rental book lists rents of 13s. 4d. due from Omeath, 3s. 4d. from Faughart, 6s. 8d. from Urney and 6s. 8d. from Rooskey.[21] In 1532 Archbishop Cromer leased the lands of Rooskey to the vicar of Carlingford for 13s. 4d.[22] The implication is that the primate was indeed able to derive some rent from those exposed borderlands.

The manor at Nobber in County Meath is not valued in Primate Dowdall's rental book. It was reckoned to be worth £5 8s. 10d. in the 1370s.[23] In the Valor in Hibernia for 1618 two thirds of the manor still held by the archbishop of Armagh was valued at £5.[24] Clearly it was not a major source of income for the primates in the first half of the sixteenth century.

The manor of Kilmoon, also in County Meath, had been worth £31 1s. 9d. in 1429.[25] Kilmoon with Primatestown, a part of the manor, were valued at £3 6s. 7d. and £9 2s. 7½d. respectively in 1544.[26] By 1618 the manor of Kilmoon was worth only £5.[27]

Together the archiepiscopal estates at Termonfeckin, Dromiskin, Monasterboice, Kilmoon and Nobber (which I speculatively suggest may have been worth about £5), were worth about £73 12s. 3d. in 1544. This accounts for less than half of the revenues of Archbishops Cromer and Dowdall in the years 1538–44.

ARCHIEPISCOPAL ESTATES 'INTER HIBERNICOS'

The manor of Armagh was the archbishop's largest landholding. In 1609 it was stated to have been composed of twenty balliboes.[28] Michael Glancy has calculated that a balliboe in the barony of Armagh was about 100 acres in size.[29] This suggests that the estate was about 2,000 acres in extent. It was organised, at least superficially, along manorial lines.

Armagh city was an archiepiscopal borough with a weekly market.[30] The tolls and customs arising from its trade were shared between the archbishop, other ecclesiastical persons, and the freeholders of Armagh city.[31] In the early fifteenth century the tolls were valued at £5 6s. 8d. a year.[32] The jurors at Armagh in 1609 did not know how much the tolls were worth then, or how they were shared between their recipients.

In the mid fifteenth century Armagh's manorial court was entrusted to a seneschal.[33] The manor had its own pillory. Archbishop Cromer seems to have continued an older practice by appointing as seneschal of Armagh the official of the church court for the rural deanery of Orior with Armagh city.[34] By combining in the hands of one man the authority to deal with both secular and ecclesiastical legal cases (which would have been difficult to differentiate on church lands) the archbishop not only rationalised the provision of justice on the manor of Armagh but gave his seneschal/official an enhanced power to maintain good order.

An early fifteenth century rental states that the primate ought to receive in rents from the manor of Armagh city and the erenagh lands associated with the churches of Clonfeacle, Derrynoose, Kilmore and Tynan, the sum of £84 a year.[35] The tenants of

Glenaul were accustomed to pay a further £20 13s. a year to the primate. His feudal dues included the use of all the ploughs in the manor of Armagh and in Clonfeacle, Derrynoose, Kilmore and Tynan too. The primate exacted a levy of trout from Clonfeacle, and his tenants were obliged to give him free carriage of coals and other fuels to Armagh, and transport other materials on the return journeys.

The manor of Armagh was not valued in Primate Dowdall's rental book.[36] Despite its great extent and former prosperity the manor seems not to have been worth a great deal in the first half of the sixteenth century. In the 1609 inquisitions the archbishop is shown to have then held only two and a half sessiaghs, approximately 0.83 of a balliboe, in demesne. The rest of the land, apart from half a balliboe rented to Armagh cathedral's master of works, was rented to seventeen septs as they had been 'time out of mind' the jurors affirmed.[37] The rents listed range from 3s. 2d. for three acres in Brynanelamackeylye to £1 9s. for seven townlands which were reckoned to be the equivalent of one balliboe. In total, the rents paid by the master of works and the seventeen septs in 1609 amounted to no more than £11 6s. 6d.

The 1609 inquisitions states that the septs who leased some of the archbishops' lands around Armagh city possessed and inherited them 'according to the Irish custom'.[38] The archbishop was not entitled to dispossess any member of the sept from the lands they rented from him without due cause.[39] No tenant on the church land in County Armagh was identified as an erenagh by the jurors in 1609, though there had certainly been erenaghs at Clonfeacle, Derrynoose, Kilmore and Tynan. Whether the ancient tenants on the manor of Armagh were erenaghs or not it seems that they enjoyed the same security of tenure as erenaghs in the later middle ages. The only recorded example of an ejectment took place in 1406 when a man lost his tenancy for having killed the archbishop's bailiff.[40]

It is impossible to determine how the land was distributed within the septs who leased church lands. However, the 1633 inquisition for the archiepiscopal manor of Armagh lists the names of a great many sub-denominations within the townlands of the manor of Armagh. The number of such parcels implies the existence of 'a large agricultural community'.[41] One might also tentatively suggest that the parcels or sub-denominations were the farms of individual sept members in the later middle ages, reflecting the kind of sedentary agricultural community one would expect to have existed on church lands.

In Glenaul,[42] the district between Armagh and the Blackwater the archbishop of Armagh held twenty townlands and one sessiagh in demesne. The archbishops leased these lands to tenants at will. There were a further thirteen townlands in Glenaul which were rented to eight septs with customary rights. In 1609 these septs paid £5 2s. 3d. in rents.[43]

The Muintir Cassely and Muintir Aghie both paid 10s rent for their lands in 1544,[44] but in 1609 paid 13s. 4d. and 6s. 8d. respectively, rents which reflected the fact that one sept rented two townlands, the other only one.[45] In 1544 the Vicar O'Corre paid £1 in rent to the archbishop,[46] but in 1609 the Muinter Corre, probably renting the same land, paid 13s. 4d. for two townlands. Clann Shane paid 10s. for the townland of Cabragh in 1544, but 8s. 10½d. in 1609.[47] It is clear then that the jurors of 1609 were presented with a more rational system of rents than the more schematic system which seems to have existed in the time of Primate Dowdall. If one compares the rents for the four septs for 1544 and 1609 one finds a 14.4% decline in rents over that period. One might have expected rents to rise instead in line with inflation but, Armagh saw tremendous military actions during the Nine Years War.

Primate Dowdall's rental book excluded all data for Armagh city and the lands in Glenaul held by Conn O'Neill, O'Neill and earl of Tyrone.[48] Consequently it is not possible to identify the lands held by The O'Neill. The jurors of the 1609 inquisition identified the 'ancient tenants' of all of the church lands in Glanaul which were not held in demesne – with the interesting exception of Anaghclare.[49] That townland was held by a tenant of James I since Hugh O'Neill's going into exile because, the jurors declared, 'there was no ancient tenant living to claim the same'. The land had yielded to the archbishop 4s. 5½d. What this signifies is that Anaghclare, and probably other parts of Glenaul besides, was usurped by the ruling O'Neills but because the ancient tenantry had died out the townland was not recovered by the early seventeenth century primates, and went instead to the British crown. Other townlands in Glenaul, whose ancient tenants survived as sub-tenants, were recovered.

It seems that O'Neill incursions were greater on the archbishop's demesne lands than on the lands with 'ancient tenants'. Primate Dowdall's rental book states that O'Neill held lands in Glenaul. It shows that other lesser O'Neills also held several townlands in Glenaul.[50]

In the district of Cosway one can identify something of this process on a large scale. In 1544 the townlands of Cosway were held by the family of Malachy (*anglice* Matthew) O'Neill, baron of Dungannon.[51] However, the jurors of 1609 identified the Slua Mc Laughlin and Slua Murtagh as the ancient tenants, and made no reference to any O'Neills.[52] According to the 1609 jurors the twenty townlands in Cosway each rendered ten silver groats to the archbishop, the equivalent of 5s. However, Primate Dowdall's rental book shows that the median rent for the seventeen identifiable townlands was then 4s, and the average rent per townland was only 2s. 10d. The 1609 inquisition clearly did not reflect the situation on the ground in the rural deanery of Orior about the middle of the sixteenth century.

While it is impossible now to determine how much land in Glenaul was held by the O'Neills, it seems that it was very great indeed. Primate Dowdall's rental book lists the rents payable in 1544 from the six townlands held in Glenaul by the Muintir Cassaly, Haughey, O'Corre, and Shane. Another two townlands, apparently in the same place were held by Mac Cowlu-na-capull, and four more by O'Cassidys.[53] Together they amount to only £4 15s. 4d. in annual rents. This compares with the £20 13s. the primates had been able to collect from the tenants in Glenaul a century earlier.[54]

The 1609 inquisition found that long before the time of Conn Bacach O'Neill (1519–59), thirteen townlands in Tiranny, on the east bank of the River Blackwater, were leased by the archbishops to the O'Neills.[55] Significantly, the jurors of 1609 could not discover how much rent was actually paid on the lands in Tiranny, and no rents for Tiranny were recorded in Primate Dowdall's rental book. One is left to suppose that the sixteenth-century primates received very little, and possibly nothing at all, from their lands in Tiranny.

The Muintir Heaney, the ancient tenants of seven townlands owned by the arch-bishops of Armagh near Tandragee, were displaced by the ruling O'Hanlon.[56] The ju-rors of 1609 do not specify the rent then paid to the archbishop, nor is there any ac-count given for the lands in Primate Dowdall's register. Six adjacent townlands were held by O'Hanlons since the mid fifteenth century and they were supposed to render eight porks to the archbishop – the equivalent of 13s. 6d.[57] Again, there is no reference to these lands in Primate Dowdall's register.

In Clanconchy the 1609 jurors found that ten townlands were leased by the arch-bishop to some O'Neills of the Fews for ten silver groats each, or 5s.[58] Some of the same lands were liable for rents of 4s. according to Primate Dowdall's register.[59] By now the pattern is clear. The archiepiscopal lands in the rural deanery of Orior were very valu-able in the early fifteenth century. However, because they comprised most of the best land in the district they subsequently fell prey to O'Neill expansionism from the north, while the O'Hanlon rulers of the retreating lordship of Orior seem to have occupied much of the archiepiscopal estates in the south east of the rural deanery by way of compensation for their losses to the O'Neills.[60]

The situation in the rural deanery of Orior was such in 1544 that the archbishop of Armagh could only hope to receive £18 0s. 7d. for their lands, excluding the rentals from the manor of Armagh and the lands held by O'Neill in Glenaul.[61] The steady erosion of the archiepiscopal estates did not end there. As late as 1555, when Primate Dowdall was promoting Catholic restoration in Armagh, and in the northern province generally, he had to engage O'Neill in legal battle to keep hold of the remaining churchland in Glenaul which was being usurped.[62] The end result, as the writer of Primate Dowdall's rental book observed, was that the summary of revenues in the old rolls 'far exceeds the present one'.[63]

The outlying manors of the archbishop of Armagh presented even greater prob-lems. The archiepiscopal manor of Inishkeen in the Mac Mahon lordship contained forty seven and a half townlands.[64] However, because of the attentions of the Mac Mahons the archbishops had difficulty in putting tenants in place for a rent of only £1 7s. 4d. in 1428.[65] In 1437 Archbishop Swayne hoped to extract a revenue from the manor by leasing it to John Gernon of Killencoole, a leading landowner in County Louth, for a rent of £4, together with six fat pigs and six vessels of butter.[66] Whether the archbish-ops ever succeeded subsequently in securing any revenue from Inishkeen is impossible to tell. The manor of Inishkeen is not referred to in the sixteenth century registers. In 1618 Inishkeen yielded £10 to the archbishop of Armagh.[67]

Archbishop Cromer held the manor of Donaghmore, comprised of twelve townlands, in the diocese of Dromore.[68] It yielded £2 a year in the early fifteenth century.[69] It was not listed in Primate Dowdall's rental book, however. It too yielded £10 to the arch-bishop in 1618.

Another manor, that of Turlagh in County Mayo, was worth nothing to the arch-bishop in 1618 according to the Valor in Hibernia. This estate of sixteen townlands was stated to have once been worth £31 11s. 4d. in annual rents but it was evidently usurped prior to Archbishop Cromer's arrival in Armagh, and was not recovered.[70]

In Derry diocese the archbishops of Armagh laid claim to five carucates in Clooney, opposite the episcopal city of Derry. It yielded a rent of 27s. 4d. in the early fifteenth century.[71] It seems that they extracted some small rent from it up until the end of the sixteenth century.[72] The archbishops of Armagh also laid claim to two quarters of land in Aghadowey parish in Derry diocese, though there is no indication as to the rent they received.[73] Finally, the archbishops of Armagh used to receive 60 large eels and 40,000 medium sized eels in the early fifteenth century from their manor of Kilrea, also in Derry diocese.[74] These are not referred to in Primate Dowdall's rental book, or the 1609 inquisitions, but in 1541 Archbishop Cromer directed his commissary *inter Hibernicos* to collect the rents from the manor of Clooney and from Kilrea in the diocese of Derry.[75]

Primate Cromer's inventory of his see lands in 1524 would have revealed very little scope for increasing his rental. Most of the acreage was leased at 'customary annual rents as set forth on the rolls' to erenaghs.[76] All leases had to receive the consent of the dean and chapter, a body likely to uphold the customs of the archdiocese. Much of the see lands were secularised, and the archbishop would be hard-pressed to halt the process of secularisation. The record of the £31 due from Turlough in Mayo diocese reflected a forlorn hope of recovering lost lands which was not to be realised by Archbishop Cromer, or his sixteenth century successors.[77]

COARBS AND ERENAGHS

In the rural deanery of Tullyhogue Archbishop Cromer found a very different system of estate management in place to that in the manors *inter Anglicos*. All of the archiepiscopal lands in the rural deanery were held by erenaghs or a coarb. The erenagh *(airchinneach)* was the head of a clan holding church lands under a bishop. All male members of the clan were entitled to farm equal portions of the erenagh's land, but the erenagh was their representative.[78] He was responsible to the bishop for the entire clan. In turn he enjoyed the privilege of being lord of the clan, 'and had of them rent, *cuid oiche* and service, as other temporal lords had of their tenants'.

In addition to paying the rent to the bishop the erenagh had certain other duties and responsibilities. According to Sir John Davies the erenagh had to make a weekly commemoration of the founder of the church.[79] He was obliged to reside permanently on his land, and provide hospitality to pilgrims, travellers and strangers.[80] This accounts for the obituaries of erenaghs recorded in the Annals occasionally making reference to their guest-houses and hospitality.[81] The erenagh was obliged also to furnish the archbishop and his household with procurations or 'noxials' whenever the ordinary came on visitation. Noxials consisted of a night's lodgings and entertainment for the bishop and his retinue. The custom in Armagh *inter Hibernicos* was for the archbishop to receive his procurations from the erenaghs only if he conducted a visitation in person, but not otherwise.[82] The one exception to this rule appears to have been the erenagh of Stuckane who rendered fifteen meaddars of oats to the archbishop if he did not visit.[83] According to Bishop Montgomery these noxials were worth thirty or forty times more than the rent.[84] Hence the very low valuations of archiepiscopal income from the lands *inter Hibernicos* are a little misleading.

Visitations were conducted to see if the erenaghs were carrying out their duties satisfactorily.[85] If the erenagh was found to be negligent he might be punished. If he failed to pay the bishop's rent, or if he committed some grievous criminal offence, he might be deprived of his office – but not otherwise.[86] On the death of an erenagh his successor was chosen by the rest of the sept and presented to the bishop for confirmation.[87] The Armagh registers contain a couple of records of in-coming erenaghs receiving charters for the archbishop's lands.[88] The bishop could reject the presentee if he had sufficient reason to doubt his qualities and he could force the clan to elect another from among themselves. If they failed to do so he had the right to nominate any one of the clan to the office. If the erenagh's clan became extinct the bishop could not keep the lands in his own hands, but was supposed to install a new erenagh family under the old rents and conditions.[89] This explains why the rents payable by the erenaghs in the rural deanery of Tullyhogue remained unchanged in almost every case to 1609 from the levels they had been in the first half of the fifteenth century.

The coarb was also the tenant of a bishop's lands, in the same manner as an erenagh. The coarb *(comharba)* was literally the 'successor' of the founding saint of a church, and he enjoyed a considerable but indefinable spiritual prestige. William Daniel, Protestant archbishop of Tuam (1609–28), stated in 1609 that 'in ancient time (as one of our ancient antiquaries, which is now with men of the age of a hundred and odd years, does confidently affirm) the coarbs were churchmen and received at least the *primam tonsuram,* and most of them wear deacon's (clothes), and vowed to keep three things besides the keeping of hospitality, viz: to keep wedlock unspotted, to marry but virgins, and to stand for the maintenance of true religion'.[90] The coarb was called by his surname, whereas the chief tenant of erenagh land was always simply called the erenagh.[91] In Armagh *inter Hibernicos* Mc Gurk of Termonmagurk was the only coarb.

According to Bishop Montgomery the erenaghs, like the coarbs, were considered to be clergymen and 'anciently they used to have *primam tonsuram*'.[92] Interestingly, Montgomery found that most of the erenaghs in his time could speak Latin. A number received priest's orders. Bishop Montgomery's survey of the parishes in Derry diocese between 1605 and 1607 reveals that several erenaghs were also rectors or vicars.[93] As well as their duties to the archbishop many erenagh were bound to maintain either the nave of the local parish church, or two thirds of a unicellular church.[94] Sometimes they maintained a hospital or school.

Table 5 indicates the sizes of the land holdings as revealed in the inquisition taken at Dungannon in 1609. The balliboe was a unit of land quality rather than simple acreage. It was possible to reclaim marginal land to create a balliboe.[95] It does give an indication of the economic capacity of the different erenagh lands. A rental preserved in Primate Swayne's register suggests that the erenaghs of Tullyhogue rural deanery in the first half of the fifteenth century paid the archbishop £16 12s. 11d. twice a year, or £33 5s. 10d. in all. The 1609 inquisitions show that the rents payable on most of the erenagh estates identical then, indicating the probable situation during the episcopates of Archbishop Cromer (1521–42) and Archbishop Dowdall (1543–58).

The total rents payable by the erenaghs as outlined in the 1609 inquisition, excluding the imponderable bloodshed fines, amounted to £26 4s. 4d., a sheep, 10 meadars of

TABLE 5 Archiepiscopal estates in the rural deanery of Tullyhogue

Location	Extent	Rent in 15th c.[1]	Rent in 1609[2]
Aghaloo	2.5 balliboes	54s. 8d.	4s.*
Ardboe	17.5 balliboes	54s. 8d.	54s. 8d.
Ardcunner	2 balliboes	6s. 8d.	6s. 8d.
Artrea	16 balliboes	54s. 8d.	54s. 8d.
Ballerenagh	?	6s. 8d.	–
Ballinderry	4 balliboes and 4 acres	20s.	20s.*
Ballyclog	18.66 balliboes	27s. 4d.	27s. 4d.
Ballydaly	?	10s.	
Ballymagumfrech	?	2s.	–
Ballynlege	?	3s. 4d.	–
Ballyonusy	?	10s.	–
Carnteel	1 quarter	3s. 4d.	3s. 4d.*
Clonoe	4 balliboes	13s. 4d.	13s. 4d.*
Crosspatrick	?	7s.	–
Derryloran	17 balliboes	54s. 8d.	54s. 8d.*
Desertcreat	8 balliboes	27s. 4d.	26s. 8d.*
Desertlyn	4 balliboes	40s.	30s.*
Donaghenry	8 balliboes	27s. 4d.	27s. 4d.*
Donaghmore	17.33 balliboes	54s. 8d.	40s.*
Donaghrisk	2 balliboes	10s.	10s.
Drumaghaviasdon	1 quarter	–	10s.
Drumfada	2 balliboes	11s. 8d.	5s. 10d.
Drumgan	?	10s.	–
Drumglass	8 balliboes	27s. 4d.	27s. 4d.*
Drummagyn	?	2s. 6d.	–
Dunnabraggy?	?	3s. 4d.	–
Errigal Keerogue	5 balliboes	16s. 8d.	10s.**
Finglush	?	6s. 8d.	–
Kildress	1 balliboe	6s. 8d.	6s. 8d.
Kileeshil	2 balliboes	3s. 4d.	3s. 4d.* 1 sheep & 30 meadars of oats
Killyboggin	?	1s. 8d.	–
Lissan	8 balliboes	13s. 4d.	13s. 4d.**
Magherabeg	?	10s.	–
Magherakilly-Kalliagh	4 balliboes	22s.	11s.*
Stuckane, alias Drumkille	6 balliboes	20s.	20s.
Tamlaght Killetra	1 quarter	13s. 4d.	13s. 4d.
Termonmagurk	16 balliboes	34s. 10d.	34s. 10d. and 10 meadars butter
Tullyniskan	?	5s.	–

1 *Swayne's register*, no. 147. 2 *Ulster inquisitions*, appendix, Armagh, Tyrone.
*denotes a bloodshed fine of 8d. per person payable to the archbishop. ** denotes a bloodshed fine payable to the archbishop only if the erenagh had shed the blood, all other fines were the preserve of the erenagh.

butter, 30 meadars of oats, and 30 meadars of seed oats worth 5s. 10d. There are inexplicable reductions of rent by the later period for Aghaloo (less £2 10s. 8d.), Donaghmore (less 14s. 8d.), Desertlyn (less 10s.) and Errigal Keerogue (less 6s. 8d.). The remaining discrepancy of something over £2 is accounted for by the failure of the jurors in 1609 to include several of the smaller parcels of erenagh lands in Loughlinsholin in their inquisition record.

The early fifteenth-century rental states that the primate ought to receive £14 13s. 4d. in procurations from the erenaghs. However, according to the 1609 inquisitions these procurations were only payable if the primates visited the erenaghs in person. Though the late medieval primates seem to have visited Armagh city quite regularly there is no evidence of them having crossed the Blackwater river to visit the parishes in the rural deanery of Tullyhogue after the fourteenth century.

TITHES AND SPIRITUALITIES

As well as their rentals from real estate Archbishop Cromer drew significant additional revenues from appropriated tithes. The archbishop, by right of his office, held the rectorial tithes of Armagh and Glenaul.[96] These tithes were worth £30 13s. 8d. in the early fifteenth century.[97] By 1458 the value of the archbishop's tithes in Armagh and Glenaul had fallen to £14 13s. 8d.[98] There is no evidence to indicate how much the tithes were worth subsequently, but one suspects that their value was further reduced.

The rectory of Derrybrusk, a little to the north of Glenaul, was part of the archbishop's mensa and was leased for £1 7s. 4d. in 1406 and 1430, though only 13s. 8d. in 1458.[99] However, Archbishop Cromer was able to farm the rectory for £1.[100]

The primate's rectorial tithes from Carlingford and Cooley were worth £20 in 1375.[101] Primate Dowdall's rental book suggests that they were then worth £30.[102] The vicar of Carlingford, with a third of the tithes of Carlingford, received an income estimated at £3 13s. 8d. in 1538.[103] The archbishop, however, held the rectorial tithes of the Cooley peninsula as well. In 1532 Archbishop Cromer leased the tithes of Rooskey alone for £3 8s. 8d., in addition to a levy of seven barrels of herring for the herring tithes, and a thousand oysters (or 3s. 4d.) on St Patrick's day.[104] Since the archbishop's revenues from Rooskey alone were so great, the valuation of the primate's two thirds of the tithes from the rest of Carlingford and Cooley in 1544 seems plausible.

The rectory of Athboy in Meath diocese was a mensal parish of the archbishop of Armagh.[105] The vicarage was worth £23 14s. 2½d. in 1539.[106] This implies that the rectory may have been worth as much as £47 8s. 5d. That seems to be a very high valuation though. In 1618 the rectory brought the archbishop a modest £10 a year.[107]

Between the lands and the tithes one can account for about the bulk of Archbishop Cromer's income. The final portion was derived from a series of charges known collectively as the spiritualities. The most valuable of these were the archbishop's procurations. Procurations were fees payable to the primate for visiting parish churches or religious houses. Through a composition made with the bishop and clergy of Meath the late medieval archbishops of Armagh were to receive £80 for a triennial visitation, or £53 7s. 4d. for biennial visitations, or £26 13s. 8d. for annual visitations.[108] In Primate Dowdall's register the procurations for Meath amount to no less than £88 7s. 11d.[109] This was the primates' single most valuable source of revenue, and it explains why the late medieval bishops took such particular interest in Meath. The other suffragan sees were also liable to procurations but they were poorer, and half of the monies involved would have had to be assigned to the commissaries who actually carried out the metropolitan visitations in the Gaelic dioceses on the primates' behalves.[110]

Within the archdiocese of Armagh too, the archbishops levied procurations for conducting annual visitations. Primate's Dowdall's rental book, again reflecting the charges levied by Archbishop Cromer, his immediate predecessor, suggests that the procurations for the benefices in Armagh *inter Anglicos* were worth £9 16s. 2d., together with another £21 12s. 5d. from the religious houses for the tithes appropriated to them.[111]

There are two very different procuration lists in Primate Dowdall's rental book for Armagh *inter Hibernicos*. In the list dated 1544 the procurations from the rural deanery of Orior were worth £5 1s. 1½d., those from Tullyhogue another £1 10s. 6½d.[112] In a near-contemporary list the procurations were worth £2 5s. 3¾d. and £1 8s. 10d. respectively.[113]

The priests attending the annual synods of the clergy of Armagh *inter Anglicos* were obliged to pay a fee called a synodal. This ranged in scale from 6d. to 12d. Altogether, they yielded £2 11s.[114] No record of a similar fee survives for Armagh *inter Hibernicos*. If it was levied it is likely to have yielded quite a small return for the archbishop.

The archbishop probably earned some money for conferring holy orders, and the sacrament of confirmation. Little evidence survives of this practice. Bishop Bale reported that the bishop of Annaghdown was confirming people in Ossory diocese in 1553, on license to the ordinary doubtless, for a fee of 2d. a head.[115] A final source of income was the Office of St Patrick. This was a voluntary levy collected from the rural deaneries of Meath diocese and Armagh *inter Anglicos* and elsewhere.[116] Apparently the collectors delegated the task of collecting to the local parish clergy who retained a portion of the dues as their fee.[117] In 1533 the *Office* was expected to yield 68 marks, or £45 7s. 4d., to Primate Cromer.[118]

For English tax purposes the archbishops of Armagh seem not to have declared any of their revenues drawn from Armagh *inter Hibernicos,* nor from any manor or spiritualities from outside the English lordship. Hence, their true income was somewhat larger than the £183 17s 5½d. recorded in the Valor in Hibernia,[119] perhaps by £50 and more.

The declared income of the archbishop was equivalent to Stg£123 2s. 10d. This sum was little more than one third of that enjoyed by the archbishop of Dublin, or by the bishop of St. Asaph, the poorest diocese in the church in England and Wales. Yet, the income of the archbishop of Armagh bore favourable comparison with that of Irish dioceses beyond the Pale.

EXPENDITURE

Having detailed the sources of the archbishop's revenues it remains to identify its destinations. The single greatest expense in the archbishop's career was his 'first fruits'. This required him to pay the equivalent of his first year's income to Rome. It was a requirement which blighted, and on more than one occasion it actually aborted, the ministries of Archbishop Cromer's predecessors at Armagh.[120] Primate Cromer was fortunate in that he seems not to have inherited a debt-burdened diocese and, more importantly, he was granted the temporalities of Armagh back-dated to eighteen months prior to his enthronement.[121] Through a papal dispensation he was able to live off the revenues from his English benefices during that time.[122] This may have allowed Archbishop Cromer to avoid incurring crippling debts.

The clergy of Armagh *inter Anglicos* were obliged to pay a subsidy to the English crown. In the early sixteenth century the subsidy stood at £19 13s. 4d.[123] Furthermore, the archbishop of Armagh had to maintain sixteen archers for service on government hostings.[124] This levy compared with one of twenty from the much wealthier archbishop of Dublin, sixteen from the bishop of Meath, and eight from the bishop of Kildare. The O Neills of Tyrone were paid a pension, equivalent to a subsidy like that paid to the English crown.[125] It seems too that local lords exacted their own levies on the church in Armagh diocese in the form of cess. A convocation of the clergy of Armagh in 1492 enacted statutes against the imposition of coign and livery on the clergy, to what effect is indeterminable. The costs associated with attendance at parliament, unless it were convened in Drogheda, were considerable. If the parliament were held in the ecclesiastical province of Dublin the primate invariably attended through two proctors, whose expenses he was naturally obliged to cover. The archbishop's proctors at Rome were liable to be very expensive. One fourteenth century proctor was paid 20 marks, or £13 7s. 4d., for his service at Rome.[126]

The archbishop's household absorbed the bulk of the revenues of the see. The chamberlain was paid £1 a year in the early fifteenth century, and earlier.[127] The lesser attendants, the archbishop's horse boys, and the horses themselves, would also have cost money to maintain. Separate establishments had to be maintained at the archiepiscopal residences at Armagh, Termonfeckin and Drogheda. The archbishop's itineraries, be they for visitations or court actions, would have involved heavy expenditure for accommodation. The archbishop maintained a number of chaplains: eight or ten chaplains were considered to be necessary for an archbishop, according to an exchequer inquisition into non-residence in Armagh *inter Anglicos* in 1545.[128] Other men might serve the archbishop on a less permanent footing, and be paid as occasion required: sums of 10s., 20s., 40s. and a robe are recorded for priests or counsellors who were of service to Primates Fleming and Sweteman.[129]

The archbishop's registrar and notary was a central figure in the archiepiscopal administration; charged with the tasks of maintaining the archbishop's archives, and producing the documents for every aspect of the archbishop's official business. A good registrar cost money. The archbishop had also, perforce, to pay the apparitors for issuing citations for the annual synods and visitations within Armagh archdiocese, and for triennial synods and visitations for the ecclesiastical province as a whole. Apparitors were also employed to issue citations and admonitions, and publish sentences in office cases processed in the archbishop's consistory and metropolitan court.

Yet the primary expense to be met from the archbishop's revenues was for hospitality. Contemporary expectations of a good bishop are well illustrated by the obituary of Tomás Mac Brady, bishop of Kilmore (1480–1511).[130] Bishop Mac Brady was lauded as 'a paragon of wisdom and piety, a luminous lamp that enlightened the laity and clergy by instruction and preaching'. It praised him too for lavishing hospitality on the rich and the poor. On the other hand, George Braua, the Greek bishop of Elphin (1499–1530), was apparently of a less generous disposition. The author of his obituary observed that the bishop's death was 'no great loss to mankind'.[131] Primate Octavian del Palatio (1479–1513), finding the archdiocese of Armagh greatly encumbered with debts, obviously tried to economise by reducing the sizes of his retinue and household but was criticised for doing so by both clergy and lay folk.[132] Such expectations were deeply rooted in the minds of people in Ireland in the sixteenth century. Hugh Brady, an Irishman and Protestant bishop of Meath (1563–84), explained in 1565 that

> I am, at this present (time), very poor, charged with a great house (and) driven to large expenses or else infamy and discredit, for these people will ... either eat my meat and drink, or else myself; ... I feed as many continually as any bishop in England does ... and to do otherwise I cannot, unless I should utterly discredit both myself and my doctrine, which both makes me to have often an heavy heart, and an empty purse.[133]

Archbishop Cromer succeeded to a greater dignity, but a smaller income than Bishop Brady was to do in Meath twenty years after the primate's death. The financial pressures on the primate are thus likely to have been all the greater. Nonetheless, Archbishop Cromer did enjoy a sufficient income from his see lands, tithes and spiritualities, augmented by his English benefices, to finance his administration of the archdiocese and to afford him more than simply frugal comforts.

CONCLUSIONS

Primate Cromer succeeded to a diocese with a modest annual revenue of £183 15s. 5d. according to the Valor in Hibernia in 1538. This sum was made up of a lot of small sums from disparate sources. Much of the patrimony of the archbishops had been lost over the preceding century. *Inter Hibernicos* the archiepiscopal manor at Armagh and neighbouring Glenaul had been occupied in a piecemeal but relentless fashion by the O'Neills, while the O'Hanlons occupied much of the church lands in Orior as they retreated into an increasingly confined enclave under pressure from the O'Neills. The archbishop's manors at Inishkeen and in Connacht were worthless by the first half of the sixteenth century. *Inter Anglicos* it seems clear that Archbishop Cromer's predecessors had alienated much land to make ends meet. The archiepiscopal manors *inter Anglicos* generated a revenue which was no greater than £73 12s. 3d. in 1544.

The modest level of the primate's income from landed sources was very significant because it made him unusually reliant on a type of revenue termed 'spiritualities'. Of these the most important were the procurations, or fees collected by the archbishop or his commissaries in the course of visitations. For Armagh *inter Anglicos* these were worth a little in excess of £30, with a further £26 13s. per annum in procurations from the suffragan diocese of Meath. Synodals from the rural deaneries *inter Anglicos* brought in another £2 11s. per annum. The significance of these fees is that it gave the archbishops of Armagh an incentive to convene synods and conduct visitations on a yearly basis. This is not to say that the late medieval primates would not have done so otherwise, but it may have helped to ensure that the synods and visitations were held more regularly in Armagh than was the case in several English dioceses.

The archbishop of Armagh could manage reasonably well financially by drawing upon his landed estates, procurations, synodals and the revenues from the voluntary 'office of St Patrick' *inter Anglicos*. Though he was the owner of extensive lands *inter Hibernicos* the revenues he could actually draw from these lands were very small indeed. The revenues received from the northern rural deaneries may have sufficed to cover his administrative costs there, with little or no surplus left to help meet the archbishop's household expenses. This is not to say that the archbishop had no incentive to give attention to the northern parishes of his archdiocese. Certainly he gave them less attention than he did the southern parishes *inter Anglicos*, but that must have owed something to the political situation in the region which made it relatively inaccessible to an English-born prelate.

Primate Cromer was very fortunate in being granted the temporalities of the see of Armagh backdated to eighteen months. That gave him sufficient funds to pay his first fruits to the Roman curia and leave him with a tidy sum with which to begin his episcopate. However, it is apparent from the experiences of several of Primate Cromer's predecessors that the demand for first fruits without some kind of financial assistance could plunge the archiepiscopal finances into crisis, for there was little real estate left *inter Anglicos* in the first half of the sixteenth century which could be alienated – either permanently or on long leases for a high entry fee and a peppercorn rent – to meet a financial crisis. Finally, the heavy dependence of the archbishops on 'spiritualities' in the first half of the sixteenth century was of tremendous importance in that any threat to these revenues, particularly the lucrative procurations could have devastating consequences for the financial stability of the archdiocese.

7

The Early Tudor Reformations

Armagh *inter Anglicos* had a dense network of churches staffed by resident priests to provide pastoral care in the first half of the sixteenth century. Drogheda, Ardee, Dundalk and Carlingford each had at least one community of mendicant friars to supplement the pastoral care afforded by the secular clergy. It has been shown that Archbishop George Cromer, like his predecessor before him, employed annual synods to exhort the parish clergy to higher standards in their priestly lives and ministries. He conducted regular visitations, either in person or through commissaries, to see that standards were being maintained by the parochial clergy and their parishioners, and he was able to use his well-ordered consistory court to correct those who failed to meet the minimum standards required of them.

In Armagh *inter Hibernicos* it has been shown that not only did the parish system continued to operate, but that the system was more flexible than was hitherto realised in that new parishes could be established by the archbishop, or chapelries activated, as pastoral needs required and material resources permitted. Though the parish clergy in Armagh *inter Hibernicos* were less well supervised and disciplined than were their counterparts in the southern rural deaneries, the 1546 visitation report seems to show that the parishes continued to be served by priests who celebrated the Mass, said the Divine Office and whose ministry provoked no criticism from the laity, though there were some accusations of concubinage made against a number of priests. The clergy of Armagh *inter Hibernicos* cannot be shown to have been either generally negligent in their pastoral duties, or immoral in their characters.

Conventional accounts of the Tudor reformations emphasised the deficiencies of the late medieval church, and lay dissatisfaction with the institution and its personnel, as the necessary preconditions for the ecclesiastical revolution.[1] A new study of the laity in Armagh *inter Anglicos* has used the evidence of widescale church building, extension and ornamentation, together with a collection of wills from County Louth, to argue that the laity (perhaps especially those who were not poor) were strongly committed to the late medieval church.[2] Certainly the evidence seems to point towards a generally positive relationship between the Catholic clergy and the wider population in Armagh *inter Anglicos* prior to the Tudor reformations. The last Catholic confraternity to be established in the archdiocese before the Henrician reformation was licensed at Ardee as late as 1534. Against such positive evidence of commitment, there is no evidence at all of disenchantment with the Catholic church or its priesthood in Armagh, or of a desire for reformation.

Further studies at diocesan and more local levels are needed to reveal more of the diversity and complexity of the church's experiences across Ireland before the Tudor reformations. Nonetheless, it is already apparent that when the Tudor reformations were transferred to Ireland they encountered a Catholic church which was vigorous and flourishing, and which enjoyed the support of the lay community, in many parts of the country, including the archdiocese of Armagh.

INITIAL RESPONSES TO THE HENRICIAN REFORMATION

The English people's strong attachment to Catholic beliefs and practices in the first half of the sixteenth century meant that the Tudor reformations involved a hard and protracted struggle to win the hearts and minds, and souls, of the people. Yet, even in the most religiously conservative regions – whether in Sussex, the West Country or Lancashire[3] – Catholicism was largely eradicated and Protestantism was, by and large successfully, imposed by the middle years of Elizabeth's reign. Hence, England's experiences of the Tudor reformations suggest, by analogy, that a 'fundamentally Catholic disposition' would not have sufficed to make the success of the Tudor reformations in Ireland impossible, though it would have ensured that the reformations would encounter strong opposition.[4]

There was one precursor to the crown's attempt to force through ecclesiastical reform on Ireland: Cardinal Wolsey's unsuccessful attempt to re-draw the diocesan map of Ireland using legatine authority over the Irish church.[5] The cardinal attempted to institute Mgr Reginald Drummin to the vicarage of St Peter's in 1528 by right of his authority as papal legate.[6] However, Primate Cromer appealed to Rome against the cardinal's claims to jurisdiction, and evidently succeeded in his appeal because in 1533 an inquisition revealed that the vicarage was then vacant because of the recent death of Mgr Michael Golding who held the benefice since 1499.[7] Primate Cromer had clear ideas about the separate nature of the church in Ireland as against the church in England.

Archbishop Cromer was in England for about two years from October 1530.[8] It is apparent that the primate of all Ireland was gravely concerned about the course of events in England. In his next diocesan synod of the clergy *inter Anglicos*, on his return to Ireland, he launched a programme of reform, doubtless to strengthen the church in Armagh before it was confronted by the maelstrom which was engulfing the church in England.[9] He would, in all probability, have done the same in the 1533 synod of the clergy of Armagh *inter Hibernicos*. Certainly there was an awareness in Ulster of the religious developments in England: the *Annals of Ulster* for 1533 recorded that 'The king of the English went against the faith and many foolish things were done by him against the church'.[10]

Henry VIII and Cromwell planned to assert control over the Irish church at an early date. In an indenture with the king in 31 May 1534, the earl of Ossory undertook to support the lord deputy in resisting the power of the bishop of Rome.[11] The deputy's instructions to resist papal authority in Ireland were contained in *The Ordinances for the government of Ireland,* a pamphlet which was printed for circulation in the early summer of 1534. However, on 11 June 1534 Lord Thomas Fitzgerald, son of the ninth earl of Kildare, publicly renounced his allegiance to the English monarch and launched a major rebellion.

The very first report to reach Cromwell informed him that Kildare's son, brothers and affinity boasted that 'they were of the pope's sect and band, and him will they serve against the king and all his partakers'. The rebels even went so far as to declare that Henry VIII was 'accursed'. Lord Offaly denied Henry's title to the lordship of Ireland, pointing out that it was a papal fief which Henry forfeited by becoming an heretic.[12] He insisted that all men in Ireland take an oath of allegiance to the pope, the emperor and to himself.[13] He made great efforts to secure papal support, and imperial involvement in his crusade against the heretical king of England.[14]

The revolt of Silken Thomas did not accord with the pattern of medieval rebellions wherein protest was combined with protestations of loyalty to the king and the established order. It was an attempt at revolution. From the very start, Lord Thomas allowed Henry VIII no scope for an accommodation, and he rejected all of the king's overtures for reconciliation.[15] If Lord Thomas had, at any stage, sought simply to wrest concessions from Henry VIII he would not have attacked the king personally, but would have scapegoated the upstart Cromwell instead. His statements and actions are not consistent with the view that he intended to make no more than a gesture of protest. From the beginning the Kildare insurrection took the form of a Catholic crusade against the heretical king and his minions. 'From the outset' ecclesiastics were prominent among Lord Thomas's closest councillors, and 'from the very outset' European observers tended to see the Kildare rebellion as a Catholic crusade.[16] As such it had the support of Archbishop Cromer and Archdeacon Roth of Armagh. This is not to say that Lord Offaly was primarily motivated by Catholic zeal. However, it can be argued that the religious appeal was central to the strategic thinking behind the Kildare rebellion from the start, that many of the churchmen who risked their lives in the rebellion were motivated by a desire to preserve the Catholic faith in Ireland from the whims of Henry VIII. The initial success of the rebellion owed something to the wide appeal of the crusade in defence of religion.

The extent of the crusade's impact is indicated by a letter from the deputy and council of Ireland which declared that 'in effect all the inhabitants of these four shires within this land, in the late commotion and rebellion of that traitor and rebel, Thomas Fitzgerald, for the most part by compulsion adhered to him'.[17] Inevitably, once the rebellion failed, many participants would claim that they had only acted under compulsion, yet the significant point is the widespread adherence of the Pale community to Fitzgerald.

Primate Cromer was implicated in the revolt at an early stage. On 16 August 1534 he was removed from office as chancellor of Ireland, a position granted to him on 5 July 1532.[18] Henry VIII subsequently ordered Lord Deputy Skeffington to examine the primate on suspicion of treason, but the deputy replied on 30 April 1535 that the archbishop was ill and unable to meet him.[19] In fact the primate's register reveals that he was active in his diocese throughout this time.[20] Indeed, after Bishop Staples fled to England along with the other English-born churchmen who did not sympathize with the rebellion, Archbishop Cromer acted as the *custos* of Meath diocese in his absence.[21]

Archdeacon Cormac Roth was identified to Cromwell as one of Lord Thomas' key counsellors.[22] Soon after Archbishop Cromer had been appointed chancellor of Ireland Archdeacon Roth was appointed to the office of Master in chancery, a sign of the primate's favour.[23] That Mgr Roth had the support of Archbishop Cromer during the Kildare rebellion, in which the former played an important part, is shown by a letter from the primate to the archdeacon dated 1 October 1534.[24] In recognition of Mgr Roth's 'great merits' and 'for purely personal reasons', Primate Cromer united the rectory of Heynestown to the archdeaconry 'to show him special favour'.

Virtually all of the known clerical supporters of the Catholic crusade were senior churchmen, like the archbishop and the archdeacon of Armagh.[25] These men were not ignorant rural priests frightened by great changes which they could not understand. They were the clerical elite; well educated men with administrative experience, and confidence. These men would have been well informed on developments in England. It would have been clear to them that the ever-widening breach with Rome could well culminate in doctrinal heterodoxy.

Steven Ellis has shown that the clergy played an active and vital part in rousing support for the crusade.[26] Though there is evidence of royal retribution having been exacted on priests in other dioceses in the Pale, the clergy of Armagh seemed to have been spared the king's wrath. Only one clergyman was promoted to a parochial benefice in the diocese by the crown over the period 1534–7, and he was presented to a benefice which had become vacant by the death of its previous holder while the patronage was in the crown's hands through wardship.[27]

Only one member of the gentry in County Louth was attainted following the Kildare rebellion; Sir Patrick Gernon of Gernonstown.[28] His son and heir, James was restored to the family estates in 1542.[29] This family was closely tied to the Dowdalls by financial and, apparently, by matrimonial connections.[30] Significantly, two marriages between Dowdall men and Gernon women were celebrated with the benefit of dispensations secured from a non-schismatic bishop in 1538.[31]

The insurrection had demonstrated something of the hostility which existed across the Pale, even to the very highest levels within the church in Armagh, towards the planned extension of the Henry VIII's religious programme to Ireland. On the other hand, the elimination of several of the leading opponents of the programme weakened the Catholic cause in the lordship. In the aftermath of the rebellion there were many who were anxious to make their peace with the English crown lest they suffered the fate of the more prominent rebels. There was a large garrison of English troops quartered in the lordship, a guarantee that the crown's wishes could not be ignored. Hence, while there was widespread dissent from the king's ecclesiastical policies, it was not likely to be expressed forcibly in the new circumstances.

On 22 December 1535 the clergy of Armagh *inter Anglicos* gathered together in convocation under the presidency of Mgr William Mann, rector of Mansfieldstown.[32]

The primate was probably keeping a low profile in the knowledge that the king wanted him apprehended on suspicion of treason. A warning was given to the clergy that a member of the council had informed the primate that the pope was no longer to be honoured in public, a pointer of things to come. A writ from the king was read to the priests in the convocation directing them to elect a proctor to represent them in the parliament which was to be convened at Dublin on 20 January 1536. After consultation and deliberation the clergy elected Mgr William Hamlin, vicar of St Peter's, Drogheda, as their proctor. The choice was virtually unanimous: only the vicar and his parishioners' proctor objected, in vain. Mgr Hamlin was one of the best educated priests in the archdiocese and would stoutly defend the Catholic order in the parliament. The clergy who elected him would have had little doubt about the significance of their choice. The crown was making great efforts to secure a Commons amenable to its will.[33]

The parliament was convened on 1 May 1536, and within a month the lords and commons had endorsed the bills for the royal supremacy, the royal succession, slandering the king and new queen, in restraint of appeals to Rome, and for the first fruits of benefices to be paid to the crown.[34] The spiritual peers seemed pliable in that they did not block the ecclesiastical legislation in the first session of the parliament. However, the crown's legislation programme ran into insuperable opposition in the Convocation House, the third house within the Irish parliament.[35] In that house the lower clergy of the lordship were represented by six or seven proctors, including Mgr Hamlin, vicar of St Peter's parish, Drogheda.[36] As early as 17 May 1536 Brabazon complained that the Convocation House refused to endorse the key ecclesiastical bills put before them: 'Loath they are', he wrote, 'that the king's grace should be supreme head of the church'.[37] A year later the proctors were still being criticised as 'froward and obstinate', and 'in nothing conformable'. It seemed to Lords Grey and Brabazon that the clerical proctors were engaged in a strategy devised by themselves and 'their masters the bishops' to block the Henrician religious changes.[38] It is certainly unlikely that the clerical proctors would have resisted Henry VIII's programme as stoutly as they did without assurances of support from their bishops.

In May 1537 the spiritual peers and proctors stone-walled proceedings in parliament. They refused to discuss any further legislation until the rights of the Convocation House were confirmed.[39] Their intention was clear, to deny parliamentary sanction to all of the bills which had not been endorsed by the Convocation House over the previous twelve months. The churchmen effectively kept the Henrician reformation at bay for an entire year. This accounts for the inaction of Archbishop Browne and Bishop Staples in promoting the king's religious programme: the programme was in limbo while the Convocation House denied it the sanction of parliament.[40]

The strength of purpose shown by the six or seven clerical proctors in the Convocation house can only mean that they were reflecting the disposition of the lower clergy in their dioceses. Significantly, perhaps, the *act for the submission of the clergy* was not imposed on Ireland, possibly in recognition of the enormous opposition it was likely to provoke.

Mgr Hamlin, the proctor of the lower clergy of Armagh *inter Anglicos*, seems to have been a leading opponent of the ecclesiastical changes promoted in the reformation parliament. This may be inferred from the pact he entered into with Patrick Barnewall M.P., the king's serjeant at law in Ireland. Barnewall was outspoken in the Commons in his opposition to the dissolution of the religious houses. He openly denied that the king 'as head of the church, had so large a power as the bishop of Rome'.[41] He was audacious enough to lead a deputation to the king to defend the monasteries. Barnewall's opposition has been dismissed as being motivated by mercenary concerns rather than religious principle.[42] However, Barnewall, on receiving a grant of the convent at Gracedieu, conveyed the manors of Gracedieu and Fieldston to six clergymen and a gentleman of Turvey.[43] One of the clergymen was Mgr Hamlin, vicar of St Peter's, Drogheda. The Barnewall family continued to support the community of nuns long after the dissolution of their house by Henry VIII.[44]

The impasse in the Irish reformation parliament was finally broken when Henry VIII sent four royal commissioners to Ireland in September 1537. The commissioners convened the fourth session of the Irish reformation parliament. They read a letter from the king to each of the houses of parliament directing them to conform themselves to the king's wishes and warning that 'if anyone will not we shall so look upon them with our princely eye as his ingratitude therein shall be little to his comfort'.[45] This threat, from a king with so much blood on his hands because of his religious programmes, could hardly be ignored.

There may have been another factor involved. In early summer 1537 Lord Grey had a conference with Archdeacon Roth.[46] No record of the meeting survives, but one may surmise that the archdeacon acted as a mediary for Primate Cromer and the Catholic opponents in the reformation parliament. It can hardly be a co-incidence that on 31 July 1537 a general pardon was issued to all of those involved in the Kildare revolt.[47] As well as the pardon Grey may have given an informal undertaking not to enforce the Henrician reformation too vigorously.

The final session of the parliament went as the king desired. The Convocation House was formally declared to have no power in the making of parliamentary legislation.[48] Thereafter the full reformation programme was endorsed by the Commons and House of Lords. Significantly, the justification for the king's supremacy over the Irish church was political rather than religious: 'like as the king's majesty justly and rightly is and ought to be supreme head of the Church of England, and so is recognised by the clergy, and authorised by an act of parliament made and established in the said realm: so in like manner of wise, forasmuch as this land of Ireland is depending and belonging justly and rightfully to the imperial crown of England'. It was an argument which side-stepped the controversial theological underpinning of the Henrician supremacy to appeal directly to the political and racial loyalties of the Old English elites in Ireland.

The one aspect of the Henrician reformation which has been the subject of a comprehensive study is the dissolution of the monasteries.[49] The dissolution campaign reached Armagh archdiocese on 23 July 1539 when the abbot of Mellifont surrendered his house to royal commissioners.[50] Within twelve months the monasteries, friaries, convents and hospitals in County Louth were dissolved, almost all 'voluntarily', or at least without resistance. The one exception which has been identified was the hospital of the Crutched friars of Ardee.[51] The prior, Mgr George Dowdall, was supposed to have retired as parish priest of Carnteel in O'Neill's lordship of Tyrone, 'in itself a sufficient indication of estrangement from the crown'.[52] In fact, Prior Dowdall became Armagh's official principal and president of the metropolitan court after Mgr Roth's death c. 1539.[53] This would have required him to reside regularly at Termonfeckin. Mgr Dowdall also became Primate Cromer's chief commissary or deputy in the administration of the archdiocese by 1540.[54] It is likely that Prior Dowdall was personally opposed to the dissolution of the religious houses, but he clearly stopped short of any action which might have caused him to be imprisoned, or worse. He did not leave the Pale.

Mgr Dowdall was identified in 1538 as a 'papistical fellow, being able to corrupt a whole country'.[55] Primate Cromer's choice of such a priest to replace his trusted Mgr Roth as official principal and commissary reflects his continuing attachment to catholicism. His choice of Brother Patrick Galtrym, the last prior of the Crutched friars of Dundalk, to be his archdeacon may reflect Prior Dowdall's influence, and in any case it re-inforces the impression that the primate endeavoured to salvage who and what he could from the Catholic order.

Some other religious also set aside their habits to join the ranks of the secular clergy of Armagh. A number of the former monks of Mellifont, as well as being pensioned off, became curates in charge of churches which had been appropriated to their monastery, including the churches of Collon, Salterstown and Tullyallen in Armagh.[56] Another monk, one Phelim O'Neill, received a paltry pension of £1 but he succeeded in taking possession of Ballymore, Derryloran and Killevy parishes in the rural deanery of Orior by means of papal provisions.[57] One of the two canons of Louth was made the curate of Louth, in addition to receiving a pension of £4.[58] Dnus John Carroll, abbot of Knock Louth from at least 1521, received a modest pension of £3.[59] He was not placed in a parish by the crown, but subsequently become the assistant curate of the parish of Darver.[60] One may conclude that the number of former monks who became secular priests in Armagh *inter Anglicos* was quite small. If the situation in the Pale bore any resemblance to that in England it is possible that the Henrician reformation brought about a collapse (or at least a significant decline) in the number of men offering themselves for ordination to the priesthood, in which circumstances the ex-religious would have met a real need in staffing the parishes.[61] The chapels of the once great monasteries at Mellifont, Louth and Knock Louth remained as parish churches under the new dispensation.[62]

The dissolution of the monasteries was of great significance in closing down the hospitals, and at least one school in County Louth. The loss of the monastic tradition of prayer and worship may, perhaps, have been softened by individual monks maintaining their accustomed round of prayer in their parish churches. In terms of pastoral care the dissolution of the mendicant orders, with their high levels of training, and their expertise as preachers and confessors probably impoverished the spiritual lives of the people in Armagh *inter Anglicos* in a more direct fashion.[63] There had been a great reliance upon the friars to deliver the quarterly sermons required in the parishes. Yet, the loss was not complete. The Observant Franciscans of Drogheda apparently survived the confiscation of their house to maintain their ministry in the city until the end of Henry VIII's reign.[64] That achievement, in the most populous city in the archdiocese, only twenty miles from the seat of English power in Ireland, says a great deal about the resilience of the Franciscans, and the degree of support which they obviously enjoyed in Drogheda.

The community of Carmelite friars from Ardee survived too. They crossed the frontier away from the English crown's jurisdiction just before their friary was dissolved in 1540.[65] Their friary was destroyed. Another friary which was destroyed by the crown was the Franciscan house at Dundalk, suggesting that the friars there too may have left the Pale to take refuge in a neighbouring Irish lordship.[66]

The most important result of the dissolution of the monasteries for the subsequent functioning of the diocesan church was the secularisation of the bulk of the revenues of the 80% of the churches in Armagh *inter Anglicos* which had been impropriated to religious houses, and the transfer of the rights of patronage to benefices and curacies from churchmen to the English crown. The dissolution not only swept away the religious houses in Armagh *inter Anglicos* but it gave Henry VIII greater power over the finances and staffing of the diocesan church than anyone had previously enjoyed. If Henry VIII had been inspired by a desire to reform the church the dissolution of the monasteries gave him an unprecedented opportunity to transform the institution.

ENFORCING THE HENRICIAN REFORMATION

Since revisionist studies undermined the conventional view that the church in late medieval England was in terminal decline, English reformation historians have been obliged to devote much attention to investigating how, and to what effect, the various stages of the 'official' reformations were enforced upon the clergy and a laity which was still committed to catholicism well into the second half of the sixteenth century. Indeed, recent English works suggest that to understand the courses of the Tudor reformations one must study their enforcement in the localities. They have highlighted the central role of the secular clergy, together with the parochial churchwardens, in implementing the crown's religious directives 'on the ground'.

The massive efforts of the crown to secure support for, or at least acquiescence in, its various religious policies in England are now reasonably well understood.[67] Coercion, intimidation and censorship were widely used to silence conservative opponents. Religious change was positively promoted with a propaganda campaign of unprecedented intensity, through the printing presses and through radical preaching in pulpits across much of England.

It is now clear that the Tudor reformations encountered much greater opposition than Dickens ever imagined. Yet, the most striking revelation of recent years has been the degree to which the leaders in England's parishes were obedient to even the most unpopular royal decrees.[68] D.M. Palliser has observed that the churchwarden accounts show that the English were 'certainly governed'. Haigh has suggested that the English grudgingly acquiesced in each 'piece' of reform because the 'piecemeal' nature of the Tudor reformations meant they could not foresee the culmination of what historians came to term 'the English reformation'.[69] Nonetheless, the obedience of the English clergy and laity to the crown's ecclesiastical decrees is striking.

The parliamentary programme

Henry VIII's religious settlement was based upon the following statutes enacted by the Irish parliament of 1536–7. The *act of supremacy* declared Henry VIII, and his successors, to be supreme head of the Church of Ireland, with all of the power and jurisdiction of that office. The *act of slander* made it high treason to stigmatise the king as a heretic, a schismatic or a usurper; anyone convicted for breaching this statute was liable for the death penalty.[70] The *act against the authority of the bishop of Rome* made anyone who supported the pope's authority, by whatever means, liable to the penalties of the statute of provisors and praemunire – in effect, everything short of execution.[71] Justices of the peace and justices of assize on circuit were directed to inquire into breaches of this statute. They were to certify all presentments made to them in the king's bench. The church authorities too were to inquire into breaches of this statute during the course of their visitations. A certificate of the case against the suspected individual was to be forwarded to the secular authorities. Any church officer who was found to be negligent in acting against suspects was liable to a massive fine of £40, half of which would go to the informer who brought the negligence to the attention of the secular powers. For the stronger enforcement of this act an oath of supremacy was prescribed for all office holders, for all of those taking religious vows or receiving holy orders, for those accepting a university degree, and for those who sued for livery or institution of the king.[72] Anyone who refused to take the oath when tendered it was liable to execution. The *act of succession* also contained an oath which acknowledged Henry VIII as supreme head of the Church of England and Ireland.[73] Refusal to take the oath, if tendered, was also punishable by death.

The act of appeals declared that appeals in all spiritual causes which were formerly made to the Roman curia now lay within the English king's competence and jurisdiction. Appeals were now to be made to the king or his deputy in Ireland, and the chancellor or keeper of the great seal, of England or Ireland depending on whom the appeal was made to, would appoint judges delegate in much the same way as the Roman curia had done heretofore.[74] The *act of faculties* provided that all dispensations and licenses which were formally sought from Rome were now to be sued for from the archbishop of Canterbury or, in certain cases, the king.[75]

The other statutes enacted included the *act of first fruits* by which the first year's income from all benefices was to be paid to the English crown. For new benefice holders in Armagh *inter Anglicos* this was a novel, and very expensive imposition.[76] An annual 5% tax, or twentieth, was imposed on all benefice holders. The chancellor or keeper of the seal was directed to have commissioners discover the value of all of the benefices, with allowances made for the cost of rents, the salaries of stewarts or bailiffs, auditors' fees, synodals and any alms which the benefice was legally obliged to disburse, and 10d for the tax collectors.[77] The bishops, or during vacancies the dean and chapter, were responsible for collecting the twentieth, as had been the case with the old clerical subsidies. However, any benefice holder who failed to pay the new tax could be deprived of his benefice by royal authority.

An *act for the probate of wills* created a scale of fees which were henceforth to be levied for processing wills by bishops, diocesan curators of wills, by notaries or scribes.[78] The intention was to eliminate the kind of abuses which the king's commissioners uncovered in the dioceses of south eastern Ireland in 1537. The act was certain to be well-received in some quarters. Primate Cromer, Dnus Hugh O'Shiel, his curator of wills, and Thomas Metame, one of his notaries, had already been sued before the baron of the exchequer in 1536 for charging excessive fees for processing wills.[79]

Under the *act of presentation to benefices* no Irishman was to be presented to any benefice, unless it was impossible to present an English speaker.[80] The statute decreed that there were to be four proclamations made in the nearest town on market days to attract English-speaking clerics for the benefice. If, after five weeks, there was no English candidate it was permitted to present an Irish cleric. Nonetheless, all new ordinands were obliged to take an oath promising to learn English, and to live in the English manner. They were to encourage others to do likewise. Any cleric presented to a benefice was to recite the bidding prayers in English, and preach the Word of God in English if he could. He was also to promote the English language and culture within his parish. All parish priests were to maintain a school to teach English to any parishioners who wished to learn the tongue, taking as a fee whatever 'is accustomably used to be taken'. The bishop, or others in authority, were to identify any who failed to maintain a school. For a first offence the priest was liable for a fine of 6s. 8d., for a second offence a £1 fine, while he could be deprived for a third offence.

It can be shown that the statutes of Ireland's reformation parliament were implemented in the archdiocese of Armagh *inter Anglicos* to no small degree. It is clear that Archbishop Cromer, reluctantly perhaps, acknowledged the king's supremacy. The primate was suspended from the exercise of his office on 23 July 1539 by Pope Paul III until such time as he canonically purged himself of the charge of heresy.[81] In the meantime the pope appointed Mgr Robert Wauchop as administrator of the archdiocese. Dr Cromer did not step down as the pope directed him to. On 29 May 1541 Archbishop Cromer formally addressed Henry VIII as the 'supreme head on Earth of the churches of England and Ireland' in an appeal to the supreme head in a dispute about the primate's visitation rights in the suffragan diocese of Meath.[82] The primate's appeal to the king reflected the new realities in the wake of the act of supremacy and act of appeals.

It is not possible to define the reasons for Primate Cromer's eventual decision to conform to the new religious regime. Possibly he was affected by the apparent futility of the sacrifices made by Bishop Fisher, Sir Thomas More and the other Catholic martyrs in England and Ireland. The absence of palpable divine intervention may have baffled many of the faithful. In the atmosphere of great uncertainty rumours abounded.[83] News, and rumours of developments in England, served to weaken Irish resistance to the Henrician reformation. The dissolution of the English religious communities, for instance, greatly demoralised their brethren and sisters in the English lordship, including even the Observant friars, whom the reformers in Ireland had repeatedly condemned for resisting the ecclesiastical changes in the Pale.[84] Archbishop Browne reported gleefully on 6 November 1538 that whereas the Observants used to have twenty friars in each house, by then they had but four through desperation, and the withdrawal of popular support.[85] This report is significant in showing how events in England served to psychologically prepare people in the crown territories in Ireland to acquiesce in religious changes which were very unpopular, and which yet seemed remorselessly irresistible. Possibly, in an atmosphere of such uncertainty, Primate Cromer allowed himself to be persuaded that the Henrician religious settlement, while schismatic, was fundamentally Catholic in essentials.

There were other considerations too which may have led Primate Cromer to reach an accommodation with the English crown. During the Kildare rebellion Conn O'Neill, lord of Tyrone, took the opportunity to plunder and take possession of more of the archiepiscopal estates around Armagh.[86] Similarly, the O'Hanlons of Orior took possession of the erenagh lands in the parish of Ballymore, and detained them into the seventeenth century.[87] Furthermore, in 1539 Irish depredations on County Louth devastated large areas and caused the church's ministry to collapse temporarily in a number of parishes which had been wasted.[88] To help prevent the outbreak of a sustained war in Ireland, and to allow the church in Armagh to recover from the turmoil of recent years, Primate Cromer probably felt obliged to come to terms with Henry VIII as best he could.

One cannot determine the number of clergymen in Armagh *inter Anglicos* who were tendered the oaths of supremacy and succession. Given the religious conservatism of Archbishop Cromer, his archdeacon and official, it is conceivable that the oaths were not imposed zealously. No clergyman in the archdiocese *inter Anglicos* is known to have been deprived or otherwise punished for refusing to swear an oath. All one may state is that Primate Cromer formally acknowledged the royal supremacy, but there is no evidence of other clergymen having done so in the archdiocese during his term of office.

The *act against the pope's authority* was not a dead letter in County Louth, as is shown by the arrest in Drogheda of Dnus Art O'Gallagher, dean of Derry, with papal provisions on his person in July 1539.[89] However, since the main responsibility for enforcing the act devolved upon the church authorities,[90] and since Archbishop Cromer and Archdeacon Roth, and the latter's successors Prior Dowdall and Prior Galtrym, were supporters of the Catholic order, it is not likely that they would have been overly zealous in seeking out dissenters from the statute, or in reprimanding them.

Archbishop Browne of Dublin found it virtually impossible to compel the clergy of Dublin to preach against the pope, and in favour of the royal supremacy. He had difficulty too in ensuring that the pope's name was excised from all liturgical books. Without a reforming prelate to oversee them, or committed government officials to coerce them, it is likely that the same situation held true in Armagh archdiocese, if the opposition to the ecclesiastical changes was not more overt than in Dublin.

It has already been shown above that the *act of appeals* was operative in that Edward Staples, bishop of Meath, appealed to Henry VIII against the primate's visitation rights in his diocese, forcing Primate Cromer to launch a counter-appeal to the king on 29 May 1541.[91] The procuration fees which the archbishops of Armagh drew from Meath diocese formed a critically large portion of their entire revenues. The very survival of the administration of the archdiocese depended upon a successful result to Primate Cromer's counter-appeal. In the event the counter-appeal did succeed.

The *act of faculties* can be shown to have been, partially at least, in effect in Armagh *inter Anglicos* soon after its enactment in the Irish parliament since Patrick Chillam and Agnes Bathe, a married couple from Drogheda, secured a matrimonial dispensation for consanguinity from Canterbury in 1538/9.[92] However, two other couples from County Louth, both Dowdall men married to Gernon women, secured their matrimonial dispensations for consanguinity in 1538 from Aodh O'Carolan, bishop of Clogher.[93] The three cases are interesting in revealing the readiness of Chillam and Bathe to secure their dispensation in Canterbury, while the Dowdalls and Gernons opted for an orthodox Catholic bishop beyond the borders of the Pale.[94] Sir Patrick Gernon was attainted for his part in the Kildare rebellion of 1534–5.[95] One of the marriages involved Sir James Dowdall, a close associate of Patrick's son, James Gernon. The dispensations granted by the bishop of Clogher probably had the prior consent of the primate since they would have been based upon documents provided by the church authorities in Armagh.

In 1538 the values of the parochial benefices in Armagh *inter Anglicos* were recorded by royal commissioners for the first fruits and twentieth tax on clerical benefices. The valuations were almost certainly derived from archiepiscopal records, as seems clear from the speed with which the commissioners carried out their surveys. One may assume that the twentieth tax was first collected in 1538 in place of the annual clerical subsidy which had been paid hitherto. If one were to judge by the Valor in Hibernia, a copy of the original of which survives from 1591, it would seem that the twentieth tax would have yielded £19 13s. This was almost identical to the clerical subsidy of £19 13s. 4d. which the clergy of Armagh *inter Anglicos* paid in the early sixteenth century.[96] The valuations of the twentieth tax levied on the benefices of Armagh *inter Anglicos* in 1544 shows variations on the Valor which indicate that deductions were made for pensions and other temporary burdens on the benefices.[97] The Valor reflects the English crown's power over the benefice holders throughout County Louth. It may be significant that the last recorded agreements to pay annates to the Roman curia for a benefice anywhere in the archdiocese of Armagh date from 1537.

The *act for presenting priests to benefices* was also widely enforced in Armagh *inter Anglicos*. Inquisitions were held regularly to identify Irish men who were appointed to benefices in contravention of the statute.[98] However, only a couple of such clergymen were identified, and they appear to have been able to purchase charters of English denizenship to overcome the legal impediment of their Irish blood. There was nothing in Armagh to resemble the 'witch hunts' against Irish benefice holders which occurred in the dioceses of Leighlin and Cashel, and some adjacent dioceses, and which must have destabilised the institutional church in the Ormond territories.

The clause in the *act for presenting priests* requiring parish priests to conduct schools for teaching English created difficulties for rather more of the clergy in Armagh *inter Anglicos*. Inquisitions appear to have been held at regular intervals in the last years of Henry VIII's reign to identify priests, beneficed and unbeneficed, who failed to maintain schools.[99] The inquisition of 1543 identified eight priests who failed to maintain a school, that of 1544 identified nine priests, but that of 1545 identified only two priests who failed to maintain schools. Evidently the imposition of fines had the desired effect. Dnus Robert Mc Laughlin, rector of Rathdrummin, was identified as having failed to hold a school by inquisitions in 1543, and again in 1548. On the latter occasion he was fined 13s. 10d., twice the fine for a first offence though less than the £1 laid down by statute for a second offence against the statute. One inquisition record indicates that it was the Old English gentry who delated the priests in County Louth.[100] On this basis one might (tentatively) suggest that on matters affecting national loyalty rather than doctrinal convictions, the Old English elites in County Louth were co-operative in enforcing aspects of Henry VIII's religious settlement.

In conclusion, it has been shown that the reformation statutes were enforced, with varying degrees of effect, throughout the period of the early Tudor reformations in Armagh *inter Anglicos*. The English crown succeeded in displacing the papacy in terms of finance, faculties and as the final court of appeal in ecclesiastical causes. The religious houses were dissolved with the co-operation of local juries, with Patrick Dowdall acting as receiver in many cases, together with Walter Dowdall and Sir James Gernon being receivers of monastic revenues in other cases.[101] Gernon was the son and heir of Sir Patrick Gernon who was attainted for his part in the Kildare rebellion.[102] Walter Dowdall, merchant of Drogheda, subsequently took a lease on the Dominican friary in Drogheda while Laurence Dowdall of Salterstown took a lease on the convent at Termonfeckin.[103] Most spectacularly, Sir Oliver Plunket, one of the great marcher lords of County Louth was made baron of Louth and was granted the extensive holdings of the priory of Louth in 1541.[104] Clearly, there were members of the Old English elite in County Louth who, though they may never previously have aspired to take the lands of the religious communities, did not hesitate to grasp a share of the spoils once they were on offer.

The greatest change enforced upon the parish clergy *inter Anglicos* seems to have been the novel requirement that they conduct schools in order to propagate the English language in their parishes. The inquisitions to identify priests who transgressed this statute could only have been carried out with the help of informants 'on the ground'. Since it was rigorously enforced it seems safe to conclude that those in authority in County Louth, in particular the gentry, supported this cultural aspect of the early Tudor reformations. The significance of this fact (i.e. that the government's will could be imposed with local assistance) is that it shows that the structures existed through which the entire Henrician reformation programme could have been enforced, if it had enjoyed stronger support among the Old English elites in County Louth.

The religious programme

The Henrician reformation is still understood as 'an act of state'.[105] However, historians now recognise that the royal supremacy involved, and perhaps necessitated, the dismantling of many aspects of traditional catholicism; most strikingly the cult of the saints, the doctrine of purgatory and the system of intercessory masses.[106] It was not simply a 'political' reformation.

The reformation statutes gave Henry VIII the authority to re-fashion the church in England and Ireland as he saw fit. The primary instrument of promoting religious change within the church was the set of royal injunctions issued in the king's name. Ireland was spared from the enforcement of the first set of royal injunctions and the kind of intense campaign associated with it, by the success of the clergy in delaying the Irish parliament's sanction of the Henrician religious programme until the close of 1537, and by the absence of any indigenous preachers of Protestant beliefs. Archbishop Browne and Bishop Staples, the two English-born reformers in the Irish church, followed in the wake of the king's religious policies rather than anticipating them.

Archbishop Browne's list of *Injunctions*, the first distinctive theological document issued in Henry VIII's church in Ireland, promoted the royal supremacy but were otherwise rather conservative.[107] The injunctions were drawn up specifically for the archdiocese of Dublin, but were ordered to be enforced across the church in Ireland by the king. However, there is no evidence to indicate whether or not they were imposed in the archdiocese of Armagh. Archbishop Browne's pretensions to authority outside the ecclesiastical province of Dublin were resisted by his fellow reformer, Bishop Staples of Meath, and are not likely to have been better received by the primate.[108] Browne could not call upon the deputy to support him for Lord Grey held the 'polshorne knave friar' in contempt.[109]

Archbishop Browne's injunctions may have been superseded by the second set of injunctions issued by Vicegerent Cromwell on behalf of the king for the Church of England and Ireland in October 1538. The Council of Ireland informed Cromwell in January 1539 that his *Injunctions* had been published not only in Dublin, but throughout south eastern Ireland by Archbishop Browne.[110] The council also acknowledged the directive to remove 'idols', extinguish the pope's authority and to levy first fruits and the twentieth tax on benefices. The *Injunctions'* decree to pluck down 'any notable images or relics to which the simple people were wont to assemble superstitiously, and as vagrants to walk and roam in pilgrimage' was carried out in 1539. The annalist of the monastery at Lough Key wrote that 'there was not a holy cross, a statue of Mary nor a venerable image within their jurisdiction that they (i.e. the English) did not destroy'.[111] Certainly in Dublin and Meath, the dioceses of the reformer bishops Browne and Staples, many shrines were despoiled and destroyed. Yet, in the archdiocese of Armagh, only one parish church is known to have suffered, that of St Nicholas' parish, Dundalk, probably at the hands of Deputy Grey who demolished the friary in the town about that time.[112] The reason why St Nicholas' church was singled out for special attention was, no doubt, the fact that it held the shrine of St Richard of Dundalk, a former archbishop of Armagh whose cult was popular with the Old English elites in counties Louth and Meath.[113] One is drawn to the conclusion that the contrasting impact of the injunction against images in the different dioceses reflected the varying dispositions of the bishops. That it was possible for a prelate to protect the religious images in the parish churches by interpreting the *Injunctions* very narrowly to refer to famous images only, is shown by the fact that the conservative Bishop Longland of Lincoln and Archbishop Lee of York managed to preserve the images in both of their dioceses, at least until Henry VIII came across them in person while travelling north from London to York in 1542.

The other articles among the *Injunctions* imposed the obligation on priests to teach the Pater Noster, Ave Maria, the creed and articles of religion to their parishioners in English, to quench the lights which used to be maintained before religious images, to excise the saints from the litany at Mass. However, Eamon Duffy has shown that in England the intensity and scope of the enforcement of the *Injunctions* varied from diocese to diocese.[114] In Armagh *inter Anglicos* it is probable that the administration of Primate Cromer would have implemented the new decrees in a resolutely minimalist manner, given his antipathy to religious innovation.

In February 1539 a commission was established in the lordship of Ireland to oversee the rigorous implementation of Henry VIII's religious decrees.[115] However, before the commission became effective the 'Six articles' were promulgated by the king on 10 June 1539. These articles endorsed most traditional Catholic doctrines and ceremonies – except those relating to purgatory, images and the cult of saints. They even upheld the obligation of clerical celibacy in Henry VIII's church, much to the discomfort of Archbishop Browne. A year later Vicegerent Cromwell was executed. James Murray has revealed that Archbishop Browne, compromised by being married and now without his patron at court, cast off the mantle of a doctrinal reformer and adopted the role of a traditional archbishop of his diocese.[116] The assault on Catholic beliefs and practices ground to a halt in Ireland.

It is apparent that the impact of the Henrician injunctions against traditional religion in the archdiocese of Armagh was very modest, in part because the enforcement of the reformation in the lordship was delayed by the Kildare rebellion and subsequently by clerical opposition in the reformation parliament. Primate Cromer's continued opposition to religious innovation further blunted the effects of the Henrician religious programme on his archdiocese. Finally, it is clear that the secular authorities, while they enforced the juridical aspects of the royal supremacy, showed no enthusiasm for religious change.

Lord Deputy Grey, from a mixture of political and (one suspects) personal reasons, was reluctant to insist that the Henrician reformation be rigorously imposed on the lordship. His over-riding aim to keep the peace in Ireland seemed most readily attainable through a rapprochement with the Geraldines and their allies across Ireland.[117] This necessarily involved a conservative approach towards religious matters which might antagonise the former Catholic crusaders. This accounts for Grey's releasing from prison of Catholic dissidents, including Canon James Humphrey of Dublin,[118] and Dean Art O'Gallagher of Derry;[119] for his licensing of a deputation of friars to visit Henry VIII in 1538 to persuade the king not to dissolve the friaries,[120] for his council's request that six specified monasteries be preserved;[121] and for his accommodation of the Catholic counsellors of the young Geraldine.[122] Lord Grey's sympathetic hearing of the vicar of Chester predicting that the king would soon restore religious images in the churches,[123] his open contempt for Archbishop Browne,[124] and his ostentatious devotion before Our Lady's statue at Trim[125] may reflect his personal religious disposition. On the other hand, such public actions conveyed deliberate political messages. At Trim, for instance, where Grey went to the pilgrimage statue and 'very devoutly kneeling before her, heard three or four masses', the trial was being held of a bishop (most probably Bishop

Staples's suffragan who had been arrested for praying publicly for the pope and the emperor, as well as Henry VIII[126]) and a number of friars arraigned on charges of infringing the statute against the pope's authority. The deputy's actions helped to ensure that the clergymen were not indicted. It is clear, then, that Lord Deputy Grey, whatever his motives, did not ensure that the Henrician reformation was imposed on the lordship with rigour. His actions accorded with the wishes of the Old English elites in the Pale who did not want religious change, and who stood condemned by one English-born reformer as 'papists, hypocrites and worshippers of idols'.[127]

The advent of Anthony St Leger as viceroy in Ireland in July 1540 merely served to confirm his predecessors' policy of avoiding religious controversy as far as possible. St Leger took advantage of the partial reversal of the Henrician reformation in England to promote the royal supremacy in Ireland shorn of doctrinal or liturgical innovation.[128] In return for their acknowledgement of the royal supremacy St Leger offered bishops, not only continued tenure of office but also, practical assistance with problems such as unwarranted lordly interference in the finances and appointments in the church.[129] In 1542 the earl of Tyrone and the lord of Tyrconnell were ordered to permit the primate and other bishops to exercise their jurisdictions unhindered, and to free churchlands of all secular exactions.[130] In 1549 Hugh O'Neill was ordered to compensate the primate for occupying some of the lands in the archiepiscopal manor of Inishkeen, while Conn O'Neill was ordered to stop interfering with the fiscal rights of the dean of Armagh.[131] St Leger exercised the crown's rights to present men to benefices in its gift, and he ensured that the reformation statutes continued to be enforced. However, the remaining years of Henry VIII's reign saw no further attempts by the crown's administration to alter the religion of the people of Ireland.

The archdiocese of Armagh engaged St Leger's attention at an early date. Recognising the serious nature of the primate's infirmities[132] St Leger suggested in 1541 that Archbishop Cromer be succeeded by the baron of Delvin's son – possibly Nicholas Nugent, a cleric of Meath who had received a dispensation to receive the dignity of archdeacon or dean at a time when he was not in full priest's orders.[133] In the event the primacy was conferred upon Mgr George Dowdall, the official principal and president of the metropolitan court of Armagh since 1540. Mgr Dowdall had a very close working relationship with the ailing primate, being his commissary – his deputy, in effect.[134] Mgr Dowdall presided over the synod of 1541 as Archbishop Cromer's commissary.[135] At the synod of 1542 Dnus Éamon Mc Cawell, dean of Armagh, and Mgr Dowdall presided as custos, *sede vacante*, and subcustos of the archdiocese *inter Anglicos* respectively.[136] By November 1542 Mgr Dowdall had been elected to succeed Archbishop Cromer as primate,[137] and Henry VIII issued the order for his consecration.[138] The new primate was a local man who was well qualified and experienced to take charge of the archdiocese of Armagh, and serve as metropolitan of the northern province of the Irish church.

THE ADMINISTRATION OF THE ARCHDIOCESE OF ARMAGH

Diocesan synods and convocations

The annual diocesan synods gave the archbishop a long-established platform for advocating reform among his priests. It was indispensable for setting out any new agenda for change within the archdiocese. It was the chief occasion each year when the archbishop could address his clergy as a body. Records survive for the diocesan synods *inter Anglicos* for all but two of the years from 1540–48.[139] There are no records extant for the turbulent years immediately preceding and succeeding that period. If one may judge from the records of convocations which survive, there appears to have been no business conducted at the convocations apart from the appointment of the collectors of the twentieth taxation from the beneficed clergymen *inter Anglicos*.[140]

The most striking feature of the annual diocesan synods over the period 1540 to 1548 is the strong continuity in format and content compared with the synods of the period immediately prior to the reformation. The synods of the clergy *inter Anglicos* continued to be held within St Peter's church, Drogheda, apart from two occasions when synods were convened in St Feighin's church, Termonfeckin, to facilitate the attendance of the terminally ill Primate Cromer.[141] The synodal records of the early Tudor reformation period refer to a roll call of the assembled priests before Mass in the morning session and/or at the start of the afternoon session of the synods.[142] The roll call is unlikely to have been a new feature of the synods, though it is not referred to in the pre-reformation records. After Mass the priests processed to the town cross, at Drogheda or Termonfeckin, depending on the location of the synod.[143] *Veni creator* was sung as usual, but during the early Tudor reformations the *Te deum* was sung also for the well-being of the church.[144]

The business of the synods of the early Tudor reformations period was remarkably conservative in character. There were the customary exhortations to the priests to observe synodal legislation ever more faithfully, and to exercise the highest standards in their priestly ministries.[145] One has the impression that the exhortations given in Primate Cromer's last synods were more earnestly made than those in his earlier synods. Primate Dowdall's synods, by contrast, seem to exude a lesser sense of urgency. His first synod as archbishop in 1544 was presided over by Conor O Cahan, the crown's bishop of Raphoe, and Mgr Robert Luttrell, official principal of Armagh.[146] Not until the synod *inter Anglicos* of 1545 did Archbishop Dowdall set out his own agenda in a series of synodal decrees.[147] Two of Dowdall's six decrees simply reminded the priests of the fees which they were obliged to pay the chief apparitor in Armagh *inter Anglicos* for citations to synods, and for delivery of the holy oils (Decrees 3 & 4). Other decrees dealt with the perennial problems of some clergymen not being properly attired at synods and convocations (Decree 2), and of priests exercising a cure of souls without securing admission from the ordinary (Decree 6). The remaining two statutes were new and they reflect something of Primate Dowdall's disposition towards the Henrician reformation in the mid 1540s. The timing is important in that the Henrician reformation had been reversed somewhat since the fall of Cromwell and the ageing king was still a Catholic of sorts by instinct.[148] Primate Dowdall chose to adopt one of the king's reformation decrees to promulgate through his synod; a direction that all parish priests study in their churches three days during each week (Decree 5). The choice is significant in that it was a measure of modest reform – not reformation.

The most important decree of Primate Dowdall's 1545 synod was undoubtedly the first on the list: a new feast day was ordered to be celebrated annually within the archdiocese of Armagh on 27 June, with nine lections no less, in honour of St Richard FitzRalph, archbishop of Armagh (1346–60). The cult of St Richard of Dundalk began soon after his death with his tomb in St Nicholas' church, Dundalk, becoming a place of pilgrimage.[149] Attempts by the church authorities in Armagh and Meath to have Archbishop FitzRalph canonised by Rome foundered because of his influence on the heretical Wyclif. However, he was widely regarded as a saint within the Pale, and the Antiphonary of Armagh included a feast of St Richard on 14 March. Primate Dowdall's provision of a new date and a more elaborate liturgy for the celebration of Archbishop FitzRalph as a saint was remarkable as it ran contrary to the Henrician act for the abrogation of certain holy days, an act which had some definite effect within the Pale.[150] More than that it contradicted the entire emphasis of Henry VIII's religious programme which was opposed to the veneration of saints.

One may conclude that, instead of being a key instrument for promoting the early Tudor reformations in the archdiocese of Armagh, the annual synods of the clergy were employed to promote traditional reformist goals. One may venture to suggest that the synods helped to thwart the early Tudor reformations by largely ignoring them, and by maintaining a high level of continuity with the pre-reformation period in terms of the format of the synods and the agendas they presented to the parochial clergy.

Visitations

It has been shown that annual visitations of the clergy of the archdiocese of Armagh had been held in the later middle ages. The loss of the visitation books deny us the possibility of determining how frequently visitations were conducted in the archdiocese in the period of the early Tudor reformations. The probability is, though, that they were conducted as frequently as in the pre-reformation period, especially since the archbishop and archdeacon of Armagh continued to demand their annual payments of procurations.[151]

That Primate Cromer's visitation rights continued to be exercised in Armagh *inter Hibernicos* seems most probable since his commissaries were certainly able to act effectively in the neighbouring diocese of Down and Connor during the metropolitan visitation of 1540.[152] In 1541 the primate was able to exercise his authority as *custos* of Down and Connor *sede vacante*.[153] He also commissioned commissaries to conduct a metropolitan visitation of Raphoe, the most remote suffragan diocese from his residence at Termonfeckin.[154] Therefore, while proof is impossible, it can be plausibly argued that since the archbishop was able to exercise his visitation rights in other Ulster dioceses he would have done the same in the northern rural deaneries of his own diocese.

Primate Cromer's successor was demonstrably active throughout the archdiocese. A comprehensive list of the churches to be visited by him during his primary visitation in 1544 survives for the southern rural deaneries of Armagh.[155] Of greater interest and value, though, are the acta of the visitation of parishes in the rural deaneries of Orior and Tullyhogue in 1546. The fact that Primate Dowdall was able to appoint commissaries to conduct a parish visitation *inter Hibernicos* shows, together with records of archiepiscopal presentations to benefices and the deprivation of incumbents, that the archbishop's authority in the northern parishes was unaffected by the Henrician reformation. Indeed, the acta reveals that Primate Dowdall had already visited Armagh *inter Hibernicos* in person at some time shortly before the visitation of 1546. It shows that both the primate and the dean of Armagh had already visited the parish priest of Tynan, and the rector of Ballyclog had already made a statement before the primate on a prior occasion. The acta allow one to identify the visitation articles of the visitors, and these in turn may be examined to help determine Primate Dowdall's disposition towards the Henrician reformation.

The chief visitor of the parishes *inter Hibernicos* was the bishop of Ardagh. The bishop in question was Patrick Mc Mahon. He was Primate Dowdall's suffragan for the parishes of Armagh *inter Hibernicos*, and vicar of Aghaloo.[156] The articles which he and Dnus Nicholas Mc Grath, canon of Clogher, put to the parish priests and their parishioners may be summarised as follows:

1   What was the state of the fabric of the parish church?

2   Was the liturgical equipment adequate?

3   Did the parish clergy celebrate the Mass and pray the Divine Office?

4   Were the parish clergy concubinary?

The striking thing about this set of articles is its wholly conservative nature. These questions would have been asked at every visitation of the later middle ages. In interpreting them two possibilities come to mind: either traditional articles were chosen exclusively because the priests *inter Hibernicos* would have baulked at any injunctions with a Protestant bias or, alternatively, they simply reflect the fact that Primate Dowdall had no wish to promote a Protestant reformation in his archdiocese. If one takes account of the conservative character of synods of the clergy of Armagh *inter Anglicos* and the record of the visitation of the parishes *inter Hibernicos* one is forced to conclude that while Primate Dowdall was prepared to accept the king as head of the church, he worked to promote traditional reform in his archdiocese – not reformation.

Church courts

The absence of church court records for the period of the early Tudor reformations precludes any discussion of how the reformations affected Armagh's ecclesiastical courts. However, it is clear that the consistory court of Armagh continued to exercise its authority effectively – except where its decrees ran counter to the wishes of the secular powers. Within Armagh archdiocese Dnus Octavian Rounsele, rector of Clonmore, was deprived early in 1542 and Dnus Malachy O'Donnelly, vicar of Donaghmore was deprived in November 1543.[157] However, Primate Cromer was powerless in the face of secular opposition (in the form of the O'Neill, perhaps) to eject Phelim O'Neill from the rectory of Killevy or the vicarages of Ballymore or Derryloran which he detained by means of papal provisions.[158] On the other hand, the metropolitan court of Primates Cromer and Dowdall was able to deprieve benefice holders in several suffragan dioceses of the northern province.[159] This shows that the consistory and metropolitan court of Armagh retained its authority, not only in Armagh *inter Anglicos* but across the ecclesiastical province of Armagh despite the turmoil of the Henrician reformation.

Once Mgr Dowdall became archbishop he appointed Mgr Robert Luttrell, rector of Kilberry in Meath diocese, to take his place as Armagh's official principal.[160] Archbishop Dowdall's regard for Luttrell is shown by the fact that, in the primate's absence, Mgr Luttrell presided over the synods of the clergy of Armagh *inter Anglicos* with a suffragan bishop in 1544 and again in 1548.[161] On 19 December 1545 Primate Dowdall appointed Dermot Mc Dewyn (his surname suggests that he may have been related to his immediate predecessor) as the ruridecanal official of Orior with Armagh city.[162] The rural deanery of Tullyhogue continued to have its own ruridecanal official, in the person of Art O'Hagan.[163] Archbishop Cromer and Archbishop Dowdall both addressed suits brought before the consistory court of Armagh from parishes in Armagh *inter Hibernicos*. On 4 April 1541 Heneas Mc Nicholl, a layman of Armagh, appeared before Primate Cromer to declare that he had fulfilled the very onerous penance which the dean of Armagh had imposed on him for strangling his son, and to seek the archbishop's confirmation of his absolution.[164] On 29 August 1544 Primate Dowdall commissioned the dean of Armagh to investigate a suit brought before him by the vicar of Tynan against the abbot of SS Peter and Paul's monastery at Armagh.[165]

Despite the absence of an act book of the consistory and metropolitan court of Armagh, there are sufficient records in Primate Dowdall's register to demonstrate that the court continued to work with effect across the archdiocese of Armagh, and across the province of Armagh throughout the period of the Henrician reformation.

Appointments to benefices

The period of the early Tudor reformations witnessed very considerable continuity in the manner in which priests were appointed to benefices. The customary inquisitions were held to establish the cause of the vacancy of each benefice, who enjoyed the right of patronage, and the suitability of the candidate being presented to the benefice as regards age, morals and circumstances.[166] There were no new questions relating to the royal supremacy.

The early Tudor reformations did nothing to enhance the very limited rights of the archbishops of Armagh to patronage of benefices in the southern rural deaneries. The primates continued to use their patronage to reward senior clergymen or administrators in the archdiocese. Primate Cromer collated his official principal and commissary, Mgr Dowdall, to the rectory of Clonmore.[167] He collated Dnus Hugh O'Shiel, a key

TABLE 6 Beneficed clergy *inter Anglicos c.*1547

Parish	Position	Name	Dates	Sources
Beaulieu	Rector	Thomas Bocume	1528	Cromer's II, f. 37v (86)
			post 1556	Dowdall's, p. 129 (95)
Carrick	Rector	Nicholas Betagh	*c.*1545	Dublin, III, Inquis 131
Clonkeen	Vicar	Patrick Bellew	1542	Dowdall's, p. 46 (42)
			post 1551	Fiants of Edward VI, no. 743
Clonmore	Rector	William Johnston	1543	C.P.C.R., i, PR 35 dorso, m. 8
			1557	Armagh clergy, p. 193
Darver	Rector	John Lymerick	1544	Dowdall's, pp 6–7 (6)
			post 1564	Armagh clergy, p. 208
Drogheda	Vicar	William Hamlin	1533	Cromer's, II, f. 73v (173)
			1556	Dowdall's, p. 129 (95)
Dromin	Vicar	John White	1544	Dowdall's, p. 50 (46)
Drumcar	Vicar	Nicholas Warren	1542	Dowdall's, p. 2 (2)
			post 1556	Dowdall's, p. 129 (95)
Dromiskin	Vicar	Richard Mc My	1542	Fiants of Henry VIII, no. 296
Dunany	Vicar	John Cantwell	1541	Dowdall's, p. 28 (23)
Dunleer	Vicar	Richard Heny	1544	Dowdall's, p. 78 (69)
			post 1556	Dowdall's, p. 129 (95)
Heynestown	Rector	Hugh O'Shiel	1542	Dowdall's, p. 42 (36)
			post 1546	Dowdall's, pp 238–9 (122)
Kildemock	Vicar	Thomas Duff	1518	Cromer's, II, f. 3 (4).
			1548	Dowdall's, p. 96 (81)
Mansfieldstown	Rector	William Hamlin	1546	Dowdall's, pp 238–9 (122)
			1556	See Drogheda
Mansfieldstown	Vicar	Robert Ardagh	*c.*1545	Dublin, III, Inquis 131
Molary	Vicar	Eamon Duff	*c.*1545	Dublin, III, Inquis 131
Rathdrummin	Rector	Robert Mc Laughlin	1518	Cromer's, II, f. 3v (6)
			1556	Dowdall's, p. 130 (95)
Stabannon	Vicar	Thomas Crieffe	*c.*1541	Dublin, III, Inquis 131
			*c.*1548	Armagh clergy, p. 418
Termonfeckin	Vicar	Patrick Morgan	1542	Dowdall's, p. 56 (51)
			post 1556	Dowdall's, p. 129 (95)

O'Shiel, a key member of the consistory and metropolitan court of Armagh, to the rectory of Heynestown.[168] He collated Dnus John Lymerick who was promoted to a canonry, to the rectory of Kene.[169] Primate Cromer promoted the long unbeneficed Dnus Patrick Bellew to the vicarage of Clonkeen, having been granted the right of presentation by Patrick Barnewall, the outspoken critic of the royal supremacy in the reformation parliament in 1536–7.[170] Unfortunately, Archbishop Dowdall's presentations to benefices *inter Anglicos* are poorly documented, but one of the primate's two known presentees was Mgr Hamlin, the steadfastly conservative vicar of St Peter's, who was awarded the rectory of Mansfieldstown *in commendam.*[171]

The dissolution of the monasteries gave the crown the right of patronage to the great majority of the benefices and parish cures in Armagh *inter Anglicos*. Together with the act for presenting to benefices this ought to have given the crown the power to refashion the secular clergy of Armagh to accord with its desires. However, the poverty of the bulk of the parish livings there greatly curtailed the crown's ability to attract the kind of clergy it wished to minister in the parishes. Two English men were presented to benefices in Armagh *inter Anglicos* by the king or his viceroy. The first, Dnus Lewis Tudor (alias Tidder) was promoted to the vicarage of Dromiskin by Lord Deputy St Leger in 1541, but he resigned the benefice in the following year in favour of a prebend in Kildare diocese, before moving on to the rich rectory of Rosslare in Ferns diocese, an office valued at no less than £39 9s. in the Valor in Hibernia.[172] The second, Mgr William Johnson, was St Leger's chaplain before being presented to the rectory of Clonmore by the crown in 1543.[173] Leslie plausibly suggested that he was the same William Johnson from Worcester who became dean of Ossory (worth £26 13s. 4d.) in 1559 and died in 1581.[174] Both of these men were presented to benefices in Armagh archdiocese whose values, at £11 9s. 2d. and £22 13s. 4d., were far greater than the average for all of the parochial benefices, yet only one of the Englishmen retained a benefice in the archdiocese for any length of time.

Three of the other crown presentees who can be identified were almost certainly English by descent, rather than birth.[175] Three Irish priests are known to have been presented to benefices in Armagh parishes by the crown; one to the remunerative vicarage of Dromiskin (worth £11 8s. 8d.), another to the impoverished vicarage of Kildemock (worth only £1 1s. 1d.), and a third to the vicarage of Dunleer (worth £4 2s. 1d.).[176] One might conclude that although the crown might have preferred to promote Englishmen to benefices in Armagh *inter Anglicos* men of English birth or blood had no monopoly of the crown's patronage to benefices.

There were twenty four parish benefices in Armagh *inter Anglicos* in 1547, two of which were held by 'pluralists'. Of the seventeen beneficed clergymen who can be identified in Armagh *inter Anglicos c.* 1547 one was English-born, nine were Old English priests, while six were Irish priests, a proportional increase from *c.* 1518–22. Another, Dnus Crieffe, has a surname which cannot be classified with confidence. Among the non-beneficed curates in charge of churches *inter Anglicos* Irish priests continued to be in a substantial majority during the early Tudor reformations, as they had been beforehand.[177]

At least eleven of the seventeen benefice holders can be shown to have served the church in Armagh before the Henrician reformation (a twelfth, Dnus Mc My, used to be a priest in Meath diocese), though the actual number of pre-reformation priests is likely to have been even greater. The failure of the English crown to establish a university in Ireland, or a training college for the ministers of the new church, meant that the parish clergy throughout the period of the early Tudor reformations had been educated and trained in the late medieval manner, by older and, in all probability, conservative priests. Only four of the parish clergymen were graduates, including Mgr William Hamlin, the conservative vicar of the key town of Drogheda. Two of the four graduates, Mgr Johnston, rector of Clonmore, and Mgr Cantwell, vicar of Dunany, were not native to Armagh and may not have resided in their parishes.

In Armagh *inter Hibernicos* the Henrician reformation threatened to tear the arch-diocese apart at first, but Primate Cromer succeeded in keeping it together, presumably with some support from O Neill. The turmoil generated by the Kildare rebellion, the Irish reformation parliament, and Primate Cromer's involvement in the Catholic cause created opportunities which were seized upon by delators in Armagh *inter Hibernicos*. In May 1534 Bernard O'Lougheran, rural dean of Tullyhogue, obligated himself to pay annates for the prebend of Ardtrea, the rectory of Magherafelt, and the rectory of Lissan.[178]

To acquire the benefices of Ardtrea and Magherafelt Dnus O'Lougheran delated Senkyn Mc Dewyn, ruridecanal official of Orior with Armagh and seneschal of the archiepiscopal manor of Armagh.[179] Dnus O'Lougheran's charges have not survived but Dnus Mc Dewyn's tuitorial letter from Primate Cromer indicates that O'Lougheran's judges delegate found in his favour, and Dnus Mc Dewyn appealed to Rome against their decision, with the support of the primate.[180] The final result of this litigation cannot be determined.

In August 1535 three men from Armagh obligated themselves to pay annates to the Roman curia for any or all of several benefices which they hoped to gain through delation. Eugene Mc Cawell delated Dnus Eoghan O'Corre, vicar of Clonfeacle, Eoghan O'Culean, vicar of Ballyclog, and Eoghan Mucgyan, rector of Ballinderry.[181] He claimed simply that the benefices were unlawfully held. Eugene Mc Cawell was identified as the vicar of Clonfeacle in 1544, suggesting that he may have been successful against one of his three defendants in 1535, but not the others.[182] It may be significant that Conor Mc Ardle, one of Mc Cawell's judges delegate, was subsequently deprived of his benefices by Primate Cromer for simony and other crimes.[183]

Art O'Hagan, rector of Derryloran,[184] and identified as ruridecanal official of Tullyhogue in 1541,[185] delated Dnus Tomás O'Connellan, rector of Kildress, and Malachy O'Donnelly, rector of Ardboe, accusing them of detaining the benefices without canonical title.[186] He obligated himself to pay annates for both benefices, if he successfully acquired them, in August 1535. No evidence exists to indicate whether he succeeded or not, but Malachy O'Donnelly was deprived as rector of Donaghmore in 1543, raising the possibility that he had had to find a new benefice after losing the rectory of Ardboe to O'Hagan.[187]

In the same month as the rector of Derryloran bound himself to pay annates to the Roman curia, Phelim O'Neill, styling himself the vicar of Derryloran, bound himself to pay annates for the rectory of Killevy, and the vicarages of Ardtrea, Muintirheny and Tynan.[188] He delated the abbess of the Augustinian convent at Killevy for the rectory, and Dnus Tadhg O'Connellan, Dnus Tomás O'Ferachan, and Dnus Tomás O'Dangusa respectively for the vicarages, making no allegations against them but claiming that they detained the benefices unlawfully. O Neill had already intruded himself into the vicarage of Derryloran 'with secular power' against Archbishop Cromer's candidate.[189] O Neill's judges delegate either decided against his suit, or he lost an appeal to Rome, because he had to intrude himself into the rectory of Killevy, and held it 'with secular power' until his death in 1541.[190] He took the neighbouring vicarage of Muintirheny too 'with secular power' and kept it too till his death. On the other hand, Tomás

O'Dangusa appears to have succeeded in keeping possession of the vicarage of Tynan.[191] The fate of the vicar of Ardtrea cannot be determined.

In February 1537 two more clerics from Armagh each obligated themselves to pay annates to the Roman curia for a series of benefices in the rural deanery of Tullyhogue. Eamon O'Quinn hoped to secure, through delation doubtless, the rectories of Clonoe, Donaghenry, Desertlyn and Lissan.[192] The charges levied against the holders of the benefices are not known, but probably involved the usual questioning of their titles. The result of the delations is not known. However, one Dnus Patrick Mc Cawell died as rector of Clonoe and Donaghenry in 1542, suggesting that O'Quinn was either unsuccessful against him, or very short lived in his success.[193]

Terence O'Donnelly, *firmarius* of the archiepiscopal lands in Tullyniskin, obligated himself to pay annates for the rectories of Tullyniskin, Ardtrea and Magherafelt, Drumglass and Kildress.[194] Again, no record survives of his success or otherwise, though it is interesting to see Dnus McDewyn's benefices of Ardtrea and Magherafelt which were coveted by a delator in 1534 attracting the attentions of another delator three years later.

The number of delations in Armagh archdiocese between 1485 and 1534 was small, and the number of successful delations was much smaller still.[195] It has been concluded that Primate Cromer had no real problem with papal provisions or delations before 1534. However, with the onset of the religious turmoil generated by the Henrician reformation, the next three years must have presented a major challenge to Archbishop Cromer's administration of the church in Armagh *inter Hibernicos*. Nonetheless, apart from Phelim O'Neill, who held three benefices *inter Hibernicos* against Primate Cromer's will, both Archbishop Cromer and Archbishop Dowdall were able to exercise their right to collate men to benefices unhindered from at least 1540 when one begins to find records in Dowdall's registers. On 2 November 1540 Primate Cromer awarded the revenues of the rectory of Carnteel to his official principal, Mgr Dowdall, for a six month term.[196] When Dnus O'Neill died in 1542 the primate promoted Mgr Dowdall to the rectory of Killevy.[197] Archbishop Dowdall presented his suffragan for the parishes *inter Hibernicos*, Patrick Mc Mahon, to the vicarage of Aghaloo in 1544.[198] The primate seems to have made Bishop Mc Mahon his chief commissary in Armagh *inter Hibernicos*, for the visitation of the parishes *inter Hibernicos* in 1546 was conducted by the suffragan. This was a novel appointment and was undoubtedly designed to increase the primate's oversight over the northern parishes of his diocese. Both Cromer and Dowdall made regular appointments to parochial benefices in the northern rural deaneries as though no reformation was taking place in Ireland.[199] However, the king's supremacy did penetrate the rural deanery of Orior in that one William Moore was presented by the crown to the prebend of Clonfeacle and the vicarage of Kilmore in 1544 after Dnus Sean O'Culean had been deprived for holding the benefices through papal provisions.[200] Such a presentation by the crown could only have taken effect with the consent of the earl of Tyrone yet, even then, it is unlikely that a man of English birth or blood would have served a cure *inter Hibernicos* at that time.

One may conclude that, continuity rather than change characterised the clergy of Armagh *inter Anglicos* throughout the first half of the sixteenth century, despite the introduction of the Tudor reformations. The English crown gained enormous power over the appointment of parish priests in Armagh *inter Anglicos* through the dissolution of the monasteries and the enactment of the act for presenting to benefices, but was not able to exercise that power to significant effect because of the difficulties in attracting suitable clergymen to the generally meagrely-endowed parish cures. After a small influx of ex-religious into parish cures following the dissolution of the monasteries, it appears that there was little change in the secular clergy of Armagh in terms of their training and professional backgrounds compared with the period immediately prior to the Henrician reformation. *Inter Hibernicos* Primate Cromer faced an initial challenge from a series of papal delators, but by 1540 at least, and possibly 1538 when the delations came to an end, he was back in control of the parishes in the northern rural deaneries.

Archiepiscopal finances

The Henrician reformation posed an enormous threat to the financial stability of the archdiocese of Armagh when Bishop Staples of Meath took advantage of the royal supremacy, and Primate Cromer's known distaste for it, to challenge the right of the archbishops of Armagh to levy procurations in the diocese of Meath.[201] Primate Cromer's appeal to Henry VIII, however, quashed this threat, and the procurations were guaranteed by an act of parliament in 1542.[202]

Primate Dowdall's concern with the finances of the archdiocese is shown by the comprehensive record of the archiepiscopal revenues preserved in the second book of the register attributed to him.[203] The greatest lacuna in the book is the lack of accounts for the properties held by Conn O'Neill, earl of Tyrone, in the archiepiscopal manor of Armagh. It is clear from the accounts which survive that the revenues drawn from the manor of Armagh by Primate Dowdall were far less than those drawn by his late medieval predecessors.

Like many of his predecessors Archbishop Dowdall would have had great difficulty in paying the first fruits – the great sum of £183 17s. 5½d.[204] There is a copy of an undated bond in his register for the payment of £58 4s. 6d. in two installments in part payment of his first fruits.[205] The primate had also to pay the annual twentieth tax of £9 3s. 10½d.[206] He appears to have been obliged to alienate some of the see properties of Armagh to pay his debts.[207]

Financial pressures weighed heavily upon the archdiocese in the period of the early Tudor reformations but Primate Dowdall seems to have garnered his resources effectively, avoided bankruptcy and does not seem to have alienated much of the see lands. No doubt his experience as prior of a hospital, and as the manager of Primate Cromer's finances in his last years, proved useful to Archbishop Dowdall when he took charge of the archdiocese.[208]

THE EDWARDIAN REFORMATION AND THE SECULAR CLERGY IN ARMAGH

There are virtually no documents in Primate Dowdall's register for the reign of Edward VI.

Three of the four that exist comprise of routine items from 1548; a record of a synod, a record of the admission of a priest to the vicarage of Kildemock and a list of the collectors of the Office of St Patrick.[209] The last document is dated 31 May 1550 and records Primate Dowdall's promotion of Dean Terence O'Donnelly to the office of rector of the Céile Dé of Armagh.[210] The other documents which would have been produced by the archiepiscopal administration have been lost. As with the period 1536–9 the loss of documents seems to have been the consequence of a period of religious turmoil.

Edward's reign saw an escalating campaign waged against the Catholic religion and the promotion of an increasingly Protestant alternative. The royal injunctions of 1547, together with a further order in January 1548, directed the clergy and laity to exterminate most traditional religious practices. Churches in England and Wales were stripped of religious imagery, whether in the form of statues, rood lofts, wall paintings or stained glass windows. Lights in churches were almost completely prohibited. The ringing of the sanctus bell at the sacring was forbidden. All religious processions were outlawed. Pilgrimages and holy days were condemned with increased vigour. The use of holy water, blessings with candles and the making of palm crosses were proscribed. In December 1547 the Chantries Act ordered the dissolution of all chantries and the transfer of their endowments to the crown.

The Edwardian regime expected that the king's injunctions and its other religious orders would be enforced throughout what it termed the 'church of England and Ireland'. In Ireland, however, there was no desire for religious change and consequently no group to lobby for the implementation of the Edwardian religious decrees. Enforcement, then, depended upon the intiative of the deputy. On 22 April 1548 the eirenic St Leger was replaced as viceroy by the bellicose Edward Bellingham, and the first evidence of the Edwardian reformation soon followed.[211]

Evidently the government commissioned a Scottish Protestant to promote the reformation in Dublin in the summer of 1548. Archbishop Browne launched a campaign against the Scot for preaching against the Mass and other religious ceremonies. The archbishop invited Mgr Hamlin, vicar of St Peter's, Drogheda, Rector Luttrell, the official principal of Armagh, and Chief Justice Luttrell (possibly a relation of Rector Luttrell) to hear his sermon against the Scottish heretic, presumably because of their known Catholic sympathies.[212] However, once Browne had been reprimanded by the government he proceeded to carry out the full Edwardian religious programme over the next two years, as did Bishop Staples in Meath.[213] Indeed, the Edwardian reformation was enforced across much of the English lordship in Ireland. In the archdiocese of Armagh, however, Edward's reformation was effectively blocked by Primate Dowdall.

Late in 1548 Lord Deputy Bellingham exhorted Archbishop Dowdall to be circumspect in his actions and his words.[214] He directed him to set forth 'the plain, simple and naked truth'. He sought a consultation with the primate in Dublin for the better setting forth of the truth and the promotion of obedience amongst the king's subjects. What transpired at that consultation cannot be determined. To judge by a letter of Archbishop Browne, dated 6 August 1551, Primate Dowdall simply ignored the crown's injunctions and other religious directives. The Mass, and even the use of holy water and candlemas candles, continued to be employed in the archdiocese of Armagh up to the point at which St Leger returned to Ireland as viceroy in September 1550.[215] Primate Dowdall attended a council meeting chaired by Deputy St Leger to answer charges that he had failed to set forth the king's proceedings and brought them into contempt by his actions. The primate, according to Browne, openly defended the Mass and 'other things contrary (to) the king's proceedings; and said that he would not embrace them (i.e. protestant beliefs)'. Despite this public declaration no action was taken against the primate, and the Catholic liturgy and traditional religious practices were maintained unabated in Armagh until after St Leger stepped down from office again on 23 May 1551.

A significant point to observe of Archbishop Browne's letter is the absence of any reference to a conference of bishops supposedly held in Dublin in 1551. R.D. Edwards demonstrated that the account of the conference was one of Robert Ware's many forgeries, as were the accounts of two further conferences involving Primate Dowdall and Protestant protagonists.[216]

Primate Dowdall's relationship with the earl of Tyrone made him useful to the crown as a maintainer of peace with Ulster.[217] Nonetheless, political expediency alone does not account for St Leger's extraordinary toleration of the archbishop's thwarting of the Edwardian reformation in his archdiocese. The deputy held the archbishop in very high esteem, referring to him as 'that good father, sage senator and godly bishop' in a letter to the earl of Tyrone.[218] The deputy himself possessed five formidable books in defense of Catholic doctrine which may have reflected his personal religious disposition.[219] Sir John Alen deposed that the deputy was negatively inclined towards the new religion.[220] At any rate, Primate Dowdall knew well that without St Leger's indulgence it would be impossible to keep the reformation out of Armagh archdiocese indefinitely. Soon after St Leger left office Primate Dowdall left the country.

It is not possible to determine what precisely precipitated Archbishop Dowdall's flight from Ireland but, since he left without his goods and chattels, it would seem that he left in haste.[221] Perhaps he was influenced by the fate of Bishop Gardiner and other bishops in England who opposed the abolition of the Mass. They were arrested and imprisoned. Perhaps he had some warning of what lay in store for himself. At any rate, Archbishop Dowdall wrote to Lord Chancellor Cusack, his cousin, declaring that 'he would never be bishop where the holy Mass (as he called it) was abolished'.[222] The primate had certainly left the country some time before 20 July 1551 when the crown presented Mgr Rory Mc Gillamura to the prebend of Dunbin, a benefice in the gift of the archbishop of Armagh.[223] On 28 July 1551 Deputy Croft wrote to the English privy council seeking instructions as to the filling of the vacancy at Armagh. In the absence of an archbishop the administration of the archdiocese would have devolved upon Dnus Terence O'Donnelly, dean of Armagh, and a subcustos from the southern rural deaneries. These men would have been simple caretakers, without the authority to promote a far-reaching reformation.

Primate Dowdall was difficult to replace because of his role in stabilising the Pale – Ulster borderland. The crown informed Deputy Croft that an Englishman would be appointed to Armagh and directed him to order the dean and chapter of Armagh 'to see God served and his holy word preached for the meantime'. Given the divided nature of the archdiocese, and the fact that the chapter, based as it was in the rural deaneries *inter Hibernicos*, was far removed from the English reformations, this order was unlikely to do much to advance protestantism in the archdiocese.

Eventually, on 28 October 1552 Mgr Hugh Goodacre was appointed to be archbishop of Armagh.[224] Mgr Goodacre was in Dublin towards the end of January 1553, and was consecrated archbishop there on 25 March.[225] He remained in Dublin until he died, some time after Easter – of poison procured by certain priests from the archdiocese of Armagh, according to Bishop Bale – never having seen the archbishopric.[226] Goodacre was not replaced as Edward VI died on 6 July 1553.

The failure of the Edwardian reformation in the archdiocese of Armagh was complete. A strong episcopal leader, backed by a conservative priesthood and people, had managed to block religious change. However, Archbishop Dowdall was fortunate in having such a good relationship with Deputy St Leger. Once St Leger was recalled the primate recognised that he could not hope to stave off the crown's reformation indefinitely. Yet Primate Dowdall was fortunate again in that the young king died prematurely and the reformation ended before protestantism could make inroads in his archdiocese during his absence.

CONCLUSIONS

Irish reformation historians have long recognised that conformity to the early Tudor reformations was general among the secular clergy and the laity of the Pale. This chapter has sought to define the impact of the early reformations upon the secular clergy of Armagh archdiocese. It has been established that, despite the enormous implications for the secular clergy in theory, the impact of the early Tudor reformations on the diocesan church in Armagh was greatly moderated in practice. The English crown's power to exact taxes from the secular clergy was enhanced in that the twentieth tax was a statutory obligation upon the beneficed clergy in place of the voluntary clerical subsidies of the later middle ages. On the other hand, the subsidies had actually been a compulsory imposition and the rate at which they had been levied was about the same as the twentieth tax. The unbeneficed majority of the parish clergy never paid the subsidy or the twentieth tax. Only the exaction of first fruits from benefice holders was a novel imposition which would have involved real hardship for incoming beneficed clergymen.

The dissolution of the monasteries and the act for presenting to benefices gave the crown enormous power over the appointment of parish priests in theory. However, the longevity of the pre-reformation benefice holders created little scope for the crown to exercise its new rights to patronage to parochial livings in Armagh *inter Anglicos*, while the poverty of the great majority of the benefices and the absolutely dismal stipends enjoyed by the unbeneficed curates made it extremely difficult for the crown to promote priests to Armagh's parishes who were graduates or men who might favour a reformation. The one English-born priest who seems to have served a parish in County Louth for any period of time during the early Tudor reformations held (significantly) the single most valuable parochial benefice in the archdiocese; the rectory of the rural parish of Clonmore (worth no less than £22 13*s.* 4*d.*). The success of Irish priests in securing benefices from the crown during the 1540s (they secured half of the six presentations, when there were only twenty four benefices in the county) suggests that there may have been increasing difficulty in securing Old English priests for promotion within the archdiocese. This coincides with a collapse in the numbers of men offering themselves for ordination across England, probably as a result of the increased uncertainty facing the priesthood in a time of reformation. In any event, it is clear that the crown's power to re-constitute the parish clergy in Armagh archdiocese was greatly curtailed by the lack of choice of priests available for promotion to parishes.

Because no records have survived from the ecclesiastical commissions established to hear appeals and issue faculties during the early Tudor reformations it is not possible to determine if these commissions affected the church courts of Armagh to any significant degree. It is conceivable that a more accessible, and hence cheaper, court of appeal in Ireland might have weakened the authority of the metropolitan court of Armagh, but there is no evidence at all with which to make even an informed guess of its impact. One can only observe that on one occasion its claim to be the ultimate court of appeal was recognised by Archbishop Cromer in order to secure his rights to procurations in the diocese of Meath. That the court of faculties conducted some business in Armagh is suggested by two legatine dispensations secured in 1555 to validate marriages contracted 'during the period of schism', despite the impediment of affinity (for which it is likely that a crown faculty had been secured).[227] However, it has also been shown that some members of the gentry preferred to secure dispensations from a non-schismatic bishop.

One may conclude, therefore, that those elements of the early Tudor reformations which had the sanction of parliamentary statute had a real impact on the diocesan church in Armagh *inter Anglicos*. Yet the impact of the legislation was moderated by difficulties in implementing it as thoroughly and effectively as in much of England.

While the reformation statutes were implemented to some degree, the doctrinal and liturgical aspects of the early Tudor reformations, which were mainly advanced through injunctions, proclamations and articles rather than parliamentary statutes, were effectively blocked by the secular clergy. During the 1530s, under Cromwell's aegis, there was a mounting campaign launched in England against pilgrimages, purgatory, the cult of saints and the whole framework of intercession for the dead which was so central a part of late medieval catholicism.[228] Ireland escaped much of these religious directives because of the Kildare rebellion and the clerical obstruction of the ecclesiastical bills in the reformation parliament. Of Cromwell's second series of injunctions, only the decree against 'feigned images' can be shown to have been enforced in the archdiocese of Armagh to any degree at all. Significantly, this isolated example of enforcement was carried out by the viceroy, not the church authorities.[229] English evidence shows that 'the intensity and scope of the Henrician assault on popular religion would vary greatly from region to region, from diocese to diocese ...'. Conservative bishops implemented the crown's religious directives in a resolutely minimalist manner.[230] Given the strength of Primate Cromer's religious conservatism, most evident in his participation in the Kildare rebellion, it is probable that he would have enforced the

Henrician decrees on religion as little as possible. Primate Cromer's estimate of the efficacy of pilgrimages is illustrated by a certificate he issued to a layman in 1541, confirming his absolution for the manslaughter of his son, on fulfilment of a penance involving a visit to a series of pilgrimage places across Ireland.[231] Primate Dowdall not only disagreed with the crown's assault on the cult of saints, he actually elevated the cult of St Richard of Dundalk to a higher status than it had enjoyed before the Henrician reformation.

The leadership of Primate Cromer and then Primate Dowdall was critically important in the preservation of Catholic beliefs, liturgical practices and traditional devotions in the archdiocese. They promoted Catholic reform within the archdiocese and did nothing to promote a reformation. Their synods, visitations and consistory court continued to operate with an agenda which owed nothing to the crown's reformation programmes. They effectively shielded the archdiocese from the assaults on traditional religion under Henry VIII, and the imposition of protestantism under Edward VI, with the willing agreement of the lesser clergy. None of the parish priests in Armagh can be shown to have had any leanings towards protestantism.

The success of the secular clergy in thwarting the early Tudor reformations was made possible by the support they must have enjoyed from the gentry and urban oligarchs. This assertion is based on the fact that the Old English elites have been shown to have enjoyed considerable authority over the parish clergy, and had they desired a Protestant reformation they had the power, as a social elite and also by right of their statutory obligations, to ensure that the crown's religious decrees were implemented in full.[232] Unlike England, where Cromwell was inundated with complaints against priests and laymen who transgressed the crown's religious decrees, no informant sent information from County Louth.

The lack of information on the religious situation in County Louth which reached the English crown or its administration in Dublin makes it impossible to define the response of the county's Old English elite towards the early reformations with any precision. It has been shown that a number of the elite availed of the opportunity presented by the dissolution of the religious orders to secure leases of former monastic properties. On the other hand, only one member of the gentry, Sir Patrick Gernon, played a prominent part in the Kildare rebellion and may be assumed to have had a strong attachment to the Catholic faith. One must conclude that outward conformity rather than resistance characterised the gentry response to the early Tudor reformations after the failure of the Kildare rebellion.

Nonetheless, there are sufficient references among the state papers referring to the religious disposition of the Pale community as a whole, and to the Old English elites in particular, to suggest that the gentry involved in law enforcement in County Louth would have shown little zeal in ensuring that the clergy implemented the crown's religious programmes, as against the juridical and non-liturgical aspects of the early Tudor reformations.[233] Indeed, the very fact that Primate Dowdall could block the entire Edwardian reformation up to the summer of 1551 suggests that he acted with the connivance of the secular authorities within the archdiocese.

Across the lordship of Ireland the strength of the opposition of the secular clergy and the local lay elites seems to have sufficed to persuade successive viceroys not to insist on the full implementation of the religious aspects of the early Tudor reformations. Grey and St Leger clearly regarded the political costs of imposing a thorough reformation against the strong wishes of the ecclesiastical and secular leadership as being too great. The Kildare rebellion may have been decisive as a lesson to the chief governors in Tudor Ireland of the risks involved in enforcing a reformation for which there was virtually no local support.

The progress of the early Tudor reformations in England was very different indeed to that in the archdiocese of Armagh, and to its progress in Dublin and across the English lordship. In England manifestly unpopular and unwanted reformations were imposed successfully.[234] Popular support for traditional religion may not have collapsed as dramatically in Edward's reign as Robert Whiting claimed, but the physical manifestations of the old religion had been erased to a remarkable degree across most of England by the time of Edward's death in 1553.[235] In England historians are struggling to account for the general compliance of a Catholic population to the reformation decrees of the Tudor regime. Rex has suggested that 'the habit of obedience to the powers that be was already deeply ingrained in English hearts and minds, and that was what allowed Henry's changes to take effect'. Indeed, 'obedience was the central theme of the ... entire Henrician reformation'.[236] Not surprisingly, then, in Tudor Lancashire, a region 'with an in-built resistance to authority', the early Tudor reformations made much less impact in the face of strong Catholic piety and an inherent conservatism than elsewhere in England. Yet even in Lancashire the Edwardian reformation was enforced through special commissions and the Catholic religion had been 'damaged' by the reformation campaigns.[237] In Armagh archdiocese, by contrast, the diocesan church was much less changed by the reformations. The parishes were still staffed by Catholic priests, many of whom had continued to serve from pre-reformation days. The Mass, holy water, candles were all in use as late as August 1551 and, without the advent of a Protestant prelate, they may well have remained in place in most of the parishes before the Marian restoration. The chantries remained in place.[238] The diocesan church in the archdiocese of Armagh seems, in other words, to have come through the early Tudor reformations relatively unscathed – at least on the surface. What our sources do not make clear, and in this regard the lack of wills is a tremendous handicap, is how attitudes had been altered by the religious turmoil of the decades prior to Edward vi's death. The dissolution of the religious communities in County Louth was most conspicuous in the towns, but its effects were felt throughout the county. The old religious certitudes must have seemed less certain.

James Murray has shown that even with a reforming bishop in place the Henrician reformation failed to make an 'impact' on the archdiocese of Dublin, that the clerical elite in the diocese defeated the reformation bishop who had been imposed upon them, and that the imposition of the Edwardian reformation in the capital was 'particularly slack'.[239] Colm Lennon found that the early Tudor reformations achieved 'fairly slight penetration' in Dublin and that, as late as 1553, protestantism had gained little currency beyond 'a small official group and its supporters in the city'.[240] The early Tudor reformation campaigns in the cities of the south and west have been characterised as 'haphazard' and 'spasmodic' by Professor Bradshaw, unsupported by evangelisation or even explanation and consequently proved ineffective.[241] Even in Kilkenny, where Steven Ellis discerned some hope of a reformation breakthrough, the citizens remained attached to catholicism and the fiery Protestant Bishop Bale left the city, never to return, after a ministry which only lasted five months.[242]

All in all, one may conclude that while the English crown was able to secure the acquiescence of the Old English elites and the church authorities over much of the lordship to the royal supremacy and the dissolution of the religious orders in Ireland, the impact of the early Tudor reformations on religious belief and religious practices in Ireland was limited. The advances made by Protestantism were virtually insignificant, even in the seat of English government in Ireland at Dublin, and seem likely to have been altogether insignificant in the archdiocese of Armagh which had strong conservative episcopal leadership, and no Protestant preachers in the pulpits.

8

The Marian Restoration and Its Aftermath

The Marian restoration has been seen as a watershed in the history of the Tudor reformations. It was suggested that Mary's reign allowed the Old English communities to take stock of their religious position, and to make a definite choice in favour of Catholicism.[1] The counter-reformation then became firmly established in Ireland and, by the 1570s, the people of Ireland were firmly fixed in recusancy. This chapter attempts to define the effects of the Marian restoration upon the church and clergy in the archdiocese of Armagh, and to investigate whether there is evidence to show that the counter-reformation had become established within the archdiocese by the time of Queen Mary's death.

The proclamation of Mary Tudor as queen of Ireland was celebrated enthusiastically in Dublin and Kilkenny, and doubtless in County Louth as well.[2] If the Catholic liturgy had not been completely in place already, then Mary's proclamation of early September declaring toleration of the Mass would have cleared the way for a complete restoration of catholicism in the parish churches.[3] Mary was anxious to purge her dominions of Protestantism as quickly as possible and in Ireland there were no political considerations to impede progress. Since the Edwardian reformation had been imposed by virtue of the royal supremacy only Mary used the same authority to undo it. On appointing Anthony St Leger as deputy in Ireland for a third occasion the queen directed him, together with the council of Ireland, to restore the old religion as far as possible.[4] Even before St Leger arrived back in Ireland Mary began to re-constitute the Irish episcopate. There were three episcopal appointments made in October 1553, of which the most important was the re-institution of Mgr George Dowdall as archbishop of Armagh.[5] The title of primate of all-Ireland, which had been granted to Archbishop Browne of Dublin after Archbishop Dowdall fled in 1551, was restored to the archbishop of Armagh on 12 March 1554.[6]

During his time of exile Primate Dowdall stayed in the monastery at Cento, north of Bologna in the Papal States.[7] It is clear that Archbishop Dowdall returned to Ireland with a strong sense of mission. He was to work closely with two counter-reformation stalwarts: Dr William Walsh, OCist, and Mgr Thomas Leverous. Dr Walsh had been one of Cardinal Pole's chaplains, while Mgr Leverous had also been part of Cardinal Pole's household at Rome.[8] Given the close co-operation between these three men, and Cardinal Pole's reliance on all three, one might suggest that during his period in the Papal States Primate Dowdall had gone to Pole to be reconciled. Not only did he win the cardinal's approbation but Archbishop Dowdall also enjoyed the confidence of the queen, demonstrated not only by his restoration to Armagh but also by her gift to him of his old priory at Ardee, worth no less than £53 7s. 4d. per annum, to hold for his lifetime without paying rent.[9]

Archbishop Dowdall's first recorded action following his restoration was the convening of one of the most important provincial synods in the history of the church in Ireland, in St Peter's church, Drogheda.[10] Eighteen statutes were enacted to restore and revitalise the Catholic religion throughout the ecclesiastical province of Armagh. The archdiocese of Armagh itself may have escaped the worse effects of the early Tudor reformations, but in the suffragan diocese of Meath Bishop Staples had endeavoured to enforce the various aspects of the religious programmes of the English crown, and his work had now to be undone.

The provincial synod ordered that the clergy and the laity restore all of the ancient rites, religious practices, feasts, customs, sacraments and sacrifices to which they had been accustomed (Art. 7). Provision was made for the reconciliation of those clergymen who had, under compulsion, celebrated the Mass or administered the sacraments according to heretical rights, or given it approval in their sermons (Art. 6). Clergymen who had presumed to marry during the period of schism were to be deprived of their office and would be prohibited from exercising a cure of souls or administering the sacraments without a dispensation (Art. 1). The work initiated by Primate Dowdall in enforcing this article in the ecclesiastical province of Armagh was strengthened and extended by a royal commission of April 1554 to remove all married clergymen in Ireland from office.[11] Archbishop Dowdall and Dr Walsh, together with Dean O'Donnelly of Armagh, Archdeacon Luttrell of Meath (formerly official principal of Armagh), Bishop Walsh of Waterford & Lismore, Bishop Devereux of Ferns and a Meath rector, Bartholemew FitzSimons, were the members of the commission. Several Henrician and Edwardian bishops were deprived of office as a result, together with a few lesser clergymen.[12] Deposing married clergymen was a special pre-occupation of Mary but also an effective, though extremely crude, means of weeding out priests who had 'sown heresies and schisms away from the true Catholic faith'.[13] Nonetheless, priests who were prepared to put their wives away and do penance for their sin were generally allowed to seek benefices elsewhere.[14] It cannot be shown that there were any priests in the archdiocese of Armagh who had been married in *facie ecclesia* during the early Tudor reformations. Given the lack of documentation for the 1550s in the archdiocese that cannot be taken as proof that no priest had married, but it seems unlikely that any Armagh priests would have been married in the face of the primate's conservative commitment.

The appointment of metropolitan and diocesan inquisitors was authorised to identify and to prosecute persons expressing heretical opinions. Parish priests were ordered to identify any such persons known to them or face suspension from office (Art. 8). Heretical books were to be burned (Art. 18). Unfortunately, there is a complete absence of any court acta for the period of the Marian restoration and it is not possible to determine what effects, if any, these articles had in the archdiocese of Armagh. One suspects, though there is no evidence to confirm the suspicion, that these articles against heresy may have had a greater impact in the diocese of Meath where Bishop Staples had promoted Protestantism, than in Armagh where Archbishops Cromer and Dowdall had opposed doctrinal innovation.

A number of decrees were of a traditional character; re-imposing standards of clerical dress (Art. 10), reiterating the long-standing obligations of the laity concerning the repair of their parish churches (Art. 11), a decree against simony (Art. 4), another against dividing the fruits of benefices between two men (Art. 3), against persons securing papal provisions through deceit (Art. 5). It was decreed that parish clergy who did not know how to preach were to commission a preacher to deliver their quarterly sermon (Art. 17). That was not a new requirement, but it was probably given a greater emphasis at a time of theological debate. It was certain to present the non-preaching parish clergy with some difficulties since they could no longer rely on the expert preaching of the friars to meet this obligation. It is conceivable nonetheless that mendicant friars from Ulster could have helped to alleviate the dearth of preaching in Armagh *inter Anglicos*. The prosperous parishes of County Louth had predominantly Irish populations and were likely to offer the friars a good financial incentive for their ministry after their years of absence. The return of the Carmelite friars to Ardee would have ensured that that town and its neighbouring parishes were well served with preachers in Mary's reign. The decree enjoining moderation in the exaction of burial fees from widows and orphans (Art. 12) was not new but, when combined with the novel decree against exacting fees for the administration of the sacraments, especially extreme unction (Art. 9), it seems clear that Archbishop Dowdall was making a great effort to defuse one of the most obvious sources of tension between the Catholic laity and their priests. Archbishop Dowdall had yet to turn his attention to the question of clerical training: but he had decided to end the system whereby students for the priesthood were sometimes supported by the fruits of benefices (Art. 2). It is, perhaps, surprising that Primate Dowdall did not make a more positive proposal for the provision of priestly formation, yet the Council of Trent did not require the establishment of diocesan seminaries until after Primate Dowdall and Queen Mary had died. Within the archdiocese of Armagh the work of restoration was quickly carried out. By the time that Primate Dowdall presided over his first annual synod of the clergy of Armagh *inter Anglicos* since his restoration, on 3 July 1554, the traditional pattern of things had been well restored.[15] Primate Dowdall celebrated Mass dressed in full pontificals and there was the customary procession to the town cross and back (customs which had been prohibited by Edward's government). The primate had Mgr Thomas Leverous deliver the sermon to inspire the assembled priests. In the afternoon session Primate Dowdall called upon and exhorted the priests in the synod to strive to reform of themselves and their parishioners. Similar exhortations were made at other synods of the remaining years of Primate Dowdall's episcopate.[16]

Though the calls for reform may have been made more earnestly than ever, the statutes endorsed by the synods were wholly traditional. The 1554 synod decreed that priests who exercised a cure of souls without having been admitted by the ordinary were to be suspended, priests who failed to pay their procurations were to be suspended and finally, any parish whose church's chancel was ill-maintained was to have its revenues sequestrated and its priest suspended. The same statutes were reiterated in the synod of 1556.[17] The synod of 1556 also re-enacted existing legislation about the obligation on parish priests to register wills with the church court officers within a month of a parishioner's decease, or face suspension. It seems clear that, after the initial urgency on his return, Primate Dowdall could feel satisfied that the work of restoration was well advanced and the problems were generally those which had been features of the late medieval period. The difficulties with defective chancels, admissions to parish cures and the payment of procurations did not constitute a moral or religious problem, but a financial one.

The persistence of the difficulties with procurations and admissions to cures (which had to be registered by a notary for a fee[18]) suggest that the parish clergy were finding it increasingly hard to cope with rising prices and (since Primate Dowdall's provincial synod of 1553) the fact that they could no longer earn fees from the administration of the sacraments. The complaints about the condition of the chancels of the churches is likely to reflect the beginnings of a new threat to the good order of the church – the failure of lay impropriators to maintain their portion of parish churches. This suggestion is based on the fact that there were very few parochial rectors in Armagh *inter Anglicos* with responsibility for maintaining the chancel; the great majority of churches had been impropriated to religious houses and thus the duty of maintaining the chancels devolved upon the beneficiaries of the dissolution of the religious houses in 1539–41. Primate Dowdall's provincial statutes of 1553 suggest that during the course of the early Tudor reformations there was also a growing problem with parishioners failing to maintain the nave of their local churches.[19] By the 1560s the churches of the Pale were said to be 'universally in ruin'.[20]

Despite the absence of visitation or court records from Armagh for Mary's reign it seems clear from the synodal records that the Catholic restoration in the archdiocese of Armagh was quickly effected. Protestantism, clerical negligence or immorality presented no problem in the primate's eyes. This impression of good order and stability seems to be confirmed by the business of Primate Dowdall's provincial synod of 1556 which did no more than to confirm a number of feast days as holy days of obligation, though agricultural labourers were not forbidden to work on those days.

When Sir Thomas Radcliffe, lord Fitzwalter, was appointed as viceroy he was instructed on 17 April 1556 to advance the Catholic religion and to help the bishops to root out heresy. He was also to prepare for a parliament which would underpin the work of Catholic restoration in Ireland. Furthermore, he was told to afford every facility to the legatine commission through which Cardinal Pole intended to conduct a visitation of the Irish church. [21] The parliament was convened on 1 June 1557 and formally endorsed the Marian restoration in Ireland. However, the legatine visitation was not conducted before Cardinal Pole was stripped of his legatine authority in April 1557.

It is not possible to say what difference a legatine commission might have made in Ireland. Cardinal Pole believed that in the short term Catholicism could best be promoted through the revival of traditional practices of worship conducted with order and ceremonial.[22] Preaching he distrusted as a two-edged sword.[23] To restore the beauty of holiness in Catholic rituals priests had to recover any vestments or ornaments that had been confiscated during the Edwardian period. To that end commissions were established in Ireland on 3 December 1557, as they had already been in England, to enquire as to the location of all chalices and ornaments, bells, houses and lands belonging to parish churches and chapels, with the aim of restoring any items which had been confiscated by the crown to the use of the church. The commission for County Louth included the primate, the dean of Armagh, Vicar Hamlin, Lord Louth and the mayor of Drogheda.[24] The Irish commissions were issued later than the English ones, possibly because the losses sustained in Edward's reign were less than in England. However, the inclusion of Vicar Hamlin on the County Louth commission suggests that the commissions were simply delayed. Dnus Walter Caddell had been vicar of St Peter's, at least from August 1556.[25] Perhaps the commissioners were chosen before then.

It is not possible to determine whether the commission made any difference to the clergy of Armagh *inter Anglicos*, though it is unlikely that many church endowments had been lost between the time of Primate Dowdall's flight into exile and the death of Edward VI about two years later.[26] Even the chantries had survived destruction.[27] There certainly seems to have been no need for the 'herculean efforts' required in England to reconstruct the ritual and sacramental framework of traditional religion.[28]

For the longer term Cardinal Pole hoped to have the church re-endowed with some, at least, of its former possessions and to use those assets for a planned assault on clerical poverty.[29] He recognised that impoverished benefices were unlikely to appeal to well educated pastors, while poor pastors were unlikely to enjoy the respect they were entitled to. He wanted to establish diocesan seminaries to educate and train an exemplary priesthood.[30]

Primate Dowdall would have approved of the thrust of Cardinal Pole's plans. Clerical poverty was a far greater problem in Ireland than in England, or even Wales. The financial difficulties of the clergy in Ireland were to be eased somewhat by an act of the Irish parliament in 1557 by which the crown surrendered its right to claim payment of first fruits and twentieths, though the latter may have been replaced by the traditional subsidy which was about as burdensome as the twentieth tax.

The financial stability of the archdiocese itself engaged the primate's attention considerably in those years. Soon after his return to Ireland he was granted the revenues of his former hospital at Ardee to supplement his income and help to make good the losses he incurred towards the close of Edward's reign.[31] On 16 December 1555, after a certain amount of disputation, Primate Dowdall succeeded in securing an indenture from Conn O'Neill, earl of Tyrone and O'Neill, to restore to the primate extensive landholdings in the manor of Armagh which the earl had seized while Dowdall himself was archbishop.[32] By 11 March 1557 Primate Dowdall succeeded, not only in recovering the archiepiscopal mansion in Drogheda which had been leased by Primate Octavian, but also in recovering the orchard attached to it.[33] Primate Dowdall's efforts were given a setback later in 1557 when English soldiers under Deputy Sussex devastated an extensive part of the archiepiscopal manor of Armagh and set fire to the primatial city.[34] Primate Dowdall sued the privy council for redress for the damages and losses inflicted upon him by Sussex and his troops, though there is no indication that his suit was successful. While at court in 1558, to discuss with the queen 'the causes of weight touching our service',[35] Archbishop Dowdall had a new copy made of a charter of the temporal rights of the archbishops of Armagh granted by Edward IV.[36] Presumably he was hoping to secure an act of resumption to recover the extensive properties which had been alienated since then by primates who had struggled to pay their first fruits.

Cardinal Pole's legatine synod in London in 1555–6 provided for the foundation of diocesan seminaries for the education of future generations of priests.[37] Primate Dowdall recognised the value of raising educational standards in Ireland. In his articles to the English privy council in May 1558 he declared that 'It shall be very expedient for that whole realm to erect a university in it with some free schools, in such places as shall be thought meet, whereby learning shall increase and, by learning (the people there) be brought to know their duty to God first and next to their prince and so then brought to obey the prince's laws'.[38] However, the idea was not adopted. The queen was unable to relinquish more than a fraction of the church's former wealth, and most of what she did return to the church in Ireland was concentrated on two major restoration projects: the re-endowment of St Patrick's cathedral, Dublin, and the Hospital of Kilmainham.

In August 1558, while visiting the queen, Primate Dowdall secured her consent to restore the former hospital at Ardee 'for the better relief of poor and sick people', of which he had been prior and whose revenues he had been granted for life in 1553. The queen directed the deputy to fund the erection of a new friary for the Carmelite community at Ardee. Primate Dowdall also persuaded the queen to sell him the lands of the former convent in Termonfeckin (worth 4 marks), and a farm there which had belonged to St Mary's abbey, Dublin (worth 5 marks 4s. 6d.) for the erection of a college.[39] However, this foundation reveals Archbishop Dowdall to have been a man of the later middle ages rather than the counter-reformation: the college was to be a chantry staffed by a number of priests 'for the maintaining of God's divine service'. He failed to see an opportunity to establish a diocesan school or seminary. In any event, the college was never founded. Archbishop George Dowdall died in London on 15 August 1558, possibly of the same influenza as was shortly afterwards to end the lives of Cardinal Pole and Queen Mary herself.[40]

For all of his zeal, and the courage he demonstrated in defending the Catholic faith in the archdiocese of Armagh, it cannot be said that Primate Dowdall was a counter-reformation figure. Rather he was one of the finest figures of the late medieval Irish church. He grasped the opportunity provided by Mary Tudor's accession to set about the full restoration of catholicism in his archdiocese, in his metropolitan province and across Ireland generally. Primate Dowdall did not anticipate the counter-reformation in Ireland. Nonetheless, through his work to defend the Catholic faith through the early Tudor reformations he laid foundations which helped to ensure that the counter-reformation would find receptive congregations during Elizabeth's reformation.

EPILOGUE

By the time of Primate Dowdall's death late in 1558, the Catholic restoration was all but complete. However, the weaknesses of the pre-reformation church remained to be

addressed: the impoverished condition of the clergy and their limited pastoral formation. Had Mary Tudor lived longer the diocesan church in the archdiocese of Armagh
would have been strengthened by the return of the impropriated tithes to the parishes,
and the extension to Ireland of the kind of reforms promoted by Cardinal Pole as papal
legate.[41] Her early death, on the other hand, left the church in Armagh with structural
weaknesses which helped to undermine the church establishment during the Elizabethan reformation.

The Elizabethan religious settlement was endorsed by the Irish parliament of 1560
in a remarkably short period of time.[42] It has been pointed out elsewhere, that 'the
differences between medieval catholicism as it was understood in Ireland in 1560, and
what the parliamentarians understood themselves to be authorising for the future, was
not at all as great as the chasm which later divided Tridentine catholicism from Calvin-
ist anglicanism'.[43] Furthermore, after the Elizabethan settlement had been endorsed
by the English parliament the Old English elites in Ireland, given their dependency on
the English crown, had no real choice but to endorse it too, especially in view of the
challenge presented by Shane O'Neill. Nonetheless, the endorsement of the religious
settlement in parliament indicates that, despite its lack of positive appeal to that date,
the failure of protestantism to become the religion of at least a substantial portion of
the people of Ireland was not inevitable after Mary's reign.

The Elizabethan settlement was intended to transform the Catholic church in Ireland into a Protestant Church of Ireland. However, the church in the archdiocese of
Armagh had depended upon the support of the laity to function as well as it did before
the Tudor reformations. The laity had financed the church building programmes of
the late middle ages, maintained the naves of the parish churches and, most importantly, they had financed the pastoral ministry of the parochial clergy not only through
the obligatory payment of tithes but also through the various fees paid to priests for the
administration of some of the sacraments, in addition to bequests made in wills. The
decay of the parish churches, and the fall in clerical incomes which can be discerned by
the 1560s, probably reflected a collapse in the laity's support of the church during the
Elizabethan reformation.

Before the reformations the church authorities in Armagh had been able to ensure
that church buildings were properly maintained *inter Anglicos* – except where war or
raids caused some parishes in the marchlands to be 'wasted'. The dissolution of the
monasteries in the English lordship undermined this ability. By 1566 Deputy Sidney
could observe of churches throughout the dioceses of Armagh, Meath and Dublin that
the chancels were decayed and 'the churches universally in ruin (and some wholly
down)'.[44] Ten years later the situation had deteriorated further and Sidney informed
the queen that the impropriated churches were entirely neglected, with those in the
queen's possession being 'the most ruined'.[45] Since the crown was the worst offender
in terms of maintaining the churches whose tithes it held impropriate, the Elizabethan
church authorities were hamstrung, not only against the government but also against
the other holders of impropriated tithes. Given the state of the churches, it is clear that
they were even powerless to compel parishioners to maintain the nave of their parish
churches. Hence, while new churches were being built across County Louth during

the later middle ages, churches throughout the Pale were falling into ruin as a consequence of the reformations.

Up to the eve of the Tudor reformations the church courts were employed to compel monastic impropriators to pay at least a 'minimum' stipend to the unbeneficed
curates who served two thirds of the churches across Armagh *inter Anglicos*. Once the
monasteries were dissolved the crown became responsible for paying their stipends.
The failure to create benefices in impropriated parishes which had none, or to incorpo-
rate adequate conditions in leases of rectorial tithes, left many unbeneficed priests with
nothing but the altarages to live on. This had been the case in many parishes in Armagh
inter Anglicos before the reformations. However, by 1566 the incomes received by
unbeneficed priests had become wholly inadequate and there was a lack of curates
available for serving parishes over much of the Pale – by contrast to the large numbers
of priests in pre-reformation times.[46] In Meath, by 1576, the vast majority of the
unbeneficed priests in charge of churches were monoglot Irish speakers with 'very
little Latin, less learning and civility'.[47] Because they had to subsist on altarages alone
they were celebrating the Mass and other Catholic services for a laity who would only
pay fees for traditional ceremonies. Even the beneficed priests were increasingly impoverished, probably by a fall-off in lay financial support as well as by the price inflation which affected the English crown's territories from the mid sixteenth century, and
a great many were unable to pay the twentieth tax.[48] They too must have been tempted
to celebrate the Mass and other Catholic rites, if not from conviction, then from the
pressing need to put bread on the table. Bishop Hugh Brady, for all of his commitment
to the Elizabethan reformation, had no choice but to tolerate such things: the priests
could hardly live otherwise. Bishop Brady could not create a Protestant ministry to
replace the conformist priests in the absence of adequately resourced benefices, the
lack of manses for the ministers to dwell in, or the want of church buildings for services. As Aidan Clarke perceptively observed, 'The resources problem, human and material, were not separable, and not easily soluble, for they proceeded from an inherited
interlocking of the structural fabric of the church with the community which made it
almost impossible for the church to act independently of those who bore it no goodwill'.[49]

The course of the Elizabethan reformation in Armagh has yet to be studied. The
Armagh registers come to a virtual close in 1558, and there are no contemporary surveys of the archdiocese of Armagh in Elizabeth's reign such as those written on the
diocese of Meath. Yet it is clear that the church in Armagh experienced tremendous
difficulties as the Elizabethan reformation was extended to the archdiocese.

The breakdown of the political and religious consensus at the start of Elizabeth's
reign caused the archdiocese of Armagh to become effectively split in two. As early as 7
February 1560 the papacy provided Dnus Donnchadh Ó Taidhg, a priest of Limerick
diocese, to the see of Armagh.[50] Primate Ó Taidhg (1560–62) was recognised by Shane
O'Neill and exercised his ministry *inter Hibernicos* – as seems clear by the fact that he
summoned a diocesan synod of the clergy of Orior and Tullyhogue circa 1561.[51] Primate Richard Creagh (1564–1685) subsequently received recognition from O'Neill and
resided at Armagh city.[52] Presumably he received any of the archdiocesan revenues
inter Hibernicos which O'Neill would leave to him.

The archdiocesan finances crashed in the 1560s. Archbishop Loftus complained that his income from the primatial see was a miserable £20 a year: 'there remains nothing to me but the bare house and four score acres at Termonfeckin'.[53] It may be that the archbishop was being economical with the truth. However, it is likely that he had been forced to alienate much of the archdiocese's residual real estate *inter Anglicos* to pay his first fruits. Furthermore, his right to levy procurations had been abrogated by the supreme governor.[54] Ostensibly this was to benefit the impoverished parish clergy, though the queen and other holders of impropriated tithes ceased to pay procurations also. It has been shown that procurations had provided the archbishops of Armagh with a great portion of their annual revenues. Without a satisfactory income Loftus felt unable to promote the reformation in Armagh; 'neither is it worth anything to me, nor am I able to do any good in it, for that altogether it lies among the Irish'.

The royal visitation of 1622 revealed the staggering extent of the collapse of the established church in the archdiocese of Armagh: most of the churches and manses were ruined, the stipends allowed to the curates of impropriated churches were often as low as 5*s*. or nothing at all, the parish clergy were greatly reduced in number and virtually all were English-born ministers. The remnants of the archiepiscopal estates *inter Anglicos* were worth paltry sums.[55]

This study does not directly address the question of why the reformation failed in Armagh. Nonetheless, by highlighting the good order of the secular clergy, and the depth of popular commitment which the parish churches enjoyed from the laity before the Tudor reformations, it suggests that historians ought to take much greater account of the strength of the pre-reformation church and of catholicism in any examination of the courses of the reformations and counter-reformation in Ireland. This is not to suggest that the Tudor reformations failed because there was a 'fundamental disposition' towards catholicism in sixteenth century Ireland. However, it is difficult to conceive how that Catholic church could have survived, and retained the allegiance of the vast majority of the population, even in the Pale, had it not possessed considerable inherent strengths before and throughout the period of the reformations.

Notes

CITATIONS FROM THE ARMAGH REGISTERS

The folio references to Primate Cromer's register are from the original manuscript in the Public Records Office of Northern Ireland (PRONI, MS DIO 4/2/11). They are accompanied by calendar numbers in brackets. The calendar numbers for Book I of Cromer's register were drawn from John McCafferty, 'The act book of the Armagh diocese, 1518–1522: a text and introduction' (unpublished M.A. thesis, U.C.D., 1991). The calendar references to Book II of Cromer's register were drawn from Laurence P. Murray (with Aubrey Gwynn), 'A calendar of the register of Primate George Cromer' in *Louth Arch. Soc. Jn.*, viii–x (1938–43). The original copy of Dowdall's register has been lost. The page numbers cited here relate to the the seventeenth century transcript in the PRONI. The calendar numbers were drawn from Laurence P. Murray, 'A calendar of the register of Primate George Dowdall' in *Louth Arch. Soc. Jn.*, xii (1929–32).

The calendar numbers for the earlier Armagh registers have been drawn from the following sources:

Sweteman's register	Henry J. Lawlor (ed.), 'A calendar of the register of Archbishop Sweteman, 1368–71' in *R.I.A. Proc.*, c, 29 (1911–12).
Fleming's register	Lawlor (ed.), 'A calendar of the register of Archbishop Fleming' in *R.I.A. Proc.*, c, 30 (1911–12).
Swayne's register	D.A. Chart (ed.), *A calendar of the register of John Swayne, archbishop of Armagh* (Belfast, 1935).
Prene's register	W.G.H. Quigley and E.F.D. Roberts, 'A history of the structure and history of the registers of archbishops Prene and Mey, with a text of Mey and a calendar of Prene' (Ph. D. thesis, Q.U.B., 1955).
Mey's register	Quigley and Roberts (eds), *Registrum Johannis Mey. The register of John Mey, archbishop of Armagh, 1433–1456* (Belfast, 1972).
Octavian's register	Canon Leslie's typescript of William Reeve's calendar of Primate Octavian's register in the Representative Church Body Library, Dublin. See also Anthony Lynch (ed.), 'A calendar of the re-assembled register of John Bole, archbishop of Armagh, 1457–71' in *Seanchas Ard Mhacha*, xv (1992).

NOTES TO CHAPTER 1

1 Henry A. Jefferies, 'The Armagh registers and the re-interpretation of Irish church history on the eve of the reformations' in *Seanchas Ard Mhacha*, xvii (1997).   2 The original manuscripts of Primate Dowdall's register did not reach the PRONI. That register survives only in the form of a transcript dating from the late seventeenth or early eighteenth century, which is preserved in the PRONI.   3 PRONI, MS DIO 4/2/11, Primate Cromer's register; PRONI, MS DIO 4/2/12, Primate Dowdall's register.   4 Richard Bagwell, *Ireland under the Tudors* (London, 1886),

pp 294–300; Robin Dudley Edwards, *Church and state in Tudor Ireland: a history of penal laws against Irish Catholics* (Dublin, 1935), pp xl–xli; John Watt, *The church in medieval Ireland* (Dublin, 1972), pp 183, 187–8, 193–202; Steven Ellis, *Tudor Ireland: crown, community and the conflict of cultures, 1470–1603* (London & New York, 1985) pp 185–92; Patrick Corish, *The Irish Catholic experience: a historical survey* (Dublin, 1985), pp 51– 62.

NOTES TO CHAPTER 2

1 J.P. Mahaffy, 'Two early tours of Ireland' in *Hermathena*, 40 (1914), p. 10.   2 P.J. Duffy, 'Geographical perspectives on the borderlands' in Raymond Gillespie and Harold O'Sullivan (eds), *The borderlands: essays on the history of the Ulster-Leinster border* (Belfast, 1989), pp 8–9, 12–14. The extents of the manors are reflected in the extents of the civil parishes (Jocelyn Otway-Ruthven, *A history of medieval Ireland* [London & New York, 1968], pp 107–8, 119–20; Otway-Ruthven, 'Parochial development in the rural deanery of Skreen' in *Journal of the Royal Society of Antiquaries of Ireland*, xciv [1964], pp 111–22).   3 Otway-Ruthven, *Medieval Ireland* , p. 115.   4 Harold O'Sullivan, 'The march of south east Ulster in the fifteenth and sixteenth centuries: a period of change' in Gillespie and O'Sullivan, *The borderlands*, p. 57; Tomás Ó Fiach, 'The O'Neills of the Fews' in *Seanchas Ard Mhacha*, vii (1977), pp 3–14.   5 O'Sullivan, 'The march of south east Ulster', p. 58–60; Victor Buckley & David Sweetman (eds), *Archaeological survey of County Louth* (Dublin, 1991), pp 302–50.   6 O'Sullivan, 'The march of south east Ulster', pp 57–8.   7 Newport B. White (ed.), *Extents of Irish monastic possessions, 1540–1* (Dublin, 1943), pp 108, 220.   8 Charles Mc Neill and A.J. Otway-Ruthven (eds), *Dowdall deeds* (Dublin, 1960), no. 567.   9 Henry F. Berry (ed.), *Statute rolls of the parliament of Ireland: Edward IV*, i (Dublin, 1914), p. 292.   10 *Monastic extents*, pp 108–10, 213–20. The reference to the growing of corn and oats at different times of the year is another indication of crop rotation (*Monastic extents*, p. 229; K.W. Nicholls, 'Gaelic society and economy in the high middle ages' in Art Cosgrove [ed.], *A New History of Ireland*, ii [Oxford, 1987], p. 411).   11 'Early tours', p. 10; Primate Kite described the Pale in 1514 as 'plenteous in corn, cattle, fish and fowl, but scant of wood' (Kite to Wolsey, 14 May 1514 [P.R.O., S.P. 60/1/ no. 3]).   12 As recently as 1489 Dundalk and its hinterland had been burnt and destroyed by Irish raiders (John O'Donovan [ed.], *Annals of the kingdom of Ireland by the Four Masters*, v [Dublin, 1846], s.a. 1489).   13 *Archaeological survey*, pp 352, 353, 357; Bradley, 'The topography and layout of Drogheda' in *Louth Arch. Soc. Jn*, xix (1978), pp 98–127; Bradley, 'The medieval borough of Ardee' in *Louth Arch. Soc. Jn*, xx (1984), pp 267–96; Bradley, 'The medieval borough of Louth' in *Louth Arch. Soc. Jn*, xxi (1985), pp 8–22; Paul Gosling, 'Dun Delca to Dundalk' in *Louth Arch. Soc. Jn*, xxii (1991), pp 296–312; *Dowdall Deeds*, no. 444.   14 Raymond Gillespie, 'The transformation of the borderlands, 1600–1700' in *The borderlands*, p. 77.   15 Wendy Childs, 'Ireland's trade with England in the later middle ages' in *Irish Economic and Social History*, ix (1982), pp 18–23, 23–4. Dr Childs also revealed that the volume of trade between Ireland and mainland Europe was very small towards the end of the middle ages.   16 *Cromer's register*, I, f. 17 (37).   17 Ibid., f. 52v (69).   18 Edmund Hogan (ed.), *The description of Ireland and the state thereof as it is at this present Anno 1598* (Dublin & London, 1878), pp 4–5 for a comprehensive list of the land owners in County Louth. Cf. O'Sullivan, 'The march of south east Ulster', p. 57.   19 *Octavian's register*, no. 15; *Statute rolls: Edward IV*, i, p. 345; O'Sullivan, 'The march of south east Ulster', p. 58.   20 Gearóid Mac Niocaill, 'Socio-economic problems of the late medieval Irish town' in David Harkness & Mary O'Dowd (eds), *The town in Ireland* (Belfast, 1981), pp 7–21; Anthony Sheehan, 'Irish towns in a period of change, 1558–1625', in Ciaran Brady & Raymond Gillespie (eds), *Natives and newcomers: the makings of Irish colonial society, 1534–1641* (Dublin, 1986), pp 99–105.   21 *Archaeological survey*, pp 342–7, nos. 1127–39. See also John Bradley, 'Ardee', pp 267–96; Gosling, 'Dundalk', pp 287–8. Urban oligarchs were not simply the urban equivalent of the rural gentry but part of a common elite (Rosemary E. Horrox, 'The urban gentry in the fifteenth century', in John A.F. Thompson [ed.], *Towns and townspeople in the fifteenth century* [Gloucester, England & Wolfboro,

New Hampshire, 1988], pp 22–38). Colm Lennon has shown that the 'lords of Dublin' invested heavily in rural estates and inter-married with families in the rural Pale, a pattern which seems to have held true of Drogheda also (Lennon, *The lords of Dublin in the age of reformation* [Dublin, 1989], chapter 3; Lennon, *Sixteenth century Ireland*, pp 32, 35). **22** Steven Ellis, *Reform and revival: English government in Ireland, 1470–1534* (Woodbridge and New York, 1986), pp 106–42, 159–64, 206–12. **23** For example, at Castletown, Clonkeen, Heynestown, Mapastown, Richardstown and Smarmore. **24** *Dowdall's register*, pp 234–6 (119, E). Though the document is undated it was clearly drawn up after Prior Dowdall became primate in 1543. Yet it is most probable that the list was made before 7 April 1544 when Dnus John White, who had been granted admission as curate of Staleban when the visitation list was compiled (*Dowdall's register*, p. 236 [119, E]), was promoted to the vicarage of Dromin (*Dowdall's register*, p. 50 [46]). That the visitation list was compiled afresh at that time seems confirmed by the fact that the rector of Killincoole was excused from the visitation for some unspecified reason. **25** *Cromer's register*, I, f. 78 (100), f. 91 (114); *Dowdall's register*, p. 10 (8). **26** *Archaeological survey*, p. 221, no. 887. **27** *Dowdall's register*, pp 230–3 (119, A, B & C). Castlering was devastated by an Irish assault in 1539 (*Monastic extents*, p. 236). **28** The tithes of Ash were appropriated to the Augustinian priory at Louth and had been leased for £10 per annum, but in 1539–40 the area was so wasted by the Mc Mahons of Farney that they were worthless in 1540 (*Monastic extents*, p. 231). **29** *Cromer's register*, I, f. 15 (35); *Monastic extents*, p. 109. **30** *Archaeological survey*, p. 256, no. 1117. **31** *Monastic extents*, p. 108. **32** *Cromer's register*, I, f. 1 (1); *Monastic extents*, pp. 237–8. **33** *Cromer's register*, II, ff 56–7 (130), ff 56–56v (131); Valor in Hibernia, p. 2. **34** Oliver Davies, 'Old churches in County Louth' in *Louth Arch. Soc. Jn.*, x (1944), p. 291; *Archaeological survey*, no. 964. **35** *Archaeological survey*, nos 884 (Ballybarrick), 887 (Barmeath), 889 (Mansfieldstown), 893 (Cappoge), 894 (Carrick), 897 (Castletown), 902 (Kilclogher), 903 (Clonkeehan), 904 (Clonmore), 910 (Darver), 915 (Dromin), 917 (Drumcar), 918 (Drumshallon), 919 (Dunany), 920 (Dunbin), 921 (Dungooly), 923 (Dysert), 924 (Faughart), 927 (Mayne), 929 (Haggardstown), 949 (Mapastown), 952 (Kildemock), 954 (Monasterboice), 961 (Newtown Cooley), 962 (Much Grange), 963 (Newtown Staleban), 964 (Parsonstown), 965 (Philipstown, Louth), 966 (Philipstown, Ardee), 968 (Port), 975 (Richardstown), 979 (Salterstown), 980 (Shenlis), 981 (Smarmore), 983 (Stickillin), 984 (Templetown), 994 (Tullyallen). **36** Ibid., nos 887, 893, 894, 902, 904, 915, 917, 920, 923, 924, 927, 929, 954, 961, 962, 963, 968, 975, 979, 980, 983, 994 for churches between 5 and 6 metres in width. Nos 897, 937, 952, 964, 984, 999 for additional churches within the range of 4.5 to 6.5 metres in width. No. 981 is narrower than 4 metres, no. 965 is wider than 8 metres. **37** For churches over 14.2 metres cf *Archaeological survey*, nos 884, 893, 897, 910, 917, 918, 919, 920, 927, 961, 984, 994. For churches less than 10 metres cf *Archaeological survey*, nos 887, 949. **38** *Archaeological survey*, nos 902, 904, 915, 923, 924, 929, 952, 968, 983, 984. **39** Ibid., no. 924 (Faughart: chancel 8.8 x 5.8 metres; nave 12.3 x 5.8 metres); no. 983 (Stickillin: chancel 7 x 3.9 metres; nave 15 x 5 metres). **40** As, for instance, were the well-known Plunkett churches in nearby Killeen and Dunsany, County Meath (Harold G. Leask, *Irish churches and monastic buildings*, iii [Dundalk, 1960], pp 12–16, 164–5). **41** Colin Platt, *Medieval England: a social history and archaeology from the conquest to A.D. 1600* (London & New York, 1978), pp 138–44. **42** *Cromer's register*, I, f. 108 (137). **43** *Archaeological survey*, nos. 897, 964, 984. **44** Bradley, 'Louth', p. 19. **45** Davies, 'Old churches in County Louth', pp 200–3. **46** Eamon Duffy, *The stripping of the altars: traditional religion in England, 1400–1580* (New Haven and London, 1992), pp 157–60. **47** *Archaeological survey*, nos 952 (Kildemock), 981 (Smarmore) and 983 (Stickillin). **48** Ibid., no. 927. **49** T.C.D., MS 808 (2), 'Provincial synod of Cashel, 1453', no. 4. **50** *Cromer's register*, I, f. 52v (68), ff 109v–110 (140). **51** Ibid., no. 927. **52** Ibid., nos 952, 984. **53** *Arch-aeological survey*, no. 981. **54** Heather A. King, 'A tiled floor at Greenoge, County Meath' in *Ríocht na Midhe* (1992–3), p. 92. **55** Opinions of Fitzwalter to Queen Mary, November 1556 (P.R.O., S.P. 62/1/22). **56** Tremayne to Burghley, 1571 (P.R.O., S.P. 63/32/40). **57** T.C.D., MS 808 Provincial synod of Cashel, 1453, nos. 3, 69. **58** *Archaeological survey*, no. 979. **59** Helen M. Roe, 'Illustrations of the Holy Trinity in Ireland, thirteenth to the seventeenth centuries' in *J.R.S.A.I.*, 109 (1979), p. 127. **60** For the

Drogheda font, now in St Peter's Church of Ireland church, Drogheda (*Archaeological survey*, no. 958). Another late medieval font, originally from Killineer, is also to be found at St Peter's (*Archaeological survey*, no. 983). Both were discussed in Roe, 'Two decorated fonts in Drogheda, County Louth' in *Louth Arch. Soc. Jn.*, xviii (1976), pp 255–62. See also Mary Cahill, 'A baptismal font at Wyanstown, County Louth' in *Louth Arch. Soc. Jn.*, xx (1983), pp 237–9. Ms Cahill suggests that the font may originally have come from Clonmore or Port. A font from Mansfieldstown is now preserved in the Church of Ireland church in Ardee, c.f. John Bradley, 'Ardee', p. 284.   **61** *Archaeological survey*, nos. 983, 995.   **62** Duffy, *Stripping of the altars*, pp 63–6.   **63** *Archaeological survey*, no. 958; Bradley, 'Drogheda', pp 114–15.   **64** Bradley, 'Drogheda', p. 114.   **65** 'Register of the mayors of Drogheda', s.a. 1548.   **66** *Dowdall's register*, pp 3–4 (3).   **67** 'Register of the mayors of Drogheda', s.a. 1515.   **68** Ibid., s.a. 1525.   **69** Ibid., s.a. 1501; 'Annals of (church of) Blessed Mary of Drogheda', s.a. 1501.   **70** King, 'A possible market cross fragment from Drogheda' in *Louth Arch. Soc. Jn.*, xx (1984), pp 334–9.   **71** Duffy, *Stripping of the altars*, pp 38, 260–1.   **72** Aubrey Gwynn, *The medieval province of Armagh* (Dundalk, 1946), p. 75.   **73** *Mey's register*, no. 313.   **74** T.G.F. Paterson, *Harvest home* (Dundalk, 1973), p. 32.   **75** *Dowdall's register*, pp 3–4 (3).   **76** *Arch-aeological survey*, no. 989; Davies, 'Old churches in County Louth', pp 16–19; Gosling, 'Dundalk', pp 310–11.   **77** Davies, 'Old churches', (1941), p. 19.   **78** G.M., 'Varia', *Louth Arch. Soc. Jn.*, xiii (1956).   **79** Gosling, 'Dundalk', p. 311.   **80** See, for instance, Christopher Dowdall's endowment of an additional chaplain at St Katherine's chapel, in St Nicholas', Dundalk [*Dowdall deeds*, no. 499].   **81** *Archaeological survey*, no. 992; Davies, 'Old churches', (1943), pp 200–3; Bradley, 'Ardee', pp 280–4.   **82** Valor in Hibernia, p. 2.   **83** *Archaeological survey*, no. 993; Bradley, 'The chantry college, Ardee' in *Louth Arch. Soc. Jn.*, xxii (1989), pp 16–18.   **84** King, 'The Ardee cross' in *Louth Arch. Soc. Jn.*, xx (1983), pp 210–14.   **85** Laurence P. Murray, 'The ancient chantries of County Louth' in *Louth Arch. Soc. Jn.*, ix (1939), pp 206–7.   **86** Paul Gosling, *Carlingford: an antiquarian's guide* (Carlingford, 1992), p. 6.   **87** Bradley, 'Louth', p. 17.   **88** *Archaeological survey*, pp 302–50.   **89** Leask, *Irish churches and monasteries*, p. 1; Glanmor Williams, *The Welsh church from the conquest to the reformation* (Cardiff, 1962), pp 266–7; Williams, *Recovery, reorientation and reformation: Wales c. 1415–1642* (Oxford, 1987), pp 120–3; Platt, *Medieval England*, pp 138 - 89; Bernd Moeller, in 'Piety in Germany around 1500' in Steven E. Ozment (ed.), *The reformation in medieval perspective* (Chicago, 1971), p. 53 observed that 'from Alsace and Upper Austria to Holland and the Baltic these (pre-reformation) decades were filled with a general resurgence of church construction'.   **90** The text of the Irish ibid., was published under the title *Valor beneficiorum ecclesiasticorum in Hibernia: or the first fruits of all of the ecclesiastical benefices in the kingdom of Ireland, as taxed in the King's Books* (Dublin, 1741). Steven Ellis highlighted the importance of this text in 'Economic problems of the church' in *J.E.H.*, 41 (1990).   **91** *Dowdall's register*, pp 193–208 (110).   **92** The Waterford valuations recorded by Walter Cowley and J. White were dated 25 February 1538, while the valuations recorded by the same commissioners for Cashel were dated 28 February 1538 (Valor in Hibernia, pp 17, 14). An interval of three days would clearly have been inadequate for a fresh survey of the fifty seven benefices valued in the archdiocese of Cashel. Clearly, the crown commissioners made use of a pre-existent schedule of the values of the benefices in Cashel, and in other dioceses (Jefferies, 'Diocesan synods and convocations in Armagh on the eve of the tudor reformations' in *Seanchas Ard Mhacha*, xvi [1995], pp 127–30).   **93** Valor in Hibernia, p. 2.   **94** TCD, MS 567, Valor in Hibernia, f. 5; PRONI, MS 4/4/2, 'The royal visitation book for the province of Ulster', pp 38–48.   **95** *Dowdall's register*, p. 243 (123 G, H, K).   **96** Ibid., p. 2 (2), p. 7 (6).   **97** *Monastic extents*, p. 239; *Dowdall's register*, p. 56 (51).   **98** This seems clear from the fact that the 1538 and 1544 valuations for the vicarage, viz. £9 7s., were identical.   **99** *Monastic extents*, pp 108–9, 214–7, 220, 229–31, 235–8, 241.   **100** Ibid., pp 212–3.   **101** Ibid., p. 229.   **102** Ibid., pp 108–10.   **103** Ibid., pp 214–20.   **104** Ibid., p. 17.   **105** *Fleming's register*, no. 225; *Swayne's register*, nos. 318, 335, 490; *Prene's register*, no. 183; *Monastic extents*, pp 108–10, p. 213, 215, 216, 219, 225, 232, 235, 238; National Archives of Ireland, Chancery Pleadings, Bundle E, no. 290; James Murray, 'The sources of clerical incomes' in *Archivium Hibernicum*, xlv (1990), p. 140.   **106** *Monastic extents*, p. 213.   **107** NAI, Chancery Pleadings, Bundle A, no.

97; *Swayne's register*, nos. 318, 335, 490; *Prene's register*, no. 183; *Monastic extents*, pp 109, 225.   **108** Murray, 'Clerical incomes', p. 142.   **109** *Monastic extents*, pp 108–10, 213–5, 225–6, 231–2.   **110** Ibid., pp 108–10, 214–20.   **111** *Cromer's register*, I, f. loose sheet (2).   **112** Ibid., II, f. 11v (26). The fish tithes of Carlingford, though valued at £6 in 1540, were leased for only £2 (*Monastic extents*, p. 122). The tithes of Drumcar were leased by St Mary's abbey, Dublin, for £9 6s. 8d., but were subleased by the farmer for £20 (*Monastic extents*, p. 17). Needless to say, the subleasee expected to make a profit on this transaction.   **113** *Monastic extents*, pp 108–10, 214–5.   **114** Ibid., pp 112, 232.   **115** Henry J. Lawlor, 'A calendar of the Liber Ruber of the diocese of Ossory' in *RIA Proc.*, c, 27 (1908–9), p. 165.   **116** Murray, 'Clerical incomes', p. 146.   **117** *Monastic extents*, pp 108–10, 232.   **118** Ibid., p. 225; Murray, 'Clerical incomes', p. 150, for tithes on the produce of gardens in Dublin.   **119** *Cromer's register*, I, ff 96–96v (121).   **120** *Monastic extents*, p. 231.   **121** Ibid., p. 110.   **122** Archbishop Swayne once commissioned the curate of Kilclogher to collect the fish-tithes at Carlingford for him (*Swayne's register*, no. 6).   **123** Murray, 'Clerical incomes', p. 153.   **124** John D'Alton, *A history of Drogheda*, i (Drogheda, 1844), pp 16–7.   **125** *Swayne's register*, nos. 114, 373.   **126** Ibid., no. 250, p. 12.   **127** T.C.D., MS 808, (5), 'Statutes of the provincial synod of Cashel, 1453', no. 34.   **128** Murray, 'Clerical incomes', p. 151.   **129** Ibid., pp 150–2.   **130** The civil parishes correspond closely enough to the medieval parishes to give an idea of their considerable extents; St Peter's, Drogheda: 3,504 acres, Ardee: 4,884 acres, Dundalk: 6,332 acres.   **131** The tithes of Dundalk were leased for £22 13s. 4d. (*Monastic extents*, p. 238). The tithes and other revenues of St Peter's, Drogheda, £18 (Ibid., p. 316). The tithes of Ardee were leased for £26 6s. 8d. (Ibid., pp 225–6).   **132** *Cromer's register*, I, f. 70 (91).   **133** TCD MS 808 (5), 'Statutes of the provincial synod of Cashel, 1453', no. 13. Offerings may have been in the order of ½d. to 1d. per adult in the parish [Murray, 'Clerical incomes', pp 153–4].   **134** Verdict of the Commons of County Kilkenny, 1537 (P.R.O., S.P. 60/5/76, presentments liv, lv).   **135** Murray, 'Clerical incomes', p. 154.   **136** K.W. Nicholls, 'Church dues', (chapter of forthcoming book on Gaelic Ireland).   **137** Nicholls, 'Church dues'.   **138** T.C.D., MS 10,383, 'Clogher, Derry & Raphoe', f. 8.   **139** H.F. Berry (ed.), *Register of wills and inventories of the diocese of Dublin, 1457–83* (Dublin, 1898), passim. See also Margaret Murphy, 'The high cost of dying: an analysis of pro anima bequests in medieval Dublin' in W.J. Sheils & Diana Wood (eds), *The church and wealth: studies in church history*, xxiv (Oxford, 1987), pp 111–22.   **140** *Dowdall deeds*, no. 486.   **141** *Cromer's register*, I, f. 77 (99), ff 78v–79 (100).   **142** Nicholls, 'Church dues'.   **143** *Cromer's register*, I, f. 77 (99).   **144** *Dowdall's register*, pp 99–106 (84, # 12).   **145** PRONI, MS DIO 4/4/2, 'State of the temporalities and churches of Armagh in 1622', pp 38–45.   **146** Robert C. Simmington (ed.), *The civil survey of the county of Meath* (Dublin, 1940), p. 372.   **147** Simmington (ed.), *The civil survey of the counties of Donegal, Londonderry and Tyrone* (Dublin, 1937), Appendix; Barony of Louth, County Louth, pp 105–7.   **148** *Monastic extents*, p. 109. The vicar's annual income was then reckoned to be a mere £1 1s. 1d. (Valor in Hibernia, p. 2). Note too that the impropriators of Ardee also kept possession of the glebe (*Mey's register*, no. 227)].   **149** *Dowdall's register*, pp 13–14 (12).   **150** *Cromer's register*, I, f. 85 (108).   **151** TCD, MS 567, 'Valor in Hibernia', f. 5; Virtually identical figures for the benefices are recorded in PRONI, MS DIO 4/4/2, 'State of Armagh in 1622', pp 38–45.   **152** Peter Heath, *The English parish clergy on the eve of the reformation* (London, 1969), p. 173.   **153** NAI, R.C./9, Exchequer inquisitions, Dublin, III, Inq. 12 (1524) ff 26–9; Dublin, III, Inquisition 120 (1537), ff 465–6; Inquisition 131 (1541), ff 489–90; Inquisition 133 (1542), f. 492.   **154** *Cromer's register*, I, ff 49–51 (67), f. 55v (74), f. 58 (77).   **155** PRONI, MS DIO 4/4/2, 'State of Armagh in 1622', pp 38–45.   **156** *Monastic extents*, p. 238.   **157** PRONI, MS DIO 4/4/2, 'State of Armagh in 1622', pp 46–7.   **158** *Monastic extents*, p. 232.   **159** Ibid., pp 225–6.   **160** Note that the extents of the parishes held by the monks of Mellifont offer no idea as to the values of altarages, indicating that they were not leased (*Monastic extents*, pp 214–20).   **161** *Cromer's register*, II, f. 60v (147).   **162** Ibid., II, f. 63v (155).   **163** Valor in Hibernia, p. 2.   **164** *Cromer's register*, II, f. 64 (156).   **165** Ibid., I, f. 13 (30), f. 35 (52), ff 40–40v (58), ff 49–51 (67), f. 55 (73), f. 58 (77), ff 64–5 (83), f. 109v (110).   **166** Ibid., I, ff 49–51 (67).   **167** Ibid., I, ff 40–40v (58), ff 106–106v (134).   **168** Ibid., I, ff 63v–64 (82).   **169** *Octavian's register*, no. 584; Bradley, 'Chantry college of Ardee', pp 16–18; *Archaeological survey*, p. 264.   **170** *Cromer's register*, I, f. 40v (58).   **171** *Monastic extents*, pp 232, 236.   **172** *Octavian's register*, no. 161; *Cromer's register*, I, f. 6v (18), f. 36v (55), f. 55 (73), f. 85 (108).   **173** Robert Cowley's vehement castigation of the bishop of Kildare as 'a simple Irish priest, a vagabond, without learning, manners or good qualities, not worthy to be a holy water clerk', offers one indication of how poorly the water clerks were esteemed (Cowley to Wolsey, September 1528 [Lambeth, MS 602, f. 56]).   **174** *Cromer's register*, I, f. 36v (55), f. 55 (73); Lehmberg found that vicars choral in English cathedrals, who were also poorly paid and regarded, were unruly and prone to incontinence in the sixteenth century (Stanford E. Lehmberg, *The reformation of the cathedrals* [Princeton, 1988], pp 35–6).   **175** *Cromer's register*, I, f. 1 (1).   **176** Ibid., II, f. 12v (28). Dnus Rathcliff was presented to the vicarage in 1520 (Ibid., II, f. 7v [12]). However, there is nothing to indicate that he ever served the cure and it seems unlikely given the canon's high position in Dublin.   **177** *Monastic extents*, pp 231, 236.   **178** *Cromer's register*, I, f. 55v (74).   **179** For the chancels see *Monastic extents*, pp 225, 253; *Cromer's register*, II, f. 60v (147), f. 63v (155). For the naves see *Cromer's register*, I, f.6v (19).   **180** *Octavian's register*, no. 362; *Cromer's register*, II, f. 60v (147), f. 63v (155); *Cromer's register*, I, f. 85 (108); *Dowdall's register*, pp 13–14 (12).   **181** *Octavian's register*, no. 52; Valor in Hibernia, p. 2.   **182** *Monastic extents*, pp 108–9.   **183** *Dowdall's Register*, pp 241–2 (123, E & F), pp 244–6 (125, A, B & C).   **184** Ibid., pp 136 - 8 (97, H, I & K), pp 230–3 (119, A, B & C), pp 239–40 (123, A, B & C), pp 247–9 (126, A & B), pp 250–3 (128, A & B).   **185** For these two extreme see *Swayne's register*, nos. 574, 522.   **186** There are indications of the levying of coyne and livery on Mellifont monastery in 1489 (*Octavian's register*, no. 650), and earlier (*Statute rolls: Edward IV*, i, p. 831).   **187** *Octavian's register*, no. 15.   **188** T.C.D., MS 808 (5), 'Provincial synod of Cashel, 1453', no. 7.   **189** Denys Hay, *The church in Italy in the fifteenth century* (Cambridge, 1977), p. 52.   **190** B. Mac Carthy (ed.), *Annals of Ulster* (Dublin, 1895), s.a. 1462.   **191** J.B. Leslie, *Armagh clergy and parishes* (Dundalk, 1911), p. 98.   **192** Brendan Bradshaw, *The dissolution of the religious orders in Ireland under Henry VIII* (Cambridge, 1974), pp 223–4.   **193** *Swayne's register*, no. 290.   **194** *Octavian's register*, no. 508.   **195** Murray, 'Ancient chantries of County Louth', pp 205–6.   **196** Grey & Council of Ireland to Cromwell, 21 May 1539 (P.R.O., S.P. 60/8/33).   **197** Sovereign & Council of Wexford to Cromwell, 29 January 1537 (P.R.O., S.P. 60/4/180).   **198** Colmcille Conway, *The story of Mellifont* (Dublin, 1958), pp 143–4, 154–7.   **199** *Statute rolls: Edward IV*, i, p. 369.   **200** Alice Stopford Green, *The making of Ireland and its undoing, 1200–1600* (Dublin and London, 1919), pp 289–302; Nicholls, *Gaelic and Gaelicised Ireland in the later middle ages* (Dublin, 1972), p. 99; Canice Mooney, *The church in Gaelic Ireland: thirteen to fifteenth centuries* (Dublin, 1969), pp 22–6.   **201** *Dowdall Deeds* , no. 517.   **202** *Cromer's register*, I, ff 40–40v (58).   **203** Ibid. II, f. 1 (1).   **204** *Dowdall's register*, p. 15 (13).   **205** Ibid., no. 517.   **206** Ibid., p. 15 (13); Leslie, *Armagh clergy*, p. 42.   **207** Ibid., p. 6 (2).   **208** Leslie, *Armagh clergy*, p. 280.   **209** Valor in Hibernia, p. 2.   **210** *Cromer's register*, II, f. 64v (158).   **211** *Dowdall's register*, p. 15–16 (13).   **212** *Monastic extents*, p. 236.   **213** *Octavian's register*, no. 279; *Dowdall's register*, pp 40–1 (35A).   **214** Mgr Mann acquired the benefice between 1515 when Dnus Robert Totayo was rector, and 1518 when he sued in the consistory court to secure his full quota of tithes (*Octavian's register*, no. 212; *Cromer's register*, I, f. 1v [2]).   **215** *Cromer's register*, II, f. 39v (93), f. 38 (88).   **216** *Octavian's register*, no. 563.   **217** *Cromer's register*, II, f. 79v (186).   **218** *Dowdall's register*, p. 42 (36).   **219** *Octavian's register*, no. 394; *Cromer's register*, I, f. 4 (11).   **220** *Cromer's register*, II, ff 72v–73(172); *Dowdall's register*, p. 3 (3).   **221** Ibid., II, f. 61v (150).   **222** *Dowdall's register*, p. 14 (12).   **223** Ibid., p. 50 (46).   **224** *Cromer's register*, II, f. 47 (121), f. 60v (147), ff 63v–64 (155–6).   **225** Jefferies, 'The laity in the parishes of Armagh *inter Anglicos*, 1518 –1558' in *Archivium Hibernicum*, 52 (1997).   **226** *Cromer's register*, II, f. 1 (1).   **227** Ibid., I, f. 1 (1).   **228** *Octavian's register*, no. 394.   **229** *Cromer's register*, I, ff 49–51 (67).   **230** *Octavian's register*, no. 279.   **231** *Cromer's register*, I, ff 6v–7v (20).   **232** Ibid., II, f. 13v (30).   **233** Ibid., I, ff 46–46v (64).   **234** Ibid., II, (30).   **235** The greatest monastic impropriators in Armagh *inter Anglicos* were the Hospitallers of Kilmainham; Cappoge, Clonkeehan, Crowmartin, Dysert, Templeton, Moreton, Dunleer, Gernonstown, Kilsaran, Kildemock with Kilpatrick, Molary, Port, Carlingford; the Augustinians at Louth; Ash, Castlering, Clonkeen, Dromiskin, Kilclogher,

Kilcrony, Killincoole, Louth, Mayne, Termonfeckin; the Crutched friars of Ardee; Charlestown, Knock Louth, Mapastown, Mosstown, Richardstown, Shanlis, Stickillin, Tallanstown, and formerly Ardee; the Cistercians at Mellifont; Ballymascanlon, Collon, Mellifont, Newtown Staleban, Salterstown, Tullyallen. **236** *Monastic extents*, p. 108. **237** *Dowdall's register*, p. 46 (42). **238** *Cromer's register*, II, f. 56 (130), ff 56–56v (131), ff 56v–57 (132), f. 52 (125). **239** Ibid., II, f. 56 (130), ff 56–56v (131), ff 56v - 57 (132). **240** Leslie, *Armagh clergy*, p. 98. **241** *Cromer's register*, I, f. 1v (2); Ibid., II, f. 38 (88). **242** Ibid., I, f. 13v (30); *Dowdall's register*, pp 94–5 (80). **243** NAI, Exchequer inquisitions, Dublin, II, Inquisition no. 12 (1524), ff 27–8; *Dowdall's register*, p. 6 (2). **244** *Cromer's register*, II, f. 39v (93); *Dowdall's register*, pp 238–9 (122). **245** A.B. Emden, *A biographical register of the university of Oxford, A.D. 1501–1540* (Oxford, 1974), p. 160. **246** *Octavian's register*, no. 140. **247** *Fiants of Henry VIII* no. 3 [*The seventh report of the deputy keeper of the Public Records in Ireland*] (Dublin, March 1875). **248** *Cromer's register*, II, f. 13v (30); f. 39v (93). **249** NAI, Exchequer inqusitions, II, Inquisition no. 12 (1524), ff 27–8. **250** Leslie, *Armagh clergy*, p. 98; *Cromer's register*, II, f. 39v (93). **251** *Cromer's register*, II, f. 65 (159); Emden, *University of Oxford*, p. 177. **252** *Cromer's register*, II, ff 72v–73 (172). **253** *Dowdall's register*, pp 238–9 (122). **254** NAI, Exchequer inquisitions, Dublin, II, Inquisition no. 12 (1524), ff 27–8. **255** Ibid., III, Inquisition no. 120 (1537), f. 465. **256** Ibid., III, Inquisition no. 133 (1542). **257** Leslie, *Armagh clergy*, p. 98. **258** *Cromer's register*, II, f. 72v (172); *Dowdall's register*, p. 42 (36), p. 50 (46). **259** Jefferies, 'The diocese of Dromore on the eve of the Tudor reformations' in Lindsay Proudfoot (ed.), *Down: history and society* (Dublin, 1997), p. 128. **260** *Cromer's register*, I, ff 49–51 (67); Ibid., II, f. 52 (125); *Dowdall's register*, p. 14 (12). **261** *Cromer's register*, I, f. 1 (1), f. 63 (81), ff 63v–64 (82), ff 66v–67 (88), ff 96–96v (121). **262** *Dowdall's register*, p. 2 (2). **263** Leslie, *Armagh clergy*, p. 1; *Cromer's register*, II, 58v (139). **264** *Octavian's register*, no. 160; *Cromer's register*, II, ff 72v–73 (172). **265** *Octavian's register*, no. 289; *Dowdall's register*, p. 40 (35A). **266** *Cromer's register*, II, f. 3 (4); *Dowdall's register*, p. 96 (81). **267** *Cromer's register*, II, f. 3v (6); *Dowdall's register*, p. 129 (95). **268** *Cromer's register*, II, f. 13v (30); *Dowdall's register*, pp 94–5 (80). **269** *Cromer's register*, I, f. 54 (72); *Dowdall's register*, p. 28 (23). **270** It was also the case in England cf A.K. Mc Hardy, 'Careers and disappointments in the late medieval church: some English evidence' in W.J. Shiels and Diana Wood (eds), *The ministry: clerical and lay: studies in church history*, xxvi, (Oxford, 1989), pp 111–2, 127–30. **271** *Cromer's register*, II, f. 11 (25). **272** Ibid., II, f. 13v (30). **273** Ibid., II, f. 61v (150); *Dowdall's register*, p. 14 (12). **274** *Dowdall's register*, p. 14 (12). **275** *Cromer's register*, I, f. 105v (132). **276** Ibid., II, f. 63v (155). **277** Ibid., II, f. 64 (156). **278** Ibid., I, f. 3 (9), f. 37 (56). **279** *C.P.R.*, xii, p. 284. **280** *Cromer's register*, I, ff 9v–10 (26). **281** Ibid., I, ff 78v–79 (100); John McCafferty, 'The act book of the Armagh archdiocese, 1518–1522' (MA thesis, UCD, 1991), pp 121–2. **282** Ibid., I, f. 3 (9), f. 37 (56), ff 49–51v (67); Ibid., II, f. 1(1). **283** Ibid., II, f. 1 (1). **284** Ibid., II, f. 13v (30). **285** Ibid., II, f. 15 (35). **286** Ibid., II, ff 72v–73 (172). **287** Ibid., II, f. 47 (121), f. 59 (140), f. 68 (167). **288** Jefferies, 'Dromore diocese', p. 135. **289** NAI, Exchequer inquisitions, Dublin, II, inquisition no. 12 (1524). **290** *Cromer's register*, II, f. 13v (30), f. 16v (38). **291** *Dowdall's register*, p. 96 (81). **292** NAI, Exchequer inquisitions, Dublin, III, Inquisition no. 43 (1529), f. 107. **293** *Cromer's register*, II, f. 38 (88). **294** Ibid., II, f. 60v (147), f. 63v (155). The fact that these indentures between Mgr O'Cahan and his curates were recorded in Primate Cromer's register show his knowledge of, and consent to, these arrangements. **295** *Cromer's register*, II, f. 47 (121). **296** Ibid., I, f. 8 (22). **297** Ibid., II, f. 68 (167). **298** TCD MS 808, (5), The provincial synod of Cashel, 1453, no. 2. **299** Ibid., no. 1. **300** The reformation of Ireland, 1515 (P.R.O., S.P. 60/1/no. 9). **301** Mgr Reginald Drummyn preached at the synod *inter Anglicos* in 1521 (*Cromer's register*, II, f. 5 [8]); the archbishop preached in 1533 (Ibid., II, f. 68 [167]); but Dnus Richard Taylor preached in the synod of 1522 (Ibid., II, f. 11 [23]). **302** *Dowdall's register*, p. 38 (32). **303** Duffy, *Stripping of the altars*, p. 57. **304** *Cromer's register*, II, f. 20v (48). **305** Roy M. Haines, 'Background to an endemic problem' in *Ecclesia anglicana: studies in the English church of the later middle ages* (Toronto, Buffalo & London, 1989), pp 134–5. **306** Duffy, *Stripping of the altars*, pp 58–60. **307** *Cromer's register*, I, ff 49–51v (67). **308** *Mey's register*, no. 179. **309** Robert E. Rodes, *Ecclesiastical administration* *in medieval England: the Anglo-Saxons to the reformation* (Notre Dame and London, 1977), p. 168 shows that the quarterly sermon became a requirement in the fourteenth century. See also *Dowdall's register*, pp 99–106 (85), Article 17.   **310** *Octavian's register*, no. 527.   **311** *Dowdall Deeds*, no. 499.   **312** Verdict of the commoners of Kilkenny, 1537 (P.R.O., S.P. 60/5/60, presentment lvi).   **313** TCD, MS 808 (5), Provincial synod of Cashel, 1453, decree no. 12 ordered that no friar was to preach without a licence from the local bishop. Decree 13 stipulated that the friars were not to collect alms on a day on which the parishioners normally gave their customary oblations to the parish clergy.   **314** Ibid., nos. 13, 14.   **315** *Prene's register*, no 37.   **316** *Cromer's register*, I, f. 15 (34), f. 107 (135).   **317** Ibid., I, f. 13 (30), ff 18v–19 (40).   **318** Ibid., I, f. 13 (30).   **319** Philip Hoffman, *Church and community in the diocese of Lyon, 1500–1789* (New Haven and London, 1984), pp 57, 70; For Irish examples c.f. Provincial synod of Dublin, 1518, which prohibited priests from playing football (Lawlor, 'Liber ruber', p. 165); Archbishop Browne's articles of 1538 prohibited priests from frequenting taverns (J. Payne Collier [ed.], *The Egerton papers: a collection of public and private documents* [London, 1840], p. 10.)   **320** Andrew Barnes, 'The social transformation of the French parish clergy, 1500–1800' in Barbara B. Diefendorf and Carla Hesse (eds), *Culture and identity in early modern Europe (1500–1800)* (Michigan, 1993), pp 141–3; Rodes, *Ecclesiastical administration*, p. 168.

NOTES TO CHAPTER 3

1 *The description of Ireland*, p. 20.   **2** Michael Glancy, 'The church lands of Armagh: the lands of the city and manor' in *Seanchas Ard Mhacha*, ii (1957), pp 336–7.   **3** *The description of Ireland*, pp 20–1; Maps of the escheated counties, 1609 (P.R.O.N.I, MS T 1652).   **4** *Description of Ireland*, pp 21, 19.   **5** Philip Robinson, *The plantation of Ulster: British settlement in an Irish landscape, 1600–1670* (Dublin, 1984), p. 15.   **6** Katharine Simms, *From kings to warlords: the changing political structure of Gaelic Ireland in the later middle ages* (Woodbridge, Suffolk & Wolfeboro, New Hampshire, 1987), pp 19, 59.   **7** Myles Dillon, 'Ceart Uí Néill' in *Studia Celtica*, i (1966), pp 1–18.   **8** Simms, *Kings to warlords*, p. 145.   **9** The term was employed in Simms, *Kings to warlords*, p. 19.   **10** Hiram Morgan, *Tyrone's rebellion: the outbreak of the Nine Years War in Tudor Ireland* (Dublin, 1993), p. 90.   **11** Morgan, *Tyrone's rebellion*, pp 89–90; For a survey of Tyrone dating from the early 1560s see A declaration of Shane (O'Neill)'s ordinary force ..., (Bodleian Library, Oxford, Carte MS 55, no. 309, f. 593v); 'Ceart Uí Néill', pp 4–11.   **12** Bodleian Library, Carte MS 55, no. 309, f. 593.   **13** *Dowdall's register*, pp 133–6; James Hardiman (ed.), *Inquisitionum in officio rotulorum cancellariae Hiberniae asservatarum repertorium, II* (Dublin, 1829) (otherwise *Ulster inquisitions*), appendix, Armagh, second page.   **14** *Dowdall's register*, pp 132–5 (97); *Ulster inquisitions*, appendix, Armagh, second page.   **15** *Ulster inquisitions*, appendix, Armagh, second page.   **16** *Dowdall's register*, p. 134 (97).   **17** Katharine Simms, 'Gaelic Ulster in the late middle ages' (unpublished doctoral thesis, T.C.D., 1976), pp 301–7.   **18** Simms, 'Gaelic Ulster', pp 304–7.   **19** D.B. Quinn & K.W. Nicholls, 'Ireland in 1534' in T.W. Moody, F.X. Martin & F.J. Byrne (eds), *A New History of Ireland, iii*, (Oxford, 1976), p. 16.   **20** Ó Fíach, 'The O'Neills of the Fews', pp 4–5, 13–8.   **21** Simms, 'Warfare in the Gaelic lordships' in *Irish sword*, xii (1975–6), p. 100; Nicholls, 'Gaelic society and economy', p. 403.   **22** *Cromer's register*, II, f. 67v (166).   **23** *Description of Ireland*, p. 20.   **24** *Prene's register*, nos. 12, 405; *Octavian's register*, nos. 406, 420b, 493; *Cromer's register*, II, f. 26v (61), f. 83v (193).   **25** *Cromer's register*, II, ff 82–83v (193).   **26** Ibid., II, f. 83 (194).   **27** Simms, 'The archbishops of Armagh and the O Neills, 1347–1471' in *IHS*, xix (1974), pp 51–5; Lynch, 'The reconstructed register of Primate John Bole', pp 178–9.   **28** *Cromer's register*, II, f. 46v (120).   **29** Nicholas Canny, *The Elizabethan conquest of Ireland: a pattern established, 1565–1576* (Hassocks, Sussex, 1976), pp 12–15.   **30** *Ulster inquisitions*, appendix, County Tyrone, sixth page; Childs, 'Ireland's trade with England', pp 6, 19; R.A. Butlin, 'Land and people, c.1600' in *N.H.I.*, iii, p. 164.   **31** T.B. Barry, *The archaeology of medieval Ireland* (London & New York, 1987), p. 187. Dr Barry's map is not

comprehensive in that it includes only surviving examples. Yet the number of tower houses identified in *Archaeological survey*, pp 302–50, far exceeds the number on Dr Barry's map and the archaeological survey may not be completely exhaustive; see Gosling, *Carlingford*, pp 45–6. **32** *Description of Ireland*, 1598, p. 27; The Maps of the escheated counties, 1609, confirm the surprising fewness of tower houses in Tyrone. **33** *Annals of Ulster*, s.a. 1470, 1471. **34** *Prene's register*, no. 11. **35** E.P. Shirley, *Original letters and papers ... of the church in Ireland under Edward VI, Mary and Elizabeth* (London, 1851), p. 81. **36** G.A. Hayes-McCoy (ed.), *Ulster and other Irish maps, c.1600* (Dublin, 1964), plate iii; Maps of the escheated counties, 1609. **37** *Cromer's register*, II, f. 60 (142). **38** *Dowdall's register*, pp 220–8 (117). This is a copy made in 1558 of a charter granted by Edward IV in the mid fifteenth century. **39** *Prene's register*, no. 17. **40** *Ulster inquisitions*, appendix, Armagh, fifth page. The church may have been built entirely of timber since no remains of it have been identified. **41** Fernand Braudel, *The Mediterranean and the Mediterranean world in the age of Philip II*, i (London 1975), pp 282–4. **42** Canny, *Elizabethan conquest*, pp 10–19. **43** *Octavian's register*, no. 15; O'Sullivan, 'The march of south east Ulster', p. 58. **44** *Dowdall's register*, p. 252 (128 B). **45** Éamon Ó Doibhlin, 'The deanery of Tulach Óg' in *Seanchas Ard Mhacha*, vi (1971), pp 155–6; *Dowdall's register*, p. 252 (128 B). **46** *Swayne's register*, nos. 203, 210, 312; *Dowdall's register*, p. 252 (128 B). **47** PRONI, MS DIO 4/2/11, Primate Cromer's register, 'Visitation of Armagh *inter Hibernicos*, 1546'. **48** *Ulster inquisitions*, appendix, Counties Armagh, Coleraine and Tyrone, passim. **49** Ibid., appendix, County Tyrone, first, second, third, fourth and fifth pages. **50** They included the chapel at Stuckane in the parish of Donaghenry, the chapel at Magheraglass in the parish of Kildress, the chapel of Drumaghviasdon in the parish of Derryloran, and the chapel at Clogherny in the parish of Termonmagurk (*Ulster inquisitions*, appendix, County Tyrone, second page, third page and fifth page). **51** *Civil survey*, p. 290. **52** For several simple graveyards which were not identified as 'chapels' in 1609 cf. Henry A. Jefferies (ed.), 'Rev. Reeve's 'Ancient churches in the county of Armagh, Dec. 1874' in *Seanchas Ard Mhacha*, xvi (1996). **53** See Hiram Morgan, 'The end of Gaelic Ulster: a thematic interpretation of events between 1534 and 1610' in *Irish Historical Studies*, xxvi (1988), pp 8–32. **54** Henry A. Jefferies, 'Derry diocese on the eve of the plantation' in Gerard O'Brien (ed.), *Derry/Londonderry: history and society* (Dublin, 1997). See also Jefferies (ed.), 'Bishop Montgomery's survey of the parishes of Derry diocese: a complete text from circa 1609' in *Seanchas Ard Mhacha*, xvii (1996). **55** *Ulster inquisitions*, appendix, County Tyrone, third page. **56** Jefferies, 'Bishop Montgomery's survey'.
57 There is a tradition of the church at Killyloughran in the townland of Urcher being in use up to the foundation of the parish church at Creggan at the end of the fifteenth century (D.O.E., Historic Buildings and Monuments Department, SMR 030:026; Smr 031:020). **58** Ernest George Atkinson (ed.), *Calendar of State Papers of Ireland, March–October 1600*, vol. ccvii, part 3 (London, 1903), no. 28. **59** *C.S.P.I., March–October 1600*, ccvii, part 4, no. 5. **60** Jefferies, 'Derry diocese'. **61** D.A. Chart (ed.), *A preliminary survey of the ancient monuments of Northern Ireland* (Belfast 1940), pp 242, 245, 233, 234, 239, 254, 255, 256. **62** Dowdall to Lord Chancellor & Privy council, 17 November 1557 (P.R.O., S.P. 62/2/no. 9). One of these churches is likely to have been Templenafertagh. St Brigid's church and Templemurry church, whose ruins are shown on the barony map of Armagh in 1609, are the other possibilities. **63** William Reeves, 'The ancient churches of Armagh' in *Ulster Journal of Archaeology*, ii (1896), p. 195. **64** Reeves, 'Ancient churches' in *U.J.A.*, iv (1898), p. 225; E.B. Fitzmaurice, 'The Franciscans in Armagh' in *U.J.A.*, vi (1900), pp 67–73. **65** H.B.M., SMR 012:055. **66** Ibid., 012:053. **67** Oliver Davies, 'Church archaeology in Ulster' in *U.J.A.*, vii (1944), p. 53. **68** Davies, 'Church archaeology in Ulster', p. 56; *Preliminary survey*, p. 62; H.B.M., SMR 008:009; Jefferies, 'The parish church and priests of Loughgall, Armagh, in 1546' in *Seanchas Ard Mhacha*, xvii (1997). **69** H.B.M., SMR 031:020. **70** Ibid., 005:005. **71** *Preliminary survey*, pp 242–9. **72** Ibid., p. 249; Y.A. Burgos, O. Davies & M. Gaffikin, 'Churches of Armagh' in *U.J.A.*, i (1938), p. 97. **73** *Preliminary survey*, p. 242; F.J. Bigger & W.J. Fennell, 'Ardboe, Co. Tyrone: its cross and churches' in *U.J.A.*, iv (1897), p. 6. **74** O. Davies, 'Carnteel' in *U.J.A.*, iv (1941), pp 149–50; H.B.M., SMR 060:012. **75** O. Davies, 'Derryloran church' in *U.J.A.*, v (1942), pp 56–7; N.F.

Brannon, 'Five excavations in Ulster, 1978–84' in *U.J.A.*, xlix (1986), pp 95–7. **76** H.B.M.,
SMR 039:024. **77** *Preliminary survey*, p. 234; H.B.M., SMR 038001. **78** These parishes all
feature in Primate Dowdall's register as being served by beneficed clergymen (*Dowdall's register*,
pp 247–9 [126], pp 250–3 (128]). **79** *Prene's register*, no. 17. An oval enclosure on the site indicates
that it may have been an early ecclesiastical site, but there is no sign of late medieval building
[H.B.M., SMR 016:044]. **80** *Ulster inquisition*, appendix, County Armagh, last page. **81**
Swayne's register, no. 129. **82** *Dowdall's register*, pp 92 (126), 251 (128). **83** A similar (modest)
scale renewal of parish church buildings has also been observed in the adjoining diocese of Dromore
towards the end of the middle ages (Jefferies, 'Dromore diocese', p. 129). **84** *Ulster inquisitions*,
appendix, County Tyrone, sixth page. **85** Simms, *Kings to warlords*, p. 145. **86** *Dowdall's register*,
pp 187–8 (106). **87** Jefferies, 'Dromore diocese', p. 127. **88** Jefferies, 'Derry diocese'. **89**
Ulster inquisitions, appendix, County Tyrone, passim. **90** Ibid., appendix, County Tyrone, second
page. **91** Ibid., appendix, County Tyrone, second page. **92** *Dowdall's register*, pp 248–9 (126
B). This record was stated to have been copied from a register of Primate Octavian, now no
longer extant. **93** Ibid., pp 187–8 (106). **94** 'The ancient estate of the dioceses of Derry, Raphoe
and Clogher', Bodleian Library, Oxford, Laud Miscellaneous MS 612, f. 8; T.C.D., MS 10,383,
'Dioceses of Clogher, Derry & Raphoe', f. 12. **95** Cf. *Cromer's register*, II, f. 3v (6). **96** C.D.,
MS 10,383, 'Clogher, Derry & Raphoe', f. 7. **97** 'Ancient estate', f. 8. **98** Ibid., f. 8. **99**
Nicholls, 'Church dues', though he was generalising about Ulster as a whole. **100** *Ulster
inquisitions*, appendix, County Tyrone, passim. So too did the vicars of Derry diocese; Jefferies,
'Bishop Montgomery's survey of Derry diocese'. **101** T.C.D., MS 10,383, 'Clogher, Derry &
Raphoe', ff 26, 28, 29, 32, 33, 34, 39, 40, 41, 42; TCD, MS 550, 'Visitation of 1622', f. 192. **102**
The 'Fearainn sagairt' identified in Derry diocese in the 1622 visitation ranged from 2 to 6 acres
(TCD, MS 550, 'Visitation of 1622', ff 189, 190, 191, 195, 197, 198, 201, 202; TCD, MS 10,383,
ff 35, 36, 43; Ulster inquisitions, appendix, County Donegal, second page. **103** Michael L.
Zell, 'Economic problems of the clergy in the sixteenth century' in Rosemary O'Day and Felicity
Heal (eds), *Princes and paupers in the English church, 1500–1800* (Leicester, 1981), pp 36–7. **104**
Ulster inquisitions, appendix, County Armagh, fourth and fifth pages. **105** *Dowdall's register*, p.
248 (126 B). **106** Ibid., pp 247–8 (126 A), pp 250–1 (128 A). **107** *Ulster inquisitions*, appendix,
County Armagh, fifth page. **108** *Fleming's register*, no. 36; *Swayne's register*, no. 485; *Prene's
register*, no. 10; *Cromer's register*, II, f. 60v (144). **109** Kenneth W. Nicholls, 'Medieval Irish
cathedral chapters' in *Archivium Hibernicum*, xxxi (1973), pp 102–11. **110** 'Visitation of Armagh
inter Hibernicos, 1546'. **111** *Ulster inquisitions*, appendix, County Tyrone, passim. **112** *Ulster
inquisitions*, appendix, County Tyrone, second page. **113** *Dowdall's register*, pp 247–9 (126 A,B),
pp 250–2 (128 A,B). **114** *Dowdall's register*, pp 248–9 (126 B). **115** *Dowdall's register*, p. 186
(106). **116** *C.P.R.*, xv, 1484–92, nos. 479, 776, 825; *C.P.R.*, xvi, 1492 - 98, nos 83, 932, *C.P.R.*,
xviii, 1503–13, nos 346, 347; M.A. Costello (with Ambrose Coleman) (eds), *De annatis Hiberniae*,
i, Ulster, (Dublin, 1912), pp 10, 12. **117** *C.P.R.*, xv, 1484–92, no. 776, 825; *C.P.R.*, xvi, 1492–
8, no. 83; *C.P.R.*, xviii, 1503–13, no. 346. **118** *Swayne's register*, no. 210. **119** J e f f e r i e s,
'Derry diocese'. **120** Eamon O Doibhlin, *Domhnach Mor: an outline of parish history* (Omagh,
1969), pp 31–3. **121** *Dowdall's register*, p. 48 (44). **122** *Cromer's register*, I, f. 5 (15). **123**
Eamon O Doiblinn, 'Domhnach Mor' in *Seanchas Ard Mhacha*, ii (1957), pp 420–7. **124** O
Doibhlin, 'The deanery of Tulach Og', p. 159. **125** *Cromer's register*, II, f. 77 (182). However, it
looks as though Dnus Christian failed to take possession of the vicarage (*Dowdall's register*, pp
42–3]37]). **126** *De annatis Hiberniae*, p. 24. **127** *Mey's register*, no. 324. **128** Barony map of
Dungannon, in Maps of the escheated counties, 1609. **129** Leslie, *Armagh clergy*, passim. **130**
Cromer's register, I, f. 4v (14); James Morrin (ed.), *Calendar of Patent and Close Rolls*, i (Dublin,
1861), Patent roll 35 dorso, Henry VIII, m. 7. **131** *Cromer's register*, I, ff 18v–19 (40). **132**
Dowdall's register, p. 26 (21). **133** Leslie, *Armagh clergy*, passim. **134** *Cromer's register*, II, f.
39v (94). **135** *Dowdall's register*, p. 46 (41). **136** *Prene's register*, no. 20. **137** *De annatis
Hiberniae*, p. 24. **138** *Cromer's register*, II, f. 91 (205). **139** *Dowdall's register*, pp 127–8
(94). **140** Shirley, *Original letters*, no xlvii, lxxviii, cxiv, cxvi. **141** *Cromer's register*, I, f. 5 (15);
A.H., p. 25. **142** *Octavian's register*, no. 620. **143** *Cromer's register*, II, ff 82–83v (193). **144**

Ibid., II, ff 78v–79 (185). **145** Simms, ' Frontiers in the Irish church – regional and cultural' in T.B. Barry, Robin Frame and Katharine Simms (eds), *Colony and frontier in medieval Ireland: essays presented to J.F. Lydon* (London, 1995), pp 196–200. **146** Mooney, 'The Franciscan Third Order friary at Dungannon' in *Seanchas Ard Mhacha*, i (1954), pp 12–23; Gwynn & Hancock, *Medieval religious houses in Ireland* (London, 1970), p. 265. **147** Nicholls, *Gaelic and gaelicised Ireland*, pp 79–83. **148** Campion, *History of Ireland*, pp 25–26. **149** Mooney, *Church in Gaelic Ireland*, p. 23. **150** Ibid., p. 23. **151** T.C.D., MS 808 (5) Provincial synod of Cashel, 1453, no. 53. **152** 'Visitation of Armagh *inter Hibernicos*, 1546'. **153** Kildare to Wolsey, 12 April 1525 (P.R.O. S.P. 60/1/11); *Cal. Carew MSS, 1515–74*, i, no. 42. **154** *Ulster inquisitions*, appendix, County Tyrone, second page. **155** *Annals of Ulster* s.a. 1478. **156** Ibid., s.a. 1487. **157** *A.F.M.* s.a. 1528. **158** Ware, 'Annals of Ireland', s.a. 1548 (recte 1547); 'Register of the mayors of Drogheda', s.a. 1547. **159** *A.F.M.* s.a. 1511. **160** Lawlor, 'Liber ruber', p. 166. **161** Michael J. Haren, 'Social structures of the Irish church: a new source in papal penitentiary dispensations for illegitimacy' in Herausgegeben von Ludwig Schmugge (ed.), *Illegitimitat im spatmittelalter: Schriften des Historischen kollegs kolloquien*, 29 (Oldenbourg, 1994), pp 224–6. **162** Jean Delumeau, *Catholicism between Luther and Voltaire: a new view of the Counter-reformation* (with an introduction by John Bossy), (London & Philadelphia, 1977), pp 154–5. **163** Williams, *The Welsh church from the conquest*, pp 325–6, 339–46; Williams, *Recovery, reorientation and reformation*, pp 339–45. **164** Delumeau, *Catholicism*, pp 154–5. **165** Barnes, 'Social transformation, pp 142–6. **166** This is amply demonstrated in the case of Derry diocese cf Jefferies, 'Derry diocese'. **167** Watt, *Church in medieval Ireland*, p. 18. **168** *Octavian's register*, no. 525; Accusations of adultery concerning two priests were dealt with by the consistory court of Armagh between 1518–22, demonstrating that concubinage was not wholly absent in the southern parishes, but also that it was dealt with effectively (*Cromer's register*, I, f. 57 [76], f. 89 [112]). **169** *Octavian's register*, no. 525.

NOTES TO CHAPTER 4

1 Biblioteca Apostolica Vaticana, Barberini MS 2878, p. 162; W. Maziere Brady, *The episcopal succession in England, Scotland and Ireland, 1400–1875*, I (Rome, 1876), p. 216. **2** Gwynn, *Medieval province*, pp 53–4. **3** *Letters and papers*, iii, nos. 1036, 1186, et al.; vii, Appendix no. 30. **4** A.B. Emden, *A biographical register of the university of Oxford to A.D. 1500* (Oxford, 1957), pp 520–1; *C.P.R.*, xviii, 1503–13, no. 72. **5** *Letters and papers*, ii, p. 1480. **6** *C.P.R.*, xvi, 1492–98, no. 1372; Emden, *Biographical register of Oxford to 1500*, pp 520–1; *C.P.R.*, xviii, 1503–13, no. 72. **7** *Letters and papers*, I, no. 3215. **8** C.P.R., xv, 1492–98, no. 180; James Ware, 'Annals of Henry VIII', s.a. 1512 in Walter Harris (ed.), *The whole works of Sir James Ware* (Dublin, 1733); *Dictionary of National Biography*, i, pp 305–06; xviii, p. 154; x, pp 431–2; xi, pp 232–3; xviii, p. 980. **9** William E. Wilkie, *The cardinal protectors of England; Rome and the Tudors before the reformation* (Cambridge, 1974), pp 73, 161–8. **10** Woleman to Wolsey, 27 August 1527 (P.R.O., S.P. 60/1/no. 47). See also Inge & Bermingham to Wolsey, 23 February 1528 (P.R.O., S.P. 6 0/1/no. 51). **11** *Letters and papers*, v, no. 528; *Letters and papers*, vii, no. 1122; Gwynn, *Medieval province*, p. 70. For other examples in the Dublin administration cf Ellis, *Tudor Ireland*, p. 331. **12** Wilkie, *Cardinals protector*, pp 161–8. **13** Gwynn, *Medieval province*, p. 54. **14** Rymer, *Feodera*, XIII, p. 796; *Letters and papers*, III, no. 3119. **15** Note how the 'first fruits' blighted the pontificates of John Bole, archbishop of Armagh (Anthony Lynch, 'The administration of John Bole, archbishop of Armagh, 1457–1471' in *Seanchas Ard Mhacha*, xiv (1991), pp 46–7); and also the episcopates of a series of his successors (Gwynn, *Medieval province*, pp 4–12). **16** *Cromer's register*, II, f. 12v (28). **17** *Fleming's register*, no. 254; *Sweteman's register*, no. 2; *Octavian's register*, nos. 294, 298, 313, 635; *Dowdall's register*, nos. 32, 79, 88. **18** *Dowdall's register*, no. 32. **19** *Cromer's register*, I, ff 83, 83v (104); ff 97, 97v, 98. **20** *Mey's register*, no. 50. **21** Ibid., no. 4, 63; *Dowdall's register*, nos. 32, 33, 34. **22** *Swayne's register*, no. 221; *Mey's* register, nos. 283, 287, 288, 289; Gwynn, *Medieval province*, pp 5–6.   23 Wilkie, *Cardinals protector*, pp 63–73, 161–8.   24 *Sweteman's register*, no. 125; *Fleming's register*, nos. 22, 23, 29, 81, 258; *Swayne's register*, nos. 40, 41, 72, 74, 76, 77, 78, 81, 201, 282, 508; *Mey's register*, nos. 299, 368, 369, 370; *Octavian's register*, no. 506; *Cromer's register*, II, f. 91 (205).   25 *Swayne's register*, no. 458.   26 *Mey's register*, no. 311.   27 *Sweteman's register*, no. 179; *Mey's register*, no. 265.   28 *Mey's register*, no. 266.   29 *Sweteman's register*, no. 179.   30 *Mey's register*, no. 319.   31 Ibid., no. 397; *Cromer's register*, II, ff 56v, 57 (132), ff 75v, 76 (179), ff 76v, 77 (181), f. 79v (186).   32 *Sweteman's register*, no. 254; *Prene's register*, no. 418.   33 Nicholls, 'Medieval cathedral chapters', p. 104.   34 *Mey's register*, nos 319, 365.   35 Ibid., no. 348.   36 Ibid., no. 378.   37 *Ulster inquisitions*, Appendix, County Armagh, last page.   38 *Swayne's register*, no. 256.   39 Leslie, *Supplement*, p. 48.   40 *Cromer's register*, II, ff 56, 56v (131).   41 Valor in Hibernia, p. 2; *Dowdall's register*, p. 148 (97, Z).   42 Ibid., p. 2; *Dowdall's register*, p. 148 (97, Z).   43 *Cromer's register*, II, f. 64v (158); *Dowdall's register*, p. 93 (79).   44 *Dowdall's register*, pp 248–9 (126, B), p. 252 (128, B).   43 *Cromer's register*, II, ff 76v–77 (181), f. 82 (193).   46 *C.P.C.R.*, i, Patent roll 35 dorso, Henry VIII, m. 7; *Cromer's register*, I, f. 4v (14); *Dowdall's register*, pp 123–4 (92); 'Visitation *inter Hibernicos*, 1546'.   47 *Alen's register*, p. 263.   48 Lehmberg, *Reformation of the cathedrals*, p. 6.   49 For England see Lehmberg, *Reformation of the cathedrals*, p. 27; for Ireland see the Valor in Hibernia, pp 2–17.   50 *C.P.R.*, xv, 1484–92, no. 776.   51 *C.P.R.*, xviii, 1503–13, no. 466.   52 Armagh Public Library, Lodge MS, Royal visitation of 1622; Thomas Fitzgerald (ed.), 'The royal visitation of 1622' in *Louth Arch. Soc. Jn.*, vi (1925), p. 7.   53 Valor in Hibernia, p. 2.   54 Ibid., p. 2; *Dowdall's register*, pp 185–6 (106).   55 *Ulster inquisitions*, Appendix, Armagh, second page.   56 Ibid., appendix, Armagh, fourth page.   57 Ibid., appendix, Armagh, fourth page.   58 Ibid.   59 Ibid.   60 Lehmberg, *Reformation of the cathedrals*, p. 6.   61 Note that it was the dean of Armagh who held the 'ancient book' of the chapter which was shown to the jury of the 1609 inquisition (*Ulster inquisition*, appendix, Armagh, fourth page); note also that in the neighbouring cathedral of Clogher it was the dean who was responsible for the cathedral library in the later middle ages) *Prene's register*, no. 451).   62 *Ulster inquisitions*, appendix, Armagh, fourth page.   63 *Sweteman's register*, no. 179.   64 Lehmberg, *Reformation of the cathedrals*, p. 6.   65 *Ulster inquisitions*, appendix, Armagh, passim.   66 Gwynn, *Medieval province*, p. 79.   67 *Sweteman's register*, no. 458.   68 Lehmberg, *Reformation of the cathedrals*, pp 6–7.   69 *Ulster inquisitions*, appendix, Armagh, last page.   70 *Sweteman's register*, nos. 179, 232; *Swayne's register*, no. 221.   71 Reeves, *The culdees of the British islands as they appear in history with an appendix of evidences* (Dublin, 1864); *Swayne's register*, no. 424.   72 *Ulster inquisitions*, Appendix, Armagh, second page, fourth page.   73 Monck Mason, *St Patrick's, Dublin*, pp 83, 89.   74 Mc Grath to Privy council, July 1584 (P.R.O., S.P. 63/111/no. 11; *C.S.P.I., 1574–85*, p. 517).   75 Nicholls, 'Medieval cathedral chapters', p. 105.   76 Reeves, *The culdees*, p. 13.   77 *Ulster inquisitions*, Appendix, Armagh, second page, fourth page.   78 Nicholls, 'Medieval cathedral chapters', pp 104–5; Lehmberg, *Reformation of the cathedrals*, pp 7–8.   79 *Alen's register*, p. 297; Mason, *St Patrick's, Dublin*, p. 87.   80 *Sweteman's register*, nos 8, 11.   81 'Visitation of Armagh *inter Hibernicos*, 1546'.   82 *Mey's register*, nos. 126, 327; Reeves, *The culdees*, pp 13, 17.   83 *Mey's register*, no. 303; *Dowdall's register*, no. 43; *Ulster inquisitions*, Appendix, Armagh, first page. Cashel cathedral also had lands to fund its maintenance (Mc Grath to Privy council, July 1584 [P.R.O., S.P. 63/111/no. 11]).   84 *Dowdall's register*, pp 47–8 (43).   85 *Sweteman's register*, nos. 149, 175, 176; *Fleming's register*, nos. 1, 2, 236; *Swayne's register*, no. 462; *Mey's register*, nos. 5, 126.   86 *Octavian's register*, nos. 132, 642.   87 *C.P.R.*, xviii, 1503–13, no. 466.   88 Ibid., xv, 1484–92, no. 776; *C.P.R.*, xviii, 1503–13, no. 466.   89 *Octavian's register*, no. 132.   90 Ibid., no. 642.   91 *Dowdall's register*, pp 47–8 (43).   92 Thomas Cusack, 'Present state of Ireland, 1553' (*Cal. Carew MSS*, i, 1515–74, no. 200).   93 Paterson, *Harvest home*, p. 32.   94 'Visitation of Armagh *inter Hibernicos*, 1546'.   95 A. Hamilton Thompson, *The English clergy and their organisation in the later middle ages* (Oxford, 1947), pp 57–63.   96 *Cromer's register*, II, f. 11 (23), f. 90 (201); *Dowdall's register*, pp 230–4 (119), pp 249–50 (127).   97 Anthony Lynch, 'The archdeacons of Armagh, 1417–71' in *Louth Arch. Soc. Jn.*, xix (1979), pp 221–2.   98 *Mey's register*, nos 362, 363.   99 Ibid., nos 271, 320.   100 *Mey's register*, no. 197.   101 *Prene's register*, no. 392.   102 *Cromer's register*, I, f.

107 (135). **103** *Octavian' register*, nos. 393, 395; *Cromer's register*, II, f. 9v (19), f. 65v (160). **104** *Cromer's register*, II, f. 66 (161), f. 66 (162), f. 77 (182), f. 90v (202). **105** *Swayne's register*, no. 256. **106** Lynch, 'Archdeacons of Armagh', p. 219. **107** *Dowdall's register*, pp 230–2 (119). **108** PRONI, MS DIO 4, 4, 2, The state of Armagh, 1622, p. 26. **109** *Cromer's register*, II, ff 56 - 56v (131), ff 56v–57 (132). **110** Ibid., I, f. 94 (118). **111** Ibid., I, f. 17 (37), ff 18v–19 (40), f. 29 (47), f. 30 (50), ff 31–31v (51), f. 35 (52) *et seq.* **112** *Octavian's register*, no. 169; *Cromer's register*, I, f. 8 (22), ff 21v–22v (43), ff 63v–64 (82), f. 87v (111), ff 92–92v (116), ff 97–98 (122). **113** *Cromer's register*, I, ff 96–96v (121). **114** Ibid., I, f. 71 (92). **115** Ibid., II, f. 79v (186). **116** Thompson, *English clergy*, pp 63–9; John A.F. Thomson, *The early Tudor church and society, 1485–1529* (London and New York, 1993), p. 118. **117** *Sweteman's register*, nos 204, 211, 152; *Swayne's register*, nos 522, 574. **118** For the financial straits of Archbishop Bole and his successors see Lynch, 'The administration of John Bole', pp 46–7; Gwynn, *Medieval province*, pp 4–12. **119** Charles Mc Neill (ed.), *Calendar of Archbishop Alen's register, c.1172–1534* (Dublin, 1950), pp 267, 269, with its references to rural deans in Kildare, and in and around Dublin city. **120** Simon Ollivant, *The court of the official in pre-reformation Scotland* (Stair Society, xxxiv, Edinburgh, 1982), pp 25–7, 32–4. **121** Lynch, 'Administration', p. 97. **122** Ibid., p. 97; *Mey's register*, no. 324. **123** *Swayne's register*, nos 172, 486. **124** *Mey's register*, no. 185; *Octavian's register*, no. 562; see also Lynch, 'Administration', pp 95–7. **125** *C.P.R.*, xii, pp 160–1; Lynch, 'Administration', p. 95. **126** *Cromer's register I*, f. 4v (14). **127** *Sweteman's register*, no. 109; *Prene's register*, no. 405; *Octavian's register*, nos 562, 620. **128** 'Visitation of Armagh *inter Hibernicos*, 1546'. **129** City of Waterford, 1537 (P.R.O., S.P. SP 60/5/80, pres. xxxviii); Jefferies, 'Derry diocese'. **130** *C.P.R.*, xv, 1484–92, no. 776; *C.P.R.*, xviii, 1503–13, no. 466. **131** Gwynn, *Medieval province*, pp 96–101; see also *Sweteman's register*, nos 131, 206; *Swayne's register*, no. 24. **132** *Cromer's register*, II, f. 83 (194). **133** Ibid., II, ff 76v–77 (181), ff 82–83v (193). **134** *Sweteman's register*, nos 209, 218.

NOTES TO CHAPTER 5

1 *Cromer's register*, I, f. 6 [18]; Ibid., II, f. 5 (8); f. 10 (21); f. 11 (23); f. 12v (27); f. 15v (36); f. 17 (39); f. 20v (48); f. 27v (63); f. 34 (77); f. 40 (95); f. 47 (121); f. 59 (140); f. 68 (167); f. 76v (180); f. 90 (201); see also *Octavian's register*, no. 585. **2** *Cromer's register*, I, f. 6 [18]; *Cromer's register*, II, f. 5 (8); f. 11 (23); f. 68 (167). **3** *Prene's register*, no. 409. **4** The market cross in St Peter's parish, Drogheda, was set up at the expense of Mayor John Ballard in 1501, c.f. An t-Ath. D. Mac Iomhair, 'Two old Drogheda chronicles' in *Louth Arch. Soc. Jn.*, xv (1961), pp 92, 95; The cross seems to have borne the image of the pieta on one side cf King, 'A possible market cross fragment from Drogheda' in *Louth Arch. Soc. Jn.*, xx (1984), pp 334–9. **5** *Cromer's register*, II, f. 5 (8); f. 10 (21); f. 12v (27); f. 40 (95); f. 59 (140); f. 90 (201). **6** Ibid., II, f. 15v (36). **7** Ibid., II, f. 17 (39). **8** Ibid., II, f. 5 (8); f. 59 (140). **9** Christopher Harper-Bill, 'Dean Colet's convocation sermon and the pre-reformation church in England' in *History*, 73 (1988), pp 191–210. **10** *Cromer's register*, II, f. 20v (48). **11** Haines, 'Background to an endemic problem', pp 133–5. **12** Michael A.J. Burrows, 'Fifteenth century Irish provincial legisaltion and pastoral care' in W.J. Sheils and Diana Wood (eds), *The churches, Ireland and the Irish* (Oxford, 1989), pp 55–67. **13** T.C.D., MS 808, (5), (20). **14** Ibid., (5), Statutes of the province of Cashel, 1453, no. 21. **15** *Swayne's register*, nos 250, 251. **16** *Octavian's register*, no. 45; N.B. White (ed.), *Registrum diocesis Dublinensis: a sixteenth century Dublin precedent book* (Dublin, 1959), pp v, 28 seq.; *Alen's register*, p. 260; '*Liber Ruber*', p. 165. **17** The reading of synodal statutes was also commonplace in the synods of Ely (D.M. Owen, 'Synods in the diocese of Ely in the later middle ages and sixteenth century' in G.J. Cumings [ed.], *Studies in church history*, iii, [Leiden, 1966], p. 219). **18** *Cromer's register*, II, f. 20v [48], f. 27v [63], f. 47 [121], f. 59 [140]. **19** Ibid., II, f. 27v [63]. **20** Barnes, 'Social transformation', pp 144–7. **21** *Cromer's register*, II, f. 47 [121]. **22** Ibid., I, f. 6 (18). **23** Ibid., II, f. 47 (121); f. 59 (140); f. 68 (167). **24** Ibid., I, f. 6 (18); *Cromer's register*, II,

f. 20v [48]; see also *Swayne's register*, no. 261; *Liber ruber*, p. 165.   25 *Cromer's register*, I, f. 5 (15), f. 6 (17).   26 Ibid., II, f. 17 [39], f. 90 [201].   27 Ibid., II, f. 17 [39], f. 90 (201).   28 Ibid., II, ff 31–31v (72).   29 Ibid., II, f. 10 [21], f. 11 [23], f. 12v [27], f. 17 [39], f. 20v [48], f. 34 [77], f. 54 [140], f. 68 [167], f. 76v [180], f. 90 [201].   30 Ibid., II, f. 12v [27], f. 40 [95].   31 Ibid., II, f. 11 [23], f. 12v [27], f. 17 [39], f. 47 [121], f. 90 [201]; the synod of 1522 declared absentees to be excommunicated, and fined each of them 6s. 8d. ([Ibid., II, f. 11 [23]); this fine was clearly considered to be a little excessive for in the synod of 1523 the fines were calibrated at more modest levels, viz. 3s. for rectors, 2s. for vicars, and 1s. for unbeneficed parish priests (Ibid., II, f. 12v [27]).   32 Ibid., II, f. 76v (180).   33 *Dowdall's register*, pp 239–40 (123 E & F), pp 244–6 (125 A, B & C); in Dublin archdiocese the synodals were levied by a simpler scale – 2s. from richer incumbents, 1s from the poorer; *Alen's register*, p. 275.   34 *Cromer's register*, II, f. 34 (77).   35 Ibid., II, ff. 33–33v (76).   36 Ibid., II, f. 68 [167].   37 The apparent exception, that for a synod of 1520, was actually for the clergy *inter Anglicos*; *Cromer's register*, II, f. 5 (8).   38 *Cromer's register*, II, f. 11 (23).   39 *Prene's register*, nos 411, 418.   40 *Dowdall's register*, pp 47–8 (43).   41 *Prene's register*, no. 418.   42 *Sweteman's register*, nos 39, 40, 41, 45, 54, 111, 112, 239; *Swayne's register*, nos. 179, 531, 537, 543, 548, 550, 552, 556, 560, 563, 577, 579, 580. Clerical proctors were also called to English parliaments in the middle ages but their attendance seems to have been more erratic than was the case in Ireland (A.K. Mc Hardy, 'The representation of the English lower clergy in parliament during the fourteenth century' in Derek Baker [ed.], *Sanctity and secularity in the church and the world: studies in church history*, x, [Oxford, 1973], pp 97, 107).   43 *Fleming's register*, no. 119; *Swayne's register*, nos 381, 531, 538, 543, 545, 551, 553; *Mey's register*, no. 123; *Prene's register*, no. 370.   44 *Fleming's register*, no. 119; *Swayne's register*, nos 561, 579; *Cromer's register*, II, f. 93 (208).   45 *Prene's register*, no. 46.   46 *Cromer's register*, I, f. 3 (4); *Cromer's register*, II, f. 16v (38).   47 Ibid., II, f. 74 (175).   48 Ibid., II, f. 4 (7), f. 13 (29), f. 74 (175).   49 Ibid., II, f. 4 (7).   50 Ibid., II, f. 4 (7).   51 Ibid., II, f. 11v (26), f. 16v (38).   52 Ibid., II, f.4 (7), f. 11v (26), f. 13 (29), f. 18 (41), f. 93v (208).   53 *Swayne's register*, no. 555.   54 *Cromer's register*, II, ff. 33–33v (76).   55 Ibid., II, f. 93 [208]; for an earlier example see *Octavian's register*, no. 525.   56 Ibid., II, f. 14v (34), ff 33 - 33v (76).   57 Ibid., II, f. 34 (77).   58 Ibid., II, f. 3 (4).   59 See also *Prene's register*, no. 404; The same problem exercised the clergy at the provincial synod of Cashel in 1453 [TCD, MS 808, (5), Statutes of Cashel province, 1453, nos 12, 13]. Doubtless this was a widespread problem.   60 *Octavian's register*, no. 525.   61 Owen, 'Synods in Ely', p. 220.   62 *Dowdall's register*, p. 244 (124).   63 *Swayne's register*, nos 65, 66, 84, 85, 86, 88, 107, 109, 210, 411, 465, 468; *Mey's register*, nos. 33, 73, 167, 172, 176, 194, 218, 222, 227, 242, 248, 251, 268, 269, 331, 334, 354, 362; *Prene's register*, nos 11, 13, 14, 15, 16, 25, 177, 436; *Octavian's register*, no. 26.   64 The value of procurations to the archbishops is indicated in *Dowdall's register*, pp 239–42 (123 A–F).   65 *Cromer's register*, II, f. 10 (21), f. 11 (23), f. 12v (27), f. 17 (39), f. 20v (48), f. 34 (77), f. 54 (140), f. 68 (167), f. 76v (180), f. 90 (201).   66 The record of a 'Visitation of Armagh *inter Hibernicos*, 1546' is inserted between the two books which comprise Primate Cromer's register (PRONI, MS DIO 4/2/11).   67 *Dowdall's register*, pp 234–6 (119).   68 'Visitation *inter Hibernicos*, 1546'.   69 *Sweteman's register*, nos 3, 13, 164, 195, 202, 204, 211, 213, 214, 215, 220; *Swayne's register*, no. 378; *Prene's register*, nos 13, 14, 177.   70 *Mey's register*, nos 73, 176; for occasions in which an archbishop visited through commissaries cf. *Sweteman's register*, no. 13; *Swayne's register*, no. 468; *Prene's register*, nos 15, 16, 25.   71 *Mey's register*, nos. 268, 269.   72 Dowdall's register, pp 47–8 (43).   73 *Prene's register*, no. 420.   74 *Sweteman's Register*, nos 203, 211, 222; *Swayne's Register*, nos 85, 86, 88, 89, 411, 468; *Mey's Register*, no. 167; *Octavian's Register*, no. 178.   75 *Sweteman's register*, nos 203, 211, 222; *Swayne's register;* nos 85, 86, 88, 107, 411; 'Visitation *inter Hibernicos*, 1546'.   76 'Visitation *inter Hibernicos*, 1546'.   77 *Cromer's register*, II, f. 20v (48).   78 Ibid., II, f. 27v (63), f. 47 (121), f. 59 (140), f. 68 (167).   79 *Swayne's register*, no. 66.   80 *Cromer's register*, II, f. 10 [21], f. 11 [23], f. 12v [27], f. 17 [39], f. 20v [48], f. 34 [77], f. 54 (140), f. 68 (167), f. 76v (180), f. 90 (201).   81 *Swayne's register*, no. 465; *Mey's register*, nos. 194, 218, 222, 248, 251, 331, 334, 354; *Prene's register*, nos. 11, 25, 436.   82 *Mey's register*, no. 248.   83 Ibid., nos 354, 379.   84 'Visitation *inter Hibernicos*, 1546'.   85 PRONI, MS DIO 4/2/11; Mc Cafferty, 'Act book of the Armagh diocese'; Jefferies,

'The church courts of Armagh on the eve of the reformation' in *Seanchas Ard Mhacha*, xv (1993), pp 1–38.   86 Mc Cafferty, 'Act book', p. 4.   87 *Cromer's register*, I, fol. 2v (7), fol. 3 (8), fol. 14–15 (26).   88 Ralph Houlbrooke, *Church courts and the people during the English reformation, 1520–1570* (Oxford 1979), pp. 7–8; Ollivant, *Court of the official*, pp 4–5; Christopher Harper-Bill, *The pre-reformation church in England, 1400–1530* (London & New York, 1989), p. 54.   89 Houlbrooke, *Church courts*, pp 8, 38–40; Ollivant, *Court of the official*, pp 21 - 22; Harper-Bill, *Pre-reformation church*, p. 55.   90 Houlbrooke, *Church courts*, p. 38; *Cromer's register*, I, fol. 52v (68). See also B.L., Hargraves MS 128, Principium procuratoris seu praxeos procuratoria breviarium (1). This manuscript reflects seventeenth century practice in Church of Ireland courts. However, given the fossilized nature of the church court system then the manuscript may still be useful for throwing light on practices which one can discern in the Armagh court book.   91 Ibid., p. 38; Ollivant, *Court of the official*, p. 36.   92 Ollivant, *Court of the official*, pp 21 –2.   93 *Cromer's register*, I, ff 18v–19 (40), ff 66v, 67v (63), fol. 95v (120); Edmund Curtis (ed.), *Calendar of Ormond deeds, III, (1413–1509)* (Dublin, 1935), no. 250; Mc Neill, *Alen's register*, p. 274; B.L., Hargraves MS 128 Principium procuratoris (1); Houlbrooke, *Church courts*, p. 40; Ollivant, *Court of the official*, pp 100–1.   94 *Cromer's register*, I, f. 17 (37), ff 18v - 19 (40), f. 35v (53), ff 40–40v (58), f. 54v (72), ff 60–60v (79), ff 66v–67v (88), f. 84 (105), ff 93–93v (117), ff 97–98 (122); *Alen's register*, pp 288–9; *Cal. Ormond deeds III*, 1413–1509, no. 250; Edmund Curtis (ed.), *Calendar of Ormond deeds IV, (1509–1547)* (Dublin, 1937), no. 79.   95 Ibid., *III*, 1413–1509, no. 250; *Cromer's register*, I, ff 18v–19 (40), ff 45–45v (63); Houlbrooke, *Church courts*, p. 28.   96 *Cromer's register*, I, ff 45–45v (63), f. 55 (73); Ollivant, *Court of the official*, p. 99; *Alen's register*, p. 274.   97 Mc Cafferty, 'Act book', pp. 16–17.   98 *Cromer's register*, I, ff 4v–5 (13), f. 30 (50), ff 66v, 67v (88), f. 85 (108), f. 107 (135); Newport B. White (ed.), *Irish monastic and episcopal deeds* (Dublin, 1936), NLI B.7 (no. 67), NLI B.10 (no. 74).   99 *Cromer's register*, I, fol. 84 (107); Heath, *English clergy*, p. 113; Houlbrooke, *Church courts*, pp 28–9.   100 *Cromer's register*, I, ff 9v, 10, 14–15 (26), f. 75v (97), ff 76, 76v (98); B.L., Hargraves MS 128 Principium procuratoris (8).   101 48 entries in the Armagh court book include depositions; c.f. Mc Cafferty, 'Act book', p. 39. For examples of copies of depositions being given to defendants cf. *Cromer's register*, I, ff 106–106v (134), f. 119 (141); *Cal. Ormond deeds*, III, 1413–1509, no. 250.   102 *Cromer's register*, I, ff 14–15 (26); *Cal. Ormond deeds*, IV, 1509–47, no. 79.   103 Ibid., I, f. 82v (103); B.L., Hargraves MS 128 Principium procuratoris (6).   104 Ibid., I, ff 97–98 (122).   105 Ibid., I, ff 66v–67 (88), f. 108 (136), ff 109v–110 (140).   106 Several late medieval instruments of judgement were preserved amongst the Ormond MSS cf *Cal. Ormond deeds*, *III, 1413–1509*, nos 226, 250; *Cal. Ormond deeds, IV, 1509–47*, nos 79, 117; *Monastic and episcopal deeds*, nos 47 (NLI A.34), 63 (NLI A.46), 67 (NLI B.7), 68 (NLI B.8), 71 (NLI C.17), 74 (NLI B.10), 76 (NLI B.ll), 77 (NLI C.18), 80 (NLI B.14).   107 *Cromer's register*, I, f. 2 (6), f. 3v (10), f. 36v (55), f. 52v (68), f. 54v (72), f. 57 (76), f. 90 (113), ff 109v–110 (140), f. 111 (144).   108 One defendent had to purge himself at the pulpit of his parish church (*Swayne's register*, no. 336). Compurgation is best discussed in R.N. Swanson, *Church and society in late medieval England* (Oxford, 1989), pp 175–8.   109 *Mey's register*, no. 354; See also Swayne's register, nos 466, 471; Prene's register, no. 211; *Mey's register*, nos 17, 405.   110 Gwynn, *Medieval province*, p. 74; *Cromer's register*, I, f. 2v (7), f. 4v (13), f. 6v (19), f. llv (28), f. 12v (29), f. 17 (37), f. 17v (38), f. 18 (39), ff 18v–19 (40), ff 21v–22v (43), et seq., and especially ff 49–51v (67).   111 Mc Cafferty, 'Act book', p. 21, calculated that for 1521 there are records of court hearings for 29 days at Drogheda, 12 at Termonfeckin, 1 at Dundalk and three elsewhere.   112 This can be confirmed by a review of court cases, bearing in mind the incomplete nature of our records, but see especially *Cromer's register*, I, ff 49–51v (67).   113 *Cromer's register*, II, f. 17v (40), f. 60 (143).   114 *Dowdall's register*, no. 45.   115 Lynch, 'Administration of John Bole', pp 86–7.   116 *Mey's register*, nos 28, 72, 129, 132, 262, 263, 361; *Octavian's register*, nos. 412; *Cromer's register*, I, f. 15 (26), ff 97–98 (122), f. loov (126); Mc Cafferty, 'Act book', pp 65–6.   117 Prene's register, no. 363; Octavian's register, nos 244, 412; *Cromer's register*, II, ff 69–70 (168).   118 *Cromer's register*, I, f. 107 (135).   119 Ibid., I, f. 107 (135).   120 Ibid., I, f. 94 (118).   121 Ibid., I, f. 17 (37), ff 18v–19 (40), f. 29 (47), f. 30 (50), ff 31–31v (51), f. 35 (52) et seq.   122 For a more thorough analysis cf. Jefferies, 'Church courts of Armagh', pp 11–21.   123

Cromer's register, I, f. 2v (7), f. 3 (8), f. 5 (17), f. 9 (25), f. 20 (41), ff 21v–22v (43), ff 41v–42 (59), f. 43v (61), ff 53–53v (70), f. 59 (78), ff 60–60v (79), ff 62–63 (81),ff 63v–64 (82), f. 68 (89), f. 74 (94), ff 83–83v (104), f. 84 (105), f. 86 (109), f. 94v (119), ff 101–101v (127), ff 102–102v (128). **124** Ibid., I, ff 83–83v (104). **125** Ibid., I, f. 20 (41), ff 21v–22v (43), ff 41v–42 (59), f. 68 (89). **126** Ibid., I, ff 41v–42 (59), f. 68 (89). **127** Ibid., I, f. 20 (41). **128** Ibid., I, f. 94v (119). **129** Ibid., I, ff 83–83v (104). **130** Ibid., I, f. 74 (94). **131** Ibid., I, f. 82v (103). **132** Ibid., I, f. 9 (25). **133** Ibid., I, f. 2v (7), f. 3 (9). **134** Ibid., I, ff 101, 101v (127). **135** Ibid., I, f. 5 (17), ff 6v–7v, 8, 8v, 9, 10v (20). **136** Ibid., I, f. 84 (105). **137** Ibid., I, f. 5 (17), ff 63v–64 (82), f. 94v (119). **138** Ibid., I, loose sheet (3), ff 4v, 5 (13), f. 6v (19), f. 8v (23), f. 11v (28), f. 12v (29), f. 14 (33), f. 35 (52), f. 48 (66), f. 56 (75), f. 57 (76), f. 65v (85), f. 71v (93), f. 75v (96), ff 79v–80 (101), f. 91 (114), f. 95v (120), f. 98v (123), f.100v (126), f. 103v (130), f. 104 (131), f. 104v (132), ff 106–106v (134), f. 110v (143); with counter-suits, Ibid., I, f. 13v (32), ff 81v–82 (102). John McCafferty, 'Defamation and the church courts in early sixteenth-century Armagh' in *Archivium Hibernicum*, xlviii (1994), pp 88–99. **139** Slanders alleging theft: *Cromer's register*, I, loose sheet (3), fol. 6v (19), fol. 14 (33), fol. 56 (75), fol. 91 (114), fol. 98v (123). Other causes: Ibid., I, ff 4v–5 (13), f. 8v (23), f. 11v (28), f. 48 (66), f. 100v (126), f. 104 (131). **140** Ibid., I, f. 48 (66). **141** Ibid., I, f. 12v (29), f. 35 (52), f. 104v (132), f. 110v (143). **142** Ibid., I, f. 13v (32). **143** Ibid., I, f. 103v (130). **144** Ibid., I, ff 79v, 80 (101). **145** Ibid., I, ff 81v–82 (102). **146** Ibid., I, f. 57 (76). **147** Ibid., I, f. 65v (85). **148** Ibid., I, f. 75v (96). **149** Ibid., I, f. 71v (93). **150** Ibid., I, ff 106–106v (134). **151** Ibid., I, f. 94 (118). **152** Ibid., I, f. 5 (15). **153** Ibid., I, f. 4 (12), f. 8v (24), f. 29v (48), f. 37 (56), f. 37, ff 40–40v (58), ff 42v–43 (60), ff 46–46v (64), f. 55 (73), f. 55v (74), ff 61 61v (80), ff 64–65 (83), f. 66v (86), ff 66v–67v (88), f. 77 (99), f. 78 (100), f. 87 (110), f. 99 (124). **154** Mc Cafferty, 'Act book', pp 121–2. **155** *Cromer's register*, I, f. 6 (18). **156** For settled suits: Ibid., I, f. 8v (24), f. 55 (73), f. 87 (110); For suits in arbitration: ff 42v–43 (60), ff 46–46v (64), f. 55v (74). **157** Ibid., I, ff 64–65 (83), ff 66v–67v (88). **158** Ibid., I, f. 2 (4), f. 21 (42), f. 29 (47), f. 29v (49), f. 58 (77), ff 97–98 (122), ff 99v–100 (125), f. 105 (133). **159** Ibid., I, f. 21 (42). **160** Ibid., I, loose sheet (2); ff 96–96v (121). **161** Ibid., I, f. 70 (91). **162** Ibid., I, f. 65 (84), f. 67 (87). **163** Ibid., I, f. 85 (108). **164** Ibid., I, loose sheet (1). **165** Ibid., I, f. 92 (115). **166** Ibid., I, ff 93–93v (117). **167** Ibid., I, ff 92–92v (116), f. 89 (112), f. 84 (107), f. 82v (103), f. 3v (10), f. 44v (62). **168** Ibid., I, f. 2 (6), f. 54v (72), f. 75v (96), fol. 90 (113), f. 109v–110 (140), f. 111 (144). For an analysis of these cases of alleged assault cf Jefferies, 'Laity in Armagh *inter Anglicos*'. **169** Ibid., I, f. 109v–110 (140). **170** Ibid., I, f. 52v (68). **171** Ibid., I, f. 36v (55). **172** Ibid., I, ff 49–50v, 51v (67). **173** Ibid., I, ff 18v–19 (40). **174** Ibid., I, f. 6v (19). **175** Ibid., I, f. 15 (34), f. 107 (135). **176** Ibid., II, f. 3 [4]. **177** Ibid., I, f. 13 (30). **178** bid., I, f. 109 (139). **179** *Mey's register's acta* for 1440, 1441, 1444; Swanson, *Church and society*, pp 167–8, 188–9; Harper-Bill, *Pre-reformation England*, pp 57–9; Jefferies, 'Church courts of Armagh', pp 29–36. **180** Swanson, *Church and society*, pp 185–9. **181** Ibid., pp 183, 185–6. **182** The best discussion of this topic is F. Donald Logan, *Excommunication and the secular arm in medieval England: a study in the legal procedure from the thirteenth to the sixteenth century* (Toronto, 1968). **183** Logan, *Excommunication*, p. 82. **184** Houlbrooke, *Church courts*, p. 39. **185** Harper-Bill, *Pre-reformation England*, p. 56. **186** *Cromer's register*, I, f. 89 (112), f. 92v (116). **187** Ibid., I, f. 92v (116). **188** Ibid., I, f. 100v (126). **189** Jefferies, 'Church courts of Armagh', pp 25–38. **190** The number of persons sued in Armagh's church courts for illicit sexual relationships seems always to have been small, for exceptions see *Swayne's register*, no. 336; *Prene's register*, nos 124, 166. **191** Houlbrooke, *Church courts*, p. 263; Harper-Bill, *Pre-reformation church*, pp 54–63; Haigh, *English reformations*, pp 49–50. **192** Lynch, 'Administration of John Bole', pp 85–7; *Prene's register*, no. 493; Simms, 'The brehons of later medieval Ireland' in D. Hogan & W.N. Osborough (ed.), *Brehons, serjeants and attorneys: studies in the history of the Irish legal profession* (Blackrock, co. Dublin, 1990), p. 71. **193** Simms, 'Brehons of later medieval Ireland', p. 71. **194** Ibid., pp 71–2. **195** *Cromer's register*, II, f. 25 (58), ff 26–26v (61), f. 43 (106), ff 69–70 (168), ff 82–83v (193), f. 83 (194); *Dowdall's register*, nos. 62, 77. **196** *Cromer's register*, II, ff 82–83v (193), f. 83 (194). **197** Lynch, 'Administration of Archbishop Bole', pp 98–100. **198** *Cromer's register*, I, f. 13 (30). **199** Ibid., II, ff 92v–93 (207). **200** Ibid., II, f. 67v (166). **201** Aubrey Gwynn (ed),

'Archbishop Cromer's register' in *Louth Arch. Soc. Jn*, x (1941), p. 121. **202** *Cromer's register*, II, f. 46v (120). **203** Ibid., II, f. 61 (145), f. 66 (163). **204** Ibid., II, f. 83 (194). **205** Ibid., II, ff 78v–79 (185); *Ulster inquisitions*, Appendix, Armagh, third page. **206** Ibid., II, f. 40v (98). **207** Ibid., II, f. 41 (99).

NOTES TO CHAPTER 6

1 English work serves to highlight the importance of wealth to underpin the social status and authority enjoyed by bishops (Christopher Hill, *Economic problems of the church from Whitgift to the Long parliament* [Oxford, 1956], pp 5–49; Felicity Heal, *Of prelates and princes: a study of the economic and social position of the Tudor episcopate* [Cambridge, 1980]. See James Murray, 'Archbishop Alen, Tudor reform and the Kildare rebellion', *R.I.A. Proc.*, lxxxix, sect. c, (1989), pp 1–16, for an important study of the struggles of a bishop in Ireland to recover lost revenues, and the consequences which befell him. By contrast see Jefferies, 'Dromore diocese', for a study of a diocese whose episcopal revenues had collapsed by the early sixteenth century. **2** *Fleming's register*, no. 32; *Sweteman's register*, no. 174; *Swayne's register*, nos 44, 384. **3** *Dowdall's register*, pp 220–7 (117). **4** *Fleming's register*, no. 50; *Swayne's register*, no. 17. **5** *Dowdall's register*, pp 144–5 (97, T). **6** For Primate Cromer's income see the Valor in Hibernia, p. 2; By 1618 the manor of Termonfeckin was valued at £23 18s. 6d. (Valor in Hibernia, pp 2–3). After allowance is made for the difference in currencies this indicates that the rental of Termonfeckin stagnated against a background of high inflation. The 1618 value of the manor suggests that it then contributed only 6% of the archbishop's revenues. **7** *Archaeological survey*, no. 1126, p. 342. **8** *Swayne's register*, nos 202, 203. **9** *Cromer's register*, I, ff 49–51 (67); Ibid., II, ff 56v–57 (132). **10** *Swayne's register*, no. 483; *Octavian's register*, no. 513; *Mey's register*, pp xxxix, xliii. **11** *Dowdall's register*, pp 220–7 (117). **12** *Swayne's register*, nos 76, 100, 258, 277, 284. **13** *Octavian's register*, no. 513. **14** *Dowdall's register*, pp 139–42 (97 L, M, P). **15** Ibid., pp 141 (97 P). **16** Ibid., p. 139 (97 L). **17** Ibid., pp 139–42 (97 L, M). **18** Valor in Hibernia, pp 2–3. **19** P.R.O.N.I., DIO 4/4/2 State of Armagh, pp 17, 20. **20** *Dowdall's register*, p. 140 (97 N); the sum of the rents listed as owing from the tenants in the Newtown of Monasterboice elsewhere in the register amounts to Ir£6 8s. 6d., but it is not clear if these were subsumed under the total given in the previous record for the estate (Ibid., pp 145–6 [97 U]). **21** Ibid., p. 140 (97 N). **22** *Cromer's register*, II, f. 64v (144). He also received two barrels of herring and a thousand oysters (or 3s. 4d. in cash). **23** *Sweteman's register*, no. 157. **24** Valor in Hibernia, pp 2–3. **25** *Sweteman's register*, no. 167. **26** *Dowdall's register*, pp 142–3 (97 Q, R), pp 140–1, 143–4 (97 O, S). **27** Valor in Hibernia, pp 2–3. **28** *Ulster inquisitions*, appendix, Armagh, first page. **29** Glancy, 'Church lands', p. 336. **30** *Dowdall's register*, pp 220–7 (117). **31** *Ulster inquisitions*, appendix, Armagh, second page. **32** *Swayne's register*, no. 147. **33** Ibid., nos 83, 206, 216. **34** *Cromer's register*, II, f. 60 (142). **35** *Swayne's register*, no. 147. **36** *Dowdall's register*, pp 132–3. **37** *Ulster inquisitions*, appendix, Armagh, first and second pages. **38** Ibid., first page. **39** For examples of individuals being enfeoffed on lands in Armagh *inter Hibernicos* c.f. *Fleming's register*, nos 22, 23, 29, 30, 32, 39, 81, 173, 174, 258; *Sweteman's register*, nos 80, 81 for lands rented to the dean of Armagh by the primate, nos 77, 79 for other tenants; *Ulster inquisitions*, appendix, Armagh, second page. **40** *Fleming's register*, no. 32. **41** Glancy, 'Church lands', pp 336–7. **42** *Ulster inquisitions*, appendix, Armagh, third page. **43** *Ulster inquisitions*, appendix, Armagh, third page. **44** *Dowdall's register*, p. 133 (97 A). **45** *Ulster inquisitions*, appendix, Armagh, third page. **46** *Dowdall's register*, p. 133 (97 A). **47** Ibid., p. 133 (97 A); *Ulster inquisitions*, Appendix, Armagh, third page; note though that the townland of Cabragh was reckoned to be the equivalent of four sessiaghs, and was hence its rent was a third more expensive than that of other townlands. **48** *Dowdall's register*, pp 132–3. **49** *Ulster inquisitions*, appendix, Armagh, third page. **50** *Dowdall's register*, p. 133 (97 A); pp 134–5 (97 B, D). **51** Ibid., p. 135 (97 E). **52** *Ulster inquisitions*, appendix, Armagh, second page. **53** *Dowdall's register*, p. 133 (97 A). **54**

Swayne's register, no. 147. **55** *Ulster inquisitions*, appendix, Armagh, second page. **56** Ibid., third page. **57** *Swayne's register*, no. 79. **58** *Ulster inquisitions*, appendix, Armagh, fourth page. **59** *Dowdall's register*, pp 135–6 (97). **60** Simms, 'Gaelic lords in late medieval Ulster', pp 303–7. **61** *Dowdall's register*, no. 97, pp. 133–6. **62** Ibid., pp 151–3 (99). **63** Ibid., p. 133 (97 A). **64** PRONI, MS DIO4/4/2 'State of Armagh', p. 17. **65** *Swayne's register*, no. 487; the manor had been leased for Ir£2 and a mease of eels in 1375 [Ibid., no. 156]; for Mac Mahon depredations see *Sweteman's register*, no. 212; *Swayne's register*, nos 145, 419. **66** *Swayne's register*, no. 343. **67** Valor in Hibernia, pp 2–3. **68** 'State of Armagh', p. 16. **69** *Swayne's register*, no. 147. **70** *Dowdall's register*, pp 131–2 (96). **71** *Swayne's register*, no. 147. **72** TCD, MS 10,383, 'Dioceses', f. 30. **73** Ibid., f. 23. **74** *Swayne's register*, no. 147. **75** *Dowdall's register*, p. 9 (9). **76** *Cromer's register*, II, f. 91 (205). **77** *Dowdall's register*, pp 131–2 (96). **78** Bodleian Library, Oxford, Laud Miscellaneous MS 612 Sir Oliver St John, 'Observations on herenachus and termon lands', f. 36. This text is edited by Jefferies in *Archivium Hibernicum* (forthcoming in 1998). **79** 'Sir John Davies' letter to Robert, earl of Salisbury, 1607' in Henry Morley (ed.), *Ireland under Elizabeth and James the first* (London et al., 1890), p. 367. **80** 'Observations', f. 36; *Ulster inquisitions*, appendix, Tyrone, sixth page. **81** *A.F.M.*, s.a. 1501, 1509; *A. L.C.*, s.a. 1432, 1519. **82** *Ulster inquisitions*, appendix, Tyrone, first to fourth pages, **83** Ibid., second page. **84** 'Observations', f. 36. **85** Ibid., f. 36. See also the end of 'The visitation *inter Hibernicos*, 1546'. **86** *Ulster inquisitions*, appendix, Tyrone, second page; 'Observations', f. 36. **87** 'Observations', f. 36. **88** *Fleming's register*, no. 173; *Ulster inquisitions*, Appendix, Tyrone, second page; *Fleming's register*, nos 174, 258; *Swayne's register*, nos 77, 79, 518. **89** 'Observations', f. 36v. **90** TCD, MS 568, 'Archbishop Daniel on herenaghs', f. 78v. **91** *Ulster inquisition*, Appendix, Tyrone, sixth and last pages. **92** 'Observations', f. 36; Davies' letter, p. 367. **93** TCD, MS 10,383 'Dioceses', ff 25, 27, 29, 32, 35, 37, 39. For an example from Armagh on the eve of the Henrician reformation see *Cromer's register*, II, f. 82 (192). **94** *Ulster inquisitions*, Appendix, Tyrone, first, second, third, fifth and sixth pages. **95** TCD, MS 10,383 'Dioceses', f. 34. **96** 'Observations', f. 8; *Ulster inquisitions*, appendix, Armagh, last page. **97** *Swayne's register*, no. 147. **98** *Mey's register*, no. 400. **99** *Fleming's register*, no. 36; *Swayne's register*, no. 485; *Prene's register*, no. 10. **100** *Cromer's register*, II, f. 60v (144). **101** *Sweteman's register*, no. 140. **102** *Dowdall's register*, pp 146–7 (97). **103** Valor in Hibernia, p.2. **104** *Cromer's register*, II, f. 64v (144). **105** *Octavian's register*, no. 398. **106** Valor in Hibernia, p. 4. **107** Ibid., pp 2–3. **108** *Fleming's register*, no. 215, see also nos 212, 216, 220, 221, 222, 253; *Swayne's register*, nos 66, 378, 434, 435; *Octavian's register*, no. 474. **109** *Dowdall's register*, pp 253–68 (129). **110** *Cromer's register*, II, ff 53v, 54 (129). **111** *Dowdall's register*, pp 136–8 (97 H, I, K); p. 138 (125 D). **112** Ibid., pp 247–9 (126 A, B). **113** Ibid., pp 250–3 (128 A, B). **114** Ibid., pp 241–2 (123 D, E, F), where D and F offer values of 11s. 6d. and 10s. 6d. respectively for the synodals of Dundalk rural deanery, of which I chose the higher sum; p. 244 (125 A, B). **115** John Bale, 'The vocacion of John Bale to the bishoprick of Ossorie' in *Harleian Miscellany*, vi, p. 452. **116** *Cromer's register*, II, f. 67 (165); f. 85v (200); for earlier references, *Swayne's register*, nos 443, 462; *Octavian's register*, no. 642. **117** *Cromer's register*, II, f. 54 (129). **118** *Cromer's register*, II, f. 67 (165). **119** Valor in Hibernia, p. 2. **120** Gwynn, *Medieval province*, pp 4–16. **121** Rymer, *Feodera*, xiii, p. 796. **122** Biblioteca Apostolica Vaticana: Barberini Lateran MS 2878, p. 162. **123** *Cromer's register*, I, f. 3 (4); *Cromer's register*, II, f. 16v (38). **124** Ordinances for the government of Ireland, 1534 (P.R.O., S.P. 60/2/no. 63). **125** *Mey's register*, no. 177.M**126** *Sweteman's register*, no. 134. **127** Ibid., no. 118; *Fleming's register*, no. 179. **128** NAI, Exchequer inquisitions for Dublin, III, Inquisition 148 (1545), ff. 508–9. **129** *Fleming's register*, no. 40; *Sweteman's register*, nos 82, 86. **130** *AFM*, s.a. 1511; See also the obituary of another highly-regarded prelate, Nicholas Maguire, bishop of Leighlin (1490–1512) in Tadhg Dowling, 'Annales breves Hiberniae' in *The annals of Ireland* (Irish Archaeological Society, Dublin, 1849), s.a. 1512. **131** *Annals of Connacht*, s.a. 1530. **132** *Octavian's register*, no. 511. **133** Brady to Cecil, 16 May 1565 (P.R.O., S.P. 63/13/39).

NOTES TO CHAPTER 7

1 The most thorough and influential exponent of this interpretation was A.G. Dickens, *The English reformation* (London, 1964). The best critique of the conventional reformation historiography in England is Christopher Haigh (ed.), *The English reformation revised* (Cambridge, 1987), and Haigh, *English reformations: religion, politics and society under the Tudors* (Oxford, 1993). **2** Jefferies, 'The laity in Armagh *inter Anglicos*' (forthcoming). **3** R. B. Manning, *Religion and society in Elizabethan Sussex* (Leicester, 1969); Robert Whiting, *The blind devotion of the people* (Cambridge, 1989); Haigh, *Reformation and resistance in Tudor Lancashire* (Cambridge, 1975). **4** Edwards *Church and state*, p. 244. **5** Peter Gwyn, *The king's cardinal: the rise and fall of Thomas Wolsey* (London, 1990), pp 252–3. **6** *Cromer's register*, II, f. 65 (159). **7** NLI, MS D. 15,973; *Octavian's register*, no. 160; *Cromer's register*, II, ff 72v–73 (172). **8** *Cromer's register*, II, ff 51v–52 (124), f. 64v (157); *Letters and papers*, v, p. 753. **9** *Cromer's register*, II, f. 68 (167). **10** *A.U.* s.a. 1533. **11** Indenture between Henry VIII and the earl of Ossory, 31 May 1534 (P.R.O., S.P. 60/2/no. 14). **12** Cowley to Cromwell, June 1534 (P.R.O., S.P. 60/2/47); Ellis, 'The Kildare rebellion and the early Henrician reformation' in *Historical Journal*, xix (1976), pp 813–14. **13** Alen to Cromwell, 26 December 1534 (P.R.O., S.P. 60/2/78); Ellis, 'Kildare rebellion', p. 813. **14** Laurence McCorristine, *The revolt of Silken Thomas: a challenge to Henry VIII* (Dublin, 1987), pp 73–8. **15** Mc Corristine, *Revolt of Silken Thomas*, pp 73–9. **16** The quotes are from Mc Corristine, *Revolt of Silken Thomas*, pp 73–4. Yet he, without offering a reason, suggests that the religious aspect of the rebellion was a mere pretext which came after the rebellion had begun (Mc Corristine, *Revolt of Silken Thomas*, pp 68, 71). For a different interpretation see Jefferies, 'Dr George Cromer, archbishop of Armagh, and Henry VIII's reformation in Art Hughes, F.X. Mc Corry and Roger Weatherup (eds), *Armagh: history and society* (Dublin, forthcoming). **17** Deputy and council to Cromwell, 1 June 1536 (P.R.O., S.P. 60/3/59); Mc Corristine, *Revolt of Silken Thomas*, p. 87. **18** James Morrin (ed.), *Calendar of Patent and Close Rolls*, I, (Dublin, 1861), Patent roll 25 Henry VIII, m. 7; Thomas Ryder, *Foedera*, xiv (London, 1712), pp 438–9. **19** Skeffington to Henry VIII, 30 April 1535 (P.R.O. SP 60/3/31). **20** *Cromer's register*, II, ff 76v–93v. **21** Ibid., II, f. 80 (187). The only other prominent English-born churchman who remained in Ireland was Dr John Travers, chancellor of St Patrick's Cathedral, Dublin, who was subsequently executed by the crown for his part in the crusade (R.D. Edwards, 'Venerable John Travers and the rebellion of Silken Thomas' in *Studies*, xxiii [1934], pp 687–99). **22** Alen to Cromwell, 26 December 1534 (P.R.O., S.P. 60/2/102). **23** *Patent rolls of Henry VIII*, patent roll 24 & 25 Henry VIII, xiii, no. 5. **24** *Cromer's register*, II, f. 79v (186). **25** Alen to Cromwell, 26 December 1534 (P.R.O., S.P. 60/2/105; Ellis, 'Kildare rebellion', p. 819. **26** Ellis, 'Kildare rebellion', pp 815–16. **27** *C.P.C.R.*, i, Patent roll 27/28 Henry VIII, m. 1. **28** *Fiants of Henry VIII*, no. 203. **29** Ibid., no. 341. **30** N.L.I., MS D. 15,980, MS D. 15,981, MS D. 15,983–4, MS D. 15, 987, MS D. 15, 998. **31** N.L.I., D. 15,981, MS D. 15,987. **32** *Cromer's register*, II, f. 93v (208). **33** Ormond and others of the council were present at the election of burgesses and knights in five Leinster counties to ensure that those elected 'should not stick in the king's causes' (*Letters and papers*, x, no. 15; P.R.O., S.P. 60/2/297). **34** Brendan Bradshaw, 'The opposition to the ecclesiatical legislation in the Irish reformation parliament' in *Irish Historical Studies*, xvi (1969), pp 291–2; Brabazon to Cromwell, 17 May 1536 (Lambeth, MS 616, f. 44). **35** Gray and Brabazon to Cromwell, 1 June 1536 (P.R.O., S.P. 60/4/74). **36** *Alen's register*, p. 300. **37** Brabazon to Cromwell, 17 May 1536 (Lambeth, MS 616, f. 44). **38** Gray and Brabazon to Cromwell, 1 June 1536 (P.R.O., S.P. 60/4/74). **39** Ibid., (P.R.O., S.P. 60/4/74). **40** Henry VIII to Browne, 31 July 1537 (P.R.O. SP 60/4/no. 55); Henry VIII to Staples, 31 July 1537 (P.R.O. SP 60/4/no. 56); Brendan Bradshaw, 'George Browne, first reformation archbishop of Dublin, 1536 - 1554' in *J.E.H.*, xxi (1970), p. 312. **41** Cowley to Cromwell, 4 October 1536 (P.R.O., S.P. 60/3/154). **42** Bradshaw, 'Opposition', pp 296–7. **43** *C.P.C.R.*, i, Patent roll 33 Henry VIII, m. 6. **44** Lennon, *Lords of Dublin*, p. 143. **45** *Letters and papers*, xii (ii), no. 388. **46** *C.P.C.R.*, i, Patent roll 27/28 Henry VIII, m. 25. **47** Ibid., dorso, m. 3. **48** Brabazon's note, 1537 (P.R.O.,

S.P. 60/5/131).   **49** The definitive study of the Henrician dissolutions is Brendan Bradshaw, *The dissolution of the religious houses in Ireland under Henry VIII* (Cambridge, 1974).   **50** Bradshaw, *Dissolution*, pp 114, 116, 121.   **51** Ibid., pp 126–7.   **52** Ibid., p. 127.   **53** *Dowdall's register*, pp 13–14 (12), pp 15, 16 (13).   **54** Ibid., p. 4 (4), p. 9 (7), p. 13 (12), p. 21 (17).   **55** Cusack to Cromwell, 1538 (P.R.O., S.P. 60/3/No. 112); Bradshaw, *Dissolution* p. 126.   **56** Mc Neill, *Monastic extents*, pp 219–20. One of the Mellifont monks, Dnus John Prowte accepted a pension of £2 and the cure of Donnore in Meath diocese before he became the abbot of the Cistercian monastery at Newry (*Monastic extents*, p. 219, 221; *Fiants of Henry VIII*, nos 77, 366).   **57** *Dowdall's register*, p. 1 (1), pp 42–3 (37), pp 43–4 (38).   **58** *Fiants of Henry VIII*, no. 86.   **59** *Cromer's register*, II, ff 83–83v (104); *Fiants of Henry VIII*, no. 92.   **60** *Dowdall's register*, p. 6 (6).   **61** Margaret Bowker, 'The Henrician reformation and the parish clergy', in Haigh, *English reformation revised*, pp 75–93, and especially pp 78–84.   **62** *Monastic extents*, pp 213, 228; *Dowdall's register*, p. 235 (119 E).   **63** Bradshaw, *Dissolution*, pp 8–16.   **64** Ibid., p. 143.   **65** Ibid., pp 140–1; Mc Neill, *Monastic extents*, p. 227.   **66** Harold O Sullivan, 'The Franciscans in Dundalk' in *Seanchas Ard Mhacha*, iv (1960–1), pp 36–8.   **67** Elton, *Policy and police: the enforcement of the reformation in the age of Thomas Cromwell* (Cambridge, 1972), passim.; Haigh, *English reformations*, pp 130–202, 235–50, 268–84; Duffy, *Stripping of the altars*, pp 379–477.   **68** Ronald Hutton, 'The local impact of the Tudor reformation' in Haigh, *English reformation revised*, pp 114–38; Duffy, *Stripping of the altars*, pp 478–503.   **69** Haigh, *Reformation revised*, pp 16–17.   **70** 28 Henry VIII, c. 7.   **71** Ibid., c. 13.   **72** The oath required the person taking it to renounce the pope's authority, to acknowledge the royal supremacy and to undertake to uphold it.   **73** 28 Henry VIII, c. 17.   **74** *Dowdall's register*, pp 187–8 (107).   **75** 28 Henry VIII, c. 19.   **76** *Dowdall's register*, pp 188–91 (108).   **77** Ibid., pp 182–93 (110).   **78** *Dowdall's register*, pp 153–67 (100).   **79** NAI, Exchequer inquisitions, Dublin, II, ff 432–6.   **80** *Dowdall's register*, pp 174–9 (108).   **81** Brady, *Episcopal succession*, p. 216.   **82** *Dowdall's register*, p. 34 (29, 30).   **83** Browne to Cromwell, 21 May 1538 (P.R.O., S.P. 60/6/129); Browne to Cromwell, 30 June 1538 (P.R.O., S.P. 60/7/13).   **84** Ibid., 8 January 1538 (Lambeth, MS 602, f. 104), Agard to Cromwell, 5 April 1538 (P.R.O., S.P. 60/6/88); Browne to Cromwell, 20 May 1538 (P.R.O., S.P. 60/6/127); Browne to Cromwell, 6 November 1538 (P.R.O., S.P. 60/7/152).   **85** Browne to Cromwell, 6 November 1538 (P.R.O., S.P. 60/7/152).   **86** *Cromer's register*, II, f. 83 (194).   **87** Ibid., II, ff 78v–79 (185); *Ulster inquisitions*, appendix, Armagh, third page.   **88** *Monastic extents*, pp 109, 231.   **89** Alen to Cromwell, 10 July 1539 (P.R.O., S.P. 60/8/42–6).   **90** Murray, 'Ecclesiastical justice', p. 40.   **91** *Dowdall's register*, pp 31–2, 33 (29, 30).   **92** Ibid., p. 209 (111).   **93** N.L.I., MS D. 15,981, MS D. 15,987.   **94** Bishop O Carolan did not acknowledge the royal supremacy until 1542 (Gwynn, *Medieval province*, p. 184).   **95** *Fiants of Henry VIII*, nos 203, 341.   **96** TCD, MS 567 (5) 'Valor in Hibernia'; *Cromer's register*, I, f. 3 (4); *Cromer's register*, II, f. 16v (38).   **97** *Dowdall's register*, pp 147–8 (97 X, Y, Z).   **98** NAI, Exchequer inquisitions, Dublin, III, Inq. 133, f. 492.   **99** NAI, Exchequer inquisitions, Dublin, III, Inq. 143 (1543), f. 503; Inq. 148 (1544), f. 509; Inq. 149 (1545), f. 510.   **100** Marsh's Library, Dublin, MS Z 2.1.7 Prosecution of the rector of Rathdrummin, 1548.   **101** *Monastic extents*, pp 221, 226, 233, 239, 242, 245, 247, 237.   **102** *Fiants of Henry VIII*, no. 341.   **103** Bradshaw, *Dissolution*, p. 242.   **104** *Fiants of Henry VIII*, no. 196.   **105** Maurice F. Powicke, *The reformation in England* (Oxford, 1941), p. 1; Richard Rex, *Henry VIII and the English reformation* (Basingstoke, Hampshire & London, 1993), pp 2–3.   **106** Duffy, *Stripping of the altars*, pp 379–423; Haigh, *English reformations*, pp 124 - 32; Rex, *Henry VIII*, pp 2–3, 6–72.   **107** Council to Cromwell, 18 January 1539 (P.R.O., S.P. 60/8/); *Injunctions* in *Egerton papers*, pp 7–10. A note on the manuscript states that they were issued circa 1543, but the references to the religious in several articles show that they pre-dated the dissolution of the religious houses in 1539 (*Injunctions*, articles 4, 8, 9, 11, 14).   **108** Staples to St Leger, 17 June 1538 (Lambeth, MS 602, f. 131; SP Henry VIII, no. ccxxxiii).   **109** Browne to Essex, 19 May 1540 (P.R.O., S.P. 60/9/62).   **110** Council to Cromwell, 18 January 1539 (P.R.O., S.P. 60/8/1).   **111** Charles Mc Neill (ed.), 'Accounts of monastic possessions' in *R.S.A.I. Jn.*, lii (1922), p. 12; Bradshaw, *Dissolution*, p. 110; Duffy, *Stripping of the altars*, p. 407; *Annals of Loch Ce*, s.a. 1538 (recte 1539).   **112** Mc Neill, 'Accounts of monastic possessions', p. 12; Mc Neill, *Monastic* *extents*, p. 249.   113 Katherine Walsh, *A fourteenth century scholar and primate: Richard FitzRalph in Oxford, Avignon and Armagh* (Oxford, 1981), pp 454–62.   114 Duffy, *Stripping of the altars*, pp 415, 431–42.   115 *C.P.C.R.*, i, Patent roll 30, 31 Henry VIII, m. 1.   116 Murray, 'Ecclesiastical justice', pp 48–51.   117 Brady, *The chief governors*, pp 19–20.   118 Browne to Cromwell, 20 May 1538 (P.R.O. SP 60/6/127).   119 Articles against Grey from the Council of Ireland, 1540 (P.R.O. SP 60/9/152; articles 29, 68, 71).   120 Browne to Cromwell, 6 November 1538 (P.R.O. SP 60/7/152).   121 Council to Cromwell, 1539 (P.R.O., S.P. 60/8/33).   122 Articles against Grey from the Council of Ireland, 1540 (P.R.O. SP 60/9/152; articles 2, 3, 4, 25, 26.   123 Butler to Cromwell, 26 August 1538 (P.R.O., S.P. 60/7/122).   124 Browne to Essex, 19 May 1540 (P.R.O., S.P. 60/ 9/62).   125 Alen to Cromwell, 20 October 1538 (P.R.O. SP 60/7/147).   126 Browne to Cromwell, 20 May 1538 (P.R.O., S.P. 60/6/127).   127 Ibid., 8 May 1538 (Lambeth, MS 602, f. 123); Alen to Cromwell, 20 October 1538 (P.R.O., S.P. 60/7/147).   128 Haigh, *English reformations*, pp 152–67; Bradshaw, *The Irish constitutional revolution of the sixteenth century* (Cambridge, 1979), pp 245–9.   129 See, for instance, St Leger's major commitments to the churchmen in the ecclesiastical provinces of Cashel and Tuam (*Cal. Carew MSS*, I, 1515–74, nos 157, 158, 170, 180, 185, 188, 193).   130 *Cal. Carew MSS*, i, 1515–74, no. 180.   131 Ibid., i, 1515–74, no. 188.   132 Cromer's illness is clear from his inability to visit Armagh city in 1542 (*Dowdall's register*, p. 47 [43]).   133 Henry VIII to Deputy St Leger and council, 26 March 1541 (P.R.O. SP 60/10/19). Such presumption as Nicholas Nugent showed suggests that he was a young man of noble background, and ambitions (*Cromer's register*, II, ff 57v–58 [136]).   134 *Dowdall's register*, pp 10–11 (8).   135 Ibid., p. 4 (4).   136 Ibid., pp 37 –8 (32).   137 Ibid., p. 39 (34).   138 *C.P.C.R.*, i, Patent roll 35 dorso, Henry VIII, m. 5.   139 *Dowdall's register*, pp 7–10 (7) for 1540; pp 35–7 (31) for 1541; p. 4 (4) for 1542; pp 37–8 (32) for 1543; pp 68–9 (61) for 1544; pp 88–90 (76) for 1545; p. 92 (78) for 1548.   140 Ibid., p. 21 (17), pp 120–1 (89); p. 121 (90); pp 38– 9 (33); Ibid., p. 13 (11).   141 Ibid., p. 7 (7); p. 4 (4).   142 Ibid., p. 7 (7); pp 35–6 (31); p. 68 (61); p. 88 (76); p. 92 (78).   143 Ibid., pp 7–8 (7).   144 Ibid., p. 36 (31); p. 38 (32); p. 92 (78).   145 Ibid., p. 8 (7); p. 36 (31); p. 38 (32); p. 92 (78).   146 Ibid., p. 68 (61).   147 Ibid., pp 88–90 (76).   148 Haigh, *English reformations*, pp 152–67, especially p. 167.   149 Walsh, *Richard FitzRalph*, pp 454–62.   150 *Dowdall's register*, p. 107 (86).   151 Ibid., pp 9–10 (8); pp 35–7 (31).   152 Ibid., pp 23–4 (19). See also Ibid., pp 21–2 (18).   153 Ibid., p. 63 (59).   154 Ibid., pp 61–2 (57).   155 Ibid., pp 234–6 (119 E).   156 Ibid., pp 51–2 (48).   157 Ibid., pp 40–1 (35A); p. 39 (34).   158 Ibid., p. 1 (1); pp 42–3 (37); pp 43–4 (38).   159 Ibid., pp 4–5 (5), pp 23–4 (65) (Kilmore); pp 21–3 (18), pp 63–6 (59) (Down and Connor); pp 24–5 (20), p. 30 (26), p. 91 (77) (Clogher); pp 29–30 (25) (Ardagh).   160 Ibid., p. 1 (1), p. 15 (13); p. 89 (76).   161 Ibid., pp 68–9 (61), p. 92 (78).   162 Ibid., p. 49 (45).   163 Ibid., pp 66–8 (60).   164 Ibid., pp 80 1 (71).   165 Ibid., pp 76–7 (68).   166 Ibid., pp 6–7 (6); pp 52–4 (49); pp 94–5 (80).   167 Ibid., pp 40–1 (35A).   168 Ibid., p. 42 (36).   169 Ibid., p. 15 (13).   170 Ibid., p. 46 (42).   171 Ibid., pp 238–9 (122).   172 *Fiants of Henry VIII*, no. 289; Valor in Hibernia, p. 12.   173 *Dowdall's register*, pp 74–6 (66, 67).   174 Leslie, *Armagh clergy*, p. 193; Valor in Hibernia, p. 10.   175 Mgr Warren was associated with one Walter Warren of Warrenstown, County Meath (*Dowdall's register*, p. 59 [54]; *C.P.C.R.*, i, Patent roll 34 Henry VIII, m. 7). Mgr John Cantwell's surname suggests that he came from south eastern Ireland and, indeed, he was anxious to minister in that region (Bradshaw, *Constitutional revolution*, pp 250–1; *Dowdall's register*, p. 28 [23]). Dnus Patrick Morgan's Christian name hints at an Irish provenance (*C.P.C.R.*, i, Patent roll 34 Henry VIII, m. 5).   176 *Fiants of Henry VIII*, no. 296; *Dowdall's register*, p. 58 (53); Valor in Hibernia, p. 2; *Dowdall's register*, p. 96 (81); Richard Hyny or Heny was admitted as curate of Tullyallen in 1531, though he may have lost his curacy to Bro Thomas Bagett on the dissolution of the monastery of Mellifont in 1539 (*Cromer's register*, II, f. 60v [146], *Monastic extents*, p. 219). When he was presented to the vicarage of Dunleer in 1544 he seems not to have held a benefice (*Dowdall's register*, p. 78 [69], *C.P.C.R.*, i, Patent roll 36 Henry VIII, m. 4). His surname suggests that he was one of the erenagh sept of O'Heny of Ballymore parish in the rural deanery of Orior (*Cromer's register*, II, ff 78v–79 [185]).   177 *Dowdall's register*, p. 6 (6), p. 14 (12), p. 66 (59); NAI, Exchequer inquisitions, Dublin, III, Inquis. 131. In further support of this assertion c.f. the situation in the neighbouring diocese of Meath in 1576 where 105 impropriated churches served by curates of whom only eighteen were found able to speak English, which number probably includes Irish priests who could converse in English (Brady [ed.], *State papers concerning the Irish church* [London, 1868], Letter xi, pp 14–19). This letter is late but it serves to show that the predominance of Irish priests among the ranks of the unbeneficed priests in the Pale continued for some decades despite the Tudor reformations. **178** *Annatis Hiberniae*, I, pp 13, 15. **179** *Cromer's register*, II, ff 76v–77 (181). **180** Ibid., ff 76v–77 (181). **181** *Annatis Hiberniae*, pp 14, 24. **182** *Dowdall's register*, pp 51–2 (48). **183** Ibid., pp 24–5 (20), p. 30 (26). **184** *Cromer's register*, II, f. 77 (182). **185** *Dowdall's register*, pp 66–8 (60). **186** *Annatis Hiberniae*, pp 14, 24. **187** *Dowdall's register*, p. 48 (44). **188** *Annatis Hiberniae*, pp 24–5. **189** *Dowdall's register*, p. 1 (1), pp 42–3 (37). **190** Ibid., p. 1 (1). **191** Ibid., p. 20 (16), pp 51–2 (48). **192** *Annatis Hiberniae*, pp 15, 25. **193** *Dowdall's register*, pp 45–6 (41). **194** *Annatis Hiberniae*, pp 15, 25–6. **195** Jefferies, 'Secular clergy of Armagh', pp 321–5. **196** *Dowdall's register*, p. 1 (1). **197** Ibid., p. 19 (15). **198** Ibid., pp 51–2 (48). **199** Ibid., p. 26 (21); pp 42–3 (37); pp 43–4 (38); pp 45–6 (41); pp 69–70 (62). Continuity is most starkly shown by the fact that one Dnus Seán O'Culean succeeded Dnus David O'Culean as vicar of Derrybrusk in 1540, and Dnus Maurice Mc Cawell succeeded the late Dnus Patrick Mc Cawell as vicar of Clonoe in 1542. **200** *C.P.C.R.*, i, Patent roll 35 dorso, Henry VIII, m. 7. **201** *Dowdall's register*, pp 31–2 (28); pp 273–80. **202** Ibid., pp 32–5 (29, 30). **203** Ibid., pp 132–281. **204** Valor in Hibernia, p. 2. **205** *Dowdall's register*, p. 192 (109). **206** Ibid., p. 147 (97 X). **207** *C.P.C.R.*, i, Patent roll 2 Edward VI, m. 7, m. 10. **208** Note that Prior Dowdall handled the expenses for the synod of 1542 (*Dowdall's register*, p. 244 [124]). **209** *Dowdall's register*, p. 82 (72); p. 92 (78); p. 96 (91). **210** Ibid., pp 127–8 (94). **211** See the interrogatories directed against Archbishop Browne for not advancing the Edwardian reformation, *c.*November 1548 (*Original letters*, pp 18–20). **212** *Original letters*, p. 19. **213** Bradshaw, 'Edwardian reformation', pp 84–5. **214** Bellingham to Dowdall, late 1548 (P.R.O., S.P. 61/1/no. 162). **215** Browne to Warwick, 6 August 1551 (*Original letters*, no. xxiii, pp 54–60). **216** The conference of bishops is reported in Robert Ware, *The reformation of the Church of Ireland … in the life and death of George Browne* (1681), p. 13. However, Edwards demonstrated the account to be a manifest forgery (Edwards, *Church and state*, p. 136). The accounts of the other two conferences in which Primate Dowdall allegedly took part include one in which the primate is supposed to have debated with Lord Deputy Croft on 1 May 1551, that is before Croft was deputy (B.L., Add. MS 4789 Disputation between Deputy Croft and Archbishop Dowdall, f. 348) and the other in 1552 when Archbishop Dowdall had already been in exile for almost a year (B.L. Add. MS 4784 Miscellaneous extracts from Ware MSS, f. 35). These too have been shown to be forgeries (Edwards, *Church and state*, pp 140–1). Robert Ware's account of a national synod of the Church of Ireland in 1560 has also been shown to be fictitious (H.A. Jefferies, 'The Irish parliament of 1560: the Anglican reforms authorised' in *I.H.S.*, xxvi [1988], p. 138). More generally, the reader is referred to Philip Wilson, 'The writings of James Ware and the forgeries of Robert Ware' in *Transactions of the Bibliographical Society*, xv (1917), pp 83–94. **217** Dowdall to Alen & Council of Ireland, 1549/50 (*Original letters*, no. xv, pp 36–8); Browne to Warwick, 6 August 1551 (*Original letters*, no. xxiii, pp 54–60). **218** Browne to Warwick, 6 August 1551 (*Original letters*, no. xxiii, pp 54–60). **219** The fact that St Leger lent the books to Archbishop Browne at a secret rendezvous suggests that he thought that the books might persuade Brown to take a less Protestant stance in religion. **220** Deposition of Sir John Alen, 1552 (*Original letters*, no. xxvi, pp 65–72). **221** *CPCR*, i, Patent roll 1 Mary, m. 2. **222** Browne to Warwick, 6 August 1551 (*Original letters*, no. xxiii, pp 54–60). **223** *Fiants of Edward VI*, no. 795. Dnus John Merriman, whose surname was known around Ardee, was presented by the crown to the prebend of Clonfeacle on 22 August 1551, another benefice in the archbishop's gift [*CPCR*, i, Patent roll 5 Edward VI, m. 15.]. **224** *C.P.C.R.*, i, Patent roll 6 Edward VI, m. 7. **225** Bale, *Vocacion*, p. 447. **226** Ibid., p. 449. **227** *Dowdall's register*, pp 83 - 90 (75, 76). **228** Duffy, *Stripping of the altars*, pp 379–423, especially p. 389; Rex, *Henry VIII*, pp 77–99. **229** Mc Neill, 'Monastic possessions', p. 12. **230** Duffy, *Stripping of the altars*, pp 413–15. **231** *Dowdall's register*, pp 80–1 (71). **232** Elton, *Policy and police*, pp 230–382; Murray, 'Ecclesiastical justice', pp 33–

4. **233** Browne to Henry VIII, 27 September 1537 (P.R.O., S.P. 60/5/49); Agard to Cromwell, 5 April 1538 (P.R.O., S.P. 60/6/88); Staples to St Leger, 17 June 1538 (Lambeth, MS 602, f. 131); Alen to Cromwell, 20 October 1538 (P.R.O., S.P. 60/7/147); Travers' device for reformation of Ireland, 1542 (P.R.O., S.P. 60/10/295); *Original letters*, no. vii, pp 22–5; no. lxx, pp 194–7; Brady, *State papers*, letter no. v, pp 8–9. **234** Rex, *Henry VIII*, p. 35; David M. Palliser, 'Popular reactions to the reformation during the years of uncertainty, 1530–70', and Hutton, 'Local impact', pp 94–138; Whiting, *Blind devotion*, passim.; Duffy, *Stripping of the altars*, pp 377–523; Haigh, *English reformations*, pp 121–83. **235** Whiting, *Blind devotion*, pp 63, 98, 145, 147; on the other hand see Duffy, *Stripping of the altars*, pp 478–523. **236** Rex, *Henry VIII*, p. 25. **237** Haigh, *Reformation and resistance*, pp 107, 116–17, 140–8, 157–8. **238** Murray, 'Ancient chantries of Co. Louth', pp 207–8. **239** Murray, 'Ecclesiastical justice', pp 50–1. **240** Lennon, *Lords of Dublin*, pp 128, 130. **241** Brendan Bradshaw, 'The reformation in the cities: Cork, Limerick and Galway, 1534–1603' in John Bradley (ed.), *Settlement and society in medieval Ireland: studies presented to F.X. Martin O.S.A.* (Kilkenny, 1988), pp 454, 456, 459. **242** Steven Ellis, 'John Bale, bishop of Ossory, 1552–53' in *Journal of the Butler Society*, ii (1984), pp 288, 292.

NOTES TO CHAPTER 8

1 Bradshaw, 'Fr Wolfe's description of Limerick, 1574' in *North Munster Antiquarian Journal*, xvii (1975), pp 50–1. **2** Ware, 'Annals of Ireland', s.a. 1553; Bale, *Vocacion*, p. 450. **3** The clergy of Kilkenny availed of the proclamation to restore the Catholic liturgy and all of the traditional ecclesiastical paraphenalia in the face of Bishop Bale's fierce opposition (Bale, *Vocacion*, p. 454). **4** *C. P.C.R.*., i, Patent roll 1 Mary, no. 2. **5** For Archbishop Dowdall see *C.P.C.R.*, i, Patent roll 1 Mary, no. 4. For the others c.f., ibid., nos 77, 79. **6** Ibid., nos. 4, 65. **7** Ware, 'Annals of Ireland', s.a. 1558. **8** Patrick F. Moran, *A history of the archbishops of Dublin since the reformation* (Dublin, 1864), pp 52, 58. **9** *C.P.C.R.*, i, Patent roll 1 Mary, no. 4. **10** *Dowdall's register*, pp 99–106 (85). **11** *Calendar of Patent Rolls, Philip and Mary*, i, (1553–54), (London, 1937), p. 71; Ware, 'Annals of Ireland', s.a. 1554; *C.P.C.R.*, i, Patent roll 1 & 2 Mary and Philip, no. 59; TCD, MS F.I.18, f. 2. **12** Ware, 'Annals of Ireland', s.a. 1554; *C.P.C.R.*, i, Patent roll 1 & 2 Mary and Philip, nos 3, 4, 5, 13, 14. **13** *C.P.C.R.*, i, Patent roll 1 & 2 Mary and Philip, no. 3. **14** Bradshaw, 'George Browne', p. 323. On the other hand, Edward Staples, former bishop of Meath, chose to stay with his wife and suffered much abuse as a result (Staples to Cecil, 16 December 1558 [*Original letters*, no. xxxi, pp 87–9]). **15** *Dowdall's register*, pp 97–8 (82). **16** Ibid., pp 98–9 (83), pp 99–101 (84). **17** Ibid., pp 99–101 (84). **18** Ibid., p. 90 (76). **19** Ibid., pp 99–106 (85), art. 11. **20** Sidney & Council of Ireland to Privy council, 15 April 1566 (*Original letters*, no. lxxii, p.235). **21** Articles sent by Queen Mary to Fitzwalter, 17 November 1556 (P.R.O., S.P. 62/1/ no. 22; *Cal. Carew MSS*, i, 1515–74, p. 252). **22** R.H. Pogson, ' Reginald Pole and Mary Tudor's church', in *Historical Journal*, 18 (1975), p. 11; David Loades, *The reign of Mary Tudor: politics, government and religion in England, 1553–1558* (London, 1979), p. 82. **23** Pogson, 'Mary Tudor's church', pp 6–7, 13, 16, 17. **24** *Fiants of Philip and Mary*, no. 181. **25** *Dowdall's register*, pp 129 (95). **26** Even in Kilkenny, despite the attentions of the zealous Bishop Bale, the Catholic clergy managed to preserve their vestments and ornaments from destruction, and were able to bring them back into use in Mary's reign (Bale, *Vocacion*, p. 454). **27** Murray, 'Ancient chantries of County Louth', passim. **28** Duffy, *Stripping of the altars*, pp 526–8. **29** R.H. Pogson, 'Revival and reform in Mary Tudor's church: a question of money' in Haigh, *English reformation revised*, pp 140–52. **30** Pogson, 'Mary Tudor's church', p. 16; Loades, *Mary Tudor*, p. 82. **31** C.P.C.R., i, Patent roll 1 Mary, no. 64. **32** *Dowdall's register*, pp 151–3 (99). **33** Ibid., p. 79 (70). **34** Dowdall to Lord Chancellor & Privy council, 17 November 1557 (P.R.O., S.P. 62/2/no. 61). **35** Queen Mary to Dowdall, 7 February 1558 (P.R.O., S.P. 62/2/no. 9). **36** *Dowdall's register*, pp 220–8 (117). **37** Pogson, 'Mary Tudor's church', p. 4; Loades, *Mary Tudor*, p. 82. **38** Dowdall's articles to Privy council, 30 May 1558 (P.R.O., S.P. 62/2/no. 44;

TCD, MS 842, f. 82). **39** Queen Mary to Sussex, 4 August 1558 (P.R.O., S.P. 62/2/no. 64). **40** *Dowdall's register*, pp 217–8 (115). Interestingly, at the synod of Armagh *inter Anglicos* in July 1558 the priests were directed to celebrate the Mass of the Five precious wounds for the health of the queen and king (*Dowdall's register*, p. 126 [93]). **41** Duffy, *Stripping of the altars*, pp 525–64. **42** Jefferies, 'The Irish parliament of 1560: the anglican reforms authorised' in *I.H.S.*, xxvi (1988), pp 128–41. **43** Ibid., p. 140. **44** Sidney to Privy council, 15 April 1566 (*Original letters*, no. lxxxii, p. 235). **45** Sidney to Elizabeth, 28 April 1576 (Brady, *State papers*, no. xi, pp 16–17). **46** Sidney to Privy council, 15 April 1566 (*Original letters*, no. lxxxii, p. 235). **47** Sidney to Elizabeth, 28 April 1576 (Brady, *State papers*, no. xi, p. 16). **48** Brady to Cecil, 27 November 1567 (*Original letters*, no. cxvii, p. 314); Zell, 'Economic problems of the parochial clergy', pp 36–40. **49** Aidan Clarke, 'Varieties of uniformity: the first century of the Church of Ireland' in W.J. Shiels & Diana Wood (eds), *The churches, Ireland and the Irish* (Oxford 1989), p. 112. **50** Brady, *Episcopal succession*, i, p. 219; W.P. O'Brien, 'Two sixteenth century Munster primates: Donnchadh Ó Taidhg (1560–62) and Richard Creagh (1564–85)' in *Seanchas Ard Mhacha*, xiv (1990), p. 37–8. **51** O'Brien, 'Two sixteenth century Munster primates', p. 40. **52** Examination of Richard Creagh, 1567 (*Original letters*, no. cxxi, p. 328). **53** Loftus to Cecil, 3 November 1566 (*Original letters*, no. cii, pp 278–80). **54** Instructions to Sir Henry Sidney, 4 July 1565 (*Original letters*, no. lxxiv, p. 209). **55** 'The state of Armagh', pp 26–48.

Bibliography

MANUSCRIPT SOURCES

Bodleian Library, Oxford
Carte MS 55, no. 309, A declaration of Shane (O Neill)'s ordinary force.
Laud Miscellaneous MS 612,
    The ancient estate of the dioceses of Derry, Raphoe and Clogher.
    Sir Oliver St John's 'Observations on heranachus and termon lands'.

British Library, London
Hargraves MS 128 (1), Principium procurationis seu praxeos procuratoria breviarum.

Marsh's Library, Dublin
MS Z 2/1/7 Prosecution of the rector of Rathdrummin, 1548.
MS Z 4/2/7 Dudley Loftus his collection of annals, civil and ecclesiastical, relating to Ireland.

National Archives of Ireland, Dublin
MS R.C./9, Exchequer inquisitions, Dublin.

National Library of Ireland
MS D. 15,973, Notorial instrument of appeal by Primate Cromer against Cardinal Wolsey.

Public Records Office, London
State Papers, Ireland Henry VIII – Elizabeth, S.P. 60–S.P. 63.

Public Records Office of Northern Ireland, Belfast
MS DIO 4/2/9, Primate Octavian's register.
MS DIO 4/2/10, Primate Octavian's register of wills.
MS DIO 4/2/11, Primate Cromer's register.
MS DIO 4/2/12, Primate Dowdall's register.
MS DIO 4/4/2, The royal visitation book for the province of Ulster, 1622.
MS T 1652, Maps of the escheated counties, 1609.

Trinity College, Dublin
MS 567, Valor in Hibernia.
MS 568, Archbishop Daniel on herenaghs.
MS 808 (5), Statutes of the provincial synod of Cashel, 1453.
MS 10,383, Dioceses of Clogher, Derry and Raphoe.

PUBLISHED SOURCES AND CALENDARS
Public records
Calendar of Carew Manuscripts, i, 1515–1574, ed. J.S. Brewer and W. Bullen (London, 1867).
Calendar of letters and papers, foreign and domestic, Henry VIII, ed. J.S. Brewer et al. (London, 1862–1932).
Calendar of the MSS of the marquis of Salisbury (London, 1893–1973).
Calendar of Patent and Close Rolls, Ireland, Henry VIII–Elizabeth, i, ed. James Morrin (Dublin, 1861).
Calendar of State Papers, Ireland, March –October 1600, ed. Ernest George Atkinson (London, 1903).
Extents of Irish monastic possessions, 1540–1, ed. Newport B. White (Dublin, 1943).
Inquisitionum in officio rotulorum cancellariae Hiberniae asservatarum repertorium, ii, ed. James Hardiman (Dublin, 1829).
Mc Neill, 'Accounts of monastic chattels' in *Royal Society of Antiquaries of Ireland Journal,* lii (1922).
Quinn, David B., (ed.), 'Bills and statutes of the Irish parliaments of Henry VII and Henry VIII' in *Analecta Hibernica,* x (1941).
Statutes at large passed in the parliaments held in Ireland, i (Dublin, 1786).
Statute rolls of the parliament of Ireland: Edward IV, i, ed. Henry F. Berry (Dublin, 1914).
The Irish fiants of the Tudor sovereigns, i, 1521–1558, ed. Kenneth Nicholls (Dublin, 1994).
Valor beneficiorum ecclesiasticorum in Hiberniae: or the first fruits of all the ecclesiastical benefices in the kingdom of Ireland, as taxed in the king's book (Dublin, 1741).

Other printed sources
Annals of Ulster, iii, ed. B. Mac Carthy (Dublin, 1895).
Annals of the kingdom of Ireland by the Four Masters, v, ed. John O'Donovan (Dublin, 1856).
Bale, John, 'The vocacyon of John Bale, bishop of Ossory' in *Harleian Miscellany,* vi, ed. T. Park (London, 1813).
Brady, William Maziere (ed.), *State papers concerning the Irish church* (London, 1868).
Calendar of the papal letters relating to Great Britain and Ireland, xiv, 1471–84, ed. Victor Tremlow (London, 1960).
Calendar of papal registers relating to Great Britain and Ireland, xv, 1484–92, ed. Michael J. Haren (Dublin, 1978).
Calendar of papal registers relating to Great Britain and Ireland, xvi, 1492–8, ed. Anne P. Fuller (Dublin, 1986).
Calendar of papal registers relating to Great Britain and Ireland, xvii, 1503–1513, ed. Michael J. Haren (Dublin, 1987).
Cheney, C.R. (ed.), *Councils and synods with other documents relating to the English church,* ii (Oxford, 1964).
Collier, J. Payne (ed.), *The Egerton papers: a collection of public and private documents* (Camden Society, London, 1840).
Costello, M.A. (with Ambrose Coleman) (ed.), *De annatis Hiberniae,* i (Dublin, 1912).
Curtis, Edmund (ed.), *Calendar of Ormond deeds,* iii, 1413–1509 (Dublin, 1935).
—, *Calendar of Ormond deeds,* iv, 1509–47 (Dublin, 1537).
Dillon, Myles (ed.), 'Ceart Uí Néill' in *Studia Celtica,* i (1966).
Dowling, Thady, 'Annales breves Hiberniae' in Richard Butler (ed.), *The annals of Ireland* (Irish Archaeological Society, Dublin, 1849).
Emden, A.B., *A biographical register of the university of Oxford to A.D. 1500* (Oxford, 1957).
—, *A biographical register of the university of Oxford, 1501–1540* (Oxford, 1974).
Frere, W.H. (ed.), *Visitation articles and injunctions of the period of the reformation,* i (London, New York, Bombay and Calcutta, 1910).
Gwynn, Aubrey, 'Documents relating to the medieval diocese of Armagh' in *Archivium Hibernicum,* xii (1947).
Hayes-Mc Coy, G.A. (ed.), *Ulster and other Irish maps c.1600* (Dublin, 1964).

Hogan, Edmund (ed.), *The description of Ireland and the state thereof as it is at this present Anno 1598* (Dublin and London, 1878).
—, *Ibernia Ignatia* (Dublin, 1880).
Jefferies, Henry A. (ed.), 'Bishop Montgomery's survey of the parishes of Derry diocese: a complete text from *c.*1609' in *Seanchas Ard Mhacha*, xvii (1996).
—, 'Rev. Reeve's 'Ancient churches in the county of Armagh, Dec. 1874' in *Seanchas Ard Mhacha*, xvii (1996).
—, 'Observations on heranachus and termon lands' in *Archivium Hibernicum* (forthcoming).
Lawlor, Henry J. (ed.), 'A calendar of the Liber ruber of the diocese of Ossory' in *R.I.A. Proc.*, c, 27 (1908–9).
Mac Iomhair, D. (ed.), 'Two old Drogheda chronicles' in *Louth Arch. Soc. Jn.*, xv (1961).
Mc Neill, Charles (ed.), *Calendar of Archbishop Alen's register, c. 1172–1534* (Dublin, 1950).
Mc Neill, Charles & Otway-Ruthven, A.J. (eds), *Dowdall deeds* (Dublin, 1960).
Morley, Henry (ed.), *Ireland under Elizabeth and James the first* (London and New York, 1890).
Nicholls, K.W. (ed.), 'The register of Clogher', in *Clogher Record*, vii (1971–2).
O'Flaherty, Roderick (ed.), *A chorographical description of west or h-iar Connaught written A.D. 1684* (ed. James Hardiman, Dublin, 1846).
Shirley, E.P. (ed.), *Original letters and papers ... of the church in Ireland under Edward VI, Mary and Elizabeth* (London, 1851).
Simmington, Robert C. (ed.), *The civil survey of the counties of Donegal, Londonderry and Tyrone* (Dublin, 1937).
—, *The civil survey of the county of Meath* (Dublin, 1940).
White, Newport B. (ed.), *Irish monastic and episcopal deeds* (Dublin, 1936).
—, *Extents of Irish monastic possessions, 1540–1* (Dublin, 1943).

PUBLISHED BOOKS AND ARTICLES

Bagwell, Richard, *Ireland under the Tudors* (London, 1886).
Barnes, Andrew, 'The social transformation of the French parish clergy, 1500 - 1800' in Barbara B. Diefendorf and Carla Hesse (eds), *Culture and identity in early modern Europe* (1500–1800) (Michigan, 1993).
Barry, T.B., *The archaeology of medieval Ireland* (London and New York, 1987).
Bigger, F.J. and Fennell, W.J., 'Ardboe, Co, Tyrone: its cross and churches' in *U.J.A.*, iv (1897).
Bowker, Margaret, *The secular clergy in the diocese of Lincoln, 1495–1520* (Cambridge, 1968).
—, *The Henrician reformation: the diocese of Lincoln under John Longland, 1521–1547* (Cambridge, 1981).
—, 'The Henrician reformation and the parish clergy' in Haigh, *English reformation revised.*
Bradley, John, ' The medieval borough of Louth', *Louth Arch. Soc. Jn.*, xxi (1985).
—, 'The medieval borough of Ardee', *Louth Arch. Soc. Jn.*, xx (1984).
—, 'The topography and layout of Drogheda', *Louth Arch. Soc. Jn.*, xix (1978).
—, 'The chantry college, Ardee' in *Louth Arch. Soc. Jn.*, xxii (1989).
Bradshaw, Brendan, 'The opposition to the ecclesiastical legislation in the Irish reformation parliament' in *Irish Historical Studies*, xvi (1969).
—, 'George Browne, first reformation archbishop of Dublin, 1536–1554' in *Journal of Ecclesiastical History*, xxi (1970).
—, *The dissolution of the religious orders in Ireland under Henry VIII* (Cambridge, 1974).
—, 'Fr. Wolfe's description of Limerick, 1574' in *North Munster Antiquarian Journal*, xvii (1975).
—, 'The Edwardian reformation in Ireland', in *Archivium Hibernicum*, xxvi (1976–7).
—, 'Sword, word and strategy in the reformation in Ireland' in *Historical Journal*, xxi (1978).
—, *The Irish constitutional revolution of the sixteenth century* (Cambridge, 1979).
—, 'The reformation in the cities: Cork, Limerick and Galway, 1534–1603' in John Bradley (ed.), *Settlement and society in medieval Ireland* (Kilkenny, 1988).
Brady, W. Maziere, *The episcopal succession in England, Scotland and Ireland, 1400–1875*, I (Rome, 1876).
Brady, Ciaran, 'Conservative subversives: the community of the Pale and the Dublin administration, 1556–

1586' in P.J. Corish (ed.), *Radicals, rebels and establishments: Historical Studies, xv* (Belfast, 1985).

—, *The chief governors: the rise and fall of reform government in Tudor Ireland, 1536–1588* (Cambridge, 1994).

Brady, Ciaran & Gillespie, Raymond, (eds), *Natives and newcomers: the makings of Irish colonial society, 1534–1641* (Dublin, 1986).

Brannon, N.F., 'Five excavations in Ulster, 1978–84' in *U.J.A.*, xlix (1986).

Buckley, Victor M. and Sweetman, David (eds) *Archaeological survey of County Louth* (Dublin, 1991).

Burgos, Y.A., Davies, O. and Gaffikin, M., 'Churches of Armagh' in *U.J.A.*, i (1938).

Burrows, Michael A.J., 'Fifteenth century Irish provincial legidslation and pastoral care' in W.J. Shiels and Diana Wood (eds), *The churches, Ireland and the Irish* (Oxford, 1989).

Butlin, R.A., 'Land and people, c.1600' in T.W. Moody, F.X. Martin & F.J. Byrne (eds), *The New History of Ireland*, iii (Oxford, 1976).

Canny, Nicholas, *The Elizabethan conquest of Ireland: a pattern established, 1565–1576* (Hassocks, Sussex, 1976).

—, 'Why the reformation failed in Ireland: *une question mal posée*' in *Journal of Ecclesiastical History*, xxx (1979).

Chart, D.A. (ed.), *A preliminary survey of the ancient monuments of Northern Ireland* (Belfast, 1940).

Childs, Wendy, 'Ireland's trade with England in the later middle ages' in *Irish Economic and Social History*, ix (1982).

Clarke, Aidan, 'Varieties of conformity: the first century of the Church of Ireland' in W.J. Shiels and Diana Wood (eds), *The churches, Ireland and the Irish* (Oxford, 1989).

Corish, Patrick J., *The Irish Catholic experience: a historical survey* (Dublin, 1985).

Cosgrove, Art, 'Marriage in medieval Ireland' in Art Cosgrove (ed.), *Marriage in Ireland* (Dublin, 1985).

—, 'The Armagh registers: an under-explored source for late medieval Ireland' in *Peritia*, vii (1987).

Costello, M.A. (with Ambrose Coleman) (eds), *De annatis Hiberniae*, i (Dublin, 1912).

D'Alton, John, *A history of Drogheda*, i, (Drogheda, 1844).

Davies, Oliver, 'Derryloran church' in *U.J.A.*, v (1942).

—, 'Old churches in County Louth' in *Louth Arch. Soc. Jn.*, x (1943).

—, 'Church archaeology in Ulster' in *U.J.A.*, vii (1944).

Delemeau, Jean, *Catholicism between Luther and Voltaire: a new view of the counter-reformation* (with an introduction by John Bossy), (London and Philadelphia, 1977).

Dickens, A.G., *The English reformation* (London, 1964).

Duffy, Eamon, *The stripping of the altars: traditional religion in England, 1400–1580* (New Haven and London, 1992).

Duffy, P.J., 'Geographical perspectives on the borderlands' in Raymond Gillespie and Harold O'Sullivan (eds), *The borderlands: essays on the history of the Ulster-Leinster border* (Belfast, 1989).

Edwards, Robin Dudley, 'Venerable John Travers and the rebellion of Silken Thomas' in *Studies*, xxiii (1934).

—, *Church and state in Tudor Ireland: a history of penal laws against Irish Catholics* (Dublin, 1935).

Ellis, Steven, 'The Kildare rebellion and the early Henrician reformation' in *The Historical Journal*, xix (1976).

—, 'John Bale, bishop of Ossory, 1552–3' in *Journal of the Butler Society*, ii (1984).

—, *Tudor Ireland: crown, community and the conflict of cultures, 1470–1603* (London and New York, 1985).

—, *Reform and revival: English government in Ireland, 1470–1534* (Woodbridge & New York, 1986).

—, 'Economic problems of the church: why the reformation failed in Ireland' in *Journal of Ecclesiastical History*, 41 (1990).

Elton, G.R., *Policy and police: the enforcement of the reformation in the age of Thomas Cromwell* (Cambridge, 1972).

Fitzmaurice, E.B., 'The Franciscans in Armagh' in *U.J.A.*, vi (1900).

Flower, Robin, *The Irish tradition* (Oxford, 1947).

Ford, Alan, *The Protestant reformation in Ireland, 1590–1641* (Frankfurt am Main, 1985).

Gillespie, Raymond, 'The transformation of the borderlands, 1600–1700' in Gillespie & O'Sullivan, *The borderlands*.

Glancy, Michael, 'The church lands of Armagh: the lands of the city and manor' in *Seanchas Ard Mhacha*, ii (1957).

Gosling, Paul, 'Dun Delca to Dundalk' in *Louth Arch. Soc. Jn.*, xxii (1991).

—, *Carlingford: an antiquarian's guide* (Carlingford, 1993).

Green, Alice Stopford, *The making of Ireland and its undoing, 1200–1600* (Dublin & London, 1919).

Gwyn, Peter, *The king's cardinal: the rise and fall of Thomas Wolsey* (London, 1990).

Gwynn, Aubrey, *The medieval province of Armagh* (Dundalk, 1946).

Gwynn, A. and Hancock, R.N., *Medieval religious houses in Ireland* (London, 1970).

Haigh, Christopher, *Reformation and resistance in Tudor Lancashire* (Cambridge, 1975).

—, *The English reformation revised* (Cambridge, 1987).

—, 'Anticlericalism and the English reformation' in Haigh, *The English reformation revised*.

—, *English reformations: religion, politics and society under the Tudors* (Oxford, 1993).

Haines, Roy M., 'Background to an endemic problem' in Haines, *Ecclesia anglicana: studies in the English church of the later middle ages* (Toronto, Buffalo & London, 1989).

Hardy, A.K., 'The representation of the English lower clergy in parliament during the fourteenth century' in Derek Baker (ed.), *Sanctity and secularity in the church and the world: studies in church history*, x (Oxford, 1973).

Haren, Michael, J, 'Vatican archives as a historical source to c. 1530' in *Archivium Hibericum*, xxxix (1984).

—, 'Social structures of the Irish church: a new source in papal penitentiary dispensations for illegitimacy' in Herausgegeben von Ludwig Schmugge (ed.), *Illegitimitat im spatmittelalter: schriften des historischen kollegs kolloquien*, 29 (Oldenbourg, 1994).

Harper-Bill, Christopher, 'Dean Colet's convocation sermon and the pre-reformation church in England' in *History*, 73 (1988).

—, *The pre-reformation church in England, 1400–1530* (London and New York, 1989).

Harris, Walter (ed.), *The whole Works of Sir James Ware concerning Ireland*, i (Dublin, 1764), p. 204.

Hay, Denys, *The church in Italy in the fifteenth century* (Cambridge, 1977).

Heath, Peter, *The English parish clergy on the eve of the reformation* (London 1969).

Hill, Christopher, *Economic problems of the church from Archbishop Whitgift to the long parliament* (Oxford, 1956).

Hoffman, Philip, *Church and community in the diocese of Lyon, 1500–1789* (New Haven and London, 1984).

Horrox, Rosemary, 'The urban gentry in the fifteenth century' in John A.F. Thomson (ed.), *Towns and townspeople in the fifteenth century* (Gloucester and Wolfboro, NH, 1988).

Houlbrooke, Ralph, *Church courts and the people during the English reformation, 1520–1570* (Oxford, 1979).

Hutton, Ronald, 'The local impact of the Tudor reformation' in Haigh, *English reformation revised*.

Jefferies, Henry A., 'The Irish parliament of 1560: the anglican reforms authorised' in *I.H.S.*, xxvi (1988).

—, 'The church courts of Armagh on the eve of the reformation' in *Seanchas Ard Mhacha*, xv (1993).

—, 'Diocesan synods and convocations in Armagh on the eve of the Tudor reformations' in *Seanchas Ard Mhacha*, xvi (1995).

—, 'The Armagh registers and the re-writing of Irish church history on the eve of the Tudor reformations' in *Seanchas Ard Mhacha*, xvii (1997).

—, 'The parish church and priests of Loughgall, Armagh, in 1546' in *Seanchas Ard Mhacha*, xvii (1997).
—, 'The diocese of Dromore on the eve of the Tudor reformations' in Lindsay Proudfoot (ed.), *Down: history and society* (Dublin, 1997).
—, 'Derry diocese on the eve of the plantation' in Gerard O'Brien (ed.), *Derry/Londonderry: history and society* (Dublin, 1997).
—, 'The laity in the parishes of Armagh *inter Anglicos* on the eve of the Tudor reformations' in *Archivium Hibernicum*, 52 (1998).
—, 'The visitation of the parishes of Armagh *inter Hibernicos* in 1546' in Henry A. Jefferies & Charles Dillon (eds), *Tyrone: history and society* (Dublin, forthcoming).
—, 'Dr Cromer, archbishop of Armagh (1521–1542), and Henry VIII's reformation' in Art Hughes, F.X. Mc Corry and Roger Weatherup (eds), *Armagh: history and Society* (Dublin, 1998).
Kenny, Colum, *King's Inn and the kingdom of Ireland: the Irish 'Inns of court, 1541–1800* (Dublin, 1992).
King, Heather A., 'The Ardee cross' in *Louth Arch. Soc. Jn.*, xx (1983), pp 210–14.
—, 'A possible market cross fragment from Drogheda' in *Louth Arch. Soc. Jn.*, xx (1984).
—, 'A tiled floor at Greenoge, County Meath' in *Ríocht na Midhe*, ix (1992–3).
Lander, Stephen, 'Church courts and the reformation in the diocese of Chichester, 1500–1558' in Haigh, *English reformation revised*.
Leask, Harold, G., *Irish churches and monastic buildings*, iii (Dundalk, 1960).
Lehmberg, Stanford E., *The reformation parliament, 1529–1536* (Cambridge, 1970).
—, *The reformation of the cathedrals* (Princeton, 1988).
Lennon, Colm, 'The counter reformation in Ireland' in Brady & Gillespie, *Natives and newcomers*.
—, *The lords of Dublin in the age of reformation* (Dublin, 1989).
—, *Sixteenth century Ireland: the incomplete conquest* (Dublin, 1994).
Leslie, J.B., *Armagh clergy and parishes* (Dundalk, 1911).
Loades, David, *The reign of Mary Tudor: politics, government and religion in England, 1553–1558* (London, 1979).
Logan, Donald F., *Excommunication and the secular arm in medieval England: a study in the legal procedure from the thirteenth to the sixteenth century* (Toronto, 1968).
Lynch, Anthony, 'The archdeacons of Armagh, 1417–71' in *Louth Arch. Soc. Jn.*, xix (1979).
—, 'Religion in late medieval Ireland' in *Archivium Hibericum*, xxxvi (1981).
—, 'The administration of John Bole, archbishop of Armagh, 1457–1471' in *Seanchas Ard Mhacha*, xiii (1991).
Mac Niocaill, Gearóid, 'Socio-economic problems of the late medieval Irish town' in David Harkness & Mary O Dowd (eds), *The town in Ireland* (Belfast, 1981).
Mahaffy, J.P., 'Two early tours of Ireland' in *Hermathena*, 40 (1914).
Marshall, Peter, *The Catholic priesthood and the English reformation* (Oxford, 1994).
Mc Cafferty, John, 'Defamation and the church courts in early sixteenth century Armagh' in *Archivium Hibernicum*, xlviii (1994).
Mc Cahill, Mary, 'A baptismal font at Wyanstown, County Louth' in *Louth Arch. Soc. Jn.*, xx (1983).
Mc Corristine, Laurence, *The revolt of Silken Thomas: a challenge to Henry VIII* (Dublin, 1987).
Moeller, Bernd, 'Piety in Germany around 1500' in Steven E. Ozment, *The reformation in medieval perspective* (Chicago, 1971).
Mooney, Canice, 'The Franciscan Third Order friary at Dungannon' in *Seanchas Ard Mhacha*, i (1954).
—, *The church in Gaelic Ireland: thirteenth to fifteenth centuries* (A history of Irish catholicism, Dublin, 1969).
Moran, Patrick F., *A history of the archbishops of Dublin since the reformation*, i (Dublin, 1864).
Morgan, Hiram, 'The end of Gaelic Ulster: a thematic interpretation of events between 1534 and 1610' in *I.H.S.*, xxvi (1988).
—, *Tyrone's rebellion: the outbreak of the Nine Years War in Tudor Ireland* (Dublin, 1993).
Murphy, Margaret, 'The high cost of dying: an analysis of pro anima bequests in medieval Dublin'

in W. J. Shiels & Diana Wood (eds), *The church and wealth: studies in church history*, xxiv (Oxford, 1987).

Murray, James, 'Archbishop Alen, Tudor reform and the Kildare rebellion' in *R.I.A. Proc.*, lxxxix, sect. c (1989).

—, 'The sources of clerical incomes' in *Archivium Hibernicum*, xlv (1990).

—, 'Ecclesiastical justice and the enforcement of the reformation: the case of Archbishop Browne and the clergy of Dublin' in A. Ford, F. Mc Guire & K. Milne (eds), *As by law established: the Church of Ireland since the reformation* (Dublin, 1995).

Murray, Laurence, 'The ancient chantries of County Louth' in *Louth Arch. Soc. Jn.*, ix (1939).

Neely, William G., *Kilkenny: an urban history, 1391–1843* (Belfast, 1989).

Nicholls, Kenneth W., *Gaelic and gaelicised Ireland in the later middle ages* (Dublin, 1972).

—, 'Medieval Irish cathedral chapters' in *Archivium Hibernicum*, xxxi (1973).

—, 'Gaelic society and economy in the high middle ages' in Art Cosgrove (ed.), *A New History of Ireland*, ii (Oxford, 1987).

O Brien, W.P., 'Two sixteenth century Munster primates: Donnchadh Ó Taidhg (1560–62) and Richard Creagh (1564–85)' in *Seanchas Ard Mhacha*, xiv (1990).

Ó Doibhlin, Éamon, 'Domhnach Mór' in *Seanchas Ard Mhacha*, ii (1957).

—, *Domhnach Mór: an outline of parish history* (Omagh, 1969).

—, 'The deanery of Tulach Óg' in *Seanchas Ard Mhacha*, vi (1971).

Ó Fiach Tomás, 'The O'Neills of the Fews' in *Seanchas Ard Mhacha*, vii (1977).

O'Sullivan, Harold, 'The Franciscans in Dundalk' in *Seanchas Ard Mhacha*, iv (1960–1).

—, 'The march of south east Ulster in the fifteenth and sixteenth centuries: a period of change in Gillespie and O'Sullivan, *The borderlands*.

Ollivant, Simon, *The court of the official in pre-reformation Scotland* (Stair Society, xxxiv, Edinburgh, 1982).

Otway-Ruthven, Jocelyn, 'Parochial development in the rural deanery of Skreen' in *Journal of the Royal Society of Antiquaries of Ireland*, xciv (1964).

—, *A history of medieval Ireland* (London & New York, 1968).

Owen, D.M., 'Synods in the diocese of Ely in the later middle ages and sixteenth century' in G.J. Cumings (ed.), *Studies in church history*, iii (Leiden, 1966).

Palliser, D.M., 'Popular reactions to the reformation during the years of uncertainty, 1530–70' in Haigh, *English reformation revised*.

Paterson, T.G.F., *Harvest home* (Dundalk, 1973).

Platt, Colin, *Medieval England: a social history and archaeology from the conquest to AD 1600* (London and New York, 1978).

Pogson, R.H., 'Revival and reform in Mary Tudor's church: a question of money' in Haigh, *English reformation revised*.

Quinn, D.B. & Nicholls, K.W., 'Ireland in 1534' in *N.H.I.*, iii.

Reeves, William, *The culdees of the British islands as they appear in history with an appendix of evidences* (Dublin, 1864).

—, 'The ancient churches of Armagh' in *U.J.A.*, ii (1896).

Rex, Richard, *Henry VIII and the English reformation* (Basingstoke and London, 1993).

Robinson, Philip, *The plantation of Ulster: British settlement in an Irish landscape, 1600–1670* (Dublin, 1984).

Roe, Helen M., 'Two decorated fonts in Drogheda, County Louth' in *Louth Arch. Soc. Jn.*, xviii (1976).

—, 'Illustrations of the Holy Trinity in Ireland, thirteenth to seventeenth centuries in *R.S.A.I. Jn.*, 109 (1979).

Scarisbrick, J.J., *The reformation and the English people* (Oxford, 1984).

Sheehan, Anthony, 'Irish towns in a period of change, 1558–1625' in Brady and Gillespie (eds), *Natives and Newcomers*.

Simms, Katharine, 'The archbishops of Armagh and the O'Neills' in *Irish Historical Studies*, xix (1974).

—, 'Warfare in the medieval Gaelic lordships' in *Irish Sword*, xii (1975–76).

—, *From kings to warlords: the changing political structure of Gaelic Ireland in the later middle ages* (Woodbridge and Wolfeboro, 1987).

—, 'The brehons of later medieval Ireland' in D. Hogan and W.N. Orborough (eds), *Brehons, serjeants and attorneys: studies in the history of the Irish legal profession* (Dublin, 1990).

—, 'Frontiers in the Irish church – regional and cultural' in T.B. Barry, Robin Frame and Katharine Simms (eds), *Colony and frontier in medieval Ireland: essays presented to J.F. Lydon* (London, 1995).

Swanson, R.N., *Church and society in late medieval England* (Oxford, 1989).

Sweetman, P.D., 'Archaeological excavations at St John's priory, Newtown, Trim, County Meath' in *Ríocht na Midhe*, viii (1990–1).

Thompson, Hamilton A., *The English clergy and their organisation in the later middle ages* (Oxford, 1947).

Thomson, A.F. (ed.), *Towns and townspeople in the fifteenth century* (Gloucester and Wolfboro, NH, 1988).

—, *The early Tudor church and society, 1485–1529* (London and New York, 1993).

Walsh, Katherine, *A fourteenth century scholar and primate: Richard FitzRalph in Oxford, Avignon and Armagh* (Oxford, 1981).

Walsh, Helen Coburn, 'The response to the Protestant reformation in sixteenth century Meath' in *Ríocht na Midhe*, vii (1987).

—, 'Enforcing the Elizabethan settlement: the vicissitudes of Hugh Brady, bishop of Meath, 1563–84' in *I.H.S.*, xxvi (1989).

Watt, John, *The church and the two nations in medieval Ireland* (Cambridge, 1970).

—, *The church in medieval Ireland* (Dublin, 1972).

—, '*Ecclesia inter Anglicos et inter Hibernicos*: confrontation and coexistence in the medieval diocese and province of Armagh' in J.F. Lydon (ed.), *The English in medieval Ireland* (Dublin, 1984).

—, 'The church and the two nations in late medieval Armagh' in *The churches, Ireland and the Irish*.

Whiting, Robert, *The blind devotion of the people: popular religion and the English reformation* (Cambridge, 1989).

Wilkie, William E., *The cardinals protector of England: Rome and the Tudors before the reformation* (Cambridge, 1974).

Williams, Glanmor, *The Welsh church from the conquest to the reformation* (Cardiff, 1962).

—, *Welsh reformation essays* (Cardiff, 1967).

—, *Recovery, reorientation and reformation: Wales c. 1415–1642* (Oxford, 1987).

Wilson, Philip, 'The writings of James Ware and the forgeries of Robert Ware' in *Transactions of the Bibliographical Society*, xv (1917).

Zell, Michael, 'Economic problems of the clergy in the sixteenth century' in Rosemary O Day and Felicity Heal (eds), *Princes and paupers in the English church, 1500–1800* (Leicester, 1981).

UNPUBLISHED THESES

McCafferty, John, 'The act book of the Armagh diocese, 1518–1522', MA, University College, Dublin, 1991.

Simms, Katharine, 'Gaelic Ulster in the late middle ages', PhD, Trinity College, Dublin, 1976.

Index